SCHINDLER'S LEGACY

ELINOR J. BRECHER

SCHINDLER'S ᴐLEGACY

True Stories of the List Survivors

Hodder & Stoughton

A MEMBER OF THE HODDER HEADLINE GROUP

First published in the United States under the title
SCHINDLER'S LEGACY by Elinor J. Brecher

Copyright © 1994 Elinor J. Brecher

Published by arrangement with Dutton Signet,
a division of Penguin Books USA Inc.

First published in Great Britain in 1994
by Hodder and Stoughton
A division of Hodder Headline PLC
10 9 8 7 6 5 4 3 2

A CIP catalogue record for this book is available
from the British Library

ISBN 0 340 63229 1

Printed and bound in Great Britain by
Butler & Tanner Ltd, Frome and London

Hodder and Stoughton
A division of Hodder Headline PLC
388 Euston Road
London NW1 3BH

To my parents,

Walter Brecher and Roslyn Kaplan Brecher.

And to the memory of my grandparents,

Dr. Ira Kaplan and Ella Rubin Kaplan;
Leo Brecher and Jeannette Kirstein Brecher.

Acknowledgments

Without the participation of the following people, this book never would have evolved from its embryonic newspaper-story stage to its current form.

I am deeply indebted to the *Schindlerjuden,* their spouses, and their children, for so generously sharing their stories, their photographs, and their time. They are brave people whose determination to tell their stories, no matter the pain, hallows the memories of those they loved and lost, and stands as a monument to the six million. I am humbled by their trust, and can only hope they feel I have repaid it with the respect and care they deserve.

Thomas Keneally had the insight, the patience, and the sensitivity to write *Schindler's List.* He recognized in this tale what so many others did not or could not. Because of his book, Steven Spielberg made a movie that changed the way a nation perceives the Holocaust. He has been genial and helpful to me throughout. I am honored by his contribution to *Schindler's Legacy.*

The photographers whose work graces these pages did a marvelous job, and I thank them all: Melissa Farlow, Jill Freedman, Eddie Hausner, Adrienne Helitzer, Beth Keiser, Jay Mather, David Rose, Gerard Simonetti, and Stan Turkula. Candace West (rhymes with The Best) copied and/or printed most of the photographs—old and new—that you see in this book. She painstakingly coaxed back to life snapshots tucked away for decades in shoe boxes, closets, and albums. I can't thank her enough.

I am indebted to the works of Elie Wiesel, Primo Levi, Martin Gilbert, and Lucy Dawidowicz. I leaned heavily on them for historical background and inspiration, as well as on Malvina Graf's *The Kraków Ghetto and the Płaszów Camp Remembered*; Abraham Zuckerman's *A Voice in the Chorus: Life as a Teenager in the Holocaust*; Michael Berenbaum's *The World Must Know: The History of the Holocaust as Told in the United States Holocaust Memorial Museum*; *A History of the Jewish People*, edited by H. H. Ben-Sasson; Nicholas de Lange's *Atlas of the Jewish World*, and the *Encyclopaedia Judaica*.

Hal Boedeker encouraged me to write about list survivors for the *Miami Herald*. Those stories led to this book. My thanks to him. I'd also like to acknowledge my (understaffed, overworked) colleagues in the *Miami Herald*'s Living and Arts section, for soldiering on without me.

I am tremendously grateful to Dr. Mitchell Borke, who read the manuscript for accuracy in the use of Polish, and saved me from making a linguistic fool of myself.

Thanks to Jackie Potts and Joyce Lewis for their help transcribing interview tapes, and to Rita Martone for research assistance.

For TLC, great meals, and a place to lay my weary head while I was on the road, thanks to Wendy and John Dougan, Melissa Farlow and Randy Olson, Adrienne Helitzer and Tammy Lechner, Irene and Al Zoot, Elaine Corn and David SooHoo, and Deborah Sanborn and Peter Quinlan.

Thomas S. Cropper of SYSOPS of Miami provided tech support and specialized programming that enabled me to make friends with all sorts of computer equipment that used to scare the daylights out of me.

Jonathan Scott Woolfson deserves special recognition for being the world's best faux stepson. From canine care to car washing, his willingness to pick up the domestic slack allowed me to concentrate on this work. And to Alexandra Beth Woolfson: Thanks for understanding why I couldn't come out and play for so long.

Lindsay Miller's professionalism and keen eye helped me get a grip on this project at a crucial time. Her physical presence, even for a few days, proved reassuring and calming.

From the moment she welcomed me to her Rolodex, my agent, Sandra

Choron, has been an ongoing source of support and encouragement. Her own special brand of "tough love" helped keep me on track. I appreciate her tolerance for my whining, and for being a pretty darn good editor herself.

My *real* editor, Peter Borland, did a superhuman job helping me bring this project to fruition. His confidence in me often outdistanced my confidence in myself. I am so grateful for the respect with which he treated this material, and for his trust in me. (And for taking me seriously when I said I don't respond well to nagging.)

And a special pat to Sara Bixler, who wrestled with the inundation of faxes and overnight envelopes I caused to descend upon the offices of Penguin . . . and for always being so cheerful on the phone.

Also at Penguin USA, I wish to thank Managing Editor Rena Kornbluh, Director of Production Cheryl Hoffman, and Senior Designer Steven Stathakis. Copyeditor Maureen Clark did a superb job. Special thanks also to Publisher Arnold Dolin, for his continuous support of this book.

Jill Bauer introduced me to both my agent and my editor. For this alone, she deserves my unending gratitude. But she also guided me through territory that seemed strange—and sometimes scary—to a newspaper girl. She always knew just the right moment to call (and exactly when not to).

And others, for their support, patience, tolerance, generosity, cheerleading, schlepping, and other acts of kindness: Evelyn Stahl, Tracey Broussard Silverberg, Joan Union, Jim Robertson, Katherine Higham, Christopher Fitzgerald, Ron Tanawaki, and Anne Bergeron.

Many of the survivors asked me about my family, and urged me to cherish them while I can. And so I do: My sister, Joanne Brecher Kay; her husband, Stanley Kay; and their son, Andrew I. Brecher Kay. My brother, Gerald I. Brecher; his wife, Louise Borke; and their kids: Liza Gail Brecher, and Laura and Louis Sciuto; also my dearest uncle, B. David Kaplan. I cannot imagine my world without them.

Mickey, Melanie, Kendall and Harpo provided loving and amusing companionship during the long days and nights at the computer (even if they did bark a lot).

My thanks to Dr. Ron Tapper, for his kindness and understanding at a time of difficult choices.

There is no way under this or any other sun that I could have completed this project—or for that matter, started it—without the enthusiasm, optimism, energy, and loyalty of my beloved Mark Woolfson. He believed when I didn't. He made me laugh when I couldn't. He never complained when I woke him up at ridiculous hours to deal with the fax modem, the tape backup, or my insecurities. He graciously talked to the back of my head for months, and managed to remodel a house around me. He obliged my every whim—reasonable and not—and always knew when I needed a hug.

Finally, my parents, Roslyn and Walter Brecher. Their commitment to Jewish heritage, laws, and traditions, their dedication to the State of Israel, the values they hold, and the standards they set provided me with the spiritual, intellectual, and cultural background essential to pursuing this enterprise. Their generosity is beyond measure, from the unbeatable daily rate on the Peugeot in New York to the long hours of talking through what this all means, to hanging in there with me through the times of doubt, exhaustion, and deadline hysteria. *Alle Yiddishe kinder* should have such parents.

CONTENTS

FOREWORD

Some months ago in Miami I met a *Miami Herald* journalist named Elinor Brecher, who had accepted the task of interviewing a range of Schindler survivors and writing about their memories in the broadest sense. That is, in terms of the total experience of their lives, as dominated as that experience might still be by their memory of the Holocaust. She knew that to speak would not be an easy exercise for the survivors, and was anxious about how she would be able to record and comment upon what the interviewees had to say in the necessary time. Here, without any sign of the stress involved in her energetic and sensitive enquiries, are the results. Here are the vigorous testimonies of the living *Schindlerjuden,* still burdened with, yet trying to utter, unspeakable memory. The focus of these personal histories is in one sense broader than that of my book and Steven Spielberg's film. The interviews I did to get information for the book, the inquiries Spielberg also made before and during the filming, necessarily centered on the remarkable Oskar. In the interviews I conducted, as in the wide and varied range of *Schindler* testimonies in Yad Vashem and in the speeches survivors made to welcome Oskar to Israel, Schindler, coruscating with *chutzpah,* glimmering equally with reckless compassions and garishly mixed motives, tended to be center-stage. Wherever he was, whether it was a bar or a prison, Oskar Schindler was the dominant figure in any landscape.

A more restrained personality such as that of Emilie Schindler, his wife, who was with him particularly in his second camp, Brinnlitz, is remembered by those who were recovering from malnutrition or typhus or scarlet fever, or by former prisoners such as Lewis Fagen, for her kindnesses to him and to his sister, Janka, who was ill with cancer.

In these accounts, though, the contact with Schindler, whether in Emalia or in

Brinnlitz or both, is in many cases a phase, important though it might be, in a long personal history.

Since the film was released, I have encountered again many of the people I had interviewed for the book and many who could not be reached at the time or were unable to give interviews. Through these contacts and conversations, the sense of Oskar as flawed hero, ambiguous liberator, strange deity, is reinforced. In my opinion he deserved to be looked upon in those terms.

The challenge in the Schindler story was to show with equal force the ambiguity of the position of the prisoners, the exceptional terror under which they lived, the struggle to deal with fear, to operate with cleverness, bravery, and native cunning. There are many individual stories told in *Schindler's List*—the stories of the Dressner family, the Fagens, of Helen Hirsch and the Pfefferbergs. But they appear under the presiding aegis of Oskar. Here, annotated and edited by Elinor Brecher, we have the memories of the Schindler survivors in their own right.

They cannot fully escape the shadow of two personages—that of Schindler, now firmly planted by Spielberg's brilliant film in the canon of Holocaust heroes, and Amon Goeth, commandant of Płaszów, a man who grew demented under the extraordinary sanction the SS and National Socialism gave him. Amon Goeth in particular still resonates in the dreams and memories of survivors of KL Płaszów. He and Oskar both still preoccupy the internal and external discourse of Schindler survivors. But perhaps, since savagery rather than kindness owns the larger psychic guns, Goeth dominates the dark hours of memory. "I was sitting," says Rena Ferber Finder, "and all of a sudden the girl next to me fell over. You didn't hear the shot. I looked, touched her, there was blood . . ."

There seems to me as a highly interested observer to have been a change among Holocaust survivors since the days I sought their reminiscences for *Schindler's List*. In the early 1980s there was a considerable reluctance among most of them to speak of their lives as prisoners of that frightful system. Many of the survivors had become successful people in their own communities, and by the early 1980s they were at the height of their powers. Omens of mortality that strike people in their sixties and seventies had not yet presented. They who had in visible terms triumphed in life were aware that they had once been by decree *Untermenschen* and *Unterfrauen*, and had been subjected to inhuman and degrading fears, herdings and inflictions they did not want now to recall or recount. Humans who have lived an "ordinary" life—whatever that is—guard the secrets of their earlier follies and degradations. How much more intense must be the impulse in survivors of exceptional cruelty, who carry with them as well as everything else a ferocious self-perceived guilt at having survived?

For whatever reason, it took considerable persuasion, especially from my mentor Leopold Pfefferberg, to convince some of the interviewees to talk about their time in either of Oskar's camps, and about the inevitable corollaries—the brutality of the SS and the shadow that camps such as Auschwitz, Mauthausen and Gröss-Rosen cast over their lives.

I remember that on the night of the premiere of *Schindler's List* in Washington, D.C., I met a woman survivor who told me that though I had written to her at the time, she had not then been able to face speaking since her husband, a Holocaust survivor, had died—in large part of grief—just before she received my request.

Among those I interviewed at the time, from whom I felt a special reluctance, to whom I feel a special debt, are the ones—some of them represented in these pages—who had been young at the time of the events of the Holocaust. It seemed to me that their sufferings and experiences were the most unutterable, and the most unassimilable to their daily lives.

In remarking on the earlier reticence of some survivors, I do not wish to diminish the success of the work of Elinor Brecher. I am not trying to say that Elinor Brecher did not face her own rejections, or found it an easy matter to put together this remarkable collection. It is a tribute to her energy and a celebration of her subjects that so many of them were willing to go on the record.

Rather, I wish to celebrate the fact that survivors are speaking to us more. Based on what survivors and children of survivors told me during recent lecture tours in the United States, a welcome change has occurred. The survivors are older now, and they are faced with deniers of their experience. While they still have voices, they want to relate the atrocities and barbarities that were practiced on them. There seems, as one speaks these days to survivors' groups, a greater urgency to do this than there once was.

I want to celebrate, too, the fact that a number of Holocaust survivors have stated that the book and, more broadly, the film of *Schindler's List* have catalyzed them into speaking. When the film was first released, there were newspaper articles about survivors needing counseling as a result of having watched it, and I feared that it might have a disorienting and painful effect on some. But if widespread anecdotal evidence can be believed, the film and the book have somehow, through the benign muses that drove both myself and Spielberg, acted as a catalyst to memory and to partial healing.

It is a matter of delight and celebration that so many survivors should all speak comprehensibly in these pages, that they should validate their own experiences of terror and celebrate the impulses that brought them to safety.

Ms. Brecher was aware that the prisoners had lives before and after Schindler, and we are able to be enlightened by the stories of these survivors both as pre–World War II Poles and as post–World War II displaced persons and emigrants to the United States. This book is among other things a record of the lost prewar world, and in its succession of individual remembrance is an index of the huge mass of talents and energies that were nullified by the Holocaust.

When the film was about to be shown, everyone including the President of the United States, Bill Clinton, wanted to know if it would feature a figure who has become known as "the little girl in red" or "red Genia." This child was the one who made a clever walk through the Kraków ghetto in June 1942. By the sort of adaptability and cunning that characterizes children in times of disaster, she evaded a rounding up of seven thousand people who would be ultimately gassed with carbon monoxide in Belżec.

Genia stands for the native cunning of the survivor, but—since she was later to die in Auschwitz—she is also an index of the impossible odds against which survivors were struggling. People showed exceptional cleverness and craft and still perished, and the awareness of masses of obliterated talents is clearly what gnaws at the souls of survivors.

But one is aware as well that the small number of survivors were never themselves less than people of nous, percipience and valor. This record demonstrates that. It demonstrates it against a recurrent slander against the Jewish people of Europe, that as a group they participated in their own destruction. *Schindler's List* tells in part the story of some who did collaborate knowingly and corruptly with the enemy—Chilowicz, Goeth's bagman, and Spira, the chief of the ghetto police. But their tales are not germane to the sometimes heard accusation I speak of—that the Jews *as a community* were passive at each stage of the process of their destruction.

This slander ignores the European Jewish reality, the tradition of getting on as constructively and with as little human cost as possible with more or less anti-Semitic civil authorities. The elders of the Jewish community by and large believed that it was better for the mass of their community if individual acts of anti-Semitic brutality and savagery were protested to the authorities, with subsequent negotiations aimed at ensuring they did not happen again soon. It is this tradition of which the SS knowingly and cunningly made use.

The brave, pained histories you are about to read demonstrate that Jews did not in any way pre-succumb to their destiny as victims, even if the past history of relationships between the Jewish community and Gentile authority might have made it easier for the community to be maneuvered into place by the successive waves of deceit which the SS brought to bear during the Final Solution.

Schindler is out there now, in the minds of millions, celebrated at the National Holocaust Museum in Washington, D.C., honored in Hollywood, a household name, etc. But these are the stories of thirty of his collaborators who, having got through the war, went on to do more than Oskar could manage—to become citizens of repute, contributors to business and to the arts, and women and men of honor.

—THOMAS KENEALLY

Author's Note

For what reason you are writing this book? Your parents, they are survivors? Your grandparents? No? Then why are you interested?

The questions generally came within the first ten minutes of introductory schmooze, right after, "You'll have a little cake?" which wasn't so much a question as a directive.

I spent four months interviewing Americans who had been on Oskar Schindler's now-famous list. Despite the astonishing popularity of *Schindler's List*, Steven Spielberg's Academy Award–winning film, a number of these men and women couldn't figure out why anyone would care about *their* stories. What had they done, except manage to survive the Holocaust? (God only knows, *that* never had counted for much.) Wasn't Schindler the real story? The hero? The star? Didn't I want to hear more about *him?*

Well, of course I did, but . . .

The idea for this project was born in December 1993, after I saw *Schindler's List* for the first of four times. Like thousands of other moviegoers, I sat in silence as the ending credits rolled, unwilling and unable to wrench myself out of the mood . . . or the seat. I come from a family of movie-theater owners, and I've seen a lot of memorable films in my life, but few ever had as much impact as this one. And at first, I wasn't sure why.

The Holocaust was hardly virgin historical territory. I was raised as an observant Jew in a family blessed—well into my adulthood—with living members of my grandparents' generation. I have known survivors, and their children, all my life. The events and lessons of the Holocaust were integral to my Jewish education. So this latest screen representation of Nazi behavior and Jewish reaction neither shocked nor surprised me. I even knew who Oskar Schindler was.

Then I realized why I couldn't move: I wanted to follow the people who walked over the hill near the end of the film, and those who lovingly placed stones on the grave of the "Righteous Gentile." They didn't just fade to black in the real world; they walked over that figurative hill and went somewhere to live the rest of their lives. Who were they? Where were they? How had the Holocaust marked them and their offspring? How had they spent the legacy of survival bequeathed to them by Oskar Schindler?

As a feature writer for Florida's largest daily newspaper, I was in the ideal position to find out. South Florida is retirement country. Dade, Broward, and Palm Beach counties are home to hundreds of thousands of elderly Jews. Surely I'd find *Schindlerjuden* among them. And I did. Some live here permanently; some are "snowbirds," as the locals call the Northerners who flock to Florida in the winter.

So it began with newspaper profiles of eight men and women who had been with Oskar Schindler at his factories in Kraków or Czechoslovakia, or both. They led me to others, and so on. It turned out to be a fairly small universe. I found galaxies of families, extended families, and psychic families: groups of friends from the camps and before, who staggered out of the flames together to discover nobody alive but each other. The bonds hold even now. "You never in the entire world could understand, unless you were there," New Yorker Roman Ferber told me. "There was no day or night. There was no happiness, just fear. There was nothing but the next thirty seconds."

The survivors treasure their shared history because there's so much history to share, and so few left to remember. The memories of these survivors are the voices of those who were lost.

They range in age from the mid-fifties to early nineties. There are certain obvious generational differences. The younger survivors tend to be more "Americanized." Nothing but an accent gives them away. Many at the upper end of the range seem to have replicated much of life as they knew it in Poland, "before." I was struck by certain lifestyle similarities in the Jewish neighborhoods and condo enclaves that attract survivors. They play cards in the evenings—the men in one room, the women in another—dine together, travel together, and decorate in the same Old-World style.

In the camps, they had shared the same simple dreams: an entire loaf of bread for themselves. Clean water to drink. A real mattress to sleep on. Thick soup. Life for another day.

And when it was over, most married other survivors. "Hitler was the matchmaker," Floridian Betty Schagrin told me.

The *Schindlerjuden* clearly understand the differences between themselves and other survivors. One of them told me, "By Schindler, we were hungry, but not starving. We were cold, but not freezing. We had fear, but we were not beaten," and that about says it all.

There's one other remarkable distinction, not unique to the Schindler experience, but, in the larger context of the Holocaust, certainly unusual: families emerged intact. Only a few, but any at all is wondrous.

The Holocaust is their perpetual gate-crasher. "By us, no matter what we're doing—if we're going to a wedding, a bar mitzvah, or getting together—this thing comes up on the table sooner or later," Californian Stanley Orzech told me. "If it's every week we get together, or every day, it comes up. We cannot get this thing out from our minds."

And no wonder. If I heard it once, I heard it a hundred times: The movie was so real, but it showed just a fraction of the brutality. Followed invariably by: "But they couldn't show these things; nobody could watch it."

Spielberg can be forgiven a certain amount of cinematic license with the story. There were no hangings in *Schindler's List.* No Jews dangled from iron rings in Amon Goeth's office. The dogs wore muzzles; audiences didn't see them gnawing men's genitals and women's breasts like so much hamburger. Spielberg's storm troopers refrained from swinging infants by their feet into brick walls, smashing their skulls like melons. He spared audiences Goeth's theoretically nonlethal punishment of choice. Every one of the *Schindlerjuden* to whom I spoke had either undergone it or witnessed it at sickeningly close range: twenty-five strokes of a lead-tipped leather whip on the bare buttocks, with the victim—laid over a slatted table—counting the blows in German for his or her tormentor. Miss a count and the series began all over again.

It must be said, though, that some survivors are upset about some of the film's more notable fictions. For example, Schindler's emotional—and well-attended— departure from the Brinnlitz factory was far less dramatic in real life than portrayed in the film. In reality, following his farewell speech on the factory floor, he, his wife, a mistress, and a small group of survivors motored out of the compound late at night without ceremony.

Yet even the *Schindlerjuden* who find fault with the presentation are loath to criticize it publicly for two reasons: First, Spielberg accomplished what neither they as survivors nor the irrefutable fact of six million murdered Jews ever could. He grabbed the world's attention. People wanted to listen. They wanted to learn. They wanted to know. They seemed inclined to believe. This, in turn, sparked a sudden and seemingly insatiable demand for the survivors, and anyone else qualified, to shine in Oskar's reflected glory. When his widow, Emilie, appears at tributes, she is mobbed like a movie star. Clearly, it is not because of her own considerable errands of mercy at Brinnlitz (for which she has received scant credit, according to survivors).

Emilie Schindler is in her mid-eighties and lives in Argentina. She was a sweet, proper, devoutly Catholic girl when she and Oskar married in 1928. By all accounts, he was a lousy husband, a prodigious philanderer, and a spendthrift. In interviews she's granted since the film's release, Emilie has gleefully discussed his less than saintly side. But she evidently reconciled herself to his behavior long ago. When she's in New York, she stays with one of Oskar's former mistresses on Long Island.

Some *Schindlerjuden* are booked for speaking engagements a year in advance. There is no question that the list has conferred a certain mystique on the listees. In fact, by the time I got to them, some had been used, abused, and burned out by the media. Over and over I heard about the invasion of the television crews. Holocaust survivors as celebrities du jour? It made their heads spin.

Second, they worry that pointing out any inconsistency or error—no matter how trivial—will further arm the deniers, the people who will say, "If *this* isn't true, and if *that* isn't true, then why should anyone believe *any* of it?"

Holocaust denial—historical revisionism, if you prefer—is a growth industry. Surveys have shown that millions of Americans believe it's *possible* the Holocaust never happened. Then there are the professional anti-Semites and hatemongers eager to capitalize on the ignorance of those millions.

It's an argument no rational person should bother joining. But it gets to one reason why I wrote this book. The youngest Holocaust survivors are in their mid-fifties; most are over seventy. Forty years from now, it's likely that they'll all be gone. These people are living history. Their stories simply must be told *by them,* in their own words, in their lifetimes. No one else can—or should—try to interpret or appropriate their experience.

"While we are still alive ... if we will not leave a good testimony—the way we were brought up and the way we came to be normal human beings, and the way we raised our families and dedicated ourselves to the family, and how we helped each other—then so much more will be lost for the future generations," New Jersey survivor Murray Pantirer told me. "We felt like we had a mission. We, the survivors, without an education, became ambassadors for our families. The way we behave, the people of the world can appreciate whom we had lost. If I am—God forbid—a nobody, then six million nobodies were killed by the Germans."

Thomas Keneally interviewed some of these people for his book *Schindler's List* in the early 1980s. Some went to Israel with Spielberg in 1993 to film the final sequences of the movie. For many years, some had been active making speeches and conducting workshops for survivor groups. British director Jonathan Blair featured others in *Schindler,* his 1983 documentary for Thames Television.

But others had never spoken about their pasts to anyone outside their families and closest friends, and never intended to. Every time they did, pain, guilt, anxiety, sadness, and fear overwhelmed them. They simply couldn't stand it. It was bad enough that nothing could banish the nightmares. Why should they punish themselves further by *intentionally* summoning the horror? Others had given up talking early on. What could they say to the American relatives complaining about wartime shortages of meat and nylon stockings?

But the senses remember, even as the intellect struggles to forget. Some survivors can't look at or listen to trains, pass smokestacks, or wait on lines. Others can't tolerate tardiness or the waste of food. They wolf their meals. The sound of spoken German makes some of them physically ill. Dogs terrify a few of them, especially big dogs like Danes, shepherds, and Dalmatians—the breeds favored by the Nazis. Many still jump when the phone rings, their voices prickly with dread when they answer. Who could it be? What do they want?

Irrational fears torment them. One *Schindlerjude* told me about American survivor friends who go to bed every night behind a forest of deadbolts, convinced that Nazis will come in the dark and drag them away.

Another reason I wrote this book is because the film *Schindler's List* starred a Nazi: industrialist/bon vivant Oskar Schindler. It costarred another Nazi: *Hauptsturmführer* Amon Goeth, commandant of the Kraków-Płaszów *Konzentrationslager.* Schindler's Jewish *Haftlinge*—his prisoners—appeared as the supporting cast: helpless Jews dependent on a gentile for their very lives, not to mention all the little details. From time to time, the film showed acts of Jewish courage and canniness—bold, split-second decisions with everything to lose *and* everything to gain.

It must be said that in the grand and grotesque scheme of the Holocaust, Jews did vastly more to save themselves and each other—to the small extent salvation was possible—than all non-Jews, especially in Poland. Too little has been offered along the avenues of popular culture about the efforts Jews made to preserve themselves, their families, their faith, and their heritage. Defiance wasn't limited to the Warsaw Ghetto uprising.

But neither can armed struggle define Jewish resistance to Adolf Hitler's Final Solution. Resist with what? Yes, the Jewish men of Camp Płaszów had shaving razors and rocks, but their German and Ukrainian guards had guns.

Escape where? Even sympathetic Poles seldom risked their own families' safety by hiding Jews. Most Poles were delighted to deliver Jews to the nearest Gestapo office for the reward of a five-pound bag of sugar, or a used winter coat.

Sanctuary? For centuries, the Polish Church preached hatefully against the Jews. Many survivors told me that their families never ventured outside during Easter, because the priests had been exhorting their flocks to avenge Christ's death by killing Jews.

Even the Polish underground was hostile to Jews. Several survivors told stories about friends or relatives escaping to the resistance, only to be shot by their confreres when unmasked as Jews.

The survivors also learned how little the rest of the world had done to save them, how Roosevelt and Churchill, the great democratic leaders, essentially turned their backs on the beleaguered Jews of Europe. It broke their hearts. Thank God they didn't know it at the time, they told me. Hope was all that kept them going.

Things didn't improve after the war. On July 4, 1946, as Americans ecstatically celebrated their first postwar Independence Day (the war with Japan ended in August 1945), a crazed mob in the Polish city of Kielce hacked, shot, stoned, and bludgeoned to death forty-two Jews. Some were children; others were Polish army officers. Some could be identified only by their Birkenau tattoos. Violent, anti-Semitic spasms already had shattered thousands of returning Jews' resettlement fantasies. The Kielce pogrom's chilling message propelled thousands more toward the nearest border. "Poland is one big cemetery for the Jewish people," a survivor told me.

But there's another reason why more Jews didn't resist or escape: collective punishment. Those who fought back or ran away brought death or, at the very least, increased suffering, upon fellow Jews. It was one of the rare guarantees in a world where nothing made sense. Sixty years before anyone ever heard of "virtual reality," the Nazis invented it.

But the Jews calculated their own small defiances. Just because the Nazis considered them *Untermenschen* and *Unterfrauen*—subhuman—didn't mean they had to act like it. Manci Rosner of Queens remembers that a woman named Anna Koenigsberg hid diamonds in the socket behind her glass eye. Prisoners "brushed" their teeth with their fingers and the brown liquid that passed for coffee. They used whatever they could scrounge for sanitary napkins and toilet paper: rags, bits of newspaper, straw. Women rubbed beet peels on their cheeks for a spot of color. They fought degradation as hard as they fought to survive.

Even more subtle were the acts of religious resistance. Many devout Jews refused to eat overtly non-kosher food, or transgress Talmudic law, even if it meant starvation or execution. Some actually refused to work on the Sabbath or eat bread during Passover. *In concentration camps.* They prayed constantly.

In all these ways—and, most important, by producing children and leading productive, honorable lives after the war—the surviving Jews of Europe thwarted the Final Solution.

Most of the *Schindlerjuden* in this country became great American patriots. The United States took them in when nobody else would, gave them the chance to raise families, own businesses, buy houses, and give their sons and daughters—an enormous number of whom are successful professionals—the educations stolen from them. As immigrants, the *Schindlerjuden* treasure the constitutional basics that native-born Americans take so much for granted.

Most also are staunch supporters of the State of Israel, of the haven it represents for all Jews, for all time. Had there been such an entity in 1939, they say, the world would be a vastly different place.

"We had no leadership that time," Californian Maurice Markheim explained to me. "We were not organized. At that time, if someone told me, 'You gonna die anyway,' and give me a gun in my hand, I would go and kill. But there was nobody who gave us the gun. That's why we have to have strong leadership today and Israel has to exist. Then it will never happen again."

The months during which I researched and wrote this book coincided with anniversary dates heavy with significance for the *Schindlerjuden*. On March 10, 1941, Nazi Governor General Hans Frank ordered the Kraków ghetto established. On June 22, 1941, Germany invaded the Soviet Union. On March 13, 1943, Amon Goeth liquidated the Kraków ghetto.

But things were happening in the here-and-now that dovetailed with the events of history. In April 1994, the University of Miami student newspaper, the *Hurricane*, accepted a paid ad from the Committee for Open Debate on the Holocaust, a denial outfit based in California. "The U.S. Holocaust Memorial Museum displays no convincing proof whatever of homicidal gassing [*sic*] chambers, and no proof that even one individual was 'gassed' in a German program of 'genocide,' " began the ad, which blathered on about the "Holocaust lobby" and "quasi-religious Holocaust zealots," and claimed no one could prove that the heaps of corpses in museum photos actually were *Jewish* corpses. And so on.

Top university administrators supported the *Hurricane*'s decision to run the ad, declaring it a First Amendment issue. Needless to say, a roiling controversy erupted in south Florida. A Jewish benefactor immediately withdrew a two-million-dollar pledge to the university in protest, and an entire community got involved in a screaming match over whether this was about censorship, academic/intellectual freedom, or—as one of the Nazis said to Oskar in *Schindler's List*—"good, old-fashioned Jew-hating talk."

Many of the survivors I interviewed during that time were livid: How could the *Hurricane* editors be so naive? How could the administration be so disingenuous? Don't newspapers, after all, reject paid ads every day for reasons that make a lot less sense?

Other survivors just seemed saddened and deflated by the whole thing. They'd shake their heads and confirm aloud what was obviously on their minds: *It just never ends.*

Then came the bombings at or near Jewish institutions: ninety-six dead in Buenos Aires, Argentina, and London. An airplane carrying mostly Jews exploded over Panama. Islamic radical terrorists triumphantly claimed responsibility for all of it.

On the positive side, in May 1994, the state of Florida mandated Holocaust education in the public schools. The Florida legislature recognized that the lessons of the Holocaust have vital meaning for students from every social and ethnic back-ground.

I would like to suggest that those seeking genuine heroes, idols, and role mod-els might find some in this book—and in the life story of nearly every Jew who man-aged to survive the Holocaust. For that reason, I have included a few survivors who worked at Schindler's enamelware factory, but didn't make it onto his list for the Brinnlitz plant. They were shipped to camps like Mauthausen, Dachau, Gusen II, Linz II, and other hellholes. The conditions these people endured represent the normative camp experience.

You will read here about people whose pain is as raw today as it was fifty years ago—people in their seventies and eighties who cannot speak the names of their mar-tyred parents and siblings without tears. People who can't get through a night without screaming in their sleep. People who lost everyone and everything they ever cared about.

In a culture drowning in its own excuses, here are men and women who have every reason in the world to exploit their trauma. Who could possibly begrudge them their hard-earned victimhood? But they don't seek to blame—even as they may not forgive and certainly will never forget. "I don't believe any of us is one-hundred-percent normal," one of the Schindler women told me. "We are all damaged, physi-cally or mentally."

If that's true—though some survivors insist it isn't—then it's all the more reason to define as heroes those who chose life, when in some cases other alternatives might have brought at least peace. As you will see, Holocaust survival did not grant them immunity from future heartbreak.

I have deliberately remained faithful to the speech and syntax patterns of these individuals. I realize that some of them have spent fifty years struggling to speak Eng-lish like "real" Americans, and I hope this doesn't upset or embarrass anyone. I felt it was important to convey the flavor of an accent headed for extinction. In certain cases, I have smoothed out quotes that seemed overly convoluted, but you will see phrases like "in ghetto" and think that there's a "the" missing. It's not. You will see the past and present tenses used interchangeably. This is how people talk.

You also will notice an obvious variation in the depth of personal exploration in these profiles. No survivor finds it comfortable to discuss the past, but some have had a lot of practice. To them, the words come easier. Generational and cultural constraints limited or structured what people said (or didn't say), as did time. In some cases, sur-vivors couldn't tolerate more than a few hours of discussion. In others cases, I returned several times. Some have secrets of their own, or keep secrets for others. Some are in-trospective and revelatory. Others preferred discussing events rather than feelings.

In some cases, I was asked to omit certain details (sometimes weeks after they'd been freely conveyed to me). Generally, the survivors who asked me to do this explained how and why such things might cause tremendous distress to others. Most of these requests made sense. A few didn't. Sometimes after we talked it through and tinkered some with the phraseology, we could achieve a mutual comfort level. If we couldn't, I bowed to the survivors' requests. It's hardly my place—nor anyone else's—to demand full disclosure about sexual dysfunction, botched relationships, rebellious children, marital infidelity, suicide, or family squabbles, from men and women whose loved ones literally went up in smoke.

Dozens of survivors in the United States who were with Schindler at Emalia or Brinnlitz or both do not appear in this book. Some didn't want to be found. Others, like the Willie S. mentioned in Roman Ferber's chapter, didn't mind being found, but didn't want to go public. (He's the head of a highly recognizable national company. He feared that disclosure of his *Schindlerjude* status would so dramatically change his life that he couldn't do his job. In addition, he was so young at the time that he remembers little of the experience.)

A few have written, or want to write, their own books. Some didn't want to be interviewed because they can't tolerate the stress. One man told me, "If I talk to you, I'll have nightmares for a month," and I believe him.

I interviewed or identified other Schindler workers whose stories are no less compelling and inspiring than those contained in these pages. Space, time, and logistics prevented their inclusion. I would like to recognize them here, and apologize for their omission: Helen and Kuba Beck of Poughkeepsie; Nathan Kreiger and Paula Fishman of Long Island; Leon Cooper of Houston; Zev Kedem of Sacramento; Max and Ala Mingal of Buffalo; Felix Kaminsky of Minneapolis; Joseph Lipshutz of Cape Coral, Florida; Halina Brunnengraber Silber of Baltimore; Salomon Pila of Tampa; Mike Tanner of Sherman Oaks, California; Samuel Klasner of Sunrise, Florida; Sam Soldinger of Phoenix; Joseph Ryba of Brooklyn; Leo Schreiber and Eugene Ginter of the Bronx.

Notable by their absence are Leopold "Paul" Page, or Poldek Pfefferberg, as he was known in Poland (and in *Schindler's List*), and his wife, Mila. Page is the Beverly Hills luggage-shop owner who collared the Australian novelist/playwright/political activist Thomas Keneally in 1980, and convinced him to write the book called *Schindler's List* (all Keneally wanted was a briefcase). Then he convinced Steven Spielberg to make the film. Both, therefore, are heavily influenced by his version of events, and those of his close friends. By now, his story is well known. He acted as an adviser to the film. Steven Spielberg praised him to the world on Oscar night. He has been feted with tributes all over the world.

Page, still barrel-chested and garrulous in his early eighties, is an influential and controversial figure among the *Schindlerjuden,* many of whom have known him since he taught physical education at the Jewish high school in Kraków before the war. As with most homogeneous social groups, within the *Schindlerjuden* there exist factions, alliances and cliques. Some support Poldek Page's position as self-appointed custodian of the Schindler legend; some do not. Yet there isn't one who won't praise his persistence in seeing that Schindler's story got the attention it deserved. Over time, he has come into possession of most of Schindler's documents, and claims the publication rights to scores of Schindler-related photos. He declined to be interviewed for this book until after the time it might have been feasible to do so.

Many survivors knew him as an *Ordnungsdienst*—or OD man, as the Jewish policemen in the ghetto and the camps were called—and as a Płaszów *Blochalteste* (barracks leader). While some OD men were justly reviled as collaborators, there were others like Poldek Pfefferberg who did what they could, when they could, sometimes at considerable personal jeopardy, to assist other Jews, especially their friends. Several *Schindlerjuden* tell stories about risks Page took, or favors he granted, on their behalf.

Page, who didn't work at Emalia, was among the small group who helped smuggle Oskar and Emilie Schindler out of Brinnlitz after Soviet troops liberated the factory. The Schindlers were in extreme danger. They were rich Germans. Oskar was a Nazi. There's no question that he met most definitions of "war criminal," and as he passed into Allied hands, he desperately needed the security of Jewish supporters.

Then, as now, Schindler had an ally in Leopold Page. It was he who sent out a letter in 1969 to hundreds of survivors worldwide. Page asked his fellow "Schindler Jews" to help provide a regular income for Oskar Schindler, by sending a minimum of fifty dollars to the "Oskar Schindler Survivor Fund," to help support their savior in comfort and security.

I am told that even those who could hardly afford it were happy to help.

Adolf Hitler came to power on January 30, 1933. He soon began restricting the rights of Germany's Jews. From the first official government act of persecution on April 1 of that year—the boycott of Jewish businesses—through the 1935 "race shame" laws prohibiting sex and/or marriage between Jews and Gentiles, the Nazis relentlessly regulated every facet of Jewish life. By 1935, 75,000 Jews had fled. After Kristallnacht—the "Night of Broken Glass"—on November 9, 1938, any Jew who didn't leave Germany was confined to a concentration camp. Thousands more crossed over to Poland, which would boast Europe's largest Jewish population on the eve of World War II: 3,300,000. By war's end, only 10 percent remained alive.

The Nazis invaded Poland on September 1, 1939. They took Kraków on the sixth, then home to 60,000 Jews, 26 percent of the city's population. By year's end, Jews lost the right to attend school, keep bank accounts, own businesses, or walk on the sidewalks. They were tagged by a yellow Star of David. By the following April, evacuation orders would pare Kraków's Jewish community to 35,000.

All this transformed Poland into the land of economic opportunity for German entrepreneurs. They swarmed the cities, snapping up forfeited Jewish firms as their Treuhanders, or trustees. One of them was a young salesman named Oskar Schindler, born April 28, 1908, in the Sudetenland. He applied

Gates to the Kraków Ghetto, around 1942.

for Nazi Party membership on February 10, 1939. By then, he was an agent of the German Abwehr, the intelligence. In fact, he had been jailed in 1938 as a spy by the Czechs (he was released when Germany annexed the Sudetenland). Oskar Schindler provided Polish Army uniforms to the German provocateurs who attacked a German border radio station the night before the invasion.

Schindler took over an idled enamelware plant at 4 Lipowa Street in Kraków, capital of the occupation government. A Jew named Abraham Bankier had owned the plant. Schindler renamed it Deutsche Emailwaren Fabrik, and began turning out pots, pans, and mess kits for the German military. He had come to seek his fortune, and with Jewish slave labor, he made one.

By the end of 1942, Schindler employed 370 Jewish workers, all from the Kraków ghetto. He paid their wages directly to the Nazi general government. Word quickly spread that his factory, outside the ghetto, in the Zablocie district, was a safe haven. With copious bribes, Schindler kept the SS at bay, so nobody was beaten on the job. He winked at the flurry of illegal "business" between the factory's Jewish and Polish workers. He lied for people so they could bring in friends and relatives. Most of his "skilled" workers had no skills at all. Eventually one thousand Jews would gain sanctuary at the DEF (called Emalia by its workers).

Hans Frank, the Nazi governor of the Kraków district, established the Kraków ghetto in March 1941; there were 320 residential buildings for 15,000 Jews (the rest had been driven off into the suburbs). Transports and massacres decimated the ghetto population over the next two years. Between June and October 1942, 11,000 ghetto dwellers were sent to the Belżec death camp. Then, on March 13, 1943, *Untersturmführer* Amon Goeth liquidated the ghetto. Those who lived through it became inmates at the Kraków-Płaszów labor camp—later a concentration camp—on the outskirts of the city, under Goeth's bloodthirsty command.

For a few months, Schindler's workers lived in the camp barracks and marched every

Emilie Schindler, Poland, around 1940.

day to the factory at 4 Lipowa Street. At the end of their shifts, they would return to Amon Goeth's hell, and the very real possibility of ending up dead on Chujowa Górka, the camp's notorious execution hill.

The literal translation of Chujowa Górka is "Prick Hill." Some say it earned the name for its shape; others say that although it was primarily a killing-ground, it also was the site of many rapes. One of the Schindler women says she has nightmares to this day of witnessing a gang rape by Ukrainian "blacks"— guards who wore black uniforms emblazoned with death's-head insignias.

The victim, a stunningly beautiful woman, was among a group taken to the hill to be shot; dying from her wounds, she was raped by guard after guard, all the while clutching the hand of her murdered husband. The same witness says she once saw Amon Goeth shoot a girl because—as he told her before pulling the trigger—he didn't like her nose. His favorite recreation was using Jews for target practice.

Oskar Schindler at a social function during the war. The Nazi figures in the photograph were torn out by Adele Gerner, a Brinnlitz worker to whom Schindler gave several photos as he fled the camp.

Daily life at Płaszów proved unbearable for some people: They lost the will to live and so they died. Conditions were so bad that only internal fortitude kept people going. "You knew when people stopped washing themselves, stopped pushing themselves in the line, they were giving up," says Cleveland survivor Jack Mintz. "They didn't answer or ask questions. They became like zombies. If they got torn shoes, they didn't try to find something else to put on."

Schindler's Emalia subcamp extracted his workers from that hell, but in August of 1944 he was ordered to reduce his workforce by about seven hundred. In September, the Emalia subcamp shut down and its remaining workers were sent to Płaszów. In October, Schindler moved his operation to a new plant at Brinnlitz, Czechoslovakia, near his hometown. A second list was drawn up, providing the nucleus of the one in circulation today. The October list consisted of three hundred original Emalia workers and seven hundred replacements for those shipped out in August.

Before Schindler's workers got to Brinnlitz, they made intermediate stops: the women at Auschwitz, the men at a transit camp called Gröss-Rosen. Memories vary, but most survivors think the men stayed about a week at Gröss-Rosen. It was nightmarish, even by Płaszów standards. Chaskel Schlesinger of Chicago remembers the humiliating body searches when they arrived: "You had to open your mouth and spread the fingers and bend over and lift up your feet because you could have [something taped] on the bottom."

The men were run through delousing showers, and then, soaking wet and naked, they were made to stand outside in frigid temperatures. Brooklynite Moses

Goldberg remembers a German officer on a white horse approaching the group and yelling to the guards, " 'Those are *Schindlerjuden!* Put them in a barracks and give them nightshirts, otherwise our hospital will be full of them tomorrow.' "

Schindler's three hundred women left Płaszów two days after his men and spent about three weeks at Auschwitz. It's clear that he knew they would have to stop there, and that a few of the women knew it, too. However, neither he nor they realized they would languish there so long. He had to bribe their way out. In one of the most dramatic scenes in the film *Schindler's List,* the women—stripped and shaved—are shoved into a locked, windowless room. Shower heads stud the ceiling. The Auschwitz gas chambers are no longer a secret. Suddenly, the lights go out, as someone throws a heavy switch. The women are hysterical. Then water blasts from the jets. The women survivors confirm that it actually happened.

"There were old prisoners who were quite rough," remembers Betty Schagrin, a Florida survivor. "They were saying, 'You go in through the big doors and you go out through the chimney.' In the shower, they waited ten minutes to panic people. We started to go crazy."

As awful as they looked, the women were a welcome sight to the worried men at Brinnlitz, where the copy of Schindler's list currently circulating was drawn up on April 18, 1945. In a clunky, manual typeface, it logs the names of 297 women and 800 men, each page headed: "K.L. Gröss-Rosen - A.L. Brunnlitz/Liste der mannl.Haftling [or weibl.Haftling, for the women] 18.4.45." *Haftling* is German for prisoner. K.L. stands for *Konzentrationslager.*

The only difference between the *Frauen* (women) and the *Manner* (men) is that the women are listed alphabetically. Otherwise, both read from left to right: list number, prisoner number, name, date of birth, job classification.

The April 18 list is a jumble of inaccuracies: phony birth dates—some off by decades—and altered identities. Some mistakes are intentional; others resulted from confusion or disinformation, or simple typos. There are German spellings, Polish spellings, and Hebrew transliterations into both languages.

By April 18, Janka Feigenbaum and a Mrs. Hofstatter had died of natural causes. About ten young boys and their fathers had been taken to Auschwitz soon after arriving at Brinnlitz in the fall, so they weren't listed. Canadian journalist Herbert Steinhouse, who interviewed Schindler at length in 1949, estimates that about eighty names were added from the "frozen transport": men from Goleszów, an Auschwitz subcamp, who had been locked in two sidetracked freight cars without food or water for ten days in subzero temperatures. Abraham Bankier, the enamelware plant's original owner, appears twice, and some people who unquestionably were at Brinnlitz don't appear at all. According to Steinhouse, Schindler also gathered in Jewish fugitives who escaped transports leaving Auschwitz, including Belgians, Dutch, and Hungarians.

All in all, the composition of the list is as much of a puzzle as Oskar Schindler's motives, a topic of endless debate among the *Schindlerjuden*. Was he an angel masquerading as an opportunist? An opportunist masquerading as an angel? Did he intend to save eleven hundred Jews, or was their survival simply one result of his self-serving game plan? Did he build the Emalia subcamp to protect Jews or to keep Amon Goeth from interfering in his lucrative black marketeering?

"I think he was a gambler and loved to outwit the SS," says Rena Finder of Massachusetts. "In the beginning, it was a game. It was fun at first. He joined the [Nazi party] to make money. But he had no stomach for the killing. He enjoyed the wheeling and dealing and doing outrageous things—living on the edge. But then he realized if he didn't save us, nobody would."

Did he have a sudden change of heart, or undergo a gradual metamorphosis? It's hard to say. Henry Rosner of Queens, New York, claims that there was a definitive moment: "Two girls ran away to Kraków. Goeth sent two Jewish policemen and said, 'If you don't find them, ten OD men will be hanged.' They found those girls. All women [were ordered] to *Appell* for hanging. Schindler came and saw Goeth shoot them two seconds before they died hanging. Schindler vomited in front of everybody. He would never be working for the Germans again, he said to me."

In 1964, a decade before Schindler's demise from alcoholic complications, a German television news crew caught up with him on the streets of Frankfurt and asked him the question directly. He replied "The persecution of the Jews under the General Government of Poland meant that we could see the horror emerging gradually in many ways. In 1939 the Jews were forced to wear the Star of David and people were herded and shut up into ghettos.

Oskar Schindler with female companions, apparently twins, about 1940.

"Then in the years 1941 and 1942, there was plenty of public evidence of pure sadism. With people behaving like pigs, I felt the Jews were being destroyed. I had to help them."

The bottom line for most is this: "If I hadn't been with Schindler, I'd be dead." And that's all that matters. (It's thought that nearly four hundred *Schindlerjuden* are still alive; about half live in Israel.)

Clearly, Oskar Schindler was a sybarite, a sexually voracious, thrill-seeking dandy. He wore so much cologne that you could smell him before you saw him. Apparently he considered his sexual magnetism negotiable capital in situations where gemstones or vodka might have had a less dramatic impact. One of the Schindler women told me that a group complained to Herr Direktor about the abuses of a female camp guard at Brinnlitz. He said he would take care of things. Later, he remarked to the women that someone should have warned him about how bad the guard smelled. He seemed to have had an infinite capacity for alcohol. When he came to New York in 1957, he stayed with Manci and Henry Rosner in Queens. Manci remembers how "every single night, we got him a bottle of cognac, and in the morning, I found an empty bottle. But he was never drunk."

One of the survivors told Steinhouse, "It's the personality more than anything else that saved us." Another, who hailed from Schindler's hometown, said, "As a Zwittau citizen, I never would have considered him capable of all these wonderful deeds. Before the war, you know, everybody here called him *Gauner* [swindler]."

He permitted the Jews to observe holidays (secretly) and, at Brinnlitz, to bury their dead traditionally. He got them extra food and rudimentary medical care. He accepted the frozen transport when no one else would, and, with his wife, Emilie, lavished personal attention and resources on the half-dead survivors.

According to Steinhouse, the Schindlers "never spent a single night" in their comfortable "villa" at Brinnlitz, sleeping instead in a small room at the factory, because Oskar understood how deeply the Jews feared late-night visits by the SS.

It's hard to say what was in that sort of thing for him, except the creation of goodwill, which in itself was a valuable commodity. Were his humane actions really planned to ensure that the grateful Jews would protect him after the Germans lost and support him for the rest of his life? Some people think so.

Sol Urbach of New Jersey has one theory: "Oskar Schindler, on April eighteenth, recognized that everything was over, so he told somebody in Brinnlitz, 'Make me a list of all the people who are here.' That's when Oskar Schindler hatched his plan of escape. There is no question in my mind that that was going through his mind. He needed this list of who survived in his camp because he was going to go to Germany and take this list into some agency."

It's commonly believed that Schindler had far less to do with compiling the list than Marcel Goldberg, the greedy Jewish policeman. (In the film, Goldberg takes Oskar's gold watch and cigarette case as a payoff to place Jewish workers at Emalia.) Most people who saw the movie will recall the scene in which Oskar and his faithful accountant, Itzhak Stern (played by Ben Kingsley), laboriously construct the list from their hearts and minds. In reality, it was

Marcel Goldberg who controlled the list, not Stern or even Schindler. According to many survivors, Goldberg demanded payment directly from those who wanted to get on the list.

What's definite is that seven hundred Emalia workers were sent to death camps. Some survived; others didn't. There's no small amount of bitterness among the former group and among the surviving relatives of the latter. After the war, some confronted Schindler, demanding to know why they had been left behind. He said he couldn't stand over Goldberg's shoulder keeping track all the time.

When Oskar left Brinnlitz, he was accompanied by Emilie, a mistress, and eight Jewish inmates as-

Emilie Schindler, 1994.

signed to safeguard him. The group left the factory on May 8, 1945, in Oskar's Mercedes. A truck pulling two trailers followed. The interior of the Benz—the seats and door panels—had been stuffed with valuables. The Schindlers also carried a letter, signed by some of his workers, explaining his role in saving their lives.

The entourage headed southwest, first getting stuck in a Wehrmacht convoy, then halted by Czech partisans. They stopped over for the night in a town called Havlickuv Brod. They spent the night at the town jail—not as prisoners, but for the accommodations—then awoke to find their vehicles stripped, inside and out. They proceeded by train, then on foot.

In the spring of 1945, Kurt Klein, an intelligence officer in the U.S. Army—a German-born Jew—encountered Oskar's traveling party near the Czech village of Eleanorenhain, on its way from Brinnlitz to the Swiss border.

Klein got permits for the group to remain in the American Zone of Occupation until it could find transportation for the rest of the trip.

"Nobody knew who he was at the time," Klein has said. "They were all dressed in prison uniforms and presented themselves as refugees from a German labor camp. They didn't let on that Schindler, their Nazi labor camp director, was in their midst, probably because they were afraid I would arrest him as a POW. They were correct, because my assignment was to interrogate and segregate Germans caught fleeing from Russian and Czech guns." Klein (now retired in Arizona) enlisted the aid of other Jewish American servicemen to ensure the group's safe passage to the Swiss border town of Konstanz.

When Steinhouse met Oskar, he found that the forty-year-old Schindler was "a man of convincing honesty and outstanding charm. Tall and erect, with broad shoulders and a powerful trunk, he usually has a cheerful smile on his strong face. His frank, gray-blue eyes smile too, except when they tighten in distress as he talks of the past. Then his whole jaw juts out belligerently and his great fists are clutched and pounded in slow anger. When he laughs, it is a boyish and hearty laugh, one that all his listeners enjoy to the full."

According to Steinhouse, Schindler helped American investigators gather evidence against Nazi war criminals by "presenting the occupying power with the most detailed documentation on all his old drinking companions, on the vicious owners of the other slave factories . . . on all the rotten group he had wined and flattered while inwardly loathing, in order to save the lives of helpless people."

But in 1949, Oskar Schindler was "a lost soul. Everyday life became more difficult and unsettled. A Sudeten German, he had no future in Czechoslovakia and at the time could no longer stand the Germany he had once loved. For a time, he tried living in Regensburg. Later he moved to Munich depending heavily on Care parcels sent to him from America by some of the *Schindlerjuden*, but too proud to plead for more help.

"Polish Jewish welfare organizations traced him, discovered him in want, and tried to bring some assistance even in the midst of their own bitter postwar troubles."

A New York woman and Płaszów survivor who had relatives on the list recalls that in the summer of 1945, Schindler told her that he'd been warned to stay out of Poland, "because he'd meet the same fate as had Dr. Gross and Kerner, the OD men [Jews killed for their war crimes]. He'd meet it at the hands of those who got knocked off the list."

The Jewish Joint Distribution Committee gave Oskar money and set up the Schindlers in Argentina on a nutria ranch, where they tried raising the minklike animals. He failed. Survivors bought him an apartment in Buenos Aires, but he left Emilie in 1957 and went back to Germany. He tried running a cement plant but failed at that, too. He just couldn't seem to adjust to the banality of life in peacetime.

He visited Israel in 1962. The *Schindlerjuden* there received him like a potentate. From then on, he never lacked for support from his "children." Before he died in 1974, he asked that the *Schindlerjuden* take his remains to Israel and bury him there. He lies in the Catholic cemetery on Mount Zion.

Whatever he was between 1939 and 1945, he has come to represent so much more than a mere flesh-and-blood mortal. He has become, in legend, what most people want to believe they themselves would become in situations of moral extremis. "Each one of us at any time, faced with the particular circumstances, has the power to stand on the side of right," a California survivor named Leon Leyson told me. "Ninety-nine percent of the time, we simply don't. This is an ordinary man, not a special hero with super powers, and yet he did it."

He also has allowed hundreds of men and women to answer at least part of the imponderable question: *Why did I survive and six million perish?* Answer: *Because of Oskar Schindler.*

THE ROSNER FAMILY

"Come! Come! I want to show you my museum."

Long, delicate fingers tremble lightly on a visitor's arm, as Henry Rosner steers a course around the quadruple-locked front door toward a room stocked with memories.

Here is his violin—the one made in 1918 that returned to him after the war like a faithful old dog. Here, on a high shelf, rests the pearly red accordion an SS guard gave his son, Alexander, at Auschwitz. Here he keeps the LPs he and his brothers made and his violin collectibles—ashtrays, miniatures, and the like. And the photographs: Henry in his dashing prime, often mistaken for Danny Kaye; his wife Manci with Oskar Schindler, smiling and free, after the war; Alexander in his U.S. Navy officer's uniform.

In the wretched mass of thirty thousand Płaszów *Haftlinge*, where nearly everyone looked the same, smelled the same, hungered, shivered, despaired, and feared the same, the Rosners kept their identity: They were the musicians. They weren't just numbers.

Henry played the fiddle; his brother Leopold, called Poldek, the accordion. They entertained *Hauptsturmführer* Amon Goeth's party guests with musical pleasantries and obsequious smiles. And sometimes, when Amon Goeth grew sleepy after a long, hard day torturing and murdering Jews, they played lullabyes at his bedside, consigning him to his dreams. "He liked German songs," says Henry. "He had such a good ear, he could tell when I changed violins." Often, the brothers would be called to play after a killing spree, "to ease his conscience," Henry has said.

Prisoners would see them trekking to the commandant's residence under guard, wearing tuxedos, instruments in hand. Incredibly, given Amon Goeth's volatile nature, they always returned. Oskar Schindler dined there often, as did the other Kraków-area *Treuhänders,* local and visiting SS brass, Gestapo bigshots, and a revolving harem of agreeable young women.

Wilhelm Rosner, the youngest brother, played the bugle. Promptly at seven each morning, he roused the camp from its uneasy slumber, blowing a reveille of his own composition. Fifty years later, some Płaszów veterans still can hum it. In the frigid winter, his lips froze to the mouthpiece, but he never missed a day. "Twelve, I played for lunch, and twelve-thirty, go back to work," he remembers. He alone was permitted a wristwatch, so he would always be on time. *Exactly* on time.

A sensitive and emotional boy, Bill Rosner was, to some extent, the camp's psychological barometer. "One night, my father's friend, who was a heavy smoker, was smoking in a place he shouldn't, and a Nazi came and shot him right away. I was so upset that I couldn't sleep one minute, and in the morning when I started to play, all the people said, 'Something is wrong. This is not the right sound.' "

Manci Rosner was well known too, not just as Henry-the-violinist's wife, but as a Płaszów *Blochalteste,* a housemother of sorts to three hundred women. Some still speak of how she offered hope simply by maintaining her dignity and humanity. Her snooty Viennese breeding served her well in these dire times.

Then there was Alexander. In *Schindler's List,* he is called "Olek," a diminutive his parents still use. He was four when the war began, and like the other unauthorized children at Płaszów, materialized and vanished as the occasion demanded. Arranging and monitoring his whereabouts consumed vast stores of his parents' energy, and allied them forever with those who helped safeguard his life.

Alex Rosner says that many years after the camps, his father told him about his deal with the Nazis: "As long as you keep my son alive, I will play for

Manci and Henry Rosner with the actors who portrayed them in the film Schindler's List: *Beata Paluch (left) and Jacek Wojcicki (right).*

you. The minute he dies or is taken away, it doesn't matter anymore what you do to me." Henry understood that the Nazis' passion for music rivaled their loathing of the Jews.

Henry Rosner is nearly ninety years old. The predictable infirmities of age have hobbled his gait, confused his speech, and short-circuited his temperament. He's sunny and clear one minute, thunder and lightning the next. As he decade-surfs through the past, waves of recollection lap and backwash over each other.

Manci is in her mid-eighties, but could easily pass for a decade younger. She copes, within a range of solicitous patience and white-knuckled exasperation. "Henry," she'll warn, if he heads down certain pathways, "I don't want you to talk about that. You know it makes you cry." It usually doesn't help: He talks, he cries. She lets out a long breath and steadies him with a firm but gentle hand.

Manci Rosner with Steven Spielberg, in Israel, for the filming of the final scene of Schindler's List.

They have been together, in love and war, for nearly seventy years. In the early spring of 1994, when he could still tolerate the shoulder pain, Henry tucked a fiddle under his chin and brought tears to the eyes of his wife with a wobbly, but quite respectable, rendition of "Nobody Loves You Like I Do." "It's from an operetta," said Manci Rosner, whose uncharacteristic display of emotion surprised even herself. "He used to play it for me."

The Rosners were pillars of the Krakovian inner circle that dominated Jewish prisoner life at Płaszów, at Emalia, and later at Oskar Schindler's Brinnlitz factory. Their connections to, and alliances with, the camp's most influential Jews stretched back years. Henry and Poldek's frequent contacts with Schindler, chez Goeth, offered Oskar's protection to the entire extended Rosner family, which included Regina Rosner Horowitz—the brothers' sister—her husband, Dolek, their son, Ryszard, and daughter Niusia.

The power of their name and status can't be overestimated. Bill says it once kept him from getting shot. He had a flashlight in Płaszów. "I was maybe fourteen. I was walking with it: tick, tick, tick"—he mimes, swinging a flashlight by his side, clicking it on and off—"and a Nazi comes in a private car: 'To whom did you make this signal?' He opened up the gun, put it in my neck. I saw a guy—a Jewish guy, who was always taking care of Amon Goeth's horses—he was going on a horse so fast. He stopped. He said, 'Officer, who are you killing? This is *Rosner!* He plays for Amon Goeth!' He said, 'Oh, I'm sorry.' This saved my life."

Still, no Jewish *Haftling* was indemnified. Henry remembers that once, at Goeth's, a "big SS man who hated Jews" got drunk and deliberately shot into the ceiling over Henry's head, raining plaster chunks down on his violin. Another time, one of the commandant's flesh-eating Great Danes growled at the violinist. "Are you afraid?" Goeth asked. Henry realized it was a test. "I said, 'No.' I pet the dog. He said, 'That's my boy,'" and proceeded to get Henry drunk on schnapps.

As for the job of *Blochalteste,* "You bet your life it was a dangerous position," says Manci. Yes, it gave her a small, private cubicle with its own wood-stove, a bit of extra food, and a decent pair of boots, but it also held her accountable for the infractions of every woman on her block and vulnerable to punishment on their behalf.

Once, during an *Appellplatz* lineup, someone turned up missing. A woman from her block had escaped. Manci Rosner paid for her disobedience with twenty-five lashes on the bare buttocks. (They never caught the woman, says Manci, "Thank God." She lives today in Australia.) "Luckily, it was an OD man who did it, so he slapped once the boot, once me. But for six weeks, anyway, I had infections."

Henry was born in 1905 in Kraków, the oldest of Henry and Francesca Rosner's nine children: five sons and four daughters. His parents actually called him Hermann, but he changed his name after the war to honor the memory of his

Manci (left) and Gertrude Robitcshek dressed as clowns, 1920s.

father, who also had been a violinist. He also abhorred sharing the name of Gestapo chief Hermann Göring.

In addition to Leopold, Regina, and Bill, Henry had a sister who died in childhood; two who died in the Holocaust: Melanie, killed in the ghetto, and Marysia, killed at the Stutthof death camp; a brother, Samek, who died of overeating two days after liberation from Mauthausen (he'd been at Płaszów with the rest of the family, but decided to follow his girlfriend to a camp in Germany rather than go to Brinnlitz). The fifth brother, George, came to the United States as a pianist with a Polish orchestra for the 1939 World's Fair. He lost a wife and child in Poland, but remarried and had a second family. He lives in Arizona.

The elder Rosners were taken on a transport in 1942. "A Gentile fellow who was involved with a Jewish girl went after the train," says Henry. He reported all on board were shot.

Manci was born Marianne Robitcshek in October 1910, the younger of Max and Ernestina Guth Robitcshek's two daughters. She and her sister, Gertrude, were pampered girls: They took dancing lessons, went to summer camp, and had nannies and fine clothes.

Ernestina Robitcshek died in 1934 of diabetes. Every year, Manci visits her grave in Vienna. Max was taken first to Theresienstadt, then to Auschwitz. Gertrude, a childless divorcée, was killed in Berlin, where she had been managing family real estate. "They confiscated the property and took her to a *Lager* [a camp] where she died" in the early 1940s, according to Manci.

Manci and Henry met in Vienna, where her father owned the Café Central. She was a sixteen-year-old dressmaker. He was playing "in a very nice restaurant orchestra." Sometimes, Max would take his daughters there. "He started to flirt, then he found out who I was. He was cute," young, slim, and suave, in his black-velvet jacket. They fell madly in love.

Her mother was appalled. "Henry made a very good living, but for my mother, it was like a gypsy, and on top of it, a Polish musician! My mother was Viennese from three generations. If it was not Austrian, not Viennese, it was not good. But she saw that there was no way out, so she gave in. My father liked him. He was not Viennese. He was Czech."

In 1929, Henry's father gave her "a beautiful solitaire with little diamonds. In the ghetto, when we had to give up everything, I gave up that ring, too."

Needless to say, thanks to Ernestina's disapproval, the wedding the next year in a Vienna synagogue was modest, followed

Manci Rosner as a young girl with her sister, Gertrude, and her parents, Ernestina and Max Robitcshek. Vienna, 1920s.

by a family dinner. "It was very simple," says Manci. "My girls in the atelier made me a white dress—crepe georgette—to the floor, with a veil." They sewed five hairs into the gown. "There was a superstition that if you sew a hair in the wedding gown, you will get married, too."

"Rosner's Players" were well known before the war, working the swanky cafés and clubs in Europe's sophisticated cities: Vienna, Kraków, Berlin, Prague. The Club Adria in Warsaw. The Moulin Rouge in Łódź. Zakopane resorts in winter. Summers at the famous Hotel Patria in Krynica. Until her son's birth, Manci traveled with her husband. Once the baby came along, she settled down in Warsaw. She, Olek, and the nanny would accompany Henry only to the resorts.

Alex Rosner, born in February 1935, recalls little of his early years, just that his father was a popular musician "in the class of Tommy Dorsey,"

Henry Rosner's band, "Rosner's Players," before the war.

and that his family led a privileged life ... until 1939. On September 1, Germany invaded Poland. Six days later they took Kraków, where Henry happened to be playing on "a very good contract." Manci and Olek moved in with relatives, while Henry ran east, to the Soviet-occupied territories. "I was thinking Henry was going to send for me, but we couldn't communicate," says Manci. "He just came walking in one night" in mid-1940, and the family returned to Warsaw.

"I said 'Heil Hitler!' to a German on the corner," Henry recalls of his reentry to Kraków. "This was very much at the beginning: no ghetto yet. You were still free to go around, but there were armbands and curfews. You couldn't ride the tramway. The cafés were closed, and Jewish businesses taken."

On the eve of the Warsaw ghetto's creation, in November 1940, the Rosners fled to the peasant village of Tyniec, south of Kraków. Manci did some sewing. They secured the most basic accommodations.

"I had my trousseau. That paid for our shed," says Manci Rosner. "I paid with embroidered nightgowns and sheets. We had the whole family there: in-laws, sisters, brothers, not far away. Henry's mother was a marvelous cook." She concocted a dish everyone called *zupa nic:* " 'soup nothing,' from just potatoes, vegetables, little onions that grew around. It tasted terrific! Then they came again with an order, and everybody had to move from there to the [Kraków] ghetto. I still had some lingerie, sheets, drapes that we could take. We had a little jewelry and cash. But we never accumulated money; we spent it."

It is difficult to imagine any daughter of the formidable Ernestina Guth Robitcshek adjusting to such grubby circumstances. "I don't think I ever did,"

Henry, Alexander, and Manci Rosner, Poland, 1936.

Manci admits. "But I had a child, and I had to live for him. He didn't know what was going on. He never asked. I was not open with my emotions then, and I am not now, either. I had thought until then it was temporary. From then, I knew it would get bad."

Fortunately, it "got bad" in stages. "In the ghetto, we had a very nice, six-room apartment with the Horowitzes" and eight other families. The bath was in the hallway.

Henry and Poldek made a little money entertaining at a café operated by Alexander Forster. He was a German Jew, the son of a piano manufacturer, and a spy for the Gestapo. He didn't wear an armband, his family had a private ghetto apartment, and he had special permission to run a business. Still, according to Henry, "in the end, they finished him off like a dog."

When Henry could no longer play at Forster's, he played at the *Luftwaffe* mess at the airbase. There, a barman befriended him. One day, the barman and his girlfriend showed up at the Rosners' apartment. The girlfriend was wearing a voluminous cape. They told the Rosners something was afoot, and they didn't believe Olek was safe in the ghetto. "So this German woman took

Alexander and Manci Rosner, Poland, 1930s.

him out under the cape, and she had him in her apartment five days," says Manci. "She was a good woman."

Manci earned pocket change catering to the card players who joined Dolek Horowitz's evening poker games at the apartment. "At eleven, they got hungry, so I baked pastry and made coffee, and they paid me."

Manci Rosner wanted another child, but not in a dirty, crowded ghetto, with an unknown future. When she found herself pregnant at the beginning of 1943, she went to the ghetto's Jewish Hospital and had an abortion. Her sister-in-law Marysia enlisted a friend, Bronia Gunz, to bring Manci her meals. "She came every day and brought me food," says Manci. "I'm never going to forget this girl as long as I live." They remain close friends.

Olek almost didn't survive long enough to enter Płaszów. Just before an *Aktion* in the ghetto, while his parents were at work, he wandered away from their apartment. "I got the urge to go exploring, and got thoroughly lost," he recalls. "I found myself face to face with a couple of nuns," who took him to an apartment. "They got friendly with me and offered me hot chocolate. They stroked my head and I fell asleep, and they kept me there. When I woke up, they packed me off, and I found my way home. I noticed that the streets were completely deserted. I was exhausted, and fell asleep on the bed. My parents came home and were hysterical. The Nazis had come and taken all the children and old people away."

In addition to his musical chores, Henry was given an easy job painting stripes on the fire buckets in the camp paint shop so that he wouldn't injure his hands.

Manci became head of Płaszów's Women's Block number 10 by popular demand. "They pushed us in a row, and they asked, 'Who speaks German?' All the women pushed me in front. I was the best speaking. I didn't even speak Polish. I got a little corner for myself, with a little stove, and I could cook there. The women who still had some money came to me and I sold them a dinner: rice, potatoes, noodles. Sometimes I got a piece of meat and made a soup. This was all from the black market: the Jewish workers who had outside jobs."

Henry, confined to the men's barracks, managed to visit her "little corner" with some regularity. "Somehow he got in. Everybody respected him because he was covered by Goeth. You couldn't touch him. We made love. We talked. We did everything that a young couple would normally do. We were young then, you know?"

The women on the block, who hailed from all over Poland, developed friendships, according to Manci. "Misery loves company. We were dreaming to sit at a table, with a white tablecloth, a pot of coffee, and loaf of bread. That was the most beautiful thing that could be. Some were dreaming about their boyfriends or their husbands and their children.

"I had a woman on the third tier, and she was singing all the time, lying on her stomach, sticking out her head. Other women got so nervous, they came to me complaining. So I said to her: 'Must you sing all the time?' She said, 'Manci, I'm so hungry; when I sing, I don't feel it so much.' When something happened in camp, we heard. When one suffered, they were crying together."

The Rosners worried most about their son. "A lot of times, he was not in Płaszów," Manci explains. "Pfefferberg [Leopold Page, a Jewish policeman, or OD man] took him to Bochnia. Moniek Horowitz [Dolek's brother] was an OD man in Bochnia. When Henry was playing by Goeth, he would sometimes say, 'Take your child away to Horowitz.' He knew when there would be *Aktions* in other towns."

Early on in her tenure as *Blochalteste*, Manci and her "colleagues" got a lesson in the kind of business Amon Goeth meant. "I remember one day, a big hole was dug, big as a room, six feet deep, in the middle of the *Appellplatz*. They called the heads of all the blocks—we had twelve women's blocks and twelve men's—and Poldek [Pfefferberg] was one.

"They told us to go to this hole. On the other side came a truck. They had to get naked, these women and men, across from us, and they had to kneel, and from the back came an SS, who shot them in the neck, gave a kick, and they fell in the hole. Then we had to put the dirt, and Goeth made a speech to us: 'I want you to see that, and tell to people in your block what is going to happen if one is going to sabotage.' They came from the outside—runaways, or were denounced by Poles. So, you see, I could have been killed for the girl who ran away. I was very lucky."

Amon Goeth, who took command of the Kraków-Płaszów camp in February 1943, occupied two less grandiose residences before he moved into the posh hillside villa shown in *Schindler's List.* One of Henry Rosner's clearest and fondest memories from his days of musical servitude involves an incident at the villa. He never tires of telling it.

Amon was entertaining the usual crowd of fun-loving Nazis, all heavily lubricated by black-market alcoholic beverages. Late in the evening, the Rosner brothers struck up a sentimental and melancholy Hungarian tune called "Gloomy Sunday," at the request of a *Waffen* SS officer. They played it once, then again and then again. Henry noticed that the guest was growing increasingly morose. They played on, a fourth time, a fifth, amazed that Goeth hadn't signaled them on to something more cheerful. ("Gloomy Sunday" is the tale of a young man who decides to die for love.)

Henry fixated on the forlorn officer. He actually convinced himself that he could fiddle the man to death. Six, seven, eight. The officer couldn't stand it anymore. Nine, ten times in a row! He lurched toward the balcony door, yanked it open, and, says Henry, *"Bink!"* He shot himself in the head. *"Bink!"*

"I felt so happy that I hurt a German," says Henry, his eyes crinkling to little more than slits as he grins. He accompanies the tale with a tape he and Poldek once made of the song. He knows precisely which crescendo lured the German officer over the brink, and it never fails to delight him.

Some people know this story from Thomas Keneally's book *Schindler's List.*

Manci says that a man from Canada once asked to kiss Henry Rosner's hand: "the hand that killed a Nazi."

For Oskar's thirty-sixth birthday, on April 28, 1944, Henry asked Goeth for permission to entertain *Herr Direktor* at Emalia. Goeth consented. Henry enlisted "Ivan the Russian," a normally bestial camp guard who happened to have a wonderful singing voice, and the two of them went to Lipowa Street. Ivan "got plastered," Henry recalls, and left the room. Henry and Oskar were alone. Oskar knew how badly the war was going for Germany, and how at any time he might be forced to shut down his subcamp.

"He wanted to take his chair and throw it on a picture of Hitler," Henry remembers. "But it fell apart in his hand."

In the late summer of 1944, when Goeth got the order to fold Kraków-Płaszów and its affiliates, Schindler devised the move to Czechoslovakia. He assured Henry and Poldek that wherever he went, he'd take the Rosner clan. And he kept his word. Everyone except the girl who would become Bill Rosner's wife, Erna Zuckerman, made the list.

On October 15, 1944, Henry, Poldek, Bill, and Olek Rosner, along with Dolek and Ryszard Horowitz, joined the cattle-car transport of Schindler men bound for Brinnlitz, through Gröss-Rosen, a transit camp. Manci, Regina, and Poldek's wife, Helena, would soon follow, with the Schindler women.

The men couldn't believe what they saw, heard, and breathed at Gröss-Rosen. Płaszów had been horrendous, granted, especially near the end, with the frantic exhumation and incineration of 10,000 decaying corpses from the Chujowa Górka. But this place was surreal. Snarling, bellowing, flailing psychopaths in uniforms ran the camp. Glazed-eyed, skeletal inmates wandered around like rag-draped scarecrows. The filth and stench could make a person swoon.

They were stripped, inspected, shaved, deloused, and divested of the few possessions to which they clung. Someone snatched Henry's cherished violin—a Guadagnini crafted in 1890 in Turin. Poldek lost his accordion. Somehow, Henry had the presence of mind to compose a brilliant lie. "I said, 'How can you take it away from me? It belongs to Oskar Schindler!'"

When the Rosners arrived at Brinnlitz without their instruments, Schindler asked Henry what had happened. "I said, 'My violin, they took away from me.'

He said, 'Why didn't you tell them it belonged to me?' I told him I did tell them that." Within days, Oskar had retrieved the instruments from Gröss-Rosen. The Rosners never learned how much that particular transaction cost.

In the meantime, Schindler's three hundred women were in cattle cars on their way to Auschwitz. "That time in Auschwitz was like a lifetime for us," says Manci Rosner, number 220 on the women's list. "I am so thankful to Oskar Schindler. I never would have survived it. At least in Płaszów, no ovens, no gas. You knew when you went to the shower, you got a shower. There is no comparison. I can remember only the smell: a terrible stench."

During the short time the women were at Auschwitz and the men were at Brinnlitz, something went seriously awry. Schindler was away from the factory for a few days (which wasn't unusual). Apparently, the Brinnlitz commandant, *Untersturmführer* Josef Liepold, decided that an ammunition factory was no place for small children. Perhaps his colleague Dr. Josef Mengele could make better use of them at Auschwitz for his medical "experiments."

Guards came and rounded up the youngest boys and their fathers. The number of boys varies: nine or eleven, depending on the account. They were sent to Auschwitz on a regular passenger train. The guard was a decent sort. He bought sandwiches for the group and actually conversed with them in a civilized manner. He mentioned to Dolek Horowitz that he had an order to bring three hundred women from Auschwitz back to the Schindler installation at Brinnlitz. Dolek and Henry were elated. They knew their wives would be in that group. They implored the guard to find their women and deliver a note.

As Henry Rosner tells it, young Olek was convinced they were about to die. "I don't want you to talk about it," Manci admonishes her husband, to no avail. "You will start to cry." "My son, he told me: 'Daddy, it's too bad you have to go to Auschwitz because of me.' Even this guard, his eyes were crying."

Manci Rosner, Regina Horowitz, and her daughter, Niusia, already had been loaded into cattle cars on a siding when Niusia happened to glimpse Olek and Ryszard through the slats. Manci and Regina convinced the guard to let them out, and, true to his word, he delivered the notes. The women crawled under the train to urinate and were able to exchange a few words. The boys pulled

Alexander Rosner's accordion, given to him at Auschwitz. At right, a silk clutch Manci filled with documents, all returned to her after the war. At left, the last letter her father wrote.

up their sleeves and showed their mothers their brand-new arm tattoos. It was the last time they'd see one another for about a year.

Apprehensive but hopeful, Manci and Regina arrived at Brinnlitz to find Bill and Poldek Rosner waiting. They were numbers 414 and 365 on the men's list. One day some months later, Oskar Schindler approached Manci Rosner on the factory floor. He had something to give her: Henry's violin. She remembers that he said, "It is the same instrument, only a different tune." She wept.

By the time Henry, Olek, and the rest of the father-son entourage got to Auschwitz, all the camp's musicians were dead. But someone—Henry thinks it was a female guard—found a small accordion for Olek, who obligingly entertained his captors.

There was to be a further separation of the group. A selection was announced. The fathers and sons lined up. Alex Rosner recalls what happened next. "The commandant winked at my father, and immediately after he did, he said, 'All children back,' at which point everybody went back except me. My father held my hand and said, 'He doesn't mean you.' That's how he interpreted that wink. We kept walking. My cousin, Ryszard, was separated from his father at that point. My father said I was the only child ever to walk out of Auschwitz alive. All the other children who survived were liberated by the army, or hid, or were tortured by Mengele. That was strictly because we played for him the night before. He told me the story recently."

Henry, Dolek, and Alexander were sent to Dachau, leaving Ryszard, then five years old, alone at the Auschwitz-Birkenau death camp.

The trip in the dead of winter was nightmarish. There were no passenger coaches this time; they were back in cattle cars. The trip took days. The men starved and suffocated. Someone got the idea to hang the stinking corpses in blanket hammocks from the ceiling to get them off the floor where everyone else had to sleep. It gave Henry an idea.

"I put Olek inside a blanket like that, so he could reach the window and get air. He got icicles from the train, and I was all bloody, because everyone was trying to take the icicles from him. We didn't eat for seven days and nights. The wagon where the bread was was the last car. We didn't get any."

Alex Rosner says that Dachau, a few miles northwest of Munich, was "kind of nice, compared to Auschwitz." He remembers a Polish prisoner of war in charge of the camp infirmary took care of him when he came down with typhus. "He kept me after I got well. He said, 'If you leave, they will kill you.' "

Alex claims he had a premonition in Dachau that liberation was imminent. When he said so, he was smacked by another Jew who thought it a sin to mention such things. But he was right: On April 29, 1945, the inmates heard heavy artillery. Soon after, one of the Nazi guards in a tall tower peeled off his white undershirt and hung it on his machine gun. "There was a big commotion," Alex Rosner says, and then came the Americans. "They took the Germans, and threw supplies over the fence for us to have."

It was over . . . at least for them. Soviet troops liberated the *Schindlerjuden* of Brinnlitz eleven days later.

The Americans found thirty-three thousand living—and dying—people at Dachau. They found reeking middens of corpses. The camp crawled with disease.

Manci Rosner and Regina Horowitz made their way to Kraków to the location where they'd prearranged to meet their husbands. Manci was carrying Henry's Guadagnini violin. They had no idea where their husbands and sons were, or if they were still alive.

After a few weeks under the Americans' care at Dachau, Henry, who had tuberculosis, and Olek were moved to a displaced persons camp set up at the *Deutschesmuseum* in Munich. That fall Manci spotted their names on a refugee list published in a Polish newspaper. Within days, she was in Munich.

An item from the *DP Express*, the camp's newsletter, proudly advertised Henry's performances (in somewhat cumbersome English):

The management of our coffee and dancing house succeeded in finding an exquisite orchester [sic] of Mr. H. Rosner and B. Smuga which gives everyday concerts from 5 p.m. to 5:30 p.m. and later dance music till 8:30 p.m. As our guests are puzzling us with questions like these: What kind of orchester is it? Where did they come from? We feel obliged to explain the following: Both these men were well known in Poland from several auditions by broadcast and modern dance music. Even many foreigners had the opportunity to hear this orchester when it appeared abroad.

Alas, from the beginning of the war, only few people knew what happened with the members of this orchester. They met themselves in the same place where most of the Polish artists were kept. Namely, they were put in concentration camps until liberated by U.S. troops. The conductor of this orchester, Mr. Rosner, young but famous violinist, possesses, besides his wonderful violin, a son, Alexander, who spent about five years in concentration camps whose life was saved many times by playing on violin.

However, the little Alex Rosner, too young to play in the orchester, beloved by the customers of the coffee house, and we often succeeded in persuading him to play on

small accordion and small harmonica. Indeed, many of our customers were aston-
ished seeing this little ten year old boy who spent half of his life as one of the most
dangerous enemies of the Third Reich. They had a great joy the last days because the
wife of the conductor Rosner, the mother of the little Alex, arrived to Munich. They
didn't see each other since a couple of years.

Manci and Henry took a large apartment in Munich. Bill Rosner and his
bride, Erna Zuckerman, moved in. Oskar and Emilie Schindler came for a
visit—with Oskar's mistress.

"He lived in one of the bedrooms and we lived in another," recalls Erna,
divorced from Bill in 1974. "He was a fantastic-looking man. He had this
savoir faire. There was not one woman who would not like to have him in bed,"
which, she says, is where Oskar spent a great deal of time (with at least one
woman, often two).

"We had a very nice life there," Manci recalls
of the Munich period, which ended in the
spring of 1946. On an affidavit of support
from George Rosner—the brother who'd
come to the United States for the 1939
World's Fair and missed the war—they arrived in New York on May 24. Olek was
eleven years old.

"George picked us up in his car at the
pier. He got us furnished rooms on Steinway
Street in Astoria. We stopped on the way and
he bought Olek ice cream. He had never had
an ice cream before! Then he had to stop
again and buy again!"

Even though her firstborn was nearly a
teenager, Manci Rosner had considered having another child . . . until she came to America. "I didn't want to have a second child in

Henry Rosner, New York City, 1950s.

Germany, then I saw these young women [in New York], how they struggled with no mother or aunt, no sister, so I decided I will bring this one up in a good way," which included doing everything possible to discourage a career in music.

"It's a very hard profession," says Manci. "Between a thousand musicians, one makes it. I tried to make my son's life very pleasant. I tried to cover up for what happened. But he was really a very serious child. He had no childhood. He was injured by the war—no doubt about it. In my opinion, every survivor is, some more, some less. Some physically, some mentally. My son didn't know how to write or read. He didn't know English. He never in his life saw a toy. He was playing with four-, five-year-old children. But he was a very good child. He never demanded things out of our reach."

There was no question, of course, how Henry would make his living. "I

Oskar Schindler visited New York in the 1970s. Standing (left to right): Roman Klinger, Henry Rosner, Oskar Schindler, Abe Zuckerman. Seated (left to right): Mrs. Roman Klinger, Mrs. Abe Zuckerman, Manci Rosner.

made money right away," he says, as Manci rolls her eyes. "Never mind how hard it was to put together a meal," she interjects. "But it was paradise compared to what we had."

Henry joined the musicians' union, and worked for a month as a substitute. "The one Russian fellow, head of some union, he [heard] I spoke German. He gave me a Russian name, Gregory Shumsky, and I got a job at a [Russian] nightclub on Second Avenue."

The Rosners heard about Polonnaise, a Polish restaurant at Fifty-first Street and Second Avenue. They went for dinner, and couldn't help noticing the absence of music. Henry and George offered their services to the owner, who accepted. Gregory Shumsky once again became Henry Rosner, and with his brother played at Polonnaise for fifteen years (after which George moved to Arizona). Until he retired in 1987, Henry Rosner also played at New York's Plaza Hotel and at Sign of the Dove, a well-known Third Avenue restaurant.

Henry and Manci own a small apartment building in Rego Park, Queens. They live in one apartment; each of their two grandsons has one for himself. In the winter, Manci and Henry go to Florida, where they have a condo a few blocks from the beach in Hallandale.

In 1947, Manci went to work for Maximilian Apfelbaum, an old friend from Warsaw. In New York, he was known simply as Maximilian, the furrier. For thirty-seven years, Manci Rosner made linings for some of the most fashionable fur coats in New York. Henry says she made more money than he did. She got her own mink in February 1972. The date is embroidered on the lining. "I paid only for the skins," she says. "My boss let me make it myself at the factory."

She displays the coat on a hanger. Its rich, dark pelts glisten, even in the fading afternoon light. After all these years, it still looks magnificent.

Not long after he started playing his precious Guadagnini at Polonnaise, Henry Rosner got a phone call from a musician with whom he'd worked before the war, a lifetime ago. During a gig on the *Queen Mary,* the band's drummer had approached the musician with an offer: Would he care to buy a violin? He recognized the instrument immediately as Henry Rosner's Holzer, one he'd given away for safekeeping in the early days, before the embers of Nazi hate burst into a Holocaust.

The violin had changed hands several times across the European continent, ending up with the *Queen Mary's* drummer. Henry's friend hopped in a cab and sped to Polonnaise, where violin and violinist were reunited after a quarter-century separation. It's the only fiddle he has left.

In the spring of 1994 one of the *Schindlerjuden* bought the Guadagnini from Henry Rosner and donated it to the United States Holocaust Memorial Museum in Washington, D.C. Henry says that bidding it farewell nearly broke his heart.

ALEXANDER ROSNER

In the early months of 1994, business took an unexpected upturn at Rosner Custom Sound. Maybe things weren't as good as they'd been in the disco seventies, when Alex Rosner created the huge disco sound systems that rocked El Morocco, Ginza, Regine's, Trude Heller's, the Copacabana, and hundreds of other dance palaces from Manhattan to Singapore, but certainly it was better than anytime in the past decade.

"I must admit, it is picking up tremendously since the movie," says Rosner, launching a pungent cloud from a Primo del Rey Aristocrat, as classical music drifts in from another room. "But unrelated to the movie, or so it would seem. There are no specific referrals, and the people we're getting business from don't even know about this, but the forces—business is raining down on us."

He sits at the desk in his wood-paneled office. Framed documents cover the dark wall behind him: his honorable discharge papers from the U.S. Navy, his diploma from Rensselaer Polytechnic Institute—a bachelor of science in electrical engineering—completion certificates from various professional courses. A bank of closed-circuit television cameras keep vigil over the property.

Tina, his wife of seventeen years, is upstairs in their apartment. Alexandra, their ten-year-old daughter, wobbles through the office on in-line skates. She's on her way out to the parking lot, which is guarded by large dogs.

The Rosners live and work in Long Island City, a few blocks from the upper-roadway ramp to the Queensboro Bridge. It's a decaying, inhospitable neighborhood of mixed residential/commercial usage. The pitted streets look as if they've come under mortar attack. Alexandra, who attends a gifted program at a Manhattan school, does not play with the neighborhood kids.

Rosner explains the odd choice of locale: His first wife got the family home when they divorced in the mid-1970s. He and Tina figured they could economize by moving in over the showroom and shop. Their sons—his two and her one—were teenagers by then, and Tina had had her tubes tied. Certainly, they never expected to raise more children—until Tina turned up pregnant.

"When [Alexandra] came along, we were buried in here. I really have no resources, and, to this day, my mother likes to rub it in: 'If you hadn't divorced Fran, you'd be rich.' To which I say, 'Probably.' "

He says it with the hint of an ironic smile. He and the former Tina Long, who had been his secretary, carried on a long-running, tumultuous affair. For this, and other reasons, family relations have remained difficult. To some of his relatives Tina is "a homewrecker first, not Jewish second, and black third."

But he says the "Schindler thing" is turning conditions around. "Not that the Schindler thing is making me any money, because obviously I have nothing to do with the movie, but somehow the fates, the forces, are making a change. We've struggled the last ten years."

It's apparent he means in the financial sense, but for Alex Rosner, there have been more intense struggles. His repeated references to forces, fates, and the "Schindler thing" hint at their complexity. He says it began soon after liberation, when the kindness of the American GIs both healed and confused him. It continues to this day, as he searches for an answer.

"I'm still with it: 'Why me and why the Jews and why was it so horrible, and what did the Jews do to deserve this?' I have opinions. I can't sit here today, in 1994, and tell you I have the definitive answers, but I'm hot on the trail and I'm going to get the answer before I die. I'm going to have an answer that I won't be able to talk about."

He speaks with the zeal of a pilgrim. "The direction of the trail is: If we take the premise that there is a God, then everything that happens is just, because it's His game, not mine. There has to be a legitimate reason by His way of looking at it, not by mine. There has to be a legitimate explanation—that we can understand through reason—why it happened, in the way it happened, why all those people died and I'm alive. But I don't know those answers right now. I can't tell you. It's knowable; it's not one of the mysteries of life. It's an answer that will eventually dawn on me."

What he does remember well is how quickly the Nazis stole his childhood. By the time Poland's Jews had been herded into ghettos, even small boys had to learn to live by their wits. His personality, emotions, and early worldview gelled in the perverse confines of the Płaszów forced-labor camp, and later amid the starvation and terror of Dachau and Auschwitz-Birkenau, where B14440 was tattooed on his arm.

From ages six to nine, his primary education consisted of daily lessons in fear, degradation, brutality, and death. For two of those years, he seldom saw his mother. For the third, he didn't see her at all, and didn't know if she was alive. In response, he says he shut down his feelings "totally. It was necessary." It's no wonder, then, that his hooded eyes—a feature inherited from his father, like the swept-back wavy hair—betray little.

He acknowledges that his sense of humor is "not well developed, not in proportion to my intelligence." Indeed, hours go by without a smile, much less anything like laughter.

Faith was another casualty. "I had none when I came to this country. It went out the window. I wanted no part of Judaism because to be Jewish was not so terrific, if I had all this *tsurris.*"

At thirteen, living in Queens, he refused to be bar mitzvahed (though his sons underwent the ritual). "It would have been totally meaningless," he says, "and who needed that?" For eighteen years, until 1991, he actively followed an Eastern religious philosophy. He refers to it as a school, though he won't say precisely where or what it is. He doesn't attend anymore, though he still meditates for a half hour, morning and evening, reciting a mantra. He says it lets his mind rest.

About twenty years ago, he recaptured a belief in God. "There came a time when I was watching some fish at a friend's house, and suddenly it hit me that this fish couldn't be created by something but a high intelligence. So my whole atheistic point of view took a flip, suddenly. I was about thirty-five, just before I started up with Tina. The philosophy was perfect, because it was one of these 'what's it all about' things. Before that, I went to est, and that was a waste of time. And, of course, I tried psychiatry for a while."

Alex Rosner never had any interest in speaking out about the Holocaust. He says he turned his back on it in 1946, a year after he was liberated at the age of ten. He wouldn't be talking now but that *Schindler's List* thrust the role upon him, compelling him to spend more time on discussing life in the death camps with high-school students than on business with his clients: the churches, hotels, nightclubs, restaurants, cruise lines, and the privately wealthy for whom he builds audio and/or video systems.

"It's not that I wanted to forget," he says. "I couldn't, even if I wanted to. But I didn't want to remember. There was no point, and, in principle, I still feel that way. I don't believe you should dig up the past. Disasters shouldn't be commemorated. That's why I'm against the Holocaust museum [in Washington]. When you go back and think about something that happened in the past that was bad, you're resurrecting negative forces. You're feeding the devil. In the Bible it says you turn into a pillar of salt if you look back, and I think there's something to that. It comes back and bites you in the leg. It makes you feel bad, makes the person you're talking to feel bad. It's not good for anybody."

People he's known for years are now calling him in amazement, saying they had no idea about his past. It tests him. "What should I do, wear a sign? I never had secrets: My first wife knew, my second wife knew, my children knew. They asked questions, I answered them. I didn't have my tattoo removed, but we just didn't talk about it. Now comes this movie, and it evidently touches some kind of nerve in people, and it's in my face, so I react to it. Now I see it as a form of service, there is something worthwhile for me to do. But it's a sacrifice play. Believe me, it doesn't make me feel happy."

Happiness. It never came easily to Alex Rosner. Still, until his mid-thirties, he thought himself untouched by the surreal horror of his childhood, "perfectly well adjusted, with no psychological problems at all. None! I think a person might have a case if he still says that. What happened to me was an ordinary American midlife crisis. Of course, other people would feel differently, but that's as legitimate an explanation as any. If I didn't have my parents when the war was over, it would have been a completely different ball game. That isn't to say there aren't wounds, but the wounds are manageable."

He insists he neither is nor was a victim. "I don't believe there is such a thing as a victim. How do I characterize people who came through the Holocaust? They are survivors. The people who didn't are dead. If there were victims, there was no God. Which would you like to have? If there is no God, there is no justice. It rejects any higher consciousness. I believe this, based on my own experience. Each one of us, our present situation and condition, is a direct result of past action. We get what we deserve." Those who see themselves as victims "are making a serious tactical error that will cost them, because you don't act right. You ask for mercy. I never did that. Life there was barbed wire, and if you weren't good, you got beaten to death, and if you stepped out of line, you got killed. You only got this much water and this much bread."

He says he never realized what he'd been through until it was over, and he met a man in the Dachau displaced persons camp named Richard Hooe, a tall, craggy-faced master sergeant from Falls Church, Virginia. "That was a real American," little Alex thought. "That was a real man." Hooe had made for him an authentic army uniform, scaled down to his size. He got him a bicycle and another GI—a black soldier whose name Alex can't recall—taught him to drive a truck: round and round, in the courtyard of the Munich museum that served as a temporary dorm for Jewish survivors. "They were real human beings, and they treated us like human beings, not like vermin."

One day, a German kid stole his bike. Hooe threw Alex in a jeep and went chasing after the kid. He told him, "When we catch him, you beat him up." But Alex didn't want to beat him up when they found him; he just wanted the bike back.

Hooe also gave him a pistol, a real one with a bent firing pin so it wouldn't shoot. After he used it to stick up a nearby cherry farmer for a bushel of fruit, he was relieved of his weapon.

Ten-year-old Alex Rosner was crazy about Hooe and the rest of the GIs: their chewing gum, their baseball, their movies, and, especially, their lighthearted Big Band music, so different from the tea-room schmaltz of his earliest years. He's particularly fond of Latin jazz, but to this day, says the evocative music of Benny Goodman, Glenn Miller, and Harry James gets him "choked up. It was lilting, with a beat and rhythm, and it lifted me up. It was like the angels talking, and it spoke to my heart."

During the months of 1945 that the Rosners lived in Munich, Alex also was befriended by a woman who ran a theater. She'd let him in for free, as often as he wanted. "I must have seen *You Were Never Lovelier* and *The Gold Rush* one hundred times."

For the boy Alex Rosner, it was a time of joy and discovery. But inevitably, as what he calls "civilizing forces" began to reconfigure his instincts and values, the questions came, along with doubts, confusion, and anger.

"When the war ended, the trauma set in, because now you're among a different species of human being. You think: 'So if this is life now, what the hell was *that*? What the hell was *that* all about? It's difficult for people to understand, but up until that time, I was perfectly well adjusted in all that misery. I never had a sleepless night [in the camps]. Yes, I was beaten. Yes, there was trouble. Yes, I was scared. But this was life, and you were scared when you lived. It was dangerous. It was hard. You saw ugliness. You saw women getting beat up. You saw people shot, killed, hanged. You saw dead bodies carried in wheelbarrows. You saw horrible things. But this was normal life."

Once in Płaszów, he was within sight and earshot of the notorious Chujowa Górka (Prick Hill), the sloped killing ground where the Nazis slaughtered thousands. "I saw limousines, and women with foxes around their necks. They'd take the foxes off and take their clothes off, and their hats. Hats and foxes. They were well dressed. They were killed and thrown into the ravine."

At the death camps, he'd see people stop in their tracks, defecate, and fall over dead. He says he saw it often, and it barely fazed him. In Birkenau, a guard beat him on the back and buttocks with a rubber pipe, and he says he didn't cry, not because it didn't hurt—it was excruciating—but because "it wasn't the right thing to do." He says that not even the stench of burning flesh at Auschwitz caused psychological problems: "Nothing threw me or shocked me."

He was just young enough to accept his father's assurances that no matter what happened, things would work out, and they'd survive. "I had a rock to lean on when there was trouble—my father—who told me everything was going to be all right, and why should I doubt him? The man was right every time he said it. He never lied to me. He was an optimist, and he had chutzpah, even when there were guns facing him and it looked like curtains. He never showed me he was afraid."

Later in life, father and son "never had conflict," according to Alex. "The only thing he didn't approve of was my choice of my present wife. But we never had any kind of ideological dispute. He supported everything I ever did. He was always good to me.

"My father was the only one to whom my interests came first. He was very protective, and he always made provisions for me. Yes, I had my uncles, and people who knew me who meant well, but if it was a choice between their life and mine, I knew they were going to choose theirs. They would only go out of their way so much for me. I knew he was where my salvation would come from. There were isolated incidents where people did a lot of good for me, but as an operating principle, everyone was out for themselves."

In retrospect, he sees his father as the agent of whatever forces ordained his survival. "Man is capable of surviving a great deal; it's just a question of being guided. Some of us are, and some of us are not."

While they were still in the Kraków ghetto, Henry and Manci Rosner prearranged a rendezvous point, should they survive the war. The family reunited in Munich in the fall of 1945. By the next year, they had come to the United States, moving in with relatives in Queens. Though Alex spoke no English beyond the few words he'd picked up from the GIs, he was enrolled in school and set on the path toward Americanization, something he wanted desperately. It didn't take long to learn the language, but it took decades to sort out his emotions.

"I grew up selfish and self-centered, and I felt that the world revolved around me," he admits. "My mother spoiled me rotten. I grew up without much consideration, and not very generous. I didn't reach out to others. My ego had husks around it. For the first twenty-five years, I hated everybody and was very antagonistic. I questioned why Jews didn't come and save us. I questioned why the wise Jews taught us how to pray, not how to escape and resist. But in time, I came to understand there was a reason for what we went through."

After high school, his longtime interest in electronics led him to Rensselaer, where he developed his audio hobby and swam competitively. This produced a love for the water, which pointed him toward the navy. He was commissioned an ensign, and spent two years on the U.S.S. *Shasta* as its only Jewish officer.

In 1957, Oskar Schindler attended Alex Rosner's college graduation party in Queens. The other guests, many of them *Schindlerjuden*, were "respectful and affectionate. He commanded attention, he had a gregarious manner, he was open and friendly and spoke with a gravelly voice. People didn't make such a big fuss over him then—it wasn't like God walked in. He gave me a stopwatch, but it got wet and I later threw it away."

In 1959, Alexander Rosner married Francine Siegel of Queens. They met at a dance in New York. "She came over to me and picked me up. I was in my navy uniform. She was a sweet girl. It was perfect timing. I was tired of traveling—I'd been two years with the navy in Europe, the Mediterranean, Scotland. I wanted to start a family."

The model for his marriage was his parents' relationship, which produced its own set of problems. "My mother waited on my father hand and foot. It was the European way, and that's what I expected. She was the most wonderful mother anyone could have, but I only learned recently that she didn't teach me about women—the difference between men and women. I had to do it by myself and I didn't do it well. My first wife treated me that [European] way, too. She didn't like it, but she did it."

Benjamin Rosner, who works with his father, was born in 1963, followed by Gregory, who is a graphic artist, in 1966. At the time, Alex Rosner was working in the defense industry, for Sperry Gyroscope Company. "They had a normal childhood," he says of his sons. "Their father was a normal person with no problems."

With Fran's encouragement, Alex quit Sperry to start his own business. Until then, he says he "never strove for excellence in anything. My mother always said to me, 'I'll be happy if you get average grades.' My goals weren't particularly high. I started building my business to supplement my income so I could buy records. Pretty soon there was as much income in my sideline as my salary. I became slightly disenchanted with my job. I wasn't getting as much credit as I deserved for what I was doing. It was meaningless. I'd work on a proposal for six months for the government, and six months later, the project got scrapped and all my work went right into the trash can. On December 31, 1967, I quit."

Along the way, he found an outlet for his love of Latin dance music in a dance group that once performed at Harlem's famous Apollo Theater with bandleader Tito Puente and songstress Celia Cruz. He still dances, though Tina doesn't have the "passion" for it he does. He says it's part of his replacement childhood, like the Porsche: "a 911T regulation sports car. The real thing."

For a time, Alex ran Rosner Custom Sound from the basement of the family home in Queens. One day in 1971, a young woman showed up to interview for a clerical job. Her name was Tina Long. She was a Manhattan native, the daughter of a tailor and a housewife. Her grandfather had been a minister. " 'It looks like we've got a winner,' " he recalls his ex-wife telling him. "She made quite an impression with both of us. I hired her instantly."

For the next year and a half, it was strictly business. Then one morning, he was shaving. He looked in the mirror, and a question popped into his mind: "Is this all there is? Is life more than I'm leading?" A few weeks later, he called his secretary into his office and asked her—with about as much ceremony as requesting the mail—whether she'd have an affair with him.

"I thought, 'What the hell do I have to lose? This woman is so unlike me, I can't get into trouble with her—no way!'

For her part, Tina Long grew curious. She thought he was "a cute guy." She finally agreed. But after six months of sneaking around, things began to change. "I was lying to my wife, and I didn't like it," says Alex. "I was very moral, and after six months, I broke down. The whole thing opened up a can of worms."

One evening, his wife came home and found him in tears. " 'What's the matter, did you kill someone?' " she asked. "I wouldn't tell her." When he finally confessed, he says she was relieved. He remembers she said, "Is that all?" He says she "consented, since she realized who the other woman was," thinking that such an arrangement couldn't last long. They all were wrong.

Alexander Rosner just about went crazy. He says he thought suicide was the only way out. Finally, a therapist challenged the two women in his life to make a decision: "He said, 'One of you ladies is going to have to take him away from here.' Fran sat silent, and finally Tina said, 'I will.' " They spent a few weeks in Puerto Rico, where he began to calm down. (Francine Rosner became a nurse and has since remarried.)

Alex says his sons paid a heavy price for what happened. They were "deprived of a stable home, and they got hurt, but it was unavoidable. I was insufficiently strong to deny myself what I really wanted, for the sake of God and country."

At this point, he says, there's not much he can do for them. "Whatever I failed to teach them, I failed to teach them. Whatever they have wrong with them, they have to fix themselves. I feel no guilt whatsoever. None. It's true they suffered as a result of my change of life, but that's tough. That's life."

Alex Rosner and Tina Long were married in 1977 by a justice of the peace in Queens. "Tina is a remarkable woman," says her husband. "She is not at all what she looks like. She sees things on a cosmic scale. Her mind is gargantuan."

They don't socialize much, he says, because most couples they know can't handle it. "The mixed marriage presents serious problems. The women think, 'There goes the other woman, and there but for the grace of God goes my husband.' It makes the hair stand up on the backs of their necks."

When the Rosners went to Israel to film the final scene of *Schindler's List,* Tina says she got a chilly reception from the other survivors. "I got on the plane, and I got *that* look. How quickly they forget." Her husband adds, "Racism is alive and well in the Jewish community. There were daggers coming from the other survivors at her."

In contrast to her husband, Tina Rosner laughs easily and broadly. At fifty, she's thin as a wheat stalk, with silvery hair cropped close. Long, graceful fingers tipped by dark-red rapier nails part the air in dramatic gestures when she talks. She loves the attention and excitement brought by the movie.

"This is tantamount to the way people feel when they win the lottery,"

Alex Rosner with the actor who played him in the film Schindler's List, *Israel, 1993.*

she says. "Rich, in terms of growth, and seeing certain spiritual aspects of living life manifest. I'm watching celebrity come from a horrible occasion in my husband's life, but it took all of our loving him to be able to sustain this media onslaught. He needed some anchorage."

It was she, says Alex, who taught him not to be a victim. "I'd be down and laying on the ground writhing in pain, and, figuratively, she'd kick me in the balls and tell me, 'A man is not supposed to be down.' It took a while to accept this. I fought it tooth and nail: 'You're supposed to help me get up!' I expected sympathy. 'At the very least, feel sorry for me. If you're not going to give me a rag to wipe the blood, at least say, "Aw, poor baby." ' You learn to live that way and all of a sudden, it's a different experience."

At this point, he says, he has few regrets. He's aiming for none at all in the last part of his life. "To live a regret-free life is a goal, and the way to start that is you don't do anything wrong each day. I started that a few years ago, so no guilt is being added and little by little it's being washed away. Pretty soon, it's going to be great. To be old and regretful is a terrible thing."

BILL ROSNER

He used to be a flirt, a prankster, the life of any party, and always—even in the Kraków ghetto—impeccably dressed.

No wonder, then, that on an ordinary Sunday at home, Bill Rosner comes to the door in a three-piece suit and a tie, goatee neatly trimmed, an over-the-ears haircut flawlessly combed, two lapel pins proudly identifying him as a Master Piano Technician and a member of the Piano Technicians' Guild.

He is, and always has been, a perfectionist, which is important when you're tuning pianos for such virtuosos as Artur Rubinstein, Vladimir Horowitz, Billie Taylor, and Gary Graffman. It also can be an unbearable burden, when perfection—or anything close to it—is beyond a person's control.

Such is the case these days with Bill Rosner. Lou Gehrig's disease bedevils him. He can't tune anymore. He can't play anymore—not the piano, the accordion, or the bass. He can barely maneuver the flatware. He is bony and gaunt, so frustrated, humiliated, and depressed that he doesn't see the point in carrying on.

Bill Rosner (left) with siblings Melanie and Samek. Kraków, early 1930s.

He seems to blame himself for his condition, as if it were some moral failing. His wife lectures him in Polish about eating properly and taking his many medications, but he seems indifferent. He says he has lots of Christian friends praying for him.

But every once in a while, you still can catch a bit of the twinkle—for instance, when he tells how Victor Borge, the famous keyboard comic, once teased him with a classic ploy.

"One day I finished tuning. I said, 'Why don't you try it?' He took the Yellow Pages"—he mimes placing a phone book on a chair and pretends to sit—"and said, 'A little too high.' He opened it up, ripped one page out, and said, 'Oh, now that's right!' " He even gets a smile out of himself.

"There was no end to his jokes," says Erna Rosner, his ex-wife (and teenage sweetheart), "and he knew how to sell a joke, how to dress it up. He was extremely well liked."

He used to have musical toilet seats and musical neckties, his nephew Alex Rosner remembers. He would delight clients by turning away from the keyboard and playing the piano backward.

At the fancy buildings on Park and Fifth Avenues, where doormen directed piano tuners to the service entrance, Bill Rosner, with his black bag of tools, was sometimes mistaken for a doctor.

During the 1950s, Bill played New York–area weddings and bar mitzvahs. He'd work the Catskill hotels in the summers. "I really enjoyed it very much," he says of those days. "I loved the sun." But making music was his avocation. He never quit his day job. He worked seven years as a technician for Steinway & Sons, then thirty-two on his own (he quit Steinway when he found out he and the janitor made the same wages). Since 1980, he has lived in Vineland, New Jersey, with Eva, his second wife. He dotes on Ebony, their fifteen-year-old gray miniature poodle, cooing at her in the tender singsong usually reserved for infants.

Jewish peasants fleeing Russia after a series of deadly pogroms settled in Vineland in the mid-1800s. Most of them raised poultry. A second wave of Jewish refugees came after World War II, and they, too, went heavily into fowl. "You didn't have to speak English to chickens," explains Eva Rosner, whose family was among the latter group. (She spent eighteen months hidden with a sister, their parents, and another woman in a hole under a barn near Sambor, Poland, that was ten feet long, six feet wide, and four feet deep.)

The couple's suburban ranch house boasts gold flocked wallpaper, heavy gold drapes, ornate gilt furniture, and crystal chandeliers. His domain is the basement den. Publicity photos, most autographed, line the walls: Bess Myerson, Peggy Lee, Burl Ives, Skitch Henderson, Benny Goodman, Oliver Nelson, Kaye Ballard, and dozens more.

He tuned for Nat King Cole twice a week at the Copacabana, and for Barbra Streisand before she became famous. ("It was on Seventh Avenue in New York. A lousy upright.") Red Buttons used to make him breakfast, and Greer Garson herself—"not the maid!"—served him coffee and cake.

"The first two years, I couldn't bear it to live here," says Bill Rosner, who initially visited Vineland for a party, then married Eva after her first husband died. "I used to live so many years in New York. But here, when you drive, nobody pushes you. Then I got used to it. Now I couldn't live in New York if I made a thousand dollars a day."

Several of his brothers' records are on display in the upstairs den, near his piano: George Rosner's *Portraits of Italy* and *Portraits of France*, and the album of Polish music Henry and Poldek made together. There's also a plaque in that room that reads: "Life is like a piano; what you get out of it depends on how you play it." It prompts a question: Why did he choose tuning pianos as a career, instead of playing them? According to his nephew Alexander, Bill has more natural talent than either of his brothers.

Bill Rosner won't answer the question directly. Instead, he replies with anecdotes: "Did you hear of this pianist, Ahmad Jamal? He was a nice man. He was washing dishes. When I finished, I did a running down the keyboard that I heard on the radio. He broke a dish and came running out. He wrote it down. He said, 'How long you study the piano?' I said, 'I never studied piano. I play maybe now a year.' He said, 'I don't believe you.' " (In fact, Bill couldn't read music then, and he still can't. It's the reason, say Manci and Henry, that the three brothers never had their own group in the United States.)

Once Steinway sent him to RCA to tune a piano, "and I didn't know this was for Roger Williams. The sound technician said, 'Hey, Mr. Piano Tuner, can you please tickle the ivories so I can adjust my levels?' He told me I was in the wrong business."

Perhaps, but he was a Steinway favorite. Popping up from a kitchen chair, he demonstrates how he charmed clients into demanding that the company send him—and only him.

"The director of traffic said to me, 'What the hell you talking to the people? Everybody calls me and says, "I want the Spanish guy who smokes the pipe." I say we don't have a Spanish guy. "Well, maybe he was a Frenchman." We don't have a Frenchman. "Maybe he was a Greek." We don't have a Greek.' He got so mad. You know what I did?"—he drops to his knees, clasping his hands as if in prayer— " 'Would you please ask for me?' He started to laugh so much, we became best friends. Later, he sent me to Carnegie Hall, RCA, WWDB radio station, and to many people making records."

The mention of his pipe-smoking days reminds him of Oskar Schindler. "I was a heavy smoker, and he was, too. Each time he saw me, he started a cigarette and threw it down. Three weeks before liberation, we were getting two slices of bread all day long. I found out that one guy had tobacco. I gave him bread and he gave me the tobacco. I took the lousy paper and made myself cigarettes. All week long, I was smoking and not eating bread." And he was getting awfully hungry.

"Two weeks before [liberation], I had a broom and was cleaning the sidewalk. I saw a sixteen-wheeler truck. Bread! I said, 'I don't give a damn, I'm gonna steal the bread.' I looked everywhere, and I didn't see a Nazi. It took me fifteen minutes to pull out the bread. Somebody kicked me in the back. I looked and it was an OD man. A few minutes later, came the Nazi guard. He put the gun in my neck. I could see Oskar Schindler about half a block away. He ran like a jet."

Oskar steered the guard away from the situation with promises of a drink, says Bill Rosner, "and that night, everybody got a quarter of a bread. Women were kissing me for this!"

He was so weak by May 9, 1945, that when a woman in a third-floor window saw him wandering the street in his striped prisoner suit and offered

Bill (left) and Henry Rosner, before Bill took sick.

to make him breakfast, it took him ten minutes to climb the flight of stairs to her flat. "She made me scrambled eggs. I took two spoons and couldn't eat more. She gave me jacket, pants, hat, everything. I'll never forget it."

Teenage Wilhelm Rosner met his first wife, Erna Zuckerman, in the Kraków ghetto, where they lived next door to each other. "He was fourteen or fifteen. I had a beautiful mother, who was always on the balcony, and he was flirting with her. She was thirty-five. After two weeks, he kissed me on the cheek and I slapped him, and my mother brought us back together."

She was in Płaszów, too, but says someone who could pay bought her spot on Schindler's list, even though all the Rosners went to Brinnlitz, and she was, by then, "part of the family. We were the whole day running after each other in Płaszów, like a cartoon." She became Auschwitz *Haftling* A26672, as her tattoo indicates.

The sweethearts promised to meet in Kraków if they lived. "I left Brinnlitz, took the train. People said she's here. I went to places we met, and after two weeks I found her. She was walking on the street. Then we went to Munich, and met up with Henry and Manci." Schindler attended Bill and Erna's 1946 wedding in Munich, surprising his former slave laborer.

They were divorced in 1974. They have two sons—Jeffrey, a Florida chiropractor, and Robert, a New York ultrasound technician—and two grandchildren. They remain cordial. In fact, Erna says, "[Bill] was a great father, a great husband, lots of fun."

In Munich, Bill played the bass with Henry and Poldek "in a big orchestra. Henry got his first car, but he never drove. Some guy used to drive for him. Then he went to America because my brother George sent for him. I was [in Munich] till 1949, then George sent for me."

In Munich, Bill Rosner learned the hip American tunes from listening to the radio, "so when I came here, I knew all the music. After six months, I got a card for the union. Always, the pianos were out of tune, and I couldn't take it." That's when he became a technician.

"One day, they got a call at Steinway from the Russian embassy. So I went there, the KGB opened up the door—I had an M.D. bag—and they looked inside the bag. I tuned the piano for an hour and a half, with the KGB walking back and forth outside the door"—he imitates the pacing. "I said to myself, 'You son of a gun; I'm gonna fix you up.' When I finished, I played a Russian song. He said, 'How did you know the Russian songs?' I said, 'I was liberated by Russians.' Later, I played the Russian tango, and he loved it so much, he gave me five boxes of cigarettes. I started to smoke. Ach! Terrible! I threw it away. What junk!"

"Uncle Bill" Steinway, as the firm's owner was known, wanted to know how the service call had gone. "He said, 'They let you in?' I said, 'Why don't you ask me if they let me out?' Then he started to laugh, and we became friends.

"Every morning," says Bill Rosner, he and "Uncle Bill" Steinway had a routine. "At eight o'clock, he gave me always a cigar, and I gave him the *New York Times*.

"*Exactly* eight o'clock!"

RYSZARD HOROWITZ

Ryszard Horowitz calls himself a "photo composer," a term he coined to describe the way he creates his startling, computer-assembled photographs. In them, fruit solar systems encircle vodka bottles, rabbits bound from monitor screens, and luxury cars float among the clouds. They're as whimsical as they are surreal, an intriguing partnership of imagination and technology.

Horowitz is one of America's premier commercial photographers. His pictures enliven dozens of magazines as illustrations and as ads for the likes of Jaguar, AT&T, Van Cleef & Arpels, Stolichnaya, and Toshiba. They've been exhibited at galleries and museums all over the world, including New York City's International Center for Photography, the George Eastman House in Rochester, New York, and the Georges Pompidou Center in Paris. He has photographed some of the world's top models and actresses, and won just about every award given in his field. In 1983, *Adweek* named him All-American Photographer of the Year.

Born May 5, 1939, four months before the Nazis invaded Poland, he is thought to be the youngest of the *Schindlerjuden*. His father, David, called Dolek, was a Kraków engineer. His mother, Regina, was a milliner. Other survivors say she was one of the most beautiful women in Jewish Krakow. He has an older sister, Bronislawa, called Niusia. In *Schindler's List*, she's the younger of the two girls who present Oskar Schindler with a birthday cake.

Niusia and Ryszard appeared in the final scene of *Schindler's List.* After that, he says, "My personal story became public, whether I liked it or not." The world media lined up at his door. He has been on Spanish, Dutch, Austrian, and French television. Most absurdly, a Bolivian presidential candidate asked him on live television for his opinion "on how to make things better in the world."

At the age of six, Ryszard Horowitz emerged from the mud and ash of Auschwitz, presuming himself an orphan. The story of his family's postwar reunion is one of the most dramatic and poignant among the *Schindlerjuden.* When Płaszów closed in September 1944, its thirty thousand inmates were scattered. The Horowitzes got onto Schindler's list because they were well connected. Dolek was camp purchasing officer in the "employ" of Franz Bosch, a civilian wheeler-dealer operating inside the Płaszów camp. This had enabled him to place his wife, son, and parents at Emalia. They also were close to Abraham Bankier, who owned the factory before Schindler took it over.

"My parents were highly respected and my father saved lots of lives because of his contacts," says Horowitz. "At some point, he was tipped off when things were getting really rough, and initially when we were at Płaszów, I was taken out of the camp a couple of times and put into hiding in a nearby town. How they did it is hard to say."

After the men arrived at Brinnlitz—but while the women remained at Auschwitz—the camp commandant culled out the youngest boys and their fathers, and ordered them sent to Auschwitz. Schindler was away, and no one could prevent it. Ryszard and his father were among them. By the time Regina and Niusia arrived at Brinnlitz with the rest of Schindler's women, they were gone.

Ryszard managed to stay with his father for a few months. Then came another selection, and Dolek Horowitz was sent to Mauthausen. Roman Gunz, a man from Kraków who'd been an Auschwitz inmate for three years, took care of Ryszard and several other parentless children until Russians liberated the camp in January 1945. Horowitz says Gunz hid him in a barracks that was supposed to be for quarantined typhus victims. It was one of the few places guards wouldn't search.

Regina Horowitz, freed from Brinnlitz in May with Niusia, had no idea what had become of her husband and son. She didn't know Ryszard had been taken to a Catholic orphanage in Kraków with the other Auschwitz youngsters, most of them true orphans. A now-famous photo shows caretakers shepherding the little ones—bundled into adult-size, striped concentration-camp jackets—past rows of barbed wire, out of the camp.

Weeks later, Regina Horowitz was watching newsreel footage of the scene in a Munich theater. She spotted her son in the crowd and ran out shrieking. By the time she got to the orphanage, a family friend had taken Ryszard into her home. She was Tosia Liebling, and she had a nephew a bit older than Ryszard—Roman Liebling, who became his lifelong friend. Today he is known as Roman Polanski, the director. Horowitz still wears the tiny, flat gold heart that Tosia Liebling gave him as a child on a thin gold neck chain. Polanski's mother was killed in the Kraków ghetto. He and his father escaped, and went into hiding with a peasant family for the duration of the war.

"There must have been a list published of the kids in the orphanage, so she took me in and inquired about the rest of the family.... A few months later, my mother and sister and Manci [Rosner, Regina's sister-in-law] came in. We found each other. The next step was looking for my father. Slowly, people began to siphon in from wherever, and my mother came across people who claimed my father had been killed, but she didn't believe it. Then one day she literally bumped into him on the street in Kraków."

Horowitz doesn't remember much about the actual events of his early childhood, but fifty years later, it is sometimes difficult for him to discuss the separation from his father. It's not that he still feels the pain; rather, he recalls that there was so much of it at the time.

"There's a lot of wishy-washy imagery prior to when I began to remember what actually took place," he says. "The most horrifying experiences I had were in my preverbal period, which is why a lot of what I recollect is a combination of what I was told by my parents and other family members. What I remember deals with what happened somewhat later, from the middle of forty-four on."

He's been told he was "a pretty vibrant little kid, running around and pulling people by their arms. Polanski recalls me as being a little brat, and I probably was one, unlike my sister; she pretty much froze. They [the older children] were numbed. Shell-shocked. They knew what it was to talk back and misbehave. Apparently I was having a ball, from all accounts."

Indeed, his artistry reflects a sensibility formed during that later, exuberant period. It tweaks the senses with colors more vivid than nature's. Above a conference table in his sleek, three-story Manhattan studio—in the shadow of the Empire State Building, on a block otherwise occupied by commercial sewing-machine shops—there's a picture of boulder-size, flame-hued oranges improbably dotting a crystalline winter landscape. Shot for *Sports Illustrated*, it's his impression of Florida in the post-ozone global deep freeze, he says, chuckling in a gentle way that comes easily.

He says his work doesn't reflect his childhood traumas, either consciously or subconsciously, "yet it obviously contains elements or suggestions that relate to it. I was working on an image, and I showed it to someone who said, 'My

The Horowitz Family. Kraków, 1953. Standing (left to right): Schahne Horowitz, grandfather; Niusia Horowitz, sister; Ryszard Horowitz. Sitting (left to right): Sabina Horowitz, grandmother; Regina Horowitz, mother; David Horowitz, father.

God, this would have been a perfect poster for *Schindler's List*,' and I said, 'Are you out of your mind?' It's a picture of a gigantic eagle that's saving an infant. Never in my wildest dream would I connect it. My pictures are narrative, and suggest a story. They're not just meaningless pictures."

As a boy discovering his vocation after the war—coming of age in communist Poland, which hardly encouraged artists to be fanciful or daring— "everything that was glossy, that was colorful, that moved and made sound, it was elation. . . . I loved Disney. I saw *Snow White* dubbed in Polish."

A clarinetist, he especially loved American music. "I'd tune

Ryszard Horowitz on a donkey. On the left, Niusia Horowitz; on the right, Regina Horowitz. Kraków, 1947.

to Voice of America to listen to jazz. The MC, Willis Conover, was my idol, and the first man I wanted to meet in America. We became great friends. He had the most incredible silky voice, and he spoke slowly and precisely. He knew that his audience was not fluent in English. He played this incredible music. When I got hold of my first tape recorder, which was so primitive it's hard to believe, I used to tape it. It was constantly being jammed by the Russians. But people would come over and listen. Polanski and I used to record programs, with all kinds of sound effects."

Some of the first jam sessions in Poland took place at his family's apartment, "for which my mother never forgave me. At that time, it was not even totally legal, because it was considered to be degenerate."

Horowitz didn't emigrate from Poland until 1959, after which his parents moved to Vienna. As far as he can recall, his parents recovered well from the Holocaust. "In my judgment, they were quite normal. They had their fights, but there was nothing really extraordinary. They definitely dwelled to some extent on their experiences, and most in their group of friends were other survivors. But they never really lingered on it or shared with me. It was not an open subject at the dinner table."

The family belonged to a society of ex-prisoners in Kraków, "initially mostly Jewish, then integrated by a Polish veterans' society. My father was a member of the Jewish congregation that still exists. We had seders and my bar mitzvah, but I had very few Jewish friends. We used to go to Remuh synagogue, a Renaissance synagogue. My father was involved in rebuilding it after the war."

His parents stayed in Poland to care for the elderly, ailing senior Horowitzes. "It's like a family tragedy. When we had opportunities to immigrate to Israel or the States, they couldn't travel. It took years before their parents died, and by then it was the height of communism. But as far as my own life is concerned, I cannot complain. I had a good family life. My father was one of very few businessmen in a time that private enterprise was taboo. He had a building-materials store, and his partner was Mrs. Liebling [whose husband was hanged after the war as a Nazi collaborator]. . . . My father was such a great guy—he managed to get along with everybody, and they let him go—he probably had to bribe some people. He was like Schindler, to some extent. I never heard a bad word about him."

The family had "a fairly good situation. We lived right in the center of town, near the old market. The apartment was on Rynek Glowny, which means Market Square. It was the top floor of what you'd call a town house, a floor-through with very high ceilings overlooking this incredible medieval market. I went to the Jewish school, in the last graduating class before Stalin had it closed, which had to be 1949.

"Early in my life, I realized what my interest was, that I was artistically inclined and talented. After grammar school, I was accepted to the High School of Fine Arts. I became close friends with teachers who were art historians and painters, and they took great interest in me."

Being Jewish in Poland remained a dicey proposition long after the war (it's estimated that seven thousand Jews live there today), but Horowitz says he was lucky. "Not that I was blind to what was going on, but I was not really exposed to anti-Semitism. I can recall one or two incidents when something could have happened, but it was prevented by my friends, who sheltered me. I remember once going to a dance party, and there was a rumor that someone wanted to beat me up, and my friends in the band took me out through the back door. I was told later on it was racially motivated."

He remembers only one other student at Kraków's Academy of Fine Arts (an orphan) and one professor ("a famous painter") who would acknowledge being Jewish. "Twenty years later, I found out the

Wawel Castle, Kraków, 1946. Rear (left to right): Ryszard Horowitz, Roma Ligocka. Front (left to right): Niusia Horowitz, Roman Polanski.

wife of my beloved art professor was Jewish. He finally admitted it."

He and Polanski joined a cinema club and pored over glossy art books published in Switzerland. "One of my professors had connections in the West, and could get them once in awhile." Because of the difficulties and deprivations, "we were all very serious about learning, very much like the GIs here after the war. There are right now a whole generation of people who are at the pinnacle of their careers: writers, film directors."

He says his most important and revealing experience, "from an emotional and artistic point of view, was the first time I left Poland and took a boat for the

U.S. The first stop was Copenhagen. The shock was incredible: the color, the smell, the whole atmosphere, the expressions on people's faces, and the way they were dressed and represented themselves. And the stores were so full! When you come from this kind of subdued, gray land, it was really a phenomenon."

When Horowitz was about fifteen, he got his first camera. "It was an East German camera called an Exacta. The company still exists: Varex. It was a thirty-five millimeter, the first reflex camera. Also, I had a Czech enlarger later on. I remember, because at the time I left Poland they had very strict control over our lives, and they entered in my passport all the so-called valuable items I was taking out of the country. I was supposed to return, so they wanted to make sure that on my return I would have it with me."

He and Polanski somehow managed to convert a German slide projector into an enlarger. "We used our bathroom as a darkroom and would develop pictures in the sink. The light switch to the bathroom was on the outside, and my sister would always turn it on." He laughs. "I never forgave her for that."

He came to the United States as an exchange student. "We were trying to find an angle to get out of Poland. My parents felt—more so than myself—there was no future in Poland. So in spite of the fact that we had been separated so many times in the past, they did everything they could to see I had a future."

His uncle Henry Rosner, already established in New York, sent an affidavit of support. "But we still needed to state why I wanted to come to the States. I could not say I wanted to study fine arts, because at the time I was at a very prestigious academy of fine arts that was very hard to get into. They had thousands of applicants and would admit thirty to forty a year. It involved week-long examinations and I was probably the only Jew in the class." (The school still exists. The last time Horowitz was in Poland, where he's had several exhibitions, he had lunch in the deans' hall, "a place I never dreamed in my life I would actually be having drinks with all these people!")

"I had this fantasy of studying animation, and there was no place to do that. . . . I convinced the dean of the academy to write a letter on my behalf to the ministry of whoever was in charge of passports, saying that I had this very unique talent and I had to go to America to study. It took over two years, but it worked."

No sooner had he left Poland than a draft-board official visited his parents. "They had to convince the woman working for the draft board that upon my return I would come right in—at the academy, you had to go through ROTC. They were very upset that I was allowed to leave, and of course I was such a brat that one of the first things I did after arriving here was send a postcard with a view of Manhattan, addressed to an officer in charge: 'Attention! Pvt. Horowitz is arriving in the States!' "

As with most of the *Schindlerjuden* who came to America—no matter how soon or late after the war—the first few years were difficult for Horowitz; in his case, culture clash combined with youthful homesickness.

"I was extracted from this highly active, artistic group of friends. Most of them became very successful—art historians, actors, filmmakers. . . . For the first few months, I lived with the Rosners. I was very unhappy. A few months later, I was accepted to Pratt [Institute] and moved to Brooklyn with five other guys."

Manci Rosner rolls her eyes when she recalls that time. Her nephew was a beatnik and a slob. Her own son, Alexander, was exactly the opposite: neat and straight. Everyone was relieved when Ryszard moved out.

Horowitz found American culture of the early 1960s "very jarring. I was in love with the American culture of the forties and fifties—Fred Astaire!— and I was a walking encyclopedia of American jazz. I was into modern jazz, like bebop."

He haunted Manhattan's jazz clubs. "It cost a buck to stay all night at these clubs—Birdland, the Village Gate. I used to travel the GG train from Brooklyn. I was a jazz groupie."

It was obvious as soon as he entered Pratt that he'd already surpassed most of his fellow students and even some instructors, and he says it upset him terribly.

"I met in class young people who were admitted to art school, were living in New York, and had never been to the Metropolitan Museum! They had no motivation. I'm still in a state of shock over it so many years later. These people felt they'd attend a course and would be certified an artist. They didn't have this inside urge to do things on their own. They were totally dependent on somebody else's direction. I always believed that if you are interested in something and show talent in it, you have to be inquisitive and make an effort on your own, regardless of what you're being told by a teacher. . . . Without that, the output is pretty banal.

"I had this art history teacher who was not very well briefed in his subject, and I used to butt in all the time and correct him, so after three times, he called me over to the side and said, 'Ryszard, I'll give you an A if you stop coming to class.' The same thing happened with my photography class."

He'd already made the decision to go into photography. "I set myself a very high standard, and I knew I could never make it in painting. . . . My great influences were painters like Magritte, Caravaggio, early Dali. New York was the center of abstract expressionism, and I had been educated in a very traditional context. My teacher would not allow us to draw from photographs, only from the classics.

"Being a realistic painter, I was out. All those kids who were doing their own Picassos. I didn't understand why they didn't learn how to draw first, and the art establishment was supporting this nonsense. I was very upset. I began to notice the art scene here, began to know [Leo] Castelli and Warhol, and I didn't want to be part of that scene. I didn't have the energy or interest to wait my time for what I do to be accepted."

Horowitz became interested in applied art at Pratt, through which he met several of the great American designers, including Alexey Lieberman Brodovitch, "the mentor to everyone from Irving Penn to [Richard] Avedon, and the art director of *Harper's Bazaar* for twenty years. Through him, I met Avedon, and was his assistant for a while."

His portfolio, after graduation, was the Pratt Institute seventy-fifth anniversary yearbook, for which he'd shot most of the pictures. It won the prestigious Art Directors Club of New York Distinctive Merit Award, the first ever to a student.

His apartment on East 30th Street became "a mecca" for immigrating

Poles. "I was the first of my generation to get out. . . . Every movie star, every performer, every writer had to come and see me and ask my advice. My reputation grew over there. One day I was even invited to exhibit my work at the National Gallery in Warsaw, which is the most prestigious place, like if you had a show at the Guggenheim or the Metropolitan. It was all arranged by the ministry of culture, and it was received with incredible reviews. I was on television. I was in Poland a couple of years ago with Bob [Bowen, his partner], invited to speak at a seminar on electronic imaging. He was amazed that I was stopped on the streets for an autograph."

After Pratt, Horowitz took a job with CBS, then dabbled in films, doing titles and trailers. He worked with Stanley Kubrick on the cold war classic *Dr. Strangelove*. But he was having immigration problems and was advised to "hook up with a very large advertising agency, because they could help me get a green card. So I went to Grey Advertising, which was one of the biggest. . . . They claimed I was irreplaceable. The whole process was very lengthy and unpleasant and expensive."

Then it got worse. "Life began to imitate *Strangelove*. At some point, I was refused my papers because somebody denounced me as a spy, because I was known to travel with cameras. I had this incredible interrogation at immigration, when they were trying to prove I was in Madrid doing intelligence work, but at the time, I had never been in Spain. This was all based on hearsay. They gave me a very hard time because they found out I was living together with my future wife without being married. They actually spied on us, to see who was coming and going."

His wife, Anna Bogusz, is also a Polish survivor. They met after his first marriage, which lasted less than a year. Her family spent the war in hiding, and remained in Poland until 1958. They moved to Venezuela, where her father became the engineering-school dean at the University of Caracas. She never knew she was Jewish until she was thirteen years old. Ryszard and Anna have two sons: Daniel, born in 1979, and Emil, born in 1984.

The couple married at City Hall in New York in 1974, then traveled to Italy and Vienna to see the elder Horowitzes. Niusia—by then Niusia Karakulska, a Kraków beautician married to a non-Jewish doctor—was there too, for what was to have been a festive reunion. Then Dolek Horowitz suddenly took sick with stomach cramps.

"We took him to an emergency room. An intern said, 'Don't worry; it's probably food poisoning,' and he gave him a laxative, which was the worst thing he could do. He had developed peritonitis, and by the time anybody realized what had happened, he had a terrible infection and he died. It happened in a matter of days, with all of us being together. He was only sixty-nine, and my mother never recovered. . . . From that moment on, my life was unsettled, because my mother insisted on staying in Vienna. She had to be near my father's grave."

Regina had always been a great cook and hostess, and even after her husband's death continued to surround herself with interesting people, especially younger women who relished gossip as much as she did, and liked listening to her stories. But she was a chain-smoker, and began to develop circulation problems.

"It was always hopping on a plane," says Ryszard. "She was, by the end, very difficult, suspicious. She gave up when they started talking about amputating her legs." She died in 1987, and was buried next to the husband with whom she'd been through so much.

Horowitz left Grey Advertising in 1967—by then he was art director—and opened his own studio. The Madison Avenue hype was just too much. "I could not believe all these highly paid, intelligent people [at the agency], the way they talked about it, it was so stupid. They wanted to believe in all this nonsense. My attitude was, if you take it seriously, you'll be destroyed. I'm also a strong believer in a personal point of view, and I've struggled all these years to find a niche, because my work is not typical of advertising work."

In the early 1980s, the British director Jon Blair asked him to participate in a documentary he was making about Oskar Schindler. Horowitz agreed.

"It was the first time I was put in the situation to face the trauma," he says. "Jon Blair was extremely gentle and knowledgeable. I was very touched by the way he handled the whole situation. Talking to him, I realized he knew much more about my past than I did. Through it, I got kind of hooked. Yet

Ryszard Horowitz in his New York City studio, in front of some of his photographs, 1994.

even then, I realized that talking about it was extremely painful, and I found it literally impossible to withhold my tears."

In the spring of 1994, the two began collaborating on a book about Horowitz's life and work. It will be published in Poland in late fall 1994 to coincide with a retrospective of his work there.

Yet not long after the documentary about Schindler was finished and shown in the United States, Horowitz "sort of forgot about the whole thing.... I didn't dwell on it. I'm always very surprised that people spend their lives being motivated by their trauma.... It takes a lot of guts to touch it, and nine out of ten efforts backfire. But I have not built my life based on that experience. I am much more interested in beauty and more positive imagery, more uplifting."

Several years ago, Ryszard Horowitz got involved with a clinic at a New York hospital. It treats posttraumatic stress, biochemical changes, and emotional problems related to Holocaust survival. "I was intrigued to find a nonconventional therapy to cope with my own experience," he explains. "Regular therapies were overly simplistic: 'You were doomed to end up in an asylum.'" He wanted help exploring the relationship between his past and his "hang-ups."

Lately, he's been looking for information and answers from relatives, from friends of his parents, and from people like Bronia "Betty" Gunz, the widow of the man who protected him in Auschwitz.

"The questions faced me when my own children reached that age, and I could physically identify myself with their size, and I still find it unbelievable that I was there."

THE STERNLICHT SISTERS:
HELEN STERNLICHT ROSENZWEIG
AND BETTY STERNLICHT SCHAGRIN

He called her Susanna. But he also called her Jewish criminal, dumb *hund*, whore, and any other insult that came to mind. Actually, her name was Helena, and at the time she became Amon Goeth's housemaid she was seventeen years old. For nearly two years, "Susanna" served Goeth's meals, ironed his shirts, swept his floors, and dusted his furniture. She fed and brushed his man-eating Great Danes. She suffered constant abuse by his hand, and never knew an hour without fear.

"I already have one Helena," he told her, as if she was nothing more than a spare part. "From now on, you are going to be Susanna and the other Helena will be Lena."

"Lena" is Helena Hirsch, who lives in Israel. The maid in *Schindler's List* goes by that name. She's about ten years older than Helen Sternlicht Rosenzweig (who dropped the *a* in the United States).

Helena Sternlicht was a dark-eyed innocent at the start of her servitude. A childlike softness rounded the luminous beauty that neither time nor heartache has hardened. She looks fifteen years younger than the seventy she'll be in the spring of 1995, and sounds now like the teenager she was then.

It can be said without hesitation that Helen Sternlicht Rosenzweig is a hero. She risked her life day after day, sneaking extra food to her mother and two older sisters in the Płaszów barracks, lifting SS documents from Goeth's files for the camp's resistance cadre, and shielding others from the commandant's homicidal wrath. Once, in an act of insane bravery, she implored Amon Goeth to save her sisters from transport to the death camps . . . and they were saved.

"I think some people envied us a lot, the Sternlicht sisters," says Helen. "But the price I paid was working for Goeth."

On May 9, 1994, the forty-ninth anniversary of the liberation of Brinnlitz, something other than her bad back—a legacy of Goeth's cruelty, along with a badly scarred cornea—is keeping Helen Rosenzweig from enjoying what the day represents. She winces, settling onto a corner of the sectional sofa in her den, an ice pack strapped to her spine.

"What today is, I push it away right away when I wake up," she says. "It brings terrible memories. To enjoy life to some extent and not be constantly depressed, you can't keep on celebrating horrors. What I'm trying to do is not live it," which is all but impossible, considering how much demand there's been for Helen Rosenzweig's time since the film's release.

Synagogues want her. Schools want her. Nonprofits want her. Audiences seem enthralled by her story, and by her. If they recognize in Amon Goeth the vile and demonic essence of Nazism, they sense in Helen Rosenzweig the tormented Jews' unquenchable determination to survive.

She tries to bear this curious celebrity with grace, but it's costing her. A ten-year-old once asked her if she ever thought about killing Amon Goeth, and an eight-year-old wanted to know how badly she'd been beaten.

"It doesn't do me good, I can tell you. I can't sleep. I have very crazy dreams—running, chasing. In my dreams, I keep going by train back to Poland, and my mother is sick. She's about to die. I reach her, but somehow I'm not doing anything about it, and that's when it stops. . . . And besides what we went through in the camp, life is not easy—losing a husband. The pain never leaves me. I'm trying not to hate, and we have all the reason to hate."

Helen's first husband, Josef Jonas, died unexpectedly in 1980. A *Schindlerjude* from the town of Czarny Dunajec, he'd been a key figure in the Brinnlitz underground. He and Helen had three children: twin daughters and a son.

A decade after his death, she married Henry Rosenzweig, a New Jersey builder, philanthropist, and Holocaust survivor. Their huge, custom home in Colt's Neck, a bedroom suburb of Freehold, backs up to a golf course. It has an indoor pool, cathedral ceilings, and a vast, pickled-wood kitchen. The average operating room is no neater or cleaner.

Helen Rosenzweig is trying to explain why May 9, 1945, was so bittersweet. "The feeling of freedom was great, but also it was very scary. Where to go? What to do? Who am I going to be? How to go about life? You see other people who have a normal life, and we came out from being locked up. You were without parents. Nobody guides you. You have to be your own self."

The Sternlicht sisters: Bronia, Helen, and Sydonia (left to right) with their mother, Lola, mid-1930s.

By then, the Sternlicht sisters of Kraków—Helena, Bronia, and Sydonia—were orphans. Their father, metals contractor Szymon Sternlicht, presumably died at Belżec in 1942. His wife, Lola, died two years later at Płaszów. It could have been heart problems compounded by pneumonia, or something else. Bronia Sternlicht Schagrin—known as Betty—has heard the stories about how ailing prisoners were finished off by lethal injections of gasoline, and she wonders. "My mother was forty-three when she died. She wasn't so sick; she had angina. Who knows if they didn't kill her."

Betty Schagrin is a woman with well-defined opinions and little patience for frivolity. She and Leon, her husband of thirty-six years, live in Sunrise, Florida, a Fort Lauderdale suburb thick with Jewish retirees. By design, they had no children. Their lives center around the activities of Holocaust Survivors of South Florida, Inc. The group, with fifteen hundred members, raises money for social-service projects in Israel and conducts Holocaust education programs in area schools. Leon, a survivor of the Tarnów Ghetto, Auschwitz, and the notorious I. G. Farben slave-labor factory at Buna, runs the group's office.

Sydonia, the oldest sister—now Sydel Abt—lives in Brooklyn. "She is the bravest, the brightest woman there was," says Helen. "Strong and intelligent. It's hard for her to talk about any of it."

The sisters describe their childhoods as happy and secure. Their parents married young and remained very much in love. "My father didn't go out, that he didn't kiss my mother," says Betty, born in 1923. "We were brought up in a very warm home."

"When I have something stressful," says Helen, "I go back home in my mind, even though home isn't there anymore. That's what I always reach for when I'm in despair."

When the war broke out, Betty had had two years of trade school and was becoming a competent seamstress. Helen, who had ambitions toward nursing, had completed the seventh grade. Betty says that their parents were among those who didn't seem unduly alarmed by the invasion. "Who believed the German Jews? When the Germans entered Poland in 1939, people were throwing flowers. But after the *Wehrmacht* came the special groups [the *Einsatzgruppen*], and they're robbing stores and beating up Jews."

She remembers seeing three gloating Hitler Youths with a bayonet slicing the beard off an elderly Jew. "There was blood all over. He was saying in Jewish: 'God, where are you?' After that, for weeks, I was so angry. Why was it happening to us? My father was a very peaceful man, and he said they were barbarians. He believed this war would only last three months. The poor guy—he was always optimistic."

Lola Sternlicht, who was "a little on the religious side," gave her middle daughter a different answer: "She said because the Jews are sinners. I said, 'What, the Christians are not?' No Jew killed anyone in Kraków."

Time has filed only the sharpest edges off Betty Schagrin's outrage. When she talks about how the Nazis degraded Kraków's distinguished Jewish leaders by forcing them to exercise naked until they dropped, about how the

Jagiellonian University professors—"the intelligentsia"—were the first to be wasted at Auschwitz, about the Jewish babies flung like rags into brick walls, it's with the righteous passion of the betrayed.

"I used to think to myself about spilling boiling water on them. If God would just punish them! There should be a miracle like with Moses. They should kill that Hitler! They were laughing at us. They were humiliating us. Since the time when I saw them throwing the children against the walls, I don't go to synagogue anymore."

The family lived on Kordackiego Street and did odd jobs for the Germans until they were forced into the ghetto in March 1941. Szymon Sternlicht, because of his business, was put to use by the Gestapo, working on their villas. His papers bore the signatures of several powerful Nazis, including Governor Hans Frank. Ultimately, his connections counted for nothing. "My father was taken in September 1942," says Betty. "He was forty-four years old. He had status from the Gestapo and somehow they didn't respect it."

"I saw my father going to death," says Helen. "We saw them sitting on that assembly place without water and food, and [the Germans] were pushing and kicking them. That feeling is with me forever. When people ask me about the movie, I hear the noise of that train. It haunts me for the rest of my life. My father, sitting in that train, knowing where he's going, and he was always so optimistic. Even there, he said, 'Don't worry; they need me. They *need* me!'—with that sweet expression, and he went with them. He spoke German fluently, and they needed someone who did that kind of work."

By then, Sydel, who'd been a bookkeeper before the war, was working outside the ghetto. Somehow, she heard about the roundup and had managed to sneak back into the ghetto the previous night. She whisked Lola away to hide with a Christian woman she'd met while sweeping the streets. ("She was such a good soul," says Betty. "A poor woman. She would bring us bread and sandwiches.") She brought her out again after the transport departed.

From then on, Lola Sternlicht was never the same. "She was a very jolly, happy person," according to Helen. "She was full of humor. She entertained people. She would go to the theater and come back and repeat the play, singing.

When my father was taken away, everything changed with my mother. A sadness came over her."

"We knew what happened," adds Betty. "A trainman, a Pole, came back right away and told us that no trains went back out with people, and they heard the screams. We knew, but we didn't want to believe." (Two people did, in fact, escape the transport: Wiktor Lezerkiewicz—Victor Lewis of Queens—and his brother.)

Helen says that Sydel and Lola went to Płaszów during the camp's construction phase. She and Betty followed shortly before the ghetto's final liquidation. Amon Goeth, appointed Płaszów's director in February 1943, orchestrated the massacre of Ghetto B and the relocation of Ghetto A's residents to the camp on March 13. More than two thousand people died that day.

Helen sneaked into Płaszów during a transport roundup. "As I was standing on the line, I saw Betty's friend pleading with the SS, giving him money from the pocket of her coat, to let her go. First he took the money from her, then with the rifle he pushed her to the bad side. I never seen her since. I saw a guy loading large cans of milk on a wagon with a horse; they were taking food from the ghetto to the camp. When he turned to get another can, I jumped on the wagon. He had a blanket over the cans, so I covered myself with the blanket. That's how I got to Płaszów."

Betty knew none of this. She'd been hiding in the basement of the family's apartment house. She remembers a neighbor trying to convince her to give herself up. "I said, 'I'm not going. Let them kill me right here . . .' I ran out to next door and all of a sudden, some SS, young Germans, saw me, but one of them said, 'Let her live; she's young.' I didn't know there were twenty people hidden there. In everything you had to have a little luck."

When the *Aktion* ended, a Jewish policeman whose mother was among the twenty let them out. "My God," says Betty, "there was blood and bodies all over the place."

Helen had been in camp for three days when the towering Goeth strode into the barracks she was cleaning. She recalls, "He was looking at all the girls and stopped in front of me and said to the woman who was in charge of us, 'If a Jewish girl is smart enough to clean a window on a sunny day, she is good for me.'"

A day later, she was taken from the camp to his residence, immediately put to work, and just as quickly introduced to Goeth's savage nature. "I was told to iron shirts. He came from the back, pulled me by my braids, slapped me twice on my cheeks, threw me down, and very loudly said to me: 'In Vienna, a girl your age knows how to iron a shirt properly and knows how to cook and do housework, but you are too stupid, Jew.' He right away started calling me names. Then I started to cry, and he hit me once more. He said, 'In my house, I don't want to see any sad faces.' From that moment on, I knew that I had to keep my emotions, and that was the hardest thing, because if I didn't, I knew I would get so much more."

Goeth didn't talk much to his maids; he gave orders. "If something didn't please him, he right away smacked you or pushed you. He had very large hands, so when he hit me, it wasn't only my cheek, but my entire head. My ears were always ringing and my cheeks were always puffy, but it didn't really matter to him. We were just Jews. Even when his mistress would praise me for something I did right, he would say, 'So what. Even if she did well and she's nice, she's a Jew, and I have to hate her. . . .' He had a lot of hatred for Jews. It was embedded in him, and he was sadistic. So when he did kill, or hit me, he had a very content expression. It satisfied him.

"Living under his roof, the fear was so enormous. You never knew what his mood would be. He could hit you for no reason at all, just because I was standing sideways and I was supposed to stand [another] way. On the slightest provocation, I would receive the most inhuman punishment. . . . He would come in the middle of the night and pick on something and slam me. Inside, I was lonely, sad, and frightened."

Yet, says Helen, she endured something worse than physical abuse: isolation. "In the ghetto, I was still in my house. It was very scary, but the security was there a little. But being with Goeth, I was completely taken away from everybody else. Removed. I stayed in front of my window in my room watching people marching to work. I envied them. I knew they were going to daily hell, with hanging and killing and mutilations in camp, but they were together for whatever happened, and I was alone. I mostly felt this at night, on duty."

Amon Goeth spread misery everywhere he went, not just in his own house. Betty remembers having to watch two of her female schoolmates being hanged. "They wanted to escape. They couldn't take it. We had to stay there on the parade square and watch. I had been there a few months. Only our youth was holding us together. The older people couldn't take it. They got sick. And I noticed that my girlfriends who were wealthy were the first to fall apart. One of them took poison."

Betty believes that Sydel—a tall, robust girl two years her senior—was the first Jewish woman at Płaszów to earn what would become the standard punishment of twenty-five lashes on the bare buttocks. She was supervising fifty women on a road crew. "It was very cold, so she let five of the girls go into the latrine and warm up, but the SS came."

It wouldn't be the last time. About a year later, she got a second lashing. "It was a Sunday," Betty recalls. "They said it was a holiday and we didn't have to work. We were sleeping. All of a sudden, an SS came in and said we're going to get punished because we didn't come to roll call. Sydel said she would go first. She said, 'Betty, don't shout, because you'll get more.' I had to listen to them beating her. A Jewish policeman was the one who hit us: Zimmerman, from Tarnów. He was hanged later in Kraków by the Polish. You bent over a chair and they hit with a whip. We couldn't sit for weeks."

Amon Goeth had two other residences before he moved to the hillside villa shown in *Schindler's List*. While inmates constructed the villa, he first occupied a small house near the barracks, then a red brick residence near the camp's entrance. It was there, says Helen, that she witnessed two unforgettable scenes of brutality.

"He asked to call the people who were in charge of building the villa— the engineer, and the one who gave the work to the people. The villa was not ready on time, so he told them to fight each other in the yard. He stepped over to demonstrate how it should be done. He stood there watching till he saw blood flowing from their faces."

The second incident involved a young servant named Lisiek. "We were on duty that night—we changed off our nights; one night I was staying on, the next Helen would, and during the day, we were together. It was almost dawn, and [Goeth] had company. One of the civilians—he was a frequent guest, a

Gestapo who would bring out the orders—came out and said to Lisiek he needed transportation to go home. We knew him so well that Lisiek ran to the barn. A horse and carriage came. As soon as he left, Goeth [asked] Lisiek why he didn't check with him. He's the boss. He didn't give him a chance; he killed him instantly. It was in the yard, in the back. I was standing there in the door to the kitchen, and I saw it all.

"Those were some of the horrible memories I have from Goeth."

After the move to the villa, Goeth forbade his maids to go to the barracks—"he said we would bring germs and lice"—but Helen went anyway.

"I really took chances. I *had* to go to my mother. I couldn't live without seeing her. I loved my mother too much. And, naturally, I always carried some food under my arms. The Jewish police [at the entrance to the barracks] wouldn't say boo to me. Those were my privileges. Everybody knew I worked for the [commandant], and he was the only authority in the camp."

When Betty's crew passed the villa on the way to the Madritsch uniform factory, where she worked, Helen would be waiting. "She used to pack me full with sandwiches so I could give some to the other people."

Twice, Helen saved her mother from transports. "One day, a friend knocked on the window and told me they took my mother out for deportation. I went to somebody on the gate where they collected them. I told him: 'This is my mother.' That was all I had to say." The second instance was similar.

Over the years, survivors have reminded her of instances, long forgotten, in which she acted to save Jews.

"Our society [the New Crakow (*sic*) Friendship Society] built a monument on Long Island with the names of all our parents, and we meet there every year for *yiskor* [a memorial service]. One year, a gentleman introduced me to his wife. He said, 'This young girl saved my life.' It seems I was called to Goeth's office. There was a glass cabinet full of medical instruments. They had first aid for the Germans next to Goeth's office. Goeth ordered these two prisoners to move that glass cabinet to the room a few doors down. He said to them, 'If anything breaks, you will die.' This man said that the minute Goeth walked out of this room, I picked up my apron, opened up the door, and scooped all the instruments into it. He said, 'Quick, quick! We'll move.' "

On another occasion, Goeth was standing in the window with his machine gun. "There were some Jews digging ditches and they were for a moment just standing. He said, 'You see those dumb *hunds?* If they don't start right away, I'll kill them all.' Like a bombshell, I ran out of the door, so fast. With him, I never went up one step—only two. Did I fly! There was like a walkway down, but I didn't take it. I turned on my back, with my white apron on, and slid down the steep hill. If I had come around, [I] wouldn't be [in] time. I knew him so well. He would start shooting. I said, 'He's watching you!' "

And yet another time, she came upon Goeth ordering a young Jewish woman to deliver a certain message to her SS supervisor. "She said, 'I can't talk that way to my boss,' and he was reaching for his revolver. I ran and turned myself with my back on her with my arms spread, facing him, and told her, 'Run, run, run!' He says, 'Why did you do that, you dumb *hund?*' Why did I protect her? He could have killed me. But it was something I knew I had to do."

The Helenas had a room in the villa's basement, next to the kitchen. They had two beds, "and maybe some drawers or a closet." They wore black uniforms with white aprons. One of "Susanna's" chores was caring for Goeth's enormous Harlequin Danes: Ralf and Alf. They were gentle with her, but Goeth trained them to attack on command. Nearly all the *Schindlerjuden* who spent time at Płaszów have a grisly story about Ralf and Alf mauling prisoners.

"He used to call me in the yard to bring out his quilted heavy gloves," says Helen, surprisingly still a dog lover. "He used to put them on and train the dogs to attack people. He would call out the name—Ralf!—and the dog would run and chase people. Those scenes are very difficult for me to talk about. When I was called in Germany for a witness [in Goeth's postwar trial], that's when I blacked out, talking about that. I came to, but they told me I couldn't be a good witness."

Betty remembers standing on the parade square and realizing that Goeth "was starting with someone, a man. He didn't like something about him. He let his two dogs go loose, and they started to tear him apart." Goeth dispatched what was left with a bullet to the skull.

Betty says that Lola Sternlicht was worried sick about her youngest daughter, "because she was living with that murderer twenty-four hours a day. When she didn't see her for days sometimes, she would say, 'She must be dead.'" Helen understood her mother's anxiety. "So I smiled and made believe everything was fine. I didn't want to up-

Helen Sternlicht Rosenzweig (left) with Ralph Fiennes, the actor who portrayed Amon Goeth in the film Schindler's List. *Edith Wertheim is on the right.*

set her. But thinking back, how could she not know? People feared him so. When they saw him from a distance, they would run. So how would she believe he wasn't like that with me?"

Lola was not only concerned for her daughters, but hiding her step-mother, Leah Weisman. Only fifty-six, Leah was nonetheless considered elderly and useless. Helen remembers that she once saw her mother's bunk piled high with pillows. Lola said, "They're coming around taking older people. I put Grandmother there.' She said, 'She's my mother; I have to save her.' (Betty says Leah Weisman later died at Auschwitz.)

Amon Goeth, scion of a publishing family, was married, but Helen doesn't think his wife ever came to Płaszów from Vienna. The woman who shared his huge, round bed was a mistress named Ruth, a vain and vacuous brunette in her mid-twenties who did little but go shopping in Kraków, pamper herself, and organize the maids' activities. It was she who planned the dinner parties at which Oskar Schindler was a frequent guest.

"She was the kind of person—she was no good if she could live with a murderer—[who] would live with anybody as long as she got what she wanted.

She was just an empty doll, indulged with her beauty and luxury. She had everything there. She was very pretty, with delicate skin. She would lie all day long with all kinds of masques. She used to come down with yolks, cucumbers, mixed. She would go up to town and bring packages of beautiful clothes.

"She was like locked in within the walls, not knowing what went on. That was the feeling I had. She tried to be completely unaware. She heard the shooting, but she was busy with the music, maybe not to hear it."

Still, she treated the Helenas with a certain basic humanity. "Once, she brought a bunch of cut flowers. She came down to arrange them in a vase, and she left some small ones behind. I took a small vase and put these flowers upstairs next to the telephone. I remember he was using the telephone and said to her, 'The flowers smell so nice,' and she pointed to me and said that I put it there. He turned around and sort of looked at me, and said, 'So even if she does things well, I have to hate her; she's a Jew.' "

(Ruth Kalder died in the early 1980s of emphysema. Days before she succumbed, British director Jon Blair interviewed her for a documentary on the life of Oskar Schindler. Between gasps, Ruth, in a poufy black wig, argued that Amon Goeth "didn't hate Jews," and "wasn't a brutal killer, no more than other SS people. He didn't kill just for the fun of it." When Blair asked if Schindler was "a good Nazi," she replied, "We were *all* good Nazis. We couldn't be anything else.")

"I saw Schindler coming with women there," Helen recalls. "They used to stay over on the second floor. Lots of times there would be dinners, with afterward coffee and cakes. Drinks they had upstairs. That's how Oskar Schindler started to come down to the kitchen, to get a bottle of wine. He would always be extremely happy. His hands were always up when he was talking, and he liked to be the center of things. He always had a pleasant expression when he came down to me.

"At first, I didn't know who he was, so I was doubtful. He was upstairs with them, and none of them were any good. He behaved just like the rest of them. But he probably felt sorry, seeing how [Goeth] humiliated me, and he came down maybe to be a little bit nice and comforting. He patted my hair. He called me 'young child.' "

But only once, says Helen Rosenzweig, did Amon Goeth favor her with an emotion resembling compassion. "It seems like almost impossible that he said it to me, but he did," she recalls, still incredulous. "My mother died, and I was in the kitchen crying. His mistress was there, and she asked me what happened. I told her, and she must have told him, because suddenly, he came down from nowhere and said to me, 'Susanna, I heard your mother died.' I was stunned! Right away I connected it with [Ruth]. He says, 'I know what it feels like when a mother dies.' I couldn't believe it! This man who always tortured me like that. He said, 'If you ever need anything, I am here.'"

Helen Rosenzweig has nothing but praise for Steven Spielberg and his film, and it's not easy for her to advance anything that sounds like criticism. Still, since she's barraged with questions about a certain scene in the movie, she feels obliged to address it. (The scene has Goeth sexually toying with his Jewish maid.)

"I'm confronted with it by every reporter, and it's very upsetting. He was pleased with us, otherwise he would not keep us there, but he treated us not even like human beings. . . . The way he was touching her hair, it made me sick. He never did that, not to me!"

On the other hand, she says actor Ralph Fiennes did such a superb job of portraying Goeth that she had a hot flash watching the scene. "In the movie, when he smacked her, I almost felt it. Slam! He would bend his head, come down [to the basement kitchen] like dancing, and his hand was like an animal's hand. Slam . . . !"

In late spring 1944, Lola Sternlicht fell ill, and went to the *krankenstube* (infirmary) for about two weeks. Her daughters never saw her again. At Płaszów, inmate bodies were burned, but Lola had a horror of cremation, "because she believed in the second world," according to Betty. Helen's boyfriend, Adam Schtab, carried her body from the *krankenstube* and had her interred on the Płaszów grounds, placing in her unmarked grave a bottle containing information about her identity. He paced off the spot from a landmark. After liberation, Helen and Sydel returned to Płaszów and searched for the site. They never found it.

Adam Schtab—green-eyed and handsome—was a leader in Płaszów's underground, which Helen says had links to a resistance movement in Kraków.

He worked on Helen for months, trying to convince her that no one was in a better position to help than she. Needless to say, Helen was terrified. "I was never scared really to die; so many times the revolver was next to my head that it was just a matter of time. But I was fighting with Adam about it. I didn't want to do it because at that time, my mother was alive, and my sisters. If Goeth found out, probably he would make me watch how he killed them."

But she overcame her trepidation. "One room was like a smoking room, with all his tobacco and some of his rifles on one wall, and a big wooden cabinet. In those cabinets were rolled up all kinds of plans. I had keys to almost all the cabinets—this is why I thought he'd probably kill us. So I took out some information from the drawer of the cabinet. There was a map showing certain drawings of large pipes underground, like a tunnel leading from the camp to the town. I guess they were planning to escape through them. It took me three days to find that one plan. I also took out some little passes to get in and out of the camp that they [the resistance] made copies from. Adam felt they were going to try and kill us all, so there was a room where they were hiding arms."

Adam's underground activities cost him his life. The day it happened, Helen was in the villa's front yard. Goeth trotted up on his white horse. "He said, 'Susanna, where is Adam?' I looked up at him—I really see him now, on that white horse. I said, 'I don't know!' and I said to myself, 'How does he know that I know Adam? Somebody is telling him things.'

"He just dismissed it and rode on his horse to his office down the road, and the next thing I heard was two shots. I said to myself, 'It couldn't be!' I found out later they brought Adam, and Goeth asked him, 'Where do you keep the arms?' And he said, 'I don't have any.' He pulled out the gun and shot him twice, and my girlfriend said he was lying with his eyes open. It seems that Adam had a connection with a Ukrainian that was selling him things, and he trusted him, but he denounced him to Goeth. Then I was told he ordered Adam to hang and assembled the whole camp, and over him there was a sign: 'Whoever will try to escape or carry arms, this is what's going to happen to him.'"

With her parents and Adam gone, all she had left was her sisters. So it was with horror that one morning, as she was dusting near one of the villa's second-floor windows, "Susanna" noticed columns of women marching down toward the camp's entrance. They were in fives, white kerchiefs on their heads.

"I ran down to the kitchen and said to Helen, 'I think there is a deportation. Maybe my sisters are in there too.' I reached for a white kerchief and ran. She tried to stop me. She said, 'Wait, let's see what we can do here.' I said no, no, no! I ran like a mad girl, and I saw Goeth standing in the front of the entrance, where the women were loading on the cattle cars. I ran straight to him. I lost my head! I thought about what he said when my mother died, but he didn't mean it! He was in some kind of a mood. How could I possibly think he was going to help me?

"He swung his hand so hard at me. He said, 'Get away, because I kill you.' I heard a voice in back of me: 'Move away.' It was an SS. He said, 'Walk. Don't look at me. We just got a message from outside that we don't have enough wagons, so we're going to take some of the women back to camp. Tell your sisters to move very slowly back.' I told them, and all the women started to call my name. Everybody was moving back, and all the SS were shooting in the air."

When she didn't come back, Helena Hirsch grew so concerned that she woke up Ruth, Goeth's mistress. "She said, 'Susanna went down. Supposedly they are taking people away, so you have to phone the Jewish police to save the sisters, because otherwise we're going to lose Susanna.' The mistress said, 'Please don't ask me to do that! I cannot do that without him.' But Helen said, 'You have to do it. Susanna is with you for such a long time.' "

Helen Rosenzweig pauses. "I'll be honest with you. The one statement Ruth made in the documentary, about when she came down to her maids—I remember—she did say, 'If I could send you home, I would.' "

Soon after, Goeth moved his maids into the basement of the barracks housing female SS guards. "He said, 'Rumors are going around that Jews live in my house and that's wrong, and you have to get out.' " The timing could not have been better. Ruth picked that day to confess that it was she who'd placed the phone call that saved Betty and Sydel from transport. "Her conscience was bothering her," says Helen. "So he came down with a gun, to kill me, and that night I was already in the next building. He beat up Helen with the gun. He got it out of his system already before he saw me the next day. She came at four-thirty in the morning, and fell on me. The next day, he said to me, 'You are lucky.' For a whole week, I thought he was going to kill my sisters. I got beatings for Helen, too. One day he came down and said he told 'Lena' something and she didn't do it, so he beat me. All you could say was *jawohl*. You admitted to a mistake even if there was no mistake."

One day in September 1944, "Susanna" was at the villa. "The doorbell rang, and two German civilians asked for Amon Goeth. I went up to call him and he came down, and they showed him some kind of papers. I was standing right down on the stairs going to the kitchen, but I was turning around, watching. When they showed him the papers, he reached for his hat and his belt with the gun, and walked between the civilians out of the villa. I said to Helen, 'I think they take him away.' And she said, 'You're such a child; who would take him away? He's the chief commander. No one can touch him.' "

But touch him they did. Amon Goeth—who'd grown rich on bribes and the Kraków black market—was hauled off to jail.

"We were alone in the villa quite a few days, then a telephone call came. His voice was completely different. He said to pack some underwear and socks, and somebody was going to pick it up. Then we knew he was arrested, and he never came back. That's the reason I'm sitting here, because I am sure he would have killed us. We knew too much. He had already killed a few people who worked for him.

"This is when Oskar Schindler came and stood at the doorway and said, 'Susanna, you're coming with me. I have a list. I built a factory in Czechoslovakia and I'm taking all the people with me, and you.' He asked me how many of my family I had. Would I have had ten people, he would have taken ten. He took down the names of my sisters. He said, 'You're going to be safe,' and that moment, I realized that all the times he spoke to me and comforted me, he meant it. All those times he was upstairs with Goeth discussing the issues of the camp and the 'Jewish problem,' he was able to work on both ends. I realized he was like a double agent. I felt safe."

Schindler told Helen that the women would have to stop at Auschwitz on the way to Brinnlitz, and that whatever she still had in the way of valuables, she'd certainly lose there. She gave him a valise containing clothes and some jewelry.

Portraits of Szymon and Lola Sternlicht from tiny photos Helen carried in her mouth through Auschwitz.

"He said you have to go to quarantine in Auschwitz, and the men have to go through Gröss-Rosen."

Betty had been working at the Madritsch uniform factory during the time Helen worked for Goeth. Julius Madritsch, a Viennese businessman, and his assistant, Raimund Titsch, were eventually declared "Righteous Gentiles" by the State of Israel like Oskar Schindler. They treated their workers kindly and provided extra rations. Betty says Titsch even managed to get some medication for her mother, though by then it was too late.

The three weeks in Auschwitz were nightmarish. It was late October, and it was freezing. The women were issued skimpy, sheer dresses and hard wooden clogs. No underwear. No socks. No towels or anything resembling toilet paper. Betty recalls tearing off pieces of a filthy cotton mattress pad to use as a sanitary napkin. ("But Helen, because she was so pretty, an SS man there threw her a sweater.") Yet as wretched as things were, Helen rejoiced in the feeling that she was no longer so alone and so vulnerable.

As the women stripped at Auschwitz, Helen took photos of her parents—the only pictures she and her sisters still had—tore out the faces, and stuck them under her tongue. After the war, she had them restored and enlarged.

In part because of Helen's influence, Betty and Sydel were still strong and healthy as they headed to Auschwitz. "I was a very lucky woman," Betty admits. But also a bit spoiled, under the circumstances. "When I first came to Auschwitz, someone was standing by the wire, a woman with whom I had always shared my sandwiches in Madritsch. She calls me, and is standing there with a pot of soup [warm water with what appeared to be leaves]. I looked at it and I said, 'I wouldn't touch it!' I had it that good in Płaszów. Later on, I ate it, because I was starving."

The transport carrying Schindler's three hundred women from Płaszów to Auschwitz included thousands of others destined for extermination. Betty watched as one of her mother's friends was pulled from a line and sent to the gas chamber.

The Schindler women finally got under way again after three weeks, their departure greased by copious bribes from Schindler. "When we came from Auschwitz, Schindler was afraid we had lice," says Betty, "so he had a delousing place built, and a boiler room where they boiled our clothes. The doctors were afraid that we would have typhus, and once that started, they would close us up."

Life at Brinnlitz was tolerable for the Sternlicht girls. Helen benefited from the interest of a boy who wooed her with crispy baked potatoes, and the work wasn't taxing. "I think it was packing stuff into boxes," says Helen. "I was doing the same thing over and over. I could see the same boxes day after day."

She's among those who recall hearing the voice of Winston Churchill piped into the factory on the eve of the camp's liberation. "We could hear on the speakers that something was very exciting. We didn't understand, but we knew it was a voice of power, and Schindler let us listen. I realized this must be the end of the war. It was a feeling of, we are free! Goeth came to my mind right away: He can never come for me anymore."

Betty remembers becoming hysterical when Schindler called his people together on the factory floor and told them they were free but he was a fugitive. "He said we shouldn't take it upon us to take revenge. We should leave it to the judges. We were holding one another. We thought we'd be left alone. He was our father."

The Sternlicht girls after the war: Bronia, Sydonia, Helen (left to right).

Betty made outfits for herself and her sisters from fabric Schindler made sure each departing prisoner got. Then the three, with Joe Jonas and others, headed by train to Kraków. They knew their mother was dead but harbored a faint hope that their father wasn't. "When they loaded us up in the train, to Kraków, I broke out in such hives on my whole body," says Helen. "Joe was running out at every station to get medication."

She learned of Joe's role in the Brinnlitz underground only after the release of *Schindler's List.* "He used to receive the communications from the Czech people. He never told me. Afterward, we didn't talk much about things like that. You know, truthfully, it was too morbid and so painful."

Jonas also helped Schindler escape from Brinnlitz. He told Helen that "they took him out in a wheelbarrow covered with straw, and put him in the car."

* * *

Kraków's Jewish federation placed Betty in an apartment with a mother and daughter. Her sisters were with a group in a dormitory. She got some work from a man named Liebermann, who'd been a tailor at Madritsch. He was making work clothes for the city. "I was there for a month and we decided to go toward the Americans. There, the Red Cross was helping you out. Under the communists, you didn't have any help."

Helen couldn't wait to leave. "I had a very bad experience. I was walking in the streets of Kraków and I felt like the ground was falling under me. I guess I felt like this was not a safe place for me, like they don't want me there. That stayed with me for life. I wanted to get out of there as quick as I could."

Crossing borders illegally, the sisters made their way to Austria—Helen and Sydel first, followed by Betty. Their new lives began in Salzburg. "We were dancing without stop, because all of us were young," says Betty. "Almost every second day, we had dances and parties. We wanted to live. Some Americans showed us the jitterbug and the swing. We were living it up. But the whole time, there was a hole in my heart."

"We all were ready to go to Israel," adds Helen. "We were waiting for our number to come up. Then my older sister remembered we had some cousins in America, and my fiancé's uncle. He wrote and pleaded with us to come to the United States. We went through so much—to give ourselves a chance. I got married just before we came so I could go on Joe's visa. We realized we had no strength to fight in Israel."

The Sternlicht girls were thrilled when they heard from their cousins. "We thought we were alone, and all of a sudden, someone cares," says Betty. "We were like lost sheep."

During that time, Helen went to Germany to testify against Goeth. "It was not enough to hang him. I felt they should torture him a little bit, like he tortured others. Oh yes, he lost a lot of weight and was half the size, but that didn't mean anything. I still feel that all the things he was taking from the executed prisoners, he must have been shipping to Vienna to his wife and kids. They still have a lot, his family."

Had she had the chance, says Helen Rosenzweig, this is what she would have said to Amon Goeth: "You wild animal. You murderer. You're no good for nothing. You don't belong in a civilized world. You're inhuman. You should be born between wild animals."

Betty and Sydel arrived in Boston three days after Helen and Joe had landed in New York. Sydel was, by then, married to a survivor, Jack Abt. They have two daughters—Lola, who lives in Baltimore, and Marilyn, who lives on Long Island—and two grandchildren.

Helen and Joe's son, Steven—now a Long Island chiropractor—was born in 1951, followed by twin sisters, Vivian and Shelly. Vivian Delman is a nutritionist and lives on Long Island; Shelly Jonas is a psychiatric nurse and lives in Manhattan. Helen has four grandchildren.

Helen describes her late husband as "a gentleman. Very bright and talented. He was

Helen Sternlicht marries Josef Jonas.

self-educated, well spoken, and sophisticated. He had class—a polish—even though he came from a small town. I don't think people knew he was a survivor. But he was troubled a lot with the fact that he was the witness when the Germans pulled away his parents and his younger brother, and he stepped forward to go instead and they pushed him back. I don't think he ever got over it.

"But we didn't talk about these things, and we felt like nobody wanted any part of what went on in Europe. They didn't want to know. I really feel people didn't like to hear sad stories.

"We didn't even bother to talk about it with each other in our group. Everybody was busy with how to make a living. Life was going to school at night and work in the day and trying to make it. We didn't want pity or to be treated as someone different; we just wanted a little understanding."

When the children asked questions about their pasts, Helen and Joe answered in short, simple sentences, then dropped the subject as quickly as possible. Now she thinks that might have been a mistake. "My children tell me now that I should have talked to them more, but at that point, we felt it was enough for them. I was raising my children strictly by my own emotions. We thought if the kids would hear, it would hurt them too much."

Joe became a supervisor at a New Rochelle die-casting company, and the family moved to Levittown, Long Island. Helen realized she'd never be happy as "just a mom and housewife. I couldn't see myself sitting with the women having coffee klatches, smoking cigarettes, and blabbing. So I went to school for electrolysis. It's a paramedical field and it's helping people.

"I went to seminars, and there were all sorts of doctors and professionals who taught us a lot. This was me. People trusted me, and it opened up new information about people and behavior. Maybe this was a healing process for me, to give to others. And at the same time, I earned a very nice living, and I was able to get the better things. We extended out the house—it was very big—and we entertained a lot. Then Joe went into the import/export business."

When he died suddenly in 1980, Helen went into deep mourning. That's why there's nothing of her story in the book *Schindler's List*, published in 1982, and, thus, the film, which was based on the book. "They did approach me for the book," she says, "but it was only two and a half months after Joe died."

Betty, meanwhile, was working in New York's garment center, at first doing piecework for a bathing-suit manufacturer. She progressed to dressmaking and alterations for wealthy private clients. These days, her sewing room is the screened porch of her condo.

She met Leon Schagrin on a 1958 vacation to Israel. He'd been there since liberation, having lost his parents, three brothers, and four sisters. His left arm bears the Auschwitz number 161744. In 1960, he covered it with the tattoo of a panther.

"My hands will never be clean again from the dirt and blood I was forced to clean off the boots by the head of Gestapo Colonel Amon Goeth, who ordered the execution of the Tarnów Jews," he once wrote in a Holocaust Survivors of South Florida commemorative booklet.

In the beginning, Betty tried to get pregnant, but when it didn't happen, she and Leon decided it was just as well. "I didn't care about children," she says. "I needed someone to love me. If we had children, whatever problems they had, we would be thinking it was because of us."

Leon worked in the maintenance department of Memorial Sloan-Kettering Hospital in Manhattan. Then the couple bought a Long Island card shop, from which Leon retired at age fifty-five. To this day, he won't eat barley soup, because it reminds him of chasing a single barley around his bowl in Auschwitz. ("Too bad," says Betty, "I make good mushroom and barley soup.")

Leon has been speaking publicly about the Holocaust for years, but Betty never did. She suffers paralytic panic attacks and takes antidepressants. Still, since the film, she has appeared on several panels with Leon and other South Florida "list" survivors. It's not easy for her, she says, "But we are stronger than the average person, and I thank God for this."

In 1990, Helen Jonas married Henry Rosenzweig, from the Polish city of Kielce, site of the postwar period's most notorious pogrom. (Forty-one Jews who'd returned from the camps to look for relatives were murdered there in a nighttime attack.)

They travel a great deal: cruises, Las Vegas, Europe. "I had to create a whole new life. At a certain point, for better or worse, it's better together, not to lean on the children. I have seen people in my office who would say, 'I love my mom dearly, but I don't have peace. When I go out Saturday night, I think, What is my mother doing? I call, I run.' I feel my children have to have their own lives.

"When I see the second generation, it must be so difficult that they had to be born to people who were so badly hurt. Most of them don't know what it is, a grandfather or grandmother. And always remembering what a horror their parents went through. But to me, having children was the greatest achievement. And the grandchildren. We have produced something."

Helen Rosenzweig never lost faith in God. "God created people, and people were the ones who failed each other," she says. "When my husband

Betty and Leon Schagrin, Florida, 1994.

died, I remember opening the Bible. God is saying, 'Don't go left and don't go right. Go straight ahead and I will guide you.' I feel there is something that leads me, gives me the inner strength to overcome, because basically I was not a strong person."

So often, she has asked herself why she was spared. Finally, she has an answer: "It was meant for me to speak for all the people that perished. This is one of the reasons I put myself out to speak so much. For me, this is the most important thing. My neighbors, Italians, say, 'Helen, we are so proud of you. We are cutting out everything about you from the newspapers and we give them to our children and make them promise to give them to their children.' It is so meaningful to me that people want to know and tell their kids."

Several years ago, Helen Rosenzweig sat down in front of a video camera and talked for three hours about her life. The tape, made by the Museum of Jewish Heritage in Manhattan, is part of Yale University's Holocaust archives. She says she did it for her children, after attending the funerals of several survivor friends.

Henry—now supportive of her public appearances—was dubious. He could see how nervous it made her, how anticipating the session disrupted her sleep. "He said, 'Who needs that? It's inside us. Why can't we live this life in peace?' But I thought, if we are all gone, who is ever going to believe it? Even if *Schindler's List* didn't come out, I made my peace with that tape."

LEON LEYSON

In the town of Narewka, about 150 miles northeast of Warsaw, there is a monument to townspeople lost during World War II. It's an unusual memorial, given the town's ethnic composition, but the casualties it notes represents a quarter of Narewka's prewar population, hardly an easy number to ignore—even if they were Jews.

The marker says, roughly: "In a common grave, five hundred people of the Jewish religion, murdered by the occupying Hitler Germans on August 5, 1941. We salute their memory."

Leon Leyson, an industrial arts teacher in Southern California, visited Narewka during the summer of 1989. It had been fifty-one years since he had last walked the streets of his boyhood home. He was called Leib Lejzon then, and in 1938, he was nine years old.

His oldest brother, Hershel, had been killed in the 1941 massacre—"a tough guy. A socialist. My hero"—as well as grandparents and cousins. They all came floating back as Leon Leyson stood there with his sister and his one living brother, the three of them quite likely the only Narewka Jews left who had survived the war in Poland. The emotion nearly flattened him. "The Holocaust was not as overwhelming to think about at sixteen as it was at sixty," he says.

Narewka had been a peaceful agricultural town before the war, and remains "primitive" today. Leon's ancestors on both the Lejzon and Golner

The monument to Jews massacred in Narewka, Poland.

sides had been farmers tilling rented acreage. In those days, Jews were not permitted to own land.

Leon's father, Moshe, worked for "the one and only industry that existed in Narewka: a little glass factory making bottles and jars," as a tool-and-die maker and form builder. He and his wife, Channah, had five children: Hershel, "our Samson. A big, strong guy"; Betsalil, called Tsalig; Pesza, who changed her name to Aviva after the war, in Israel; David; and Leon, who was born on September 15, 1929, two weeks before the U.S. stock market crashed.

As the Great Depression cast dank shadows across the economies of Europe, the citizens of Narewka didn't feel a thing. Their town had just about made it into the twentieth century by then. "The mode of transportation was horse and horse-drawn vehicles," says Leon. "There was one automobile very late in my experience there. It belonged to one of the people who was ferrying passengers from the railroad station, like a taxi. We lived in a small house located on one long main street. There was no indoor water or plumbing. There was a well but not a pump. You drew water by dropping a bucket inside and pulling it up. It was a chore that the kids did, summer and winter." Wood stoves heated the rooms, the bathwater, and the food.

The Leysons and Golners were "straight, gentle, plain people living in the countryside that at the time offered a very quiet kind of life. They were making a living and observing the sabbath. To be a farmer, you had to be practical, logical. They were all that, and strong. The basis of their existence was religion."

Leon Leyson too is straightforward, gentle, and practical, but with a sneaky, ironic sense of humor. For a recent Mother's Day, he gave his wife, Elizabeth, an electric drill. Early on, he wooed her with handmade garden tools and a meat tenderizer.

Leyson seems as self-assured as he is self-effacing, a man at peace with his conscience. Drafted for the Korean War—six years after his liberation from a concentration camp—he went, without much protest. But when *People* magazine sought to include him in an article on *Schindlerjuden,* he stunned them by declining. "I told them I was not a *People* kind of person. I didn't care to be exhibited."

He plans to retire in 1995 from the job he's had since 1958: teaching shop at the largely Latino Huntington Park High School in Los Angeles. He and the former Elizabeth Burns, the Ohio-born teacher who turned his head the instant they met, have lived in the same split-level ranch house in suburban Fullerton for twenty-three years. With its putting-green lawn and antiques, it has a reassuring, neo–Norman Rockwell flavor. "We're steady, us Leysons," Leon says.

His choice of occupation isn't surprising. The Leyson brothers all were technically or mechanically inclined, taking after their father and their paternal grandfather, who was a blacksmith. "Everything that could be taken apart, we had it apart," says Leon, chuckling. "We did not always put it back together! At one time in Narewka, there were two crystal sets—two radios—and one of them belonged to Tsalig, who had the most talent of any of us. He built it himself. We could pick up the station from Bialystok and the larger cities in the area. In those days, it was a miracle that you could put your earphones on and hear something.

"Years later, Tsalig did electrical installations outside the Kraków ghetto. He had a pass, and I was his assistant. He never had a day of schooling in it."

Though a pogrom in the early 1900s sparked a significant Jewish exodus from that part of Poland—"these people were not strangers to violence against us"—Jews and gentiles "tolerated each other's holidays" and coexisted in relative peace. The Poles would warn their children that if they didn't behave, a Jew would come and get them. Once in a while, rocks flew after a Pole baited a Jew with a remark like "Why don't you go to Palestine?" A certain neighbor would chase the Leyson children away from her house because she didn't want Jews near it. But until 1941, that was about the worst of it.

Soon after Leon's birth, the glass company for which Moshe worked re-

Leon Leyson's family before the war (clockwise from top right): Hershel, Channah, David, Aviva, and Betsalil.

located to Kraków. It was a good opportunity for a young man, and Moshe took it, leaving his wife and five children behind. This wasn't a great hardship for Channah, says Leon, "because we lived in such a small town where everybody was related. We sort of were taken care of by everybody."

Moshe made the 350-mile trip to see his family at least twice a year, but planned to have them follow as soon as he got established. That was in 1938, and, says Leon, "that's what saved our lives."

The move offered young Leon his first train ride. The glitter of the city lights mesmerized him as they approached in the dark. Narewka had only recently replaced its kerosene lamps with electricity.

Krakowska Huta Szkła, the glass firm, made bottles for the state-run vodka monopoly. Its employees lived in company housing near the factory, and there Moshe installed his family, though it was a largely gentile enclave. Leon says he encountered overt anti-Semitism as soon as he enrolled in the neighborhood public school.

"I was called on to recite something. I knew the teacher was calling on me because he was pointing at me, but he did not call me by name. He called me 'Mosiek,' which is the diminutive for Moshe. That was my father's name, and I thought he was pretty good to impose my father's name on me. But it was a Polish joke. As soon as I got home, I realized he did not know who my father was. It upsets me more now than it did then."

At the start of the 1939 school term, anti-Semitic teachers were no longer a problem, because the Germans closed the schools. By year's end, Moshe was unemployed. Still, says Leon, "everyone thought that this was not going to last. That was the big discussion, that several months from now, it was all going to be over." That was before the Gestapo dragged Moshe Leyson off to jail.

"My father was arrested as soon as the Germans came in. There was another Jewish family living in our unit. He was the accountant to the glass factory. He had his family, and when the invasion came, they decided to leave. They had some family in Warsaw. They gave my father the keys to their apartment. They thought that when the war was over, they would be back. But in the meantime, certain types in the neighborhood wanted to have the keys so that they could get in. My father said no way. Of course they broke in and robbed the apartment immediately.

"When the Gestapo came into the area, one of those whom my father refused the key to pointed out that there were some Jews living right here. That was before any of those laws or anything, before the armbands, before the ghetto, before we had any idea of what might happen—there were just indications of unruly soldiers grabbing people on the street: beating them up, shaving their beards, just having fun."

From time to time, Moshe met with government officials about glass company business. When two Gestapo officers confronted him, he warned them not to "give him a hard time," or he would report them. Says Leon: "That's all they needed to hear. So they hauled him off, and we didn't know where he went. There was no such thing as *habeas corpus* or due process."

For weeks, Leon and David searched all over Kraków for their father. "We went to every agency and every Gestapo office. We went to some lawyer and talked to him about finding our father. But after all the running around, I ran across those two Gestapo officers. I chased after them to find out where they took him, and one of them told me! Sure enough, he was there. We started bringing him packages of food and stuff. We couldn't see him, but we could leave something for him."

Moshe Leyson languished behind bars for three months. He was not brutalized, but by the time he was freed, something fundamental in him had changed. In hours of discussion about the hard times and heartbreak of life under the Nazis, only this brings tears to Leon Leyson's eyes. His voice drops to little more than a whisper.

"I think that was my worst experience with the German Army. I just didn't like to see my father in that position. It pretty much broke his spirit. He was a proud craftsman, and people respected him. For somebody like me—nine or ten years old, watching his father helpless and he watching me—that was the worst. They roughed him up right in front of us."

The Leysons were booted out of their company-owned apartment and herded with the rest of Kraków's Jews into the ghetto. "We picked up what we could and moved, with a horse-drawn wagon. If you saw the people moving into the ghetto in the [Spielberg] movie, that was exactly right."

By then, Moshe and David were working for Oskar Schindler. Moshe already was well known at the enamelware plant. It stood across Lipowa Street from the glass factory. He'd often done side work there, because, Leon says, "not every company had its own resident tool-and-die maker. In fact, he worked for several companies in that area—a soft-drink company on the other side of the glass company, where he did some machinery repair. In those days, you had to make the part to fix the parts, and he did that.

"So when Schindler came and my father could no longer work [legally] in the glass company, Schindler asked him to move over to Emalia. Ironically, he did some work for [the glass company] on the sly while he was working at Emalia, and not without Schindler's knowledge. He went to work at the glass factory, then the following day came back and worked at Emalia, so he worked right around the clock. In those days, he felt a responsibility toward the glass company."

Moshe had met Schindler soon after he took Emalia over. "He needed the safe opened, and my father had the tools."

At that point, everyone in the family had valid working papers. Aviva got hers through her job at Kabelwerk, a Kraków electrical company. Like Emalia, it too would eventually establish a Płaszów subcamp. Leon, David, Tsalig, and Channa were covered under Moshe's "blue card" from Emalia.

Leon and Tsalig worked at a brush and broom factory. In his off hours, Leon went to *cheder* (religious school) in someone's home, "learning the Torah to the footsteps of the German Army on the outside." But he never had a bar mitzvah. "By the time I was ready, it was just about the time the ghetto was being closed. David was not bar mitzvahed, as I remember. Tsalig was, and I remember that he got a fountain pen."

What the sixteen-year-old Tsalig did not have, in the late summer of 1941, was a *Blauschein*, a "blue card." For some reason, when he tried to get one on his own, he was refused.

Moshe and David were at work when the soldiers swooped down on the ghetto. The rest of the family was home. "The soldiers were running all over our house and all over the building," Leon recalls, "chasing people out, asking for their IDs and just shoving people out the door. This was the second time that they had a transport, and stories were beginning to come back that those people were being murdered. But there was nothing certain, or at least nothing certain that we were aware of."

They took Tsalig, who probably died at the Belżec death camp, though according to Leon he might have been saved. It seems that Oskar Schindler was at the station, looking to pull someone off the train. He had seen Tsalig at Emalia with Moshe—"he had the memory of an elephant"—and offered to take him off. But Tsalig didn't want to leave his girlfriend.

As soldiers shoved Tsalig out the door, Channah and Leon stood frozen. "It was a feeling of absolute fear, because we had incidents by that time where people were being murdered for no reason, so anything that anybody would have done at that point [to resist] was suicidal."

When it was over, Channah Leyson came apart. "I don't remember my father ever in despair about we were not going to make it," Leon says, "but my mother—sure she was. When [we were] under fire, then she was solid. When everything was quiet, she would go to pieces."

Hershel, the oldest, was among thousands of men who tried to outrun the German Army in 1939 as it rolled across Poland from the west. He fled Kraków for Narewka, and with the eastern part of the country under Soviet occupation, "it seemed like a good move, and until 1941, he really was in a better place. We all wished we were still there.

"But as it turned out, when the Germans invaded the Soviet Union and went into Narewka, they murdered all the Jews. They went house to house and chased everybody out in the street. They put the women in a barn, then drove the men down to the edge of the forest and killed them."

Hershel had been working at a Soviet coal mine, but took sick and went home to recuperate at precisely the wrong time. "We didn't find out about it till the war was over. We thought that he'd be coming back," says Leon.

As the Germans slashed away at the Jews in the Kraków Ghetto with transports, *Aktions,* and random killings, the Leyson family had a ringside seat. They lived at Lwowska 18, and anyone headed for the railroad station had to pass their building.

"In front, where one of our neighbors lived downstairs, we could kneel down and look over the edge of the window and see them. People who couldn't make it, who carried bundles that were too heavy, were just simply shot."

Still, even the Nazis could not squash the cultural life of the Kraków Jews. "We had theater, dance, lots of music and lots of talent," Leon says. "It was like a miniature society inside a crazy world. I used to climb walls to see cabaret performances in empty lots. You can't suppress it. Maybe that's why we survived."

For a time, the Leysons lodged a Jewish couple, the Lustigs, who had been deported from Germany. "We divided the bedroom with a blanket on a string and put them up over there on the other side. They were wonderful, gentle people. They were taken away—grabbed. They had no apparent employment. I was watching them march down the street, and I was really sad. Mr. Lustig was always promising to take me to America. His son lived in the United States, and he said, 'One day, after the war, I'll take you to America.' "

(In 1989, Leon visited his old ghetto apartment, and its occupants let them in. "I was looking at that bedroom, and I couldn't believe how small it was. That section we let them use was wide enough for a bed sideways, and just maybe enough room to walk past it.")

Leon and a friend almost got themselves shot one night, breaking the ghetto's nine p.m. curfew to carry a woman on a stretcher to the hospital. "On the way back, we had to pass the guard near the gates. He took his rifle off his shoulder; my friend ran around the corner and he missed him. I ran into a building with a recessed entrance. A shot rang out and ripped a piece of brick off the building. I pounded on the door and the people let me in and I stayed the night. I thought maybe I was shot. It scared the dickens out of me."

The sixteen-square-block area of Jewish confinement had been split into Ghetto A and Ghetto B. Channah and Leon, who by then had no work cards, were on the B side. Moshe, David, and Aviva were already at Płaszów. "The wise thing to do," says Leon, "was to go over to the A side while it was still possible, because those people who were left on the B side were eventually taken out and killed. My mother stayed on that B side until almost the last minute. She wasn't going to go until she got what she wanted to take: pots, dishes, spoons. We told her, 'Don't take that; we don't need it,' but it sure came in handy."

And then came March 13, 1943. Under the direction of *Untersturmführer* Amon Goeth, the two thousand Jews of Ghetto B were hunted down and slaughtered. The ten thousand from

The shed where Leon Leyson and his mother hid during the 1943 Kraków Ghetto liquidation.

Ghetto A were rounded up and sent to Płaszów. The previous evening, Schindler had warned his workers not to return to the ghetto, so Moshe and David were at Emalia and Aviva was at Kabelwerk.

The rest of the family survived by hiding in the crawlspace of a shed in the building's courtyard. "It didn't look like it would have an attic; it was leaning up against the wall of the building. We crawled all the way over to the end, across the wooden rafters. There were a couple of kids in the building that belonged to the shoemaker. His wife was the manager of the house." The woman refused to hide and continued working in the courtyard. "She was thinking that they wouldn't take her if she was busy working."

Channah didn't want to hide either, Leon remembers. "She was going to do the same thing like this woman, and take her chances, but she gave us some food to take with us up into the crawlspace. Then she remembered maybe we should have some water, so she filled a teapot full of water and she was going to bring it up. But by that time, things were really happening. The Germans were already yelling and screaming down the street, next house, next building. She was going to hand the water over, and the soldiers were already beginning to come into the courtyard, so she decided to crawl up in there with us."

In her haste, Channah Leyson left the teapot on the ground, outside their tenuous sanctuary. It could have given them all away, but fortunately, says Leon, "there was so much debris everywhere in the backyards, with people leaving stuff all around, that they didn't notice."

Channah's change of mind saved her life. "We were listening and watching what you could see in the courtyard: people being dragged out, including the mother of those two boys who were with us."

The building wasn't far from the ghetto's assembly square. "There was constant shooting and yelling. We could hear the transport being marched off, and we just kept up there. Later on, somebody came to tell us that it was safe to come out, but we didn't because that could have been a trick. The Germans used all kinds of ploys to get people out. We stayed there not knowing who it was. Then sometime the next night, someone came that my father sent. They called us by name and said who they were, and we knew that person. We thought it was probably safe, so we came out."

Channah belonged to a work group of women who cleaned houses and did laundry. "When the ghetto was liquidated and everyone was going to be shipped to Płaszów, everyone lined up by the companies where they worked. My mother's group left through the gate and marched on to Płaszów." But when the brush factory group started toward the gate, a guard pulled Leon from the ranks. "He told me that I would come later—not to worry. So I went out and started circulating around with my friends who were all about my age—about twelve. They said that they would go hide, but I decided that I wouldn't. I went back to where people were lining up with their companies and got in with some other company. That time I succeeded. The guard didn't see me, which was strange, because when I was getting into the group, somebody standing there said, 'You don't belong in this group. What are you doing here?' and somebody else told them to shut up. I didn't know if it was the right thing to do. I ended up at Płaszów, and everybody was surprised."

At first, Leon and his mother worked on the camp road—the one paved with broken headstones from the Jewish cemeteries on which the camp was built. On that detail, he had the first of two traumatic encounters with Amon Goeth.

"He came by and didn't like the way the work was going. He lined everybody up on the assembly grounds. He set up tables and had the guards hand out twenty-five lashes. I can tell you that the first crack is equal to having somebody cut you with a knife. They were using whips with little ball bearings at the end. I suspect that I didn't get as heavy a blow as the adults did. I just can't imagine that I would have made it through it if I had. My rear end was black and blue for the longest time."

The brush factory had moved into the camp. One night while Leon was at work, Amon Goeth came by, seeking diversion.

"He shot the foreman right in front of us—for nothing. It was late at night and he didn't have anything else to do, so he shot him. He lined everybody up and started segregating people. It was a very bad sign in those days when they started grouping these people on the side and the others on the other side. I was segregated already to another group. It did not look very good to me. There were a couple of other kids about my size and some older people.

I began to think about what I should do. They were marching back and forth between us. When their backs were turned, I skipped over to the other side.

"We stood there for some time waiting to find out what was going to happen, but Goeth simply left. He took his people and left. He lost interest in the whole business. We stood there for about another thirty minutes and nothing happened. Then somebody came in and said to go back to the barracks. We went, and that was when everyone really started to get into hysterics. We had come too close to being killed."

Channah Leyson lived out her days deaf in one ear, courtesy of a Płaszów guard. "She was trying to lift up some kind of a board or something. He didn't think she was doing a fast enough job and he just hit her with his open hand, and broke her eardrum."

Because the men and women were separated, the family couldn't get together at Płaszów. "We saw each other from a distance every now and then by chance, as they were being hauled off to a job someplace." They reunited at Emalia. "[Schindler] was going to increase his Jewish workforce for the third or fourth time, and each time he did that, my father would ask him to put one of us on the list. The list became kind of a precious thing. When it came out, my mother and I were on it, but I was not allowed to leave, I guess because I was working in the brush factory and I already had a job.

"I went to see my mother off as they were getting ready to be marched off to Emalia from Płaszów. Somehow I went up to the officer—a mean-looking SS officer, one of Goeth's henchmen who was going to accompany the group to Emalia—and I told him that I was on the list. He asked the man with the clipboard to see if that was true, and he said, 'He is on the list here.' Then he was going to tell him something about why I couldn't go. The officer told him to shut up. He got mad at him and he told me to get in line. I had a momentary benefit of the German mentality, so I got to go to Emalia."

The incident stuck with Leon. "I think I recognized that every individual is a person on his own, and cannot be judged by anything other than what he does. I could have been helped by an SS who maybe five seconds later might have shot me."

Aviva was still at Kabelwerk, living at that plant's subcamp. From time to time, someone from Kabelwerk would go to Emalia. "There was some connection about work, and through the official messengers, word came back from Aviva that she was over there, and we sent back word that we were okay."

Moshe Leyson may have been "a small-town boy coming into a big city, but he was a pretty fancy dresser," according to his youngest son. "So he left his suits with one of his Polish friends from the glass company. Periodically, [Moshe] got the word to [the friend] that he should sell one of the suits and exchange it for food, and he did. This was one wonderful guy. He didn't have to do it, and our chances of coming back were slim. He would show up in Emalia, around the corner, and let it be known that he had the stuff. It was at considerable risk to himself."

At Emalia, Leon learned the skills that would support him for the rest of his life. "I was doing production work on the machines. My father was doing tool-and-die work. My mother was a cleaning woman. Schindler called me 'Little Leyson.' "

The whole family got KL tattoos, though Leon's is gone. "I sucked it out right after they tattooed me. Not all of it came out; it was just a thin line that was still there, but eventually I grew out of it. My father, mother, and brother still had theirs."

In 1944, a forced population reduction sent hundreds of Schindler's workers back to Płaszów. Channah was allowed to stay, but her husband and sons had to leave. When Schindler learned of the situation, he changed it.

Leon says, "Schindler came to see the people who were leaving, and we were all lined up. I was ready. I had a Thermos bottle with me. I tried to get his attention. I worked my way toward the front, and the German guard standing there saw me and tried to get me back in line. He hit me with his rifle and he knocked the bottle out of my hand. It made a big noise. Schindler saw me, and I raised my hand and told him that we were not on the list to stay, so he immediately ordered that we be put back on. Not only did he do that, but he actually went over to where my mother was and told her that we were coming. She told us afterwards. She said that she didn't believe him at first. I didn't even know that he knew her."

A couple of months later, Płaszów and all its subcamps shut down.

Schindler's men went briefly to Gröss-Rosen, his women to Auschwitz. "Some people will tell you that they knew exactly that if you weren't on Schindler's list, you were going to die. We weren't exactly certain what was going to happen. We knew that Płaszów was a thousand times worse than Schindler's company, but as far as future survival, nobody knew. It is all in retrospect now."

Gröss-Rosen terrified "Little Leyson," just as it terrified men twice and three times his age. "We could have been there twenty-four hours or a week or a month—it all ran together. We were on our own in a camp that also exterminated people, in the hands of murderers. Anything could have happened."

That first night at Gröss-Rosen "was the most incredible scene. We had been standing there most of the night out in the cold. That itself was an absolutely unreal scene. We were all huddled up together, and if you could move your way inside the group, it got a little warmer. I realized that when I stood still long enough, I ended up on the outside again, so everybody else was doing it. This whole of mass of humanity was just standing there, twisting and moving around constantly."

Finally the freezing, naked men were shoved into a barracks suited for less than half their number. "People sat up and had the next group sit right in between the legs, stacked up. As you know, after a while in a closed room, it gets warm. I just fell asleep, like dead. When I woke up there were bodies twisted every direction you can imagine. Nobody was in the original spot where they sat."

Moshe and David were nearby, as they tried always to be. "You can see here"—Leon points to page 5 on Schindler's men's list where his brother, his father, and he appear as numbers 287, 288, 289—"that it was purposely arranged so that David could come first, because he was a little bigger, then me, sandwiched in between him and my father."

For years he nurtured an unfulfilled childhood fantasy from those days: slapping Marcel Goldberg in the face for the way he manhandled David in the cattle car bound for Gröss-Rosen.

Soon after leaving Gröss-Rosen, Leon Leyson almost lost his mother to the ovens of Auschwitz. She was shunted off to a barracks for the old and sick, "the ones they simply don't feed, then finally take them to the gas chamber. But because Schindler insisted that he have all his women—all those women were all 'very highly trained' and 'irreplaceable'—they actually got her out."

With the smallest boys taken to Auschwitz soon after arriving at Brinnlitz, "Little Leyson" was among the youngest children at the munitions factory. "I was noticeable, because when I first started working for Schindler, I was little enough that I couldn't really reach the handles on the machine. I used to stand on an upside-down box."

In Leon's shop today, "everything I touch reminds me of it. Every time I step up to one of the machines, I remember the box I stepped up on.

"Now, old Schindler—he got kind of a big kick out of that, because he used to point me out when he brought in his superiors, doing his PR to show how his company was really operating—how well they were doing, the Jews were working, and all that. I was never certain what he was going to do. I knew then that I should not be conspicuous, because I was a kid, so when he singled me out for certain things, I'd worry. He used to point me out by pointing to my father. You could tell—you didn't have to be a genius to find out what he was saying: that was my father over there. That was my brother and me. And then they would come up real close and watch me work. Now, *that* was really scary. He'd bring in huge, monstrous-looking SS with the skull and crossbones on their uniforms. They'd walk up and I'd be petrified. They would stand real close to me, on the other side of the machine. I wouldn't dare look up, so all I could see was these big belt buckles on the uniforms."

Schindler once caught "Little Leyson" goofing off—an offense that might have gotten him killed elsewhere. Instead, it got him a better job.

"I was once watching someone set up a machine, and was not at my work station. He caught me—I could smell him before I saw him, from the cologne and cigarettes. I just stood there, and he went past and didn't say anything. The following day, he ordered that my brother and I be put in the tool-and-die-making department, which took much higher skills. My father was in there, and it was not that easy to get in. Occasionally, when he was by himself, he would come and talk to me. He ordered that I get extra rations of food. I found out that he ordered whoever was making up the schedule [for the tool room] to take me off nights. That was really close to the end of the war, and we were on very, very short rations in Brinnlitz, and were getting to the point where I was beginning to get double vision, and my brother was developing these sores on his legs that weren't healing. My father was beginning to become ill too. He had to spend a little time squatting down."

Leyson remembers a day when Schindler told him to follow him into a certain room, "and he gave me this hunk of bread. That was the most exciting thing I had had in a long time. Of course, what I did immediately was to hide it and take it over to my father and brother and share it with them."

He also got extra food from the kitchen staff: the "Budzyńers," a group of burly political prisoners from the city of Budzyń, brought to Brinnlitz by its commandant, *Untersturmführer* Josef Leipold. They formed the nucleus of the camp's underground resistance.

"They came from the same area we did and they spoke Yiddish with the same accent as we did. We were not Galicianers [from the region of Galicia]; we were Litvaks [from Lithuania], and so were they. There was a little guy in that group who was about my age, like their mascot. They made the soup and distributed the bread. The soup was made in these big kettles. When they had to clean the kettles, they swished water around in them and they let me collect all the water after. I took that and boiled it until it evaporated, and there was a little bit of food left."

Nonetheless, "Little Leyson" was "undernourished, undersized, and always hungry" at liberation, a process that took about two days. "There were no guards for a whole day before the Russian soldier came. We were in limbo, in shock, and waiting to see what was going to happen, maybe like being in the eye of a storm."

He thinks the film missed a bet with the scene in which a lone Russian soldier rides up to the Brinnlitz gates. "It was a very dramatic scene, when the Russian came in. He got off his horse, and once he found out who we were, he said we were free, and made us rip off the numbers [from our uniforms]. I thought"—he grins—"that would have been as good a scene as what Spielberg could dream up."

As the Brinnlitz gates swung open, each of the *Schindlerjuden* faced a decision at least as crucial as where he or she would go. Each had to draw new lines between right and wrong, good and bad. The Nazis had obliterated the old ones. At the age of fifteen, Leon Leyson understood the choices, and for him, there was only one possible course of action.

"German POWs were being sent down the road right past us by the thousands, twenty-four hours a day. Some other people and I were just standing, watching them march with their heads down, hour after hour. Some of the boys would grab and trade boots with [the Germans]. They would take the shoes off and say, 'Here—have my wooden shoes,' and take their boots. I wouldn't have his boots if he gave them to me for nothing! I was just glad to see them with their heads down, on their way.

"To take revenge would have been absolutely insane. This one particular person I picked on might have been a perfectly innocent person with a family and children. I would not

Leon Leyson holding the document identifying him as a Brinnlitz survivor, 1994.

even then take myself down to that level. There is no way that we could get even. Trading some of those shoes for the boots in the short run is a gain, but in the long run, it is a loss. In the long run I am better off than the person who did that. I know what kind of a person I am. I could stand up taller."

Leon Leyson stayed "high on liberation" for days. "I don't think I hit the ground until after I got back in Poland and then ran across some of the unpleasantness." As they headed toward Kraków by train—"open cattle cars, but not crowded, and with bunks"—passengers disembarked along the way. "They drifted off, dazed, to different places, not knowing what awaited them. In Kraków, we were still running around in prisoners' striped clothing, and it was a strange feeling. I had the feeling that not everybody else was as euphoric as we were about us returning."

Except for Wojek, the man who had sold Moshe's suits, and a neighbor.

"He took us to his place and we stayed overnight. They brought out the vodka. It was pretty great. The first few days were devoted to getting lodging, and Father's job. He returned to the factory."

The atmosphere in Kraków was indeed tense. "Rumors spread that Jews were so emaciated that they were using gentile children's blood for transfusions. They were beating up people on the street and throwing rocks at the synagogue," exactly what had gone on five and six years earlier. There was a riot at the dormitory housing Jewish refugees, when an anti-Semitic mob stormed the place. But Moshe Leyson had no problem at the glass factory. "They felt 'He is *our* Jew.' Nobody could touch him, and on the day of the riot he stayed in the factory. They didn't want him to go home."

In 1946, Leon and his parents sneaked out of Poland to Germany. David and Aviva went back to Czechoslovakia, looking for a fresh start.

"We ended up in a DP camp in Wetzlar, and that was a cooling-down experience. It was open, and you could come and go as you please. We interacted with the German population, some by commerce and some by just friendship, My father arranged for a little bit of education for me because my education was lacking." Through a friend, they found a tutor, "a German engineer who was a Nazi during the war. He had a family of five children, and lived in this nice, modest home in Wetzlar. He turned out to be a great person."

But living conditions in the camp were not much better than they had been in the ghetto: "three in one room separated by blankets on ropes. But to be honest, having the freedom to come and go, it didn't seem quite as terrible then as it seems now."

The camp teenagers naturally grouped together, and arguments ensued about who had had it the worst. "Some were from the death camps. Others didn't go through the camps at all—they had lived through the war hiding out or in Russia. So there was sometimes a bit of suspicion or jealousy, and occasionally in anger someone might say something like, 'You don't know anything; you never saw anybody get hanged.' "

Czechoslovakia didn't work out for David and Aviva, who went to Israel in 1948. "They got caught up in the fighting, and they've been fighting in every war since, either my brother or his children or my sister or her children."

Moshe, Anna, and Leon Leyson becoming United States citizens.

Through Jewish organizations, the Leysons found relatives in the United States. "It turned out that my mother's sister and brother were in L.A." They sailed to Boston, then headed west by train, with identification tags on their shirts. Five days later, they arrived in Los Angeles.

"My uncle came to pick us up in his Chevy," Leon remembers. "We took a one-bedroom apartment in his complex. I had my own cot in the kitchen area and my parents had the bedroom, but we had the freedom to come and go, so we felt like we were uptown."

Moshe Leyson found work as a janitor. "That was difficult for him, and it hurt his pride permanently. He was depressed. But eventually, he did get a job as a machinist. Their English wasn't great, but my mother learned enough to go to the grocery store and talk to the neighbors."

And Leon Leyson learned how to move beyond his past. "I had a certain amount of cushioning when I came to this country. I had time to go to school. I had time to be drafted in the Army, in fifty-one. All those things were places for adjustment, and I think that kind of helped. The Army for me was a good experience. If you are in civilian life in a country with inalienable rights and personal privacy, being drafted is a catastrophe, because you do lose some of your rights. But when you start out thinking you have no rights whatsoever, it is a wonderful experience. I went to basic training in Atlanta. This is where I received my first great compliment: 'You damn Yankee!' I thought it was great."

He spent sixteen months in Okinawa with a unit of Army engineers, supervising twenty-one Okinawans in a machine shop. Returning to California, he finished school, got a teaching degree, and soon after landed the job he still holds, "so there wasn't a whole lot of time to dwell on anything. But my real therapy began when I met my wife. She came to Huntington Park and rescued me."

On paper, they're an unlikely pair: he a Polish Holocaust survivor, she a blond California girl, by way of Sandusky, Ohio. They met during a "get acquainted with your school" day. She was the new teacher of English as a second language. "It was love in the machine shop," she jokes. "I think we knew right away."

She had already married him in her head before she knew anything about him. " 'My parents are going to be so surprised when they find out I'm marrying an Italian Catholic,' " she remembers thinking of this exotic, black-haired foreigner. Her first clue to the truth: "I asked him what his last name was and he said, 'Leyson.' I said, 'That doesn't sound Italian,' and he said, 'I'm not.' "

Bit by bit, he told her about what he'd been through. "I will say that dealing with the initial news caused a few nightmares," Liz admits, "but it was not a dominant factor. We had a romance and a marriage and children, and our lives were very normal. I suppose it was in the back of our minds, but Leon wanted to make sure his children didn't have a burden like that to adjust to."

She credits his parents with his stability. "If you had known the kind of people that his parents were, you would see that that was larger than the experience of the Holocaust."

Leon admits that it wasn't easy telling his parents he intended to marry a woman who wasn't Jewish. "The fact that I had to break it to them was"—he searches for the right word, then gives up—"but you know, they were the kind of people that, if I decided that was what I wanted to do, that was fine."

"And there was never any indication to me that they felt any other way except that they loved me," adds Liz. They got married in 1966—twice. "One wedding was Episcopalian and one was Jewish."

Leon insists that his decision did not repudiate his heritage. "I never felt that marrying out of the religion meant I was abandoning anything. I was going to be the same person that I would have been if I married in the religion, and my children were going to be just the same kind of people that they would have been if their mother was Jewish."

The couple have two children: Stacy Wilfong and Daniel Leyson. "We raised them a little on the free side," says Leon. "We gave them choices. I did not insist on any Jewish education, though any education you miss out on is a pity. They went to services and they had friends who were Jewish."

Dan, water polo team captain during his senior year in 1992 at the University of Southern California, is practicing with the U.S. national team and hopes to make the 1996 Summer Olympics. He had an impromptu bar mitzvah at Jerusalem's Western Wall, when the USC team was in Israel competing in the Maccabea Games. "Somebody grabbed him and said, 'Have you been bar mitzvahed?' "

Stacy became a Catholic. "She married a Catholic, and she needed some spiritual grounding," says her mother. Stacy lives at the Pensacola Naval Air Station in Florida with her husband, a Navy flier, and their toddler son.

"It bothered me some," says Leon, "but it doesn't bother me when you see the kind of life they are making. He's a great guy." Not that it would have made any difference to the Nazis, Leon notes. "According to Hitler's philosophy, Stacy is still Jewish, no matter what, and so is her son."

Moshe Leyson died in 1971, during surgery for a ruptured spleen. Channah died in 1976. "Dad had been her project. Her life. He always was. After he died, she pretty much lost interest in things for herself; she only cared about me and the kids."

Leon saw Oskar Schindler once after the war, in 1972, when a group of survivors invited Schindler to Los Angeles. Leon was among those who welcomed him at the airport. He wasn't sure Schindler would recognize him, but no reminder proved necessary. " 'I know who you are,' " said Schindler. " 'You're Little Leyson!' "

Leon was not surprised that Herr Direktor didn't do well after the war. "I couldn't see how somebody who was operating in that way could succeed operating in a normal way. He thrived on crisis and a lot of wheeling and dealing. People related to him like he was still kind of a benefactor, even though he didn't have the stature he had then. But in my eyes, he was still that person."

In 1989, the Leysons took their children to Poland. David and Aviva met them in Warsaw, and together they made a pilgrimage to Narewka. Aviva and her husband had been there the previous year. They picked up a guide in Bialystok who drove them to the town. The guide was young and had never heard of the Narewka massacre. He took them to the monument, which was overgrown with weeds.

Aviva had arranged for the same man to drive them again. This time, when they arrived at the monument, the grass had been cut and the weeds pulled. Clearly, someone had attended to the site. They noticed stubs of votive candles, too.

"I looked back," says Liz, "and the driver was crossing himself." He and his brother-in-law had been there the previous day and cleaned it up.

The town's mayor was living in the house that once had belonged to Leon Leyson's maternal grandparents. "We got a nice reception with vodka," Leon says. "I can't tell you what it was like being there in the living room where we did our homework at the table, and there had been a bed for Tsalig."

The woman who used to shoo the Leyson children off her sidewalk was eager to talk about how good she'd been to the town's Jewish women when they were locked up in the barn. "They dug underneath the wall and put a hand out, so she told me what a wonderful person she was to actually go over there and give them water. But her son just happened to come on a visit that day. He remembered a lot of things, and he could hardly speak, he was so emotional. That was really an incredible meeting. I remembered him. He never bothered us."

After Narewka, the group went to what had been their home in the Kraków Ghetto. "My sister went up and knocked on the door and told them who we were. She wanted to know if we could see the place, and they said yes, why not? So we went in. I looked at it and I just came apart. This is where Tsalig was taken away from, right out the door."

He and Liz returned the following summer, and Aviva went again the summer after that. She told Leon that the man living in their family's old house was beginning to wonder why these Leysons kept reappearing. Exactly what did they want?

Here is what Leon Leyson will tell him the next time if he asks: " 'We came to visit our people and our roots.' He can have the house; we came to visit with the ghosts."

JULIUS EISENSTEIN

*I*n February 1994, retired New York restaurateur Julius Eisenstein married a widow named Ann Grosman in his cheery, red-and-gray condo in Sunrise, Florida. But a few days before the ceremony, another wedding was on his mind: his sister Dora's, fifty-seven years earlier, in Kraków.

Julius Eisenstein was a teenager then, a blurry figure at the edge of a family portrait taken that day. There's an older woman in a dark dress in the picture, unsmiling, at the bride's right shoulder. "That," he says, pointing to her, "that is my grandmother."

Her name was Rachel Holzberg and she died during the liquidation of the Kraków ghetto on March 13, 1943. By then, two of her grandsons, Julius and his brother Joe, were at Płaszów. The liquidation left the ghetto's streets awash in blood and littered with corpses. Survivors were forced to clean up the carnage, loading bodies onto horse-drawn wagons bound for the camp. There, prisoners grabbed the bodies—one took the legs, another the arms—and pitched them into a mass grave. They repeated the routine all day and into the night, without stopping.

The prisoner who grabbed the lifeless legs of Rachel Holzberg was her grandson Julius.

"What could I do?" he asks, with an anguished shrug. "Nothing. She

Eisenstein family wedding, 1937. Julius is the blurry figure at the far right.
His sister, Dora, is the bride. To Dora's left is Rachel Holzberg.

was dead already. But I felt like dying myself. How could I feel? The tears were coming down from my eyes, but the other guy wouldn't let me wait even for a minute. He was afraid if they see us not doing a fast job, they would kill us. Every minute, your life was on the line. They had those whips with the lead tips. They would hit you over the head with it."

Born in 1921, Julius was the third son of Yankiel and Feigel Eisenstein. His brother Joe is five years older. His brother Aaron, now in his mid-eighties, living in New York, left Poland before the war. Julius had four sisters: Binka, Mania, Rivka, and Dora, the 1937 bride.

Yankiel Eisenstein had run a delicatessen before the invasion. In 1941, he sent most of his family to Miechów, the town where Julius had been born, about twenty-five miles from Kraków. It was a shtetl, and he believed they'd be safer there. Julius remained in the city with Dora and her family, doing what he could to help them get by.

Not long after the rest of the family left for Miechów, soldiers snatched

Julius off the street and trucked him off to work at a local brick factory, a tolerable situation, as it turned out. "We still had a little bit of freedom and could sneak out. If they catch you, they kill you, but I always used to go back to Miechów to visit my family. . . . I was living at the factory, with a group of fifty guys. They were blasting out the clay and we were loading it on wagons, and this was our work. There were a lot of Polacks there, so we could give them some money for food from the outside. It was not that bad; that's why I always went back."

By the time he was transferred to Płaszów in 1942, it was too late for choices—and for his family. He believes most of them were transported to the Belżec extermination camp.

Julius and Joe Eisenstein were among the first to arrive at the forced-labor camp, assigned to build the barracks that eventually would house more than thirty thousand Jews. "The moment they had it all secure," says Julius, "we all went in." They were there when Diana Reiter, a young architect, was shot in the head after insisting that Amon Goeth permit the reconstruction of an improperly built barracks. The incident is depicted in *Schindler's List.*

If life in the ghetto was miserable, life at Płaszów, under the vicious and capricious Amon Goeth, was worse. Joe had to watch the brother of a friend hang after a failed escape attempt. "The rope broke," he remembers. "Goeth said to these two guys [the hangmen]: 'If it breaks again, I'm going to hang you too.' For the smallest infraction, they could kill you."

Julius worked on a road crew, breaking up stones for gravel along the thoroughfare that led to Goeth's villa. "Next to me was sitting a guy doing the same thing I was. He takes his stones away in his wheelbarrow. Goeth comes down two minutes later with his dogs, looks around, and he goes over to this guy and says in German: 'How come he has so many stones and you don't? You don't work? Huh?' He takes out the gun and shot him right on the spot. His blood spilled on me. He didn't speak German, this guy. He didn't understand."

He tells of the time his work group and several other crews were headed back to camp after a day of street cleaning. Goeth was waiting inside the camp gate, which slammed shut just as Julius's group approached. Goeth noticed that some of the inmates had bulging pockets. One had bread, one had a salami, and one had canned food.

"So Goeth started to holler, *'Alle töten!'* 'Shoot them all!' The 'blacks' were there [black-uniformed Ukrainian guards]. [They] picked up the whole group—fifty, sixty people—and marched them up the hill and killed them. Maybe three or four had contraband, but it didn't make any difference to him."

One of the SS men took a fancy to a pretty Jewish girl who was a friend of the Eisenstein brothers. "He was coming in for weeks, and throwing all the girls out," Julius remembers. "Then one day he comes in and takes her behind the barracks and he kills her. Maybe she was pregnant, or someone told him to stop."

The brothers were chosen to work at Emalia: Julius built concrete slabs for the machines, Joe operated a press. Julius remembers having one encounter with Oskar Schindler, while playing soccer. "He said, 'How come you didn't give the ball to this guy?'"

By the time Emalia shut down in October 1944, "we were already spoiled," says Julius. "We felt like we were already liberated." For Julius, the year spent at Schindler's camp was heaven compared with the hell of Płaszów. "We ate a little better and we didn't get a beating every day and you could relax a little. The work was easier and we weren't tired every day. We still had a little strength left for that cattle drive [deportation to the Flossenburg camp], and to work in Germany." Both Julius and Joe believe they would not have survived the rest of the war if they hadn't been at Emalia.

Before Schindler's workers were disbursed, some were given the gruesome task of exhuming and burning thousands of bodies buried at the Płaszów camp. Julius and Joe were among them. They don't remember how they felt because they can't recall feeling anything. "We were like zombies," says Julius. "You were trembling, but you did the work. The stench was so bad it was impossible not to be sneezing and coughing."

The brothers didn't make it to Brinnlitz. (Ann Grosman's first husband, Abe, did make it, along with his father and brother.) Packed eighty deep in a cattle car, they didn't know where they were headed. After three days and two nights without food or water, the survivors were released at the Flossenburg concentration camp. "So many people remained inside, dead," Julius recalls.

"From there, we traveled a day to Schachwitz, where there was a tank factory. We were living in a barracks on top of the factory. There were two *Kapos* who were beating everybody. They were worse than the Nazis. One was living with a Jewish young boy. He was a homosexual. They were German murderers let out of prison to take care of the Jews. The Russians hanged them after the war."

The inmates were guarded by civilians from the town who were very strict, but not nearly as vicious as the guards at Płaszów. . . . "I found some kindness," says Joe. "There was one German superintendent at the factory. He was a good guy. I got sick with typhus. Whoever got sick, got dead. My brother was bringing me food. This guy came in, and he said for me to come and sit behind the electric furnaces. He took a chair and put me there. I was sitting quite a few days. He wouldn't let me go back to work. He used to pass by and throw me a cigarette that I'd give to my brother, and he'd trade for food. He told me: 'The war will be over, and if you stay healthy, you will be able to survive.'" There was sabotage at the factory: "Maybe the steel wasn't so hard and a wheel would collapse. But you didn't want to do something that would get you killed, with the Americans so close."

In the early days of 1945, an air raid and a direct hit on the factory sent fifteen hundred people running for cover. One of the Eisensteins' cousins was trampled in the crush. "We saw him the next day dead on the floor," says Julius. "I pulled myself out of a pile of people and lost my shoes. My feet were in the mud, and people were laying on top of me. We ran out into the street, but two hours later, we went back. Why didn't we run away? It was dark, and it was Germany."

During the frantic final months of the war, the tank factory shut down, and its slave laborers were ordered to evacuate. "They took us all out and we started to march. The ones who were too weak, they took them on a truck into the woods and shot them. We were walking and walking for three nights and four days, and overnight we were staying in barns. At six in the morning, we were walking. Fifteen hundred started, and maybe remained four hundred people. We had only wooden shoes and no socks. Our feet were bloody. Whoever couldn't walk, they shoot."

Julius Eisenstein right after liberation, 1945.

The group marched past Dresden, later destroyed by fire. "We saw the Americans bombing. I'll never forget the sight. An awful lot of people died over there, before the fire. Naturally, people were very happy about it and didn't want to [continue to] walk, so [the guards] started to shoot into the crowd, and most of the people died at that time."

Their destination was Theresienstadt, the "model" camp where fifty thousand Jews are believed to have died. (To hoodwink a Red Cross inspection team, the Germans gave the camp a fresh coat of paint, erected a monument to fallen Jews, and issued currency to the inmates.) "We found there a terrible situation. People were sleeping three and four to a bunk. There was no food. The sickness was unbelievable. We spent three months in the barracks. There was no work, you would talk and cry."

The camp was liberated on May 5, 1945. Julius says the inmates didn't see the Germans for about two days, then saw columns of Russian troops passing by. "There was no announcement, but we know we are free already. We went to the city and tried to get something like bread, and to steal shoes. At that time, there were a lot of German soldiers taken prisoner, and some of them were sent into the camp to clean up after us. I said to [one guy] 'Give me your shoes,' and he said he didn't want to because he had to go a long way. A Russian soldier passed by and said, 'What's happening over here?' I said, 'He doesn't want to give me the shoes,' so the Russian soldier takes out a gun and gives it to me in my hand and says, 'OK, shoot him and take the shoes.' So this guy starts crying and says, 'OK, I'll give you the shoes.'

"I gave the gun back to the Russian. I couldn't shoot him. Maybe there was a time, when I found out that my mother and father and family had such a terrible death, and I found someone involved in it and they left me alone in the room [with him], maybe I could do it. But after the war, I see this guy crying his eyes out and I figured maybe he's not so guilty—I don't know. I didn't have the heart to kill him. What can I tell you?"

"The Russians were very good to us," adds Joe. "They said, 'Go out, rob them, do whatever you want.' But the town was so poor, we wouldn't get nothing."

The brothers made their way to Prague with a group of friends, on foot and by train, and stumbled into a luxury hotel called the Flora. "We told them we ran away from the camp and didn't have anywhere to sleep, so they said, 'Bring in all your friends,' and they gave us all a room, seven or eight guys in three big rooms, like a suite. We thought we are dead and in heaven. They give us hot water and soap. It was so emotional for us. We're not only crying, but fainting. We couldn't get over it. I was afraid to get under the sheets. It was so clean, and we got to shave! My God!"

Julius was twenty-three years old. It was a chance to make up for lost time, to go "wild" at parties, dances, and nightclubs. He got so drunk at a wedding during those days that he never drank again. "I had a girl doing my manicure and cutting my hair," says Joe, now a Toronto widower. "It was a lot of fun, but it was sad, too, because we knew we lost the whole family. You couldn't not be sad."

Through Jewish relief organizations, the brothers searched for Aaron in the United States. They located him in the Bronx. "We wrote him a letter," says Joe. " 'We are alive, but we don't know if anybody else is.' He said he would try to [arrange] papers for us. In the meantime, we found out it was a hundred percent. Nobody was alive."

Julius had gone back to Kraków, to the street where the family used to live. There wasn't a trace. "I felt completely lost and didn't know what to do," he says. "It was very sad to have no home, no sisters, no parents. We realized this is it, they'd killed our whole family and we didn't have nothing to look forward to but being on our own. I can only tell you, it's a very devastating thing to find out you have no family. You can't sleep at night. You wake up screaming. You were feeling so guilty about it, that you remained and the whole family is not here anymore, and maybe you could have done something else to save them."

In Prague, the brothers took a room with an elderly woman, did some black-market trading, and got jobs—Julius in a pharmaceutical factory. What he wanted more than anything was a new family. He'd met a pretty brunette named Rene at the Flora and had begun courting her, but Aaron had written that it would be easier for a single man to get a visa than a married man, so they waited. Others didn't, he says. "A lot of the women would marry older men just to get close to someone. They were afraid they were all dried up and couldn't have children. Rene's sister was twenty-five and married a guy who was fifty, a Czech, a Jewish man. His wife died with two daughters in the camps."

Courtship wasn't easy. "I didn't think there would be any feelings left after what happened to us. I didn't know how to approach the whole thing, how to talk about love or marriage."

Canada granted the brothers visas, and they emigrated in 1946. Rene followed a few months later. Julius and Rene married in 1949 and settled in Toronto. "The wedding was at my cousin's house, with my two brothers and an uncle and a couple of cousins. A rabbi came. It was a very emotional thing thinking that the mothers, the fathers, the sisters, nobody lived to see it. What can I tell you?"

Rene was also a survivor. "Whatever we were doing, even if we were kissing and necking, afterward we were right away remembering what happened to our families. I don't know if there was a feeling of love, [or] a feeling of need. After a while, you started to love, and it becomes very intimate. This bond that we had together—what we went through—was making us even closer, even if we came from different backgrounds. After awhile, you couldn't live without each other. As far as I know, there are very few Holocaust survivors who cheated on their wives."

The bond lasted throughout their lives. "When you would have a disagreement, you would remember what she went through, so what was I going to do, holler at her and make her aggravated? It stopped you right in the tracks. I can honestly say that in forty-four years, I never had a serious argument with my wife. If she was angry, I kept quiet."

The couple stayed in Canada until their U.S. visas came through in 1952. By then, they were the parents of a daughter, and Rene was pregnant with a second child. Still they went, and moved in with Aaron. "He had a two-bedroom apartment, with one bedroom rented out. It was bad. We lived in the living room on a cot. My wife had to keep her arm under my daughter so she wouldn't fall out of bed."

Their first home was a forty-nine-dollar-a-month apartment on Pelham Parkway in the Bronx. Julius worked two jobs—at a silver-plating factory and at a supermarket—to make ends meet. Their second child was a son. "He was carrying on the family name. If I won one million dollars, it could not be better." The son, Jack, is a New York podiatrist. Daughter Frances Flamenhaft is married to a podiatrist and lives in Indianapolis.

Julius went on to operate several businesses: a dairy store, then an appetizer store in the Bronx (where he made his own pickles), followed by a series of Manhattan coffee shops. He raised his children as traditional Jews, though he couldn't reconcile his family's fate with the faith his religion demanded. "How they could not be rescued? I wanted to remain a Jew, but I was not believing. It was important for the kids to know they came from something, but I still don't know if there is a God."

Rene Eisenstein, a smoker for fifty years, died of lung cancer in 1992. Julius didn't think he'd ever bounce back from her death—"it was losing again something precious." Only his five grandchildren kept him afloat. Then friends began urging him to call Ann Grosman, a charming widow who lived nearby. During the war, Ann, her mother, and her sister had been hidden by sympathetic Poles. But in 1946, her mother was murdered in the notorious Kielce massacre. Her father and three brothers had been killed in 1942 in a trap set by Poles who claimed to be resistance fighters.

The widow and the widower talked on the phone for three weeks, like teenagers, before he summoned enough nerve to ask her to lunch. They met at a huge outlet mall. He figured it was safe there, surrounded by thousands of shoppers. He blushes with delight as she tells the story. He's a man with an easy smile under ordinary circumstances, but around his new wife he beams like the sun on a Florida tourist brochure.

These days, when he's not playing golf (he wears a gold golfer charm on

Joe (left) and Julius Eisenstein, Florida, 1994.

a thick chain around his neck) Julius Eisenstein works with Holocaust Survivors of South Florida, Inc., a group devoted to furthering Holocaust education. He is a vice president. It sponsors "student awareness days" in the public schools and social activities for members. The January 1994 meeting drew nearly seven hundred people. It was billed as "a gathering of survivors to share our past and enjoy ourselves!"

Julius Eisenstein is among those who believe it's possible—indeed preferable—to both remember and enjoy, though it wasn't always that way. For forty years, he remained silent. "Talk to my own children? Never! It was too painful. We didn't want to remind ourselves." Then the deniers started to gain visibility, and silence was no longer an option. "We remained alive to tell people what happened," he says. "The world should not be quiet like it was when we were dying. We need to educate so it can never happen again."

IRVIN AND PHYLLIS KARP
CELINA KARP BINIAZ

For her fourteenth birthday, May 28, 1945, Celina Karp wanted just one gift: a movie ticket. She didn't really care what she saw, as long as she could put on real clothes and go to the theater.

As it happened, a 1938 Deanna Durbin film was playing in Kraków. In English it was called *Mad About Music*, in Polish *Pensionarka*. It was a silly bit of Hollywood fluff about girls at a Swiss boarding school. All those sparkly American actresses with their long, wavy hair and their cute little outfits—it was just perfect.

Celina borrowed a skirt and blouse and headed alone to the theater, where full-length mirrors lined the lobby. She can't recall whether she glanced toward the glass while entering or leaving, but she'll never forget what she saw.

"I was absolutely shocked," says the woman who is now retired teacher Celina Biniaz of Camarillo, California. "I couldn't believe that was me. It made such an impression to see myself looking so gawky and scrawny, like a scarecrow."

Celina and her parents had been free of Nazi captivity for all of three weeks. Her hair, sheared at Auschwitz the previous autumn, hadn't grown out much, and she weighed only seventy pounds. The borrowed skirt was wrapped nearly twice around her waist. She was beside herself by the time she got back home. "I can't remember if I cried," she says, "but I do know I felt so ugly."

Celina Karp hadn't seen her own head-to-toe reflection in four or five years, and what stared back at her bore scant resemblance to the person she remembered. Could this be the refined little girl whose mother made her wear white gloves to play in the park? This Celina was a teenager who'd talked her way out of an Auschwitz crematorium, who'd witnessed so much mayhem and depravity that she no longer believed in God.

"I became a total, total atheist at the age of twelve," she explains. "I remember asking my mother and other people how God could let certain things happen, and getting the answer that in Judaism, the sins of the forefathers are visited upon the children. I just couldn't accept that. I said, 'There is no God, because no God would allow children to be smashed against walls and killed.'"

Today Celina Karp Biniaz lives in a place with few Jews—outside the local Leisure Village retirement community—and no synagogues. Camarillo is high and dry, about fifty miles northwest of Los Angeles. The chamber of commerce calls it "the bougainvillea capital" of California. Celina Biniaz calls

Celina Biniaz and her parents, Phyllis and Irvin Karp, 1989,
at Oskar Schindler's tree on the Avenue of the Righteous at Yad Vashem.

it "very WASP." She and her Iranian-born husband, Amir, moved there from Long Island in 1993. Home is an airy, hilltop ranch house on more than an acre, with a courtyard pool, hummingbird feeders, kumquat and other citrus trees, white-on-white decor, and Middle Eastern *objets*.

Celina is the only child of Izak and Feiga Wittenberg Karp—now Irvin and Phyllis—of Des Moines, Iowa. Her father, born in January 1903, may be the oldest of the *Schindlerjuden* in the United States. Her mother, born two years later, isn't far behind. Irvin spends much of his time in a wheelchair, his command of English gradually slipping away. Phyllis is in good health, though increasingly frail.

The elder Karps were accountants before, during, and after the war. They came from Radomsko, a Polish city of thirty-five thousand—ten percent Jewish—known for its steel and furniture industries. They married in 1929 and moved to Kraków, about one hundred miles to the southeast. Irvin Karp's main account there was the Hogo shirt company, a concern he would later compare in stature to the American firm Arrow. Feiga did the books for a café where the Rosners played.

Poland at the time had a "professional middle class, with certain trappings that went with it and a certain kind of lifestyle," says Celina. The Karps lived it and enjoyed it. Their apartment at 22 Krupnicza Street—in a "mixed" Kraków neighborhood—had beautiful furniture. "The dining room table extended to seat eighteen, and there was service for twenty-four: china, crystal, and sterling. My parents' bedroom set was light African burled wood, very elegant. I remember all that because they sold all of it to a neighbor, and my mother felt bad about it because it was her trousseau."

Phyllis and Irvin kept a Telefunken shortwave radio in their bedroom. As the summer of 1939 wound down, they spent more and more time listening to the increasingly ominous news. Men gathered to talk politics in the building's courtyard, aware of what the Germans were up to, disbelieving that it would affect them and their families.

"When it did come," Celina says of the September 1 invasion, "we discovered that the people we were talking to were Fifth Columnists, supporters of the Anschluss. The next day, they appeared with [swastika] armbands."

According to Celina Biniaz, one of the first bombs that fell on Poland destroyed her maternal grandparents' house in Radomsko. She remembers clearly the day her mother got the news. "Mother was not feeling well and was lying on a divan. The maid came in with a letter for Mother. She started reading and crying, and I couldn't figure out why. It was a letter from a former maid from Radomsko, saying how sorry she was. I still have that picture before my eyes."

It was very painful at the time to have lost loved ones that way, says Celina, "but at the end of the war, in retrospect, we realized that at least they were lost in their own home, together."

The bomb killed Phyllis's parents, who ran a general store; a sister; a brother; and many other relatives. Another sister lived with the Karps in Kraków, but died during the war in a particularly sadistic massacre. Another brother also perished in France.

Celina's father ultimately lost two sisters. One brother was living in the United States, another in Palestine. A third, who had been in the Polish Army, survived the war as a Soviet POW.

Life changed dramatically for Celina after the invasion. Her father joined the flight of men to eastern Poland. She was sent, briefly, to the small village of a family maid. But what hurt the most was giving up her puppy, a Spitz named Leda. "That was very painful for me, and I could not quite understand why my parents were making me do this. But they felt we couldn't take care of a dog."

A Viennese gentleman named Julius Madritsch took over the shirt company, Hogo. He converted it to a uniform factory bearing his name. "My father ran the factory," says Celina. "What Stern did for Schindler [in the film], my father did for Madritsch. That's one reason we got on the list."

In the early spring of 1941, the Karps had to leave their home and move into the Kraków Ghetto. They shared one room and a kitchen with Phyllis's sister, Gucia, and Gucia's husband. He survived the war. Gucia was transported to Auschwitz, then shipped out to the North Sea, where hundreds of Jews were told that they must walk out on the ice to eventually reach Sweden. "All of them were shot," Celina says.

She and her parents could have been among them, but at the last minute her father managed to extract them from the Auschwitz transport. He couldn't do as much for Gucia, who had traded places with someone to remain with her family.

Everyone in the Kraków Ghetto had to work or risk transport. While her parents went every day to Madritsch's factory, Celina spent her days at an envelope cooperative, then at a brush factory. But neither granted her the coveted *Blauschein,* the "blue card" that designated its bearer an "essential" worker. In a 1983 videotaped lecture, Phyllis Karp explained how Celina finally got a card.

"One Friday, someone came out [to Madritsch] and told us they [had] killed everyone who wasn't working, in the ghetto. On the street you could see corpses. [Celina] was sick in bed. Thank God she was home. I vowed she would be with me all the time, and what happened would happen to both of us. We had a [Polish] neighbor who worked in the place where they made the ID cards, and we asked if she would do us the favor to make [Celina] two years older, twelve." It helped that Celina was tall for her age.

Celina went to work as a seamstress at Madritsch, igniting a lifelong avocation. For years, she made all of her children's clothes and her own—this despite poor circulation in her hands, a painful reminder of the frostbite she suffered clearing the Kraków streets of snow, barehanded.

For a time, Madritsch's workers marched from the ghetto to his factory in another part of the Podgorze section of Kraków. Then they moved to Płaszów continuing the daily trek. It took about ninety minutes each way, no matter the weather, but Celina says no one minded. "We were so glad to get out of Płaszów. Just like Schindler people felt safe [at Emalia], we felt safe at Madritsch. Then they brought all the factories inside the camp."

Madritsch—"more elegant and classy than Schindler," says Celina—set up his operation in several barracks: one for offices and storage, one for cutting, one for sewing. He and his manager, Raimund Titsch, treated their workers kindly.

"He was a very capable man, very organized," says Phyllis Karp. "He was a good human being with a heart." She says that when word reached him that Amon Goeth had slaughtered eight hundred Jewish children in the ghetto—after giving their Płaszów-bound parents his "word of honor" that the children would follow—Julius Madritsch wept uncontrollably.

Celina says Raimund Titsch was "out of his element" among the Nazis, "a wonderful man who got caught in the wrong place at the wrong time." He and his boss saw to it that their workers got extra food and, when possible, medication. "Because [Madritsch] was on good terms with Goeth, that's how he protected us."

The protection, however, went only so far. "We would come out on the *Appellplatz*, be counted and dispatched to work areas. But as soon as we walked back through the gates, we were no longer protected."

Unlike Schindler, Julius Madritsch did not establish a camp-within-a-camp at his Płaszów factory. His workers lived in the barracks, exposed to every caprice of Amon Goeth's reign. Neither Celina nor her parents ever were beaten, "but there was always the fear that we could be, and we were forced to watch it happening to other people. It was horrible."

Celina Karp witnessed the assassinations of the Chilowiczes, the camp's ruling Jewish family, on a day Julius Madritsch wasn't around. "Chilowicz was working at Madritsch. Goeth shot him. His wife ran out to see what was happening and he shot her too. There were the bales of fabric stacked up in a barrack. Rumor was that Goeth was coming, and I climbed up and hid in the bales. The little ones used to do this often, so we wouldn't be so obvious. When he came, if you didn't need to be around, you weren't around."

Celina Biniaz says that fear was "the ruling passion" at Płaszów. "I was petrified all the time, incredibly tense. I had horrible migraine headaches all the time, for which Madritsch got medication. You just didn't live any other way but afraid, and that has stayed with me the rest of my life. I'm very fearful of authority. It was a problem even with the principal at school."

In spite of the fear, and of Goeth, and of their lives' stultifying baseness, the Jewish slaves of Płaszów determined to preserve their culture. Adults taught. Children learned. The community clung to its values.

"I remember reading a great deal," says Celina Biniaz. "They brought in books for burning, and the crew assigned to bring in the books, under penalty of death, would smuggle them into the barracks. You would read at night and pass it on. At the end of the war, I knew how to read but couldn't write. I hadn't held a pencil in my hand for six years. Women would sing and tell stories. That's where I learned all my Shalom Aleichem."

It is said that Oskar Schindler tried to talk Julius Madritsch into moving with him to Czechoslovakia when Płaszów shut down, but that Madritsch declined. He and Raimund Titsch did, however, make sure that sixty of their workers, including the Karps, got on Schindler's list.

"I was doing very well until the train pulled into Auschwitz," Celina recalls of the transition to Brinnlitz. "My mother kept saying that she would always be with me. I asked her at Auschwitz if I was sent to the crematorium, would she go with me? She said yes. I fully realized what was happening there. I could see life around me. It was bitter cold, rainy, miserable, filthy, mud up to your ankles. The latrines were overflowing. And they made us stand to be counted for long periods of time. We stood in fives, so we took turns being in the middle. They had fur coats on, and we were naked. And hungry! All we got was water with a few vegetables in it."

Phyllis Karp had promised her daughter that they would never be separated, but at Auschwitz she made an exception to her own rule. Celina says, "One day they came into the barracks and said they needed twenty-five, thirty women to go and peel potatoes, and Mother volunteered because she thought she could get me something to eat. While she was gone, they took the rest of the barrack for another selection."

Dr. Josef Mengele was in charge, sending some to the left, some to the right. With his own hand, the murderous physician—"he was a handsome devil"—pushed Celina Karp into the line headed for the ovens. Then, for no apparent reason, he decided to winnow the doomed left line again.

"He made us go through a second time, and when we went through, I looked at him and said three words in German: 'Lassen Sie ich.' 'Let me go.' He pushed me to the right, and I ran out. I wouldn't be this brave now. My mother came back, running around hysterical, stark raving mad."

The women arrived at Brinnlitz "haggard and shaved," says Celina. "My mother was very sick with pneumonia; they were not ready for us—there were no bunks—and we slept on the floor. But it was warm, on top of the factory, and there was such an overwhelming feeling of relief that we were reunited. That was the thing about Schindler; he saved families."

Celina was among a handful of teenagers at Schindler's Brinnlitz factory, including Niusia Horowitz, Leon Leyson, and Janka Feigenbaum. She spent part of the seven-month stay in the camp's infirmary, in a bunk above Janka, who was thought to have bone cancer. Janka died at nineteen, shortly before liberation.

"I had picked up scarlet fever; then, because of poor sanitation, that left me with jaundice and an impaired liver," Celina says. She remembers that Janka was in great pain and suffered terrible bedsores. "But I got to know her very well. It was so sad that she didn't make it."

Celina and Niusia Horowitz had make-work jobs cleaning the big machines. But at least once, she picked up some lucrative work on the side. "My father made needles, and there was a woman in the kitchen who got some white thread from someplace. I knitted a pair of underpants and a camisole for her, and she gave me *two* loaves of bread! We shared that with my father. I was very pleased I was able to do that."

She also remembers Raimund Titsch visiting Schindler at the factory. "He was walking through with him, and he asked if there was anything I wanted. I had a pair of wooden clogs, and I said I would really like other kinds of shoes. After that, a load of shoes with wooden soles but leather uppers came in. I don't know if that was Titsch or Schindler."

On May 9, 1945, first one Soviet soldier, then others, liberated the slave laborers of Brinnlitz. "One of the hardest things to get used to was to be able to walk by yourself or with one other person, because we always had to be in fives," Celina says, chuckling. "It was so strange. I kept thinking, 'Where is my five?' My parents and I walked into the village. It was so strange to be able to walk out of the camp to begin with."

The Karps lost no time heading for Kraków. Like the other *Schindlerjuden*, they carried several yards of cloth and other trade items left to them by Schindler. Celina got five pairs of scissors. Four she traded, but she still uses the fifth in her sewing room. (Phyllis still has her red enamel Brinnlitz soup bowl.)

The Karps stayed in Kraków until the end of September. During the summer, Irvin and Phyllis went to Vienna, where they testified on behalf of Madritsch and Titsch. Celina studied with a tutor, took high school entrance exams, and prepared to enroll in classes for the first time since the second grade.

"Then there was a pogrom that had to do with Rosh Hashana, and my parents decided not to stay. We were smuggled over the border in a Russian truck, stayed in Prague a few days, then crossed the border to Germany."

The family spent the next two years in Mindelheim, Bavaria, supported by Jewish relief agencies and relatives in the United States. They lived near the Landsberg Displaced Persons' camp, in a room requisitioned from the widow of a Nazi.

"Those two years among normal German families were my salvation," says Celina. "I would have hated Germans for the rest of my life, but what I saw there was that not all Germans were bad, that people are people."

Her parents wanted Celina to learn English. They signed her up for tutoring at a nearby convent of the English Sisters, a British order. Her instructor was a nun called Mater Leontina, who'd been cloistered since the age of sixteen. When she took on the school's only Jewish pupil, she was ninety-two.

Celina Karp Biniaz with her scissors from the Brinnlitz factory, Camarillo, California, 1994.

"She had gone in after a broken love affair," according to Celina. "She had no idea what was going on in the outside world, and she gave me the acceptance and stability I needed to recover."

Celina Biniaz is not given to outbursts of emotion, but here she breaks down, surprising even herself. Mater Leontina lived just two years after they met, but they enjoyed a deep affection to the end.

"She was a very sweet and gentle person. She never judged. She knew I was Jewish and it didn't make any difference. I know I must have told her things about what happened. I remember sitting in a garden with her and talking. She was a good human being, and she was instrumental in making me feel good."

A collage of Celina Karp Biniaz's letters and cards from Mater Leontina.

From Mater Leontina, Celina learned German and English. Understanding came quickly, she says, because she was "starved" for learning. She took a class in embroidery and another in gymnastics. "I was very weak. I had no strength in my arms. I remember that I couldn't do the parallel bars, and one of the German girls started making fun. She made a remark, something like, 'Why are you proud of being Jewish?'"

A Nazi tutored her in math, "and I know I prompted myself to excel at it to prove I was as good as he was. It made me feel pretty good that he was dependent on whatever money I was giving him."

The teenager Celina Karp couldn't get enough of the movies. Today she owns an amazing collection of German playbills for American films of the era: *Kitty Foyle, Young Tom Edison, I Married a Witch, Keys of the Kingdom.* Just as Mater Leontina taught her English, Barbara Stanwyck, Ida Lupino, Gregory Peck, and Loretta Young taught her about America.

The Karps sailed for New York in June 1947, aboard the decommissioned troopship *Marine Marlin.* "Everybody else was sick," Celina recalls, "so I ate everybody's ice cream. Nobody could look at it for eleven days! They also offered Coke. I *hated* it! How could anybody drink this awful stuff?"

Irvin Karp's brother, David Karp, had come to New York from Des Moines to fetch them in his Cadillac. They stayed for a few days at the Hotel Chesterfield before heading west. Celina remembers going for breakfast and "astounding" her uncle by ordering a sliced tomato. "The waitress looked at me, but I hadn't had any and I craved it. My uncle said, 'If she wants a sliced tomato for breakfast, you give it to her.'"

When they got to Des Moines, Celina Karp thought she had "arrived in hell. It was the hottest summer on record. There was no air-conditioning, it was humid, impossible to sleep. I broke out in a heat rash all over."

Some of the media attention surrounding the Karp family's arrival in Des Moines.

Inside the photo, newspaper headline text:

Refugees Tell of 'Eternity' of Horror

BROTHER BRINGS KARPS TO D. M.

By Florence Swihart.

With the statement, "We were just lucky," three newcomers to Des Moines Wednesday shrugged off five years—an eternity—of horror in German concentration camps.

Isadore (Isac) Karp, 44, his wife, Phyllis (Pajra), 40, and their daughter, Celina, 16, arrived June 7 in New York, N. Y., from the Jewish Displaced Persons (D. P.) camp at Landsberg...

Irvin's brother, who owned an auto parts store, put Irvin to work as a bookkeeper. He would go on to become office and credit manager for H. E. Sorensen, a Des Moines home furnishings company. Phyllis became in-house accountant for the local office of Peat, Marwick, the national accounting firm.

Celina plunged into summer school and "the intricacies of baseball, which went over my head completely." She remembers becoming a curiosity among the locals. "They were used to people coming from the farms. We were the first [immigrant] city people. They kept asking: 'Do you know what electricity is? Running water? Did you have a toilet?' It was strange to us because we had all these things and in some ways lived a more sophisticated life in Poland. My parents had gone to theater, the opera, concerts, all the time."

That fall, Celina Karp enrolled at Des Moines' North High, which has enshrined her in its Hall of Fame. She didn't think much about her life in Europe, unless someone or something called it to her attention.

"In high school, during lunch hour, they would show a movie in ten- or fifteen-minute segments after lunch. One of them was a newsreel. Families were being reunited, crying and hugging, and kids started laughing. I walked out and couldn't contain myself. I had to go home for the rest of the day."

She made friends with several girls, "but the idea of going out on a date was something very uncomfortable. I had no experience with boys, and I had a hard time fitting into my age group. Socially and emotionally, I was four or five years older in my experience. It wasn't until my senior year in college that I felt they finally caught up to me."

What she couldn't understand, both at North High and at Grinnell, the Iowa college she attended on full scholarship, was how her American-born classmates could take their educational opportunities for granted. Less than a year after arriving in the United States, she graduated second in her high school class.

"For me it was such a gift. I had all kinds of odd jobs to put myself through school, and there were girls there who were not learning. It took me many years to realize that was normal behavior for Americans. I was too intense, I'm sure."

Celina spent the summer between high school and college at the Encampment for Citizenship in Riverdale, New York. It was a program sponsored by the Ethical Culture Society, "with the idea to bring together people of different cultures, races, and religions. It was an experiment in democracy. Mrs. Roosevelt was on the board. There were lectures, workshops, field trips to museums, and a picnic with Mrs. Roosevelt at Hyde Park."

At Grinnell, Celina majored in philosophy. She also worked in the lunchroom, the library, and the dean's office, on the switchboard, and as a doorkeeper (in those days of single-sex dorms and curfews). She spent the summer after graduation studying social work at Smith College in Massachusetts. But midway through the course, she received astonishing news. She had been awarded half of a $10,000 fellowship to Columbia University, given by the Necchi Foundation—of the sewing-machine Necchis—to students who had been displaced persons.

"At the time, Columbia was charging twenty-five dollars a credit, so you can imagine how much money that was. I hadn't even intended to try for it— there were two hundred and forty applicants—but my professor said he wasn't going to write me another recommendation unless I applied for this thing. I was supposed to [intern at] a family agency in Baltimore, but everyone said I'd be crazy not to take this."

In 1952, Celina Karp met Amir Biniaz at Columbia's International House, a dorm on Riverside Drive. He had come to the United States from Iran as a teenager, and served as an Army paratrooper in the Pacific theater during World War II. They married in New York the following year.

"He feels the same way about religion as I do," she says. "An atheist met an agnostic. We both feel that organized religion has done more harm than good, that it has divided people."

Amir Biniaz established a dental practice in Wantagh, Long Island. Their son, Robert, was born in 1954. He's now CEO of Universal Interactive, MCA's interactive software publishing division. His office is in the same Universal City complex as Steven Spielberg's. He and his wife have a daughter.

The Biniazes' daughter, Susan, born in 1958, is a State Department legal adviser in Washington, D.C. She and her husband have a son.

Robert says he knew almost nothing about his mother's past until his early twenties. "My first conversation with her was after I had just finished the book [*Schindler's List*]. They talk about tools and fabric, and I flashed on Mom's old black iron scissors. I remember calling her and asking her about it."

"I didn't want them to hate," Celina explains, her voice shaky and urgent. "I wanted them to accept people for what they were and not be prejudiced. What happened to me was because people hate. I didn't want them to be different or feel guilty. I watched a film on TV of a woman doctor from Canada who took her son to Auschwitz and walked him through. I could *never* do that to my children! Put them through that kind of guilt and pain? If they love you, they would feel terrible. I did not want to have second-generation kids feeling that way, and they don't. They had a very happy childhood, and they are well-put-together individuals."

Celina says she owes this to her parents. "When we came to the United States, they made a conscious decision only to speak English. They didn't dwell on the past, and we forged a life—they for themselves, I for me. And it worked, it really did. I wanted people to accept me for what I achieved and not feel pity for me."

Besides, she adds, she simply couldn't abide the stupid questions: " 'Were you cold? Were you hungry?' Nobody could understand it. I didn't talk about it for forty-five years. But I know there are those who live it, and it's the validation for their life somehow. They go on lecture tours, talk to people. They use all kind of excuses for it—that everybody needs to know about it. But there are other ways to know about it."

Celina stayed home until her daughter was in the third grade, then started volunteering at Susan's school, though her degree was in college-level teaching. Susan's teacher asked her to work with a "difficult" child who couldn't read and disrupted the class. "She asked if I could spend time with him, to keep him out of the classroom. I got him to read and was so successful at it that they proposed a program for underachievers, a pilot program funded by the state for three years," after which the local school board took it over. Celina was asked to direct the program, and did so for twenty-four years.

Occupied with her job, her family, and her determination to leave the past behind, Celina Biniaz thought little of Oskar Schindler. Then sometime in the early 1980s, she picked up a *New York Times* and "almost flipped out." There was a review of a book called *Schindler's List.*

"I called my mother: 'You won't believe it!' Up to that point, I never even talked about it. Never! Then I started admitting it: This was my life. I said to my son, when I first heard about the movie, 'Why make a movie out of that? Nobody is going to see it.' "

She certainly never expected that the film would create such demand for the list's survivors to come forward, a demand she has steadfastly resisted. "I have feelings like my mother, who has been asked to appear on TV: I can't wait for [the Schindler phenomenon] to be over, because of the memories.

"Why not have a pleasant life? These are not pleasant thoughts."

MARGOT AND CHASKEL SCHLESINGER

"Oh, you came in through the kitchen! My house is upside down from Pesach."

Margot Schlesinger—a tiny, cheerful woman in a smart wool suit and open-toe gold shoes—is busy amid the seasonal clutter of the holiday. With eight days to go, there's still plenty to do, and plenty of *hometz* to banish. "Eat a lot!" she urges, proffering a plate of homemade brownies, obviously not kosher for Passover.

This holiday, like the rest on the Jewish calendar, gets more than symbolic recognition from Margot and Chaskel Schlesinger. Some *Schindlerjuden* emerged from the Holocaust stronger in their faith. So it was for them. "We had too many miracles in our lives," explains Chaskel, straight and trim at eighty-four. "We had miracles until today." Adds Margot, "I was saved twenty-five times! Absolutely!"

The first miracle is that the Schlesingers, who married in the Tarnów ghetto, managed to stay together through the Holocaust, from beginning to end. Now living in the Chicago suburb of West Rogers Park, they celebrated their fiftieth anniversary in 1992. Another is that Margot escaped transport to the Stutthof death camp, then slipped through Dr. Josef Mengele's grasp at Auschwitz.

It's miraculous that all of Margot's siblings got out of Poland alive: one brother to Shanghai, twelve days before the German invasion; a brother and a

Margot and Chaskel Schlesinger, Chicago, 1994.

sister to Palestine; two brothers to the United States in 1938. (One of her brothers is graphic designer Willie Wind, who created the United Nations stamps.)

And what else but a miracle could have saved Chaskel after a fall in 1993 caused a blood clot on his brain?

Born in September 1910 in Wielopole, Chaskel Schlesinger was the youngest of Hersch and Chaya Schlesinger's nine children, descendants of the Chief Rabbi of Tarnów. Six of the siblings were alive at the start of the war; three survived.

Margot Wind was born in July 1918 in Berlin, where her parents, Tsimma and Yakov Wind, originally from Poland, had lived since 1911. They ran a linens store.

Both families lived well. Hersch, a leader of Wielopole's Jewish community, was in the timber business. But Chaya died in a tuberculosis epidemic when Chaskel was six, and after that, he says, "we raised ourselves, because our father got sick."

By the age of twelve, Chaskel was an orphan. In 1923, he left Wielopole for Tarnów, an apparel-manufacturing center northeast of Kraków. By nineteen, he and brothers Moishe and Chaim had their own fabric store. They prospered and had a lot to lose by September 1939.

Moishe was married and had three children. Chaskel and Chaim, the bachelors, shared an apartment. "Then the war broke out, and five days later, they entered my town," says Chaskel. "The army came in and took over parks, hotels, the school buildings, and they made a mess of them. They caught up people in the street to clean it up."

Chaskel and Chaim's apartment, across the street from Gestapo headquarters, offered an uncomfortably intimate view of life among the Nazis. "They took over two Jewish buildings, brand-new—the most beautiful buildings." In the mornings, they'd wander outside in their undershirts, casually shooting birds with their handguns.

Even so, like most Tarnów Jews, Chaskel Schlesinger refused to accept the obvious. "We knew what was going on in Germany," he says, "but we thought, 'They cannot do that in other countries.'"

The Winds offered a perfect example of "what was going on in Germany." Margot had been designing lingerie and beachwear at a Berlin factory. She was active in a sports club, competing in handball and swimming. She belonged to a theater group, and had "a good, German education."

Then came Kristallnacht, the two-day orgy of destruction in early November 1938 that signaled the end of life as Germany's Jews had long known it. When it was over, seven thousand Jewish businesses had been destroyed. Jewish institutions of all kinds had been looted, desecrated, or demolished, including hospitals, libraries, cemeteries, and schools. One thousand synagogues, nearly every one in Germany, had been pillaged or set aflame. Crazed mobs hunted down Jews in the streets and in their homes. At least one hundred Jews died, and thirty thousand were arrested. Germany then expelled its Jews. Margot's parents went to Tarnów. She followed six months later, with no Polish identity papers at all.

The Nazi Government General began issuing orders (with all violations punishable by death): Jews had to surrender their radios, furs, and jewelry at collection points. They had to wear armbands and get off the sidewalks. They had to register their business inventories. The Schlesinger brothers complied—to some extent—but engaged in creative accounting when it came to the business.

"I didn't put in the whole inventory, because I was afraid if they took it over, I wasn't going to have anything to live on," Chaskel explains. That was January or February 1940. The day before Passover, a German showed up at the Schlesingers' apartment and demanded the keys to the store. He was a *Treuhänder*, as was Oskar Schindler. These generally were Germans or *Volksdeutsche* (ethnic Germans) rewarded for service to the Reich with the commercial enterprises of Poland's Jews—in Schindler's case, the enamelware factory.

By chance, Chaskel had just made a second set of keys for the store. So late on the night of the Passover seder, he and Chaim, shoeless, crept into the building. In the dark, they managed to secrete sixty forty-meter bolts of cloth under the floorboards. "I was stealing my own merchandise in my socks," he says. They also hid jewelry, linens, and heirloom silver, some of it more than a century old. They brought more bolts of fabric home in a box with a false bottom.

In May 1940, on the day the German army occupied Belgium and Holland, the *Treuhänder* began carting off the Schlesingers' merchandise, an exercise that took two days. The man told Chaskel's hysterical sister-in-law, "You don't have to worry; you're going to Madagascar and you're going to get your money there and live like a king." (Hitler had floated the notion of exiling Jews to the French island.)

From their apartment (they had moved away from Gestapo headquarters), Chaskel and Chaim continued to do business with Jewish customers. Women would buy a few yards of cloth, wrap it around their middles, and cover up with long coats even in summer. They'd joke about how often the same women got "pregnant."

The Schlesinger brothers invested their income in the only tangibles sure to retain value: gems and "several thousand" American dollars. These Chaskel hid in a hollowed-out log on a woodpile next to the stove. The stash almost came to grief once during a card game, when an unknowing player got chilly and reached for the wrong log to toss on the fire. Chaskel also hid currency in a door frame.

The *Treuhänder* told the Schlesingers to bill him for the confiscated goods. They billed 130,000 złotys, "a lot of money before the war." But the man reduced it to eighty-five thousand, "and from that, he put in twenty thousand złotys to the bank, and I was allowed to take out two hundred fifty a week. I argued that there were three brothers, so finally they allowed seven hundred fifty a week." Two weeks later, Jews were shut out of the banks.

The brothers lived thereafter on black-market earnings. It was a risky business, but the only way for Jews to survive. Anyone caught was taken away by the Gestapo and shot, "and plenty of people got caught." It was said that the Nazis would call the undertaker in the victim's presence to announce an impending body pickup. And that, says Chaskel, "was still the good times."

Even before the creation of the ghetto, it was crucial to hold the right kind of working papers. Those in the trades and crafts, those with practical skills, had the best chance of surviving. Chaskel knew that his papers, identifying him as a businessman, were worthless. "So I went to a locksmith and I paid him to give me the seals that I worked for him."

By this time, he'd met Margot Wind. She was interested in another young man. Her first day in Tarnów, this young man happened to be with Chaskel when he spotted Margot on the street. She claims Chaskel announced, "If you aren't going to marry her, I will."

On June 10, 1942, the Gestapo demanded that Tarnów's Jews register. The next day, there would be a transport. Tsimma and Yakov Wind stayed home. They sent their daughter to a friend in the suburbs, with their remaining valuables—diamond jewelry—and hunkered down in the apartment. Margot returned the next day. Her parents had disappeared. The apartment was sealed. Everything of value was gone. "I went crazy," says Margot. It was small consolation when a Jewish OD man [policeman] found and returned a few suitcases of her clothes. She didn't know it then, but her parents probably had been shot.

"They sent about seven, eight thousand people to Belżec," according to Chaskel. "The same amount of people were killed in Tarnów. People were standing and digging graves at the cemetery for two or three days, and when they couldn't do it anymore, [the Germans] shot them and they fell into the graves."

Margot moved in with Chaskel. He obtained a marriage license, dutifully stamped by the *Judenrat.* He hoped that it would protect Margot by tying her to him "officially," because he had a ghetto pass and working papers, and she had none. Soon after, there was another transport. "They shot all the people who lived in the same building," says Margot. "I showed [an officer] the license, but it didn't make any difference."

But Chaskel's labor card and ghetto pass did. "That's better," said the Nazi. He not only let Margot stay, but gave her a valid pass: another miracle! The couple married on Margot's birthday, July 24, 1942.

The Schlesingers admit that their material losses bothered them . . . for a time. "I'll tell you the truth," says Margot, "you had to be a person. You had to be dressed. But I came to a point that I decided if I will live, I will have. If I don't live, I won't need. The important thing was life itself. I was very happy that I knew my two brothers were in America. I knew if I lived, I would have the support from my family."

In the summer of 1942, soon after the Tarnów ghetto was created, a friend came from Kraków to tell Chaskel that Julius Madritsch, the uniform manufacturer—also a *Treuhänder*—wanted to open a branch factory in Tarnów. Would he be interested in organizing the operation? Chaskel said he would.

"A few days later, Madritsch came and brought me a pass to go out [of the ghetto], and I was in this building for several days without anything, just a telephone. A few days later, they started shipping in the merchandise. Everybody was pushing themselves to work for Madritsch." Chaskel, his brothers, and Margot worked for Madritsch from July 1942 to September 1943.

The Madritsch operation offered a certain measure of safety, but even there Jews risked their lives. "I had the gun once to my head at Madritsch, from a Gestapo, and one who didn't hesitate to shoot," says Chaskel. "There was a man assigned to stay by the door, not to let any Polish people in. But we needed to buy something. So whoever wanted to buy something, he let them go down and stay for fifteen minutes. The Polish people came with a chicken, some eggs, butter.

"One day, I was buying some butter, and under the stairs was a little hiding place. I came back, and all of a sudden I saw the Gestapo was here, and his gun was near my head. 'What are you doing here?' he asked in German. I said, 'I'm watching that the Polish people shouldn't come in.' He had a tailor on the second floor, so he went up. That's another miracle, that he didn't shoot me right away."

This same officer almost nabbed Chaskel spiriting two live chickens into the ghetto. At the last moment he untied them and set them free. But Margot got caught in the same shakedown. The crazed Gestapo officer, Grunów—"he had syphilis or something"—saw a pound of butter sail over the fence, and mistakenly identified Margot as its source. "I had a raincoat on with a hood, and next to me was a woman. [The officer] took me by the hood and yanked me. He wanted to shoot me, but in the meantime he let me go. He took the next woman and gave her one shot, and she just was laying there dead. My husband saw this and thought it was me. This was another time I was saved."

She pauses. "I tell you, there were so many miracles that this by itself tells me there is a God. The only problem is, I cannot understand why six million did not live and we did. I still ask. I will never resolve it. But there is a certain purpose: that I had my family, and I believe my parents had something to do with it. Maybe after they were dead, they could do something for me."

Like Kraków, Tarnów had two ghettos: Ghetto A for nonworking people, children, and the elderly and Ghetto B for working people. Chaskel, Margot, and Chaim lived in B. Moishe, his wife, and three children lived in A.

After the Germans confiscated Moishe's apartment in 1940, the Tarnów *Judenrat* assigned him and his family "a basement which I wouldn't let a dog [live] in," according to Chaskel. Moishe's in-laws lived in the suburbs, and Chaskel suggested that he move his family there. They lived safely for a while, until Chaskel found out that the Nazis had that suburb on a hit list. "I wrote him, and he got the letter the day before. I told him, 'When they say everybody should go to the marketplace, don't go.' " From a hiding place, they watched the whole town die, including his wife's family. One by one, Moishe Schlesinger's family made it back to the ghetto. "A Polack brought the little girl to us [at] Madritsch," recalls Chaskel. "She was three, and full of lice."

Tarnów had been a city of twenty-eight thousand Jews before the war. The population swelled to forty thousand as the Germans forced Jews out of the outlying towns, villages, and smaller cities into the Tarnów ghetto. Then, on September 2, 1943, *Untersturmführer* Amon Goeth began to liquidate the ghetto.

"They came on a Thursday morning. This day I remember because this is my birthday," says Chaskel. "At six in the morning they came, and my nephew said the ghetto was surrounded. They told us to come out on the *Appellplatz.* The A ghetto, they marched out right away to the train station to Auschwitz. My sister-in-law and the little girl were with them. Her two boys tried to get with our group to Madritsch, but Goeth chased them out. Three times my nephew was chased out of the line to Madritsch. Goeth said if he came back once more, to shoot him. We were there till the next day at noon, with no food, nothing to drink."

During the night, Chaskel convinced one of the regular soldiers that it would be worth his while to let him return to his apartment. "So we went up, and I pried the money out of the door frame: dollars. I gave him all the złotys I had in my pocket. I never would have tried that with the SS." The next afternoon, "they marched us to the train and packed us one hundred and five people in a car. We had the idea that we were going to Płaszów, to Madritsch, but you could never trust them."

Families that had managed to remain intact found themselves wrenched apart. Chaskel remembers a neighbor, a dentist "with two children and a beautiful wife. He had the little boy in a backpack and had given him sleeping pills.

He got him on the train, and the SS came in. This kid woke up, and the people were anxious that this boy should go out. They started pushing, and the little boy said, 'Don't push me; I know I'm going to die.' They took out the kid, and they pushed the father back in. They took out about thirty kids and took them about a block away, and right away we heard the shooting."

Moishe managed to join the Madritsch group, naively figuring he'd be in a better position to rescue his family from wherever they were headed (even then, Jews refused to accept reality). The error in judgment would torture him for the rest of his life: He lived; they died.

Jewish policemen—the *Ordnungsdienst,* or OD men—greeted the newcomers at Płaszów. "They took apart all your clothes to see if there was something hidden," says Chaskel. "They cut off the lapels. I had a bundle of dollars, but so far I had it in my pocket."

Margot kept her valuables in a condom "inside. The only place that was safe was inside the body, but it was terrible. I had to sleep with it, eat with it. Even in Auschwitz, I had fifty dollars in a condom."

Madritsch's Płaszów factory worked around the clock. Workers never knew if shortly after going to bed from a day shift, someone would roust them from their bunks for some ridiculous task like carrying rocks from place to place all night long.

The Schlesingers got jobs in the shipping department—prized positions, as the shippers didn't work nights. Chaskel recalls an argument with Irvin Karp, who assigned Jewish workers to shifts. He wanted to shift Margot to a machine. Chaskel told him, "When your wife goes on a machine, mine will go." Neither went.

Madritsch's workers lived in the Płaszów barracks, not in a subcamp. This exposed them to Amon Goeth's full fury. On Yom Kippur, soon after arriving at the camp, "they piled up ninety-five people in a hole, naked. They were praying. Then they opened up with the machine gun and shot them, and buried them a little bit. We had to look at other things, too. Six boys going to the salt mines decided they were going to hide, then run away. In the meantime, [the Germans] saw there were six missing and they came with the dogs and right away discovered them. So they took the six boys and they hanged them. There were two brothers, and the mother had to go by and see this."

"I'm sure she went out of her mind," adds Margot, "but what good would it do to scream? You did not believe that anything like this could happen, and when it did, you were just, like, 'What could I do?' I'm sure her life is shattered. Over. But what could she do to help them?"

Then Dr. Josef Mengele, the medical butcher of Auschwitz, came to Płaszów for a selection. The scene in *Schindler's List* shows thousands of naked, panicked men and women running past the doctor and his assistants, who nod one direction for life, the other for death.

Chaskel recalls, "We were all ordered to come out very early in the morning, and we had to get undressed, the men on one side, the women on the other. I had a hernia at that time, so I put all my clothes in my jacket and held it with the sleeves hanging down, so when I came in front of him, it was covered up, and I went to the right side. He came in a uniform, and he had a coat over his shoulders—it was cold, the first of May 1944—and there we were, naked, standing and waiting for him about four hours."

They both survived the selection, but a few months later, Margot nearly was swept up with eight thousand Płaszów women in a transport bound for the infamous Stutthof death camp. (Stutthof was on the Baltic Sea. The Nazis frequently drove prisoners into the water, machine-gunning them from behind.)

"They took us to the trains, and a Jewish policeman who knew me came with a little water. The SS told him to go back, but he managed to tell me to stay toward the back, because they would not have enough room for all eight thousand women. This transport went straight into the water in Stutthof. They drowned."

Not even the camp's most powerful prisoners enjoyed immunity from Amon Goeth's recreational bloodshed. Chaskel remembers how Goeth, by then promoted to *Hauptsturmführer*, for his fine work at Płaszów, wiped out the Chilowiczes, the "first family" of the camp's Jews.

"We were working in the warehouse, the shipping department, and in the back there was a warehouse with materials. [Wilek] Chilowicz wanted to get something, so I went in with him. I was always afraid to look at this Chilowicz—he was also a monster. He said, 'We're not going to let them get away with this. We're going to fight!' He felt already that something was building under his feet. But I didn't say anything and he walked out.

"The next day, his sister came to work and went to the latrine with Margot, and said Goeth made a search of her brother's barracks and he found a gun, but he didn't remember he gave it to him. I knew already this smelled bad. About a half hour later, her husband—Chilowicz's brother-in-law—was walking in the barracks where the officers were. Goeth called him out and said, 'Where is your wife?' He called her, and she came out. Goeth took out the gun and shot him and her. We were ordered to go down an hour, two hours later, and there was Chilowicz, his wife, his sister, his brother-in-law, and two of his nephews [including Roman Ferber's brother, Moniek]. They were all laying shot, and there was a sign: 'Because they want to run away, and they had jewels and guns.' Everybody had to go by and look at this."

This was not long before Płaszów shut down and Schindler moved to Brinnlitz. Raimund Titsch, Madritsch's manager, placed sixty of his workers on Schindler's list. According to Margot, only four were from Tarnów. "I said, 'Mr. Titsch, I have a husband and a brother-in-law,' and he said, 'OK, they are going on the list, too.' This Marcel Goldberg [the Kraków OD man who manipulated the list] could not touch us because he was afraid of Titsch." Like Schindler, Titsch and Madritsch were eventually declared "Righteous Gentiles" by Yad Vashem, Israel's Holocaust memorial institution.

"Mr. Titsch brought me every week a package with food," says Margot. "We had to go to the Kraków people to get it. They were upset that these Tarnówers got a package. Titsch went every evening to Kraków and came back in the morning. Nobody checked his trunk."

Amazingly, as they headed toward Brinnlitz, the Schlesingers still had valuables. "At Gröss-Rosen, I had several gold rings from my wife," says Chaskel. "Undressed, I had to do something with them, so there was a brick wall. I counted up and from the side, and pulled out a brick and put them in there. I figured I was going to come back and I'd get them. In the meantime, they took us to a shower and we never got back to this place. They had barrels with [caustic] detergent. Your whole body got red, then only a few drops of water came out.

"We stood outside naked. The bosses were German criminals from jail. They gave you a nightgown, a pair of striped pants, and a jacket and a pair of shoes. One of the soles was open. Luckily, the nightgown was very long, so I ripped off a piece and used it for a towel. The suit, I pulled out a thread. I'm from this line, so you pull a thread: Is it wool? Is it cotton? It was paper."

The men went from freezing outdoors to sweltering inside an over-crowded barracks. "In the middle of the room was an iron oven, and the windows were closed with tar paper. The oven was so red hot that everybody was sweating terrible, sitting there. That's the way we slept. They had fifty bowls for the whole group. You had to stand in line and come get it and pass it to the next one, and if you didn't do it fast enough, they knocked the bowl from your hands. The beating was all day long. For every little thing, we got beaten. I never met anyone after that time who didn't get beat up.

"Finally they took us to the train, and gave us soup. It was grass and water, not cooked at all. Nobody ate it, but we had a sandwich wrapped in paper, very nicely. But we were told if you ate it before you got into the train, you would be shot. You could believe them, so regardless how hungry we were, we didn't. Then, when they locked the car, everybody grabbed the sandwiches: two slices of bread with jam in the middle."

No one treated the women bound for Auschwitz to such delicacies. "First of all, we had to be naked," says Margot. "They said they were going to X-ray us, and I saw a lot of people throw away diamonds and everything." She didn't believe it. She still had her fifty dollars in the condom "inside," and that's where it stayed, safely, until she got to Brinnlitz.

"We were in rows of five, always counted. Mengele was there, looking us over." Teenager Celina Karp Biniaz stood at the head of her row. Then came Margot, then Celina's mother, Phyllis Karp. " 'Would you switch with me?' " Phyllis whispered to Margot. She wanted to stay close to Celina. Margot switched. She realized Mengele saw it, and she "went pale." He motioned her to the side, next to four women he already had selected. In her flawless German, Margot tried to explain that she was young and frightened, and had made a mistake.

"Here was another miracle!" Mengele let her go.

The Brinnlitz-bound women spent three weeks at Auschwitz. "Miraculously," during that time, Margot Schlesinger succeeded in adding a woman to Schindler's list who'd never been in Płaszów or Emalia. She was the fiancée of

Margot's cousin, and they met for the first time in the shadow of the crematoria. The young woman was working in the *Krankenstube*, the camp infirmary. "She was hiding a diamond," according to Margot. "When came time for making up the list of the three hundred women, I asked can she come with me?" She did, and is listed as Maria Wiener, number 280, though that's not her real name. (She survived and lives in Canada.) Margot, who also was known as Maria and Miriam, is called Hania on the list: She is number 233.

Three weeks in Auschwitz devastated most of the Schindler women, but Margot says she found comfort and strength in something her mother once told her: " 'They can never take away your education or your self-worth, even if you are naked and have nothing to eat.' So I don't let myself go down all the way. I never let it get to the point where I didn't believe. Other people have the problem: 'I cannot find myself.' I found myself and I kept myself. I knew I was as good as the next one, and that stayed with me all my life, thank God."

On the other hand, "they took my trust. I'm still afraid that after an interview like this, someone will come and shoot me. I have a thing in my head that somebody can still do something to me and my children, too."

It is said that even under such uninspiring conditions, couples managed to make love at Brinnlitz. Not the Schlesingers, Margot says. "You had so many other problems, that this was not a problem to you. Somehow we saw each other and kissed each other, but it never came to the point where you could have any feelings left. You were always afraid for the next moment to be alive."

As liberation drew near, inmates couldn't fail to notice how things were changing. Chaskel says that a few days before the end, a German engineer who never looked at or spoke to the Jewish workers—apart from issuing orders—made a point of greeting Dr. Lewkowitz, who was from Lodz. "He tried to shake hands with him. Lewkowitz said to him, 'Yesterday you wouldn't shake hands with me; tonight I don't want to shake hands with you.' He left with his head down."

Schindler left, "and we were told we didn't have to work anymore. The next morning we went out, and we saw the German army running back home." It was a Friday. "By the camp, there was a big poster that we were criminals and [the Czechs] should not talk to us," Margot recalls. She ventured out of the factory, and met a German woman. "She was afraid they were going to put some people in her apartment. She liked me and said, 'Would you like to come into my house?' I said, 'I have a husband; I have to ask him. And I have a brother-in-law.' I was still afraid they might shoot me.

"We had the material [fabric Schindler gave the survivors] so she said, 'You can use my machine.' I made myself a skirt and blouse, and I looked like a person again. Like a mensch. She had all this wonderful food there. I baked a cake, and nobody could eat it. Your stomach was in such pain. Everything was so raw inside you." Chaskel was six feet tall, and he weighed 110 pounds. Five-foot-four-inch Margot weighed 90 pounds.

They stayed for a week, until Chaskel noticed a framed photograph of a man in an SS uniform in one of the rooms. Margot says he asked the woman who it was. "She said, 'This is my husband, but I do not know where he is or if he is coming back.'" They left and returned to Tarnów.

"We met a few Jews we knew," says Chaskel. "I met a [former] customer, and I asked if he could lend me five hundred złotys. I went to the marketplace and bought bread and butter and a little milk. Then I went to a place where they sold used clothes—like a bazaar—and I found a suit, just my size. ["I remember that suit," says Margot. "It was gray."] It was the first time I ever had a zipper in my pants, not buttons."

Incredibly, the valuables Chaskel and his brothers hid from the *Treuhänder* remained right where they'd left them. "The Polish people who were in the apartment did not even know what we were coming for. We had to have a policeman. I told them I would pay them off. I told [the residents], 'This is my apartment. I have a right to chase you out and take it back. If you want to stay here, you have to let me take out whatever I see.' They were happy. When I opened this [cache] up, they pulled their hairs out of their head!"

They spent most of the next year in Kraków, trading on the black market. Before they left Poland, the Schlesingers saw Amon Goeth one more time: at his trial. They watched one day as Goeth's secretary, Mietek Pemper, testified against him. "Pemper had a very good memory and kept a diary," Margot recalls. "So after the war, he went to the authorities. They found Goeth in a san-

Margot and Chaskel Schlesinger's working papers from Emalia, along with the family silver and a tablecloth hidden under floorboards during the war.

itorium at Bad Tolz. They brought him with a truck. He looked pathetic. I put myself up on a windowsill, and we were all clapping, and happy to see the way he looked."

She says Pemper appeared in "a nice suit every morning, so elegant, with a briefcase, shined shoes, shaved. I could imagine [Goeth] was sitting there thinking, 'Why didn't I kill him?' A lot of people demanded that they should hang him publicly, but the court didn't allow it because it would be too demoralizing."

The Schlesingers went to France. "We lived in Paris five or six months, then moved to Lyon. It was a small Jewish community. We stayed seven years and had three daughters there." Margot Schlesinger had contemplated motherhood with a certain ambivalence. She desperately wanted children, but was convinced they "would not be normal, not only physically, but mentally."

Amon Goeth (second from left) going to trial in Kraków, 1945. He was hanged on September 13, 1946.

Daughter Aline, born in 1947, weighed three pounds at birth. Margot spent most of the pregnancy in bed. Then, for three weeks, she didn't want to touch the baby. "I was afraid she might die under my supervision. I had to have someone come and diaper her. The second one, I prayed to God every day during pregnancy she should be normal, and God gave me a miracle. She was eight pounds." This was Sabine, born in 1949. Regine was born in 1951. (Aline Yolkut is a teacher in Southfield, Michigan. Sabine Himmelfarb is a psychologist in Silver Spring, Maryland. Regine Schlesinger Meisel is a Chicago radio newscaster. The Schlesingers have eight grandchildren.)

Margot never would have tried to get pregnant if she and Chaskel had lost children to the Nazis. "I could not be normal anymore if that happened. When the kids were taken to Auschwitz [from Płaszów], it still haunts me. It was always in the back of my mind that this could happen to my children. I was so grateful to God that we didn't have children then. If we lost a child, I would commit suicide."

Margot, Chaskel, and their daughters emigrated in 1953, joining her brothers in Chicago. Chaskel became a cutter at Kuppenheimer, the men's clothier. "I stayed nineteen years. Then came the hippie times and [the owner]

Margot and Chaskel Schlesinger, after the war.

liquidated the company." He worked two years after that for Hart Schaffner & Marx, then retired.

The Schlesingers decided that no matter what it took, Margot would stay home and raise the children. "Economically, we had a hardship, but I wanted the children to have my attention completely. I was always here when they came home from school."

"We had a happy home because there were never any of these secrets," says Regine. "I've read about other children of survivors who said there was always this pain and sadness in the house, but they had no idea why. Somehow they blamed themselves. For us, because it was out in the open, we could deal with it."

"Whatever they asked, we answered," says Chaskel. "My daughter had a girlfriend, her father was also a survivor. He lost a wife and children. He re-married and had this daughter. She never knew, until she had grown-up children, that he had had a family. Then he had a heart attack, and she was looking for his insurance card in his wallet and came upon a picture of him with his family. It was the first inkling she ever had."

Regine says that she and her sisters tried to spare their parents as much heartache as possible. As she talks, she reduces her father to tears. "We knew the sacrifices they made for us. They didn't spend money on themselves. They didn't take vacations. They didn't go out to movies. The money went strictly for things that were important to them: Jewish day schools and excellent secular educations. They always put us ahead, so we put them ahead."

The girls never went to overnight camp or slumber parties. "I had to know every minute of the day where they were and what they were doing and whether they were OK," says Margot.

She begins to talk about how close supervision shaped the girls' behavior. Regine shakes her head. "It was something more than that. Because we knew what they had gone through and the pain they had already suffered in their lives, we were never going to do anything that was going to add any more pain. I don't think that was guilt. Everything else seemed trivial next to the Holo-caust. We never got into drugs or radical politics [in the sixties] because we knew it would hurt them, and their feelings were more important than that."

Chaskel Schlesinger says his daughters share his feelings about the Germans. "I hate everything that's German. I wouldn't have a German car. If my children got gifts that were from Germany, they would not want them."

"I could not go back to Germany," says Margot. "They hurt me too much. They didn't want me. Maybe I could go again to Poland, to see Auschwitz, because I was there numb. But I cannot hate. Hate makes your [own] life miserable; it's not that you make somebody else miserable. But I do not forget and I cannot forgive. When I see the skinheads on television, I want to rip the TV apart."

West Rogers Park, Chicago, is right next to Skokie, the heavily Jewish community through which neo-Nazis marched in 1977. It's also not far from Northwestern University, where the following year a professor named Arthur Butz published a book called *The Hoax of the Twentieth Century*, which claimed that the Nazis killed no more than a quarter million Jews.

"Ach! I cannot tell you how angry I was!" Margot storms. "I would say to Butz, 'The same thing that happened to us Jews could happen to you, if somebody else would hate you as much as you hated us, and for no reason.' I have evidence that it happened. He has no evidence that it didn't."

The Schlesingers lived with that evidence for decades. Chaskel's brother Moishe also moved to Chicago. He spent the rest of his life punishing himself for what happened to his family. "He said he should have been with them," Margot explains. "He didn't eat any meat for forty, fifty years. He said, 'That's the way my children were cooked at Auschwitz.' He lived on just enough to survive: bread, butter, and tea. Maybe on a *yom tov* [holiday] to do me a favor, he would eat real food." He has since died.

Moishe Schlesinger never sought or received help for his problems. Apparently, he didn't feel he needed it. "He was normal," Chaskel insists. "He knew exactly what he was doing. He didn't need any help. He didn't do this because of a sickness; he *wanted* to do it. In a way, he was traditional, a believer. He *davened* [prayed] every day. He was punishing himself, that's all."

RENA FERBER FINDER

There's a standard joke that offspring of Holocaust survivors often crack about their hyper-watchful parents: "If you go to the other room, call your mother." Most survivor mothers and fathers—at least among the *Schindlerjuden*—admit they have earned the barb.

But if they've hovered, who can blame them? Between 1939 and 1945, the Nazis exterminated one million Jewish children. Even if fate spared a parent this unique bereavement, a survivor was never far from one of the afflicted.

Rena Ferber and Mark Finder met and married after the war. She was a *Schindlerjude*, he a survivor of the Mauthausen death camp system. They bore three daughters in the United States, far in time and distance from the living hell of the camps. Yet they speak of an "urgency" in the way they raised their girls. They couldn't relax as parents, and didn't realize for years how overprotective the Holocaust had made them.

But when the killer came for their firstborn, their vigilance counted for nothing. Diamonds couldn't bribe this murderer. Begging brought no mercy. And with the pitiless amorality of a storm trooper, the killer took her life.

"We always felt that if love could cure, she would be cured," says Rena Finder. But neither love nor medicine could halt the voracious malignancy that

Rena Finder and her late daughter, Anita Finder Rappaport, 1981

devoured Anita Finder Rappaport. She died on March 3, 1990, forty-nine years to the day after the *Krakauer Zeitung* newspaper announced the establishment of Kraków's Jewish ghetto. She was thirty-nine years old.

"We feel it was the worst thing that ever happened to us," says Rena Finder, a fortress of quiet control. "It still is."

Worse than Płaszów? Mauthausen? Auschwitz? "Worse," the Finders say, in unison, without hesitation.

It is a warm April day during the Finders' last scheduled visit to their seasonal condo until next winter. Up north in Framingham, Massachusetts, their permanent home, the trees are barely budding. Here in Delray Beach, the green of Florida's perpetual summer draws Rena's dark-eyed gaze toward the window.

"Anita used to say to me, 'Don't worry, Mommy. You went through so much more than I did, I'm going to get through it.' I never believed that she wouldn't live—maybe not be cured, but that she would live longer." As Rena's husband loses the struggle to contain his tears, she adds, "Our plans never work out. We roll with the punches."

Coming from most people, that would sound like self-pity. Not Rena Finder, although it's hard to imagine anyone more entitled to it. Rather, she projects the spiritual tranquillity of a person who has learned to accept the unimaginable. Other *Schindlerjuden* seem to have tremendous respect and affection for her.

A longtime lecturer for Facing History and Ourselves, a Boston-based Holocaust education group, she has told her story time and again. She speaks in a high, almost girlish voice, but with dignity and restraint. She is a reflective person who has thought as much about the meaning of her experience as about the events that comprise it.

"I think I am probably a more compassionate kind of person because of what we went through," she says. "And I think that we don't spend that much time saying, 'Am I happy?' We do what we have to do, whether it's good or bad. I know my friends always feel that they are going to have me for a friend in good times and bad, when some only want to be your friend when it's good."

Rena Ferber, a girl with dark, heavy braids, was ten years old when the war started and she became "an enemy of the state." Her family was part of the group that some other *Schindlerjuden* call "the big shots from Kraków." Her father, Moses Ferber, had one sister and eight brothers. One of them, Leon, was married to a sister of Wilek Chilowicz. Their older son, Monick, served as Chilowicz's secretary. Their younger son is Roman Ferber (see the following chapter).

Rena Finder's childhood sounds like a fantasy. She was the only child of Moses and Rose Ferber and, until the war, the only grandchild living in Kraków, of her maternal grandparents. She says the family treated her "like a little princess."

Moses was a sales representative for a surgical supply company. They lived next to Wawel Castle, across from the river Vistula. "It was a brand-new apartment when I was born in 1929. My mother's parents [the Windisches] lived around the corner. When I was sent to school around the corner, my mother could see me at recess. I remember that we had seders in the bedroom, and my grandfather and I sat on the bed. He was supported by all those down pillows. My grandmother was making raisin wine. I was saying the 'four questions' at the age of two."

She still remembers every inch of the apartment. "We were the first apartment on the left, on the third floor. From the table and chair in the kitchen, you could see the back of my grandparents' apartment. I would call to them from the window. We went on Saturday to my grandparents', and you had to make the whole circle and kiss everybody's hand, when you came and when you left. This was a sign of respect."

Her room was an alcove at the back of the dining room. "I even remember sleeping there in my crib—like a metal bed with nets on the side—and, when I got older, a daybed. There was a bookshelf under the window, and I did my homework after school on the dining room table. In each room, there was a stove for heating. In the dining room, I remember, it was celery green. My parents' bedroom had a peachy-color one, and two chifforobes, for clothes and linens. They had a big bed in a light wood, and two night tables, and a dressing table with a big mirror. My mother had a Chinese tea set on the dressing table that was her pride and joy."

Rena kept her pride and joy there too. "On one side, on a shelf, I kept my precious books. For birthdays, I was always given books. My books had leather bindings. I also had a Shirley Temple doll and a little doll carriage of wicker, and a scooter. When I had my tonsils out, I had a choice between another Shirley Temple doll and a subscription to the library—we did not have public libraries then. I chose the subscription."

Sunday mornings, the Kraków movie theaters ran children's features. "I remember seeing the Keystone Kops. I cried when [crooks] were chasing them. I was afraid they were going to be caught. They had to take me out. We were into opera. I remember going to children's theatre in the mornings, like *Peter and the Wolf* and *Puss in Boots.*"

Her father's store was around the corner from Kraków's famous Phoenix café. He'd take her there for napoleons and iced coffee, "like sherbet you ate with a spoon, with whipped cream on top, and Italian ices that tasted like real pineapple."

The storybook summers of Rena's childhood were spent at Zawoja, a village in the Carpathian Mountains. "The farmers moved out of their cottages into the barns and rented the cottages out. There were mountains, rivers, and forests where we would pick strawberries, raspberries, and mushrooms. It was paradise. We would go the day after school ended. Everybody we knew went."

The summer of 1939 saw the end of those bucolic interludes. "Father used to come Friday and stay till Monday. He came and said, 'We have to leave.' There was talk about war. We went back to Kraków. But people had lived through one war and had very high hopes that England and France would not allow anything to happen, that if Hitler would dare to attack Poland, they would attack Hitler.

"I remember that my father was saying to Mother that some of their friends were talking about leaving. But how could they leave their parents? They knew Hitler was taking away Jews' civil rights in Germany, but they never expected he would get away with it when he came into Poland."

There was another reason why the Ferbers didn't want to leave. "I remember they had just painted the apartment and gotten new chandeliers."

Rena had heard this kind of talk before, about pogroms and how everyone hated the Jews. "As long as I can remember, the Jews were not first-class citizens. Jews would always stay away from the university at Eastertime because the students were taught that the Jews killed Christ."

Her family had little social contact with gentiles. "Our one Polish friend was superintendent of the building. She always invited us for Christmas Eve dinner. And my teachers." One teacher offered Rena, then a third grader, her first personal lesson in anti-Semitism.

"An art teacher gave me a failing mark for not wanting to draw a swastika. I refused because I [had] heard about Hitler, and we had family in Berlin. We organized a little demonstration against that teacher: a stand-up strike. My mother came in, and they changed my grade because I was an excellent student. But I had to apologize to the teacher whose class we did it in."

She remembers that the Polish Jews kicked out of Germany would arrive destitute. "The Jewish community [in Kraków] would raise money and find places for them to stay. One of my uncles was a tailor. They were told to leave, and they came in the middle of the night with nothing, and two little kids."

Even so, Rena's idea of war came mainly from what she read in books: "The 1812 war. The French on one side, the Russians on the other. I expected them to come fight at the soccer field, and I would be able to watch from my grandmother's window like we were watching soccer games."

Then the air raids started. "We were going to the cellars. Then the men decided to flee and go toward Russia, again thinking, 'As soon as England and France realize what's happening, they will come and rescue us.' That was traumatic, having my father leave. His departure was very sudden."

The men returned two months later. "When they came, they had to smuggle themselves," Rena recalls. "They had to swim the river. I was told that my father saved a lot of people. Some drowned, but he saved a lot because he was a good swimmer. I will never forget that I was outside and I saw my father coming home. Oh, did I run! The day before, one of my friends' father came, and I knew in my heart [my father] was going to come."

About that time, her parents got her a puppy. "Once I was walking him late at night so he wouldn't mess up, and the German patrol came and told me I was outside too late. After that, we gave [the dog] to the woman who delivered milk."

In November 1940, Hans Frank, Kraków's German governor, decreed that from then on Jews needed permits to live in the city. Anyone under the age of twelve or over fifty was denied a permit and had to leave. Rena was too young, and her grandparents were too old. "But my father was always able to arrange things. They made me two years older. He was able to get permits for his parents and my mother's parents."

A *Treuhänder* (trustee) took over Moses Ferber's business. Fortunately, he was the son of their building's superintendent, the woman who always invited the family for Christmas Eve. Moses stayed on for a time; Rena recalls bringing him dinner at the store "so he wouldn't be exposed to walking on the streets."

In March 1941, the family moved into the ghetto, and Moses Ferber became an *Ordnungsdienst,* a member of the Jewish police force, as did two of Rena's uncles. She believes that her father arranged for the infamous Marcel Goldberg to become an "OD."

Goldberg, the character in *Schindler's List* who took Schindler's watch and gold cigarette case, exercised enormous power at Płaszów, where he assigned inmates to jobs. He was primarily responsible for compiling the list and is widely loathed by the survivors for selling spots on it to the highest bidder.

The Jews who lived outside the boundaries of what was to become the ghetto were given ten days to vacate their homes, taking whatever they could carry. "We had a pushcart. Mother had linens, bedding, some pots and pans. Each of us had a little suitcase with personal stuff. I had to leave most of the books, only being able to take a couple. *David Copperfield* was my favorite.

"I think I gave the dolls away. I must have given a lot of things to the superintendent. I remember leaving my mother's dressing table with the china tea set on it, and walking out of the house, past the dining room table, with the dining room set still on it. We were assigned an apartment, but we were fortunate because one of my father's brothers lived there with his wife and child."

Marcel Goldberg's wife, Lusia, and his sister, Sidka, "who were very nice, moved in with us," Rena remembers. "We shared the same bedroom. We hung a rope and a blanket to divide it." Marcel was already at the Płaszów camp.

The Germans established workshops in the ghetto, "because people had to be kept busy, so my mother and I worked in a paper shop. They brought in huge bales of paper for printing. It would come out ruled and lined. My father knew the people, and this was why we didn't go to Schindler right away. [These were] terrible circumstances, but people were together in a house, while the people who went to work for Schindler had to leave the ghetto. There was always a danger that if they left and came back, they would find their families gone. The Germans were constantly ripping families apart."

Her father lost his best friend in the ghetto. The friend was shot by a patrol in front of the Jewish hospital. "They played cards together before the war," Rena says. "They were so funny, because if the doorbell rang, they would both go. They didn't trust each other with the cards. But you had no time to grieve for anyone special, because two hours later, people were killed in the hospital. The doctors killed them because if they didn't, the Germans would."

During a subsequent *Aktion*, Rena and her maternal grandparents hid under thick bushes in the building's courtyard. "We stayed a whole day. You could hear people being collected on the Plac Zgody, and hear screaming and shooting. My mother was coming with her younger sister and saying, 'It's all right to come out.' We came out and were shaking the dirt off, and the German patrol came into the courtyard. It was the last patrol, and they took my grandparents away. My grandparents had papers, too. They yanked them. We wanted to go, and they were hitting us with the rifles, and they were hitting my grandparents. My mother was foaming at the mouth. We felt so helpless. We ran to look for my father; he was helpless too. That made me feel much more vulnerable. I thought my father could fix anything." The grandparents died at the Bełżec death camp.

The relatives deported from Berlin fled to Tarnów; then that ghetto was liquidated. Moses Ferber smuggled one of the daughters, a five-year-old named Jenny, back to Kraków. Then, says Rena Finder, "they came and took my father away."

He and Marcel Goldberg were arrested together on New Year's Eve

1942. Goldberg was released. Moses Ferber was sent to Auschwitz. After the war, someone who had seen him there confirmed his death.

Three months later, Amon Goeth liquidated the Kraków Ghetto, sending thousands to Płaszów and other camps and killing thousands more on the spot. "They didn't want to waste a bullet on the children, so they told people to leave the children behind—they would be cared for. My little cousin, Jenny, we didn't want to leave her, but in the end, we had no choice. I took her to the orphans' home and left her with a friend of my mother's." All the children at the home were killed.

Others did sneak children into Płaszów. "We were always hiding the children," Rena says. "One day, a group of SS and Gestapo was coming for an inspection. We had to stand on the *Appellplatz* and go to work, so we took one barracks and painted 'infectious' on it. The SS didn't go near it. We were gone a long day, but the children were safe. Some of the very young had to be drugged."

Amon Goeth already had claimed one member of the Ferber family. "One of the first victims was Uncle Romek, who was painting the barracks and all of a sudden he was shot in the back. Those people were hoping that by obeying orders and working hard, they would survive. My grandfather, Aryeh Ferber, was next to him." Goeth was on his balcony, using Jews for target practice.

Rena says she was careful never to make eye contact with Goeth, who liked to watch his Great Danes eviscerate prisoners. "I thought if I didn't look at him, he wouldn't see me. . . . I was sitting on the ground, breaking up tombstones for the road, and all of a sudden the girl next to me fell over. You didn't hear the shot. I looked, touched her, there was blood coming from her head."

Mark Finder, Rena's future husband, already was at Płaszów when Rena and her mother arrived, but they didn't meet until after the war. He was assigned to the metal shop. His mother had been transported from the ghetto to a death camp. His sister died at Bergen-Belsen. "My father went with me to Mauthausen. He couldn't make it from the train. He was taken to the *Krankenstube* [infirmary]. There he probably died."

Goeth tolerated the children at Płaszów, to a point. "One day on the *Appellplatz*," Rena says, "they told us the children were going to be rounded up and sent away, and if anyone moved, the children would be shot. People started to whisper that the children were going to be taken to an orphanage and be taken care of by nuns and maybe adopted." Instead, they were transported to Auschwitz and gassed.

Rena and Rose Ferber lived one year in the Płaszów barracks. When Schindler built his Emalia subcamp, Marcel Goldberg moved them into it. "Emalia was like going to heaven," Rena says. "Schindler tried to feed us better and give us clothes. You could be on the *Krankenstube* and not worry about being killed. We got the KL, but I kept scratching it and it went away."

Rena and her mother worked at the ammunition factory in the subcamp (not in the building that made enameled pots and pans). "One of my new memories, since the movie, is about an incident I had with Schindler in the factory," Rena says. "They had changed me from a small machine to a big press. The machine broke, and there was a lot of yelling and screaming. The [German] foreman said I sabotaged the machine."

She remembers now how badly the episode shook her. "I became the center of attention, and the thing to be in camp was *not* to be, and just to blend in. All of a sudden, there were so many people. Everyone was looking at me and blaming me. I was terrified.

"Somebody went for Schindler. He inspected it, very seriously, and said I couldn't have sabotaged it. He put me back on a small machine, and from then on, he told them not to put anyone but a man on the big presses.

"He was very dashing. He made me think of Clark Gable. He winked at me."

Sometimes at night, Rena and other girls cleaned the factories' offices. It was coveted duty, "because we used to take turns sleeping."

Until the Schindler women embarked for Auschwitz, no one had laid a hand on Rena Ferber in anger. "But when we were loaded on the train in Płaszów, an SS woman hit me on the head. They were so vicious and brutal and sadistic, more than men. I think because some of them were women and you expect kindness, it was so shocking. But of course, some were fat and big and ugly."

Auschwitz, she says, almost defies description. "The first thing that struck me was the terrible stench, and the smoke so heavy you could feel it. The ashes were landing on you. Your eyes were burning. You could taste it."

When she and her mother arrived at Brinnlitz, her grandfather was waiting. He was seventy years old, though his papers lopped twenty years off his age.

She remembers that Emilie Schindler "came to live with us [at Brinnlitz]. She fed the younger girls half a cup of farina in the mornings. My mother had scurvy, and she got her a lemon."

After liberation, Rena and Rose Ferber joined a group headed for Kraków. It included Joe Lipschutz, now of Cape Coral, Florida, who would marry Rena's first cousin, Hanka Ferber—Roman's sister—after the war. "We arrived in the late afternoon and went to the school across the street from where Roman and Hanka used to live. They brought cots; we slept there the first night. Then we went to the Jewish community center and registered, and looked to see if anybody was looking for us. We found out nobody was because everyone was dead."

Rena still believed she would find her father. "I was sure he could not have died. He was such a strong man and so smart and resourceful, I was convinced he would be alive. I went to quite a few pharmacists who used to be his friends, asking if they had seen him. Even in America when I first came, I thought he would be alive, even though there were witnesses he was killed [in the Auschwitz gas chambers]. I was hoping he would come and look for me. You're always a little princess to your father, especially when you're an only child."

When they reached Kraków, Rena and Rose went to their old apartment. "The superintendent was not there anymore, but they told us where she was. She was very happy to see us and gave us back some things, like linens. Her son had been killed by the Germans, in the underground. Then I went to the ghetto, to the house of my grandparents. Nobody was there. I went upstairs to the attic, and in the sawdust I found family pictures."

She says she didn't cry when she found them. "I don't think we had any tears left. I think we were so traumatized, we were numb."

They stayed in Kraków only two months, then went to the Bindermichel displaced persons' camp in Linz, Austria. They shared an apartment with the Levensteins, relatives of Murray Pantirer. That was where Rena Ferber met Mark Finder.

"Mark spoke English, and was translating German to English for the American military," Rena says. "He was paid with K-rations." This made him extremely popular.

Mark says, "Three beautiful girls found out and came to visit us, to see the cans of fruit and ham and eggs! One of them was Rena. She was sixteen and gorgeous. A year later, we decided to marry."

Rena, the avid reader and music lover, luxuriated in postwar Austria's rich cultural life. "We went to every opera, and some several times. I used to go with my girlfriend to *Madame Butterfly*, and before it even started, we were already crying. I must have seen it one hundred times. It was cheap—less than a dollar—and I was working in

Rena Ferber marries Mark Finder, Austria, 1946.

the office of the UNRRA [United Nations Relief and Rehabilitation Administration]. This was part of our determination to build a new life. You were grieving and lost, but you wanted to be normal and do what your parents had done before the war."

Rena and Mark married in a cousin's apartment. Rena wore a pleated white skirt and smocked overblouse. Rose Ferber made raisin wine and, alongside Sala Levenstein, walked her daughter to the *chuppah* [wedding canopy]. "We had a friend who was a dentist who had a gold wedding band [to use as a filling], so he gave it to us. I still have it. It's got someone else's date engraved in it."

Rena remembers her wedding as "bittersweet. My mother was going back to Poland to remarry. She [had] met in Austria an old friend whose wife and son did not survive. He had a younger son in a [tuberculosis] sanitarium. She lived ten years in Poland, waiting for the boy to recover, before she came to the U.S."

(Rose Halpern died in Massachusetts in 1967, at the age of sixty-four. Grandfather Aryeh Ferber died in Connecticut in 1956 at eighty-five. "For me," says Rena Finder, "it's a big comfort that I was able to engrave the names of her family on my mother's gravestone.")

The newlyweds couldn't wait to start a family. "We wanted to go on with our lives and be normal again and start living, and do all the things like normal people did. I felt I survived to go on with my life, that I had won over Hitler. They killed almost all of us, yet we were going to go on in spite of him and all the other anti-Semites who really wanted us to disappear."

In the DP camps, the initial period of relief and healing gave way to confusion, frustration, and further pain. Conditions ranged from tolerable to oppressive. Few seemed to understand how deeply the survivors had been wounded. General Lucius Clay, the American commander of Bindermichel, for instance, wanted to house the refugees in barracks. General Dwight D. Eisenhower intervened, insisting that they be given SS officers' apartments.

"We thought that when the war ended, the world would roll out the red carpet for us and honor us because we survived," says Rena Finder, with a sad, ironic smile. "Of course, that did not happen. They still had very strict immigration laws. We still couldn't go where we wanted and were stuck in DP camps."

Gradually, the survivors began to learn how "the world" had responded—or, more accurately, failed to respond—to their plight.

"It is so horrifying that there was a murderous machine bent on killing us, and there was nobody who wanted to help us," Rena Finder says. "It was beyond our comprehension that everybody knew what was going to happen—Roosevelt, Churchill—and they let them kill us. It made me lose faith in God. I couldn't believe that God could exist and let innocent children be murdered, but after a while, I realized I needed my faith, and maybe God didn't have anything to do with it. Like Elie Wiesel said, 'Where was man?'"

Years later, when the Korean War ended, it struck Rena Finder that the freed American prisoners of war were accorded a much different reception than the Holocaust survivors. "There was an army of psychologists waiting for them, and I remember thinking, 'Nobody was waiting for us. Nobody wanted to find out how we were feeling.'" She found the Korean War "a frightening experience. When we survived, I thought there would never be another war, that the world must have learned."

Mark Finder adds: "Right after the war, when survivors came to this country, Americans did not want to listen to us. Jewish or not Jewish, they were not ready to talk to us or hear us."

The Jewish relief organizations concentrated on the basics: food, clothing, and shelter. "Who knew about our minds?" asks Rena. "They expected us to act normal. Mostly the survivors got together and talked and were each other's psychiatrists. That's why lot of survivors have friends who are survivors."

Rena Finder had someone else: her mother. "I never had the feeling of abandonment so many had, and, being on Schindler's list, we went every step of the way together."

Rena hungered for details of the lost years. "I wanted to know everything that I missed, not having all this education. I read everything I could get my hands on, on the Civil War, and the war in Japan. I did not know America was at war with Japan! The men, maybe, had more opportunity to listen to the news [at Brinnlitz]. I was too preoccupied with trying to survive."

In November 1948, Rena and Mark Finder sailed to Boston aboard the USS *Omar Bundy.* "When the ship leaned one way, the showers were hot; the other way, cold. Eight hundred people were sick on that ship. I was the only one who was not. The men and women were separated, and it took eight days."

They went to Boston because the uncle of a friend, in Peabody, Massachusetts, had agreed to sponsor them, even though he didn't know them. "Uncle Harry" White became a lifelong friend. His daughter and her husband, Sadie and Charlie Loten, "adopted" the Finders, introducing them to American culture via films, Chinese food, and lobsters.

They arrived the day before Thanksgiving. "I wanted to go to work right away," recalls Mark Finder, a businessman. "I never heard of Thanksgiving."

He got a job in a leather goods factory. Rena became a light bulb tester, then moved on to a shoe factory. She became pregnant with Anita. Marilyn and Debbi followed.

The family moved to Framingham in 1958. "As soon as we saved enough money, we bought a house," says Mark. "We worked hard and didn't look for charity. We didn't have a car for the first six or seven years."

Like many survivors, they told their children nothing about their lives during the war years. Rena says that when Marilyn was ten or eleven, one of her friends asked, " 'Do you know your parents were in concentration camps?' She came home, and she didn't want to ask me. She wanted to look through my night table because she knew there were all kinds of papers there. The newspaper did articles when we [came]. But somehow she didn't ask any questions. When the movie *Holocaust* was on television, then we started to talk."

But Rena Finder didn't speak publicly until the Holocaust revisionists began to get a lot of attention. "We realized we had to say something. Time was growing short, and people were dying. I feel it is my duty to talk. Mark was very much against it, because it does take a lot out of me. We had a lot of arguments about it. Mark does not like to talk about it or listen about it, but he has changed now since *Schindler's List.*"

Rena became involved with Facing History and Ourselves in 1981. It was started by two Boston teachers who wanted to educate people about the Holocaust but couldn't find appropriate material. Rena Finder and other resource speakers train teachers to instruct at every level from middle school to adult education.

For her, the Holocaust is "part of your thinking and feeling and living. It's there all the time. Whatever you do, it's part of you." But she is aware that it's different for others. The film, she says, "opened a flood of memories for people who never wanted to confront it. People are using it as their own private therapy."

She is candid about the compulsions and aversions that vex her to this day (along with the numbness in her toes caused by the frostbite she suffered in the camps). "I am compelled to always be on time. I am a nervous wreck if I'm a minute late. I hate to stay in line—I get really nervous. Also uniforms, especially Massachusetts state troopers. They have to be very tall, they wear those high, shiny boots, and a cap that was modeled like the Nazis'. No matter how slow I go, I will always slow down when I see one. I know they are here to protect you, but . . ."

She is "absolutely petrified" of dogs. "I didn't realize why until I started talking [about the Holocaust]. Intellectually, when I see a dog, I say it's just a

Rena Ferber Finder and her husband, Mark, 1994.

dog, but when I go for a walk, I go to another street when I see one coming. But my granddaughter has one, and I've had to make friends with it."

Indeed, Rena and Mark Finder will do just about anything for Amy Rappaport, the child who was only two when doctors finally diagnosed her mother's cancer (as well as for grandsons Zach, Adam, Jason, David, and Joseph).

Anita, Bert, and Amy Rappaport lived in Upper Nyack, New York, where Anita worked for American Express. She complained for months in 1985 that her hip and shoulder hurt. A chiropractor began treating her for bursitis. "She was pregnant with her second child, and they never took X rays," says Rena. "She suffered more and more with walking, and I was very upset. I told her she had to see somebody else, so she finally went to see an orthopedic doctor, and they took X rays, and made an appointment with an oncologist the very next day."

It is not easy for Rena Finder to talk about this, but she continues, softly, wearily. "They took bone marrow. They said the primary was in the breast. She was in such pain, they sent her to the hospital right away to start chemo. A month before, I was watching her walking, and the thought went through my head and out—'Anita has cancer.'"

From the end of July 1986 to the following January, Rena Finder lived with her daughter, helping care for Amy as Anita underwent chemotherapy. Mark commuted from Framingham on weekends.

"Then she got better," says Rena. "She responded. She started to drive again, and they went on vacation. I came home. She had about a year after that. She was disabled. Her bones were so brittle. But she was taking care of her child. Then she had two femur replacements."

Mark interjects: "Rena was there for almost another year, July until [Anita] died on March 3, 1990. They had put her through all kinds of chemo again, and she said, 'No more.'" The family decided on hospice care. They were all together at the end. Amy was not quite six years old.

"She is so smart," says Amy's proud grandmother. "She said, 'How come Mommy couldn't be cured?' And we tried to tell her that there was no cure for it but someday there will be, and she said, 'It will be too late for my mommy.'"

Bert Rappaport has remarried. Rena says his wife is "a wonderful mother to Amy. We are close to them, for which we have to thank God."

The Finders' next daughter, Marilyn Sandperl of Lanton, Massachusetts, a teacher, has three sons. Their youngest, Debbi Katz, lives in Framingham. She has two sons.

Inevitably, someone gave the Finders *When Bad Things Happen to Good People,* by Harold Kushner, rabbi emeritus of a nearby congregation in Natick.

"I read it three times," says Rena. "Then I thought, 'I guess it is true: God does not give you the cancer cells or make the car crash; he gives you the strength to go on.'"

ROMAN FERBER

*I*f you live or do business in New York City, there's a good chance Roman Ferber has had some impact on your life. He's not exactly a household name, but he has held key urban-planning and economic-development positions in every mayoral administration since John Lindsay's. His tax-abatement recommendations enabled the mega-developers to shape the city of the 1990s.

As Industry Relations Specialist in the New York City Economic Policy and Marketing Group, Office of the Deputy Mayor for Finance and Economic Development, he has been researching ways to comply with court mandates covering the feeding of jail inmates. The courts have ordered the city to accommodate inmates' special dietary needs—*halall* (for the Muslims), kosher, vegetarian, and so on—as well as to serve more "wholesome" food to the general inmate population.

As Roman Ferber studies the steak-and-peach-cobbler-studded menus from other jurisdictions and the reports of jailhouse lawsuits over peanut-butter consistency, the irony nettles him. "I read newspapers about prisoners complaining that they don't have this and that: television, sufficient access to telephones. I've thought, 'My God, how things have changed.' "

As Birkenau prisoner B14435, nobody worried about what he ate, or, for that matter, *if* he ate. Incarcerated for the capital crime of being Jewish, it's doubtful anyone but his father cared whether prisoner B14435 lived to his twelfth birthday.

A delicacy for this inmate? Toast, of a sort. "They distributed food in the barracks," he recalls. "They brought pots of soup and occasionally a piece of bread. I remember putting the bread on a stick and trying to toast it a little in the oven. We had no butter, so we used salt, and made a sandwich out of it."

Entertainment? The deadly serious game of hide-and-seek with rifle-toting Nazis.

Born on January 25, 1933, Roman Ferber was one of the youngest *Schindlerju-den*. His father, Leon, and Rena Finder's father, Moses, were brothers. Roman was among the boys snatched from Brinnlitz in the early weeks and sent to Auschwitz. The boys' fathers went, too—if they still had fathers. The group included one little boy who didn't: Willie S., another of Roman's first cousins. Roman's mother, Malia, and Willie's mother, Feiga, were sisters. For the better part of a year, Roman Ferber considered Willie S.'s survival his responsibility.

Ask most *Schindlerjuden* why they made it, and they'll credit God, Oskar Schindler, and just plain luck—not necessarily in that order. Roman Ferber credits luck, timing, and himself—not necessarily in that order.

"I'm not one of those who attribute survival to God. Some of us had much better intuition, survival instincts, tenacity. I happen to be one that fit that picture very well. My survival is based on being very opportunistic. I took many more chances. I was the product of the environment. I adapted, adjusted, took the opportunity that was there. I look at myself and think, 'How come I'm here and so many others are not?' Sheer guts, stamina, cunning. Actually, I did very well in Auschwitz. I had a lot of bread. I was an expert at stealing."

One could make the obvious snide crack about how well this prepared him for a career in New York City government, but there's nothing funny about it. At the age of eleven, he was on his own in Birkenau. The fathers went to one barracks, the sons to another. "Take care of yourself" was Leon Ferber's last bit of advice to his boy, who did his best to heed it.

"My mind was always conniving to see how I could survive and make the best of it," he says. "We all had to do chores. The crematory by then [late 1944] was blown up, and it was being closed down. There were no cars. There were no horses, because the Germans were killing and eating them. I organized myself and talked to the *Kapos* and said, 'Why don't you use us as horses? We are small, and you can put about twenty of us in one of these wagons and we can pull it and we can collect garbage and make ourselves useful.'

"They bought the idea, and that gave me freedom of movement. We would remove things from the concentration-camp garbage and we were able to go into the kitchen while our *Kapo* was making love with the kitchen supervisor. We used to steal the kitchen blind, and load up the whole wagon, instead of taking the garbage. I don't think I was tougher than most of the kids; I was just self-confident."

After all, he had another mouth to feed (and to monitor): Willie S. was seven when they left Brinnlitz. "He was a crybaby," says Roman Ferber, with grudging, big-brotherly affection. "I kept his mouth shut in Auschwitz. I had to stuff his hat in his mouth every time they came [to search for children]. At night, when Mengele used to come and pick kids for experiments, I used to have to hide this kid, and he was always crying. I used to put him in a soup pot and put the cover on it, because the noise wouldn't penetrate."

Willie S. was an orphan for the same reason Roman Ferber no longer had a brother. Amon Goeth shot Moniek Ferber, along with Feiga and Chaim S., and just about everyone related to Wilek Chilowicz, in the late summer of 1944. Malia Ferber and Feiga S. were Chilowicz's sisters.

As head of Płaszów's Jewish police, Chilowicz exercised enormous power. In hundreds of instances, his word meant life or death, suffering or solace. For this, he was loathed and feared by many of the inmates. He also was Goeth's flunky, helping him amass a fortune on Kraków's black market. Before the commandant's rapacious greed toppled him, he'd sent much of the booty to his family in Vienna, prosperous publishers to this day.

It's said that Chilowicz collected quite a nest egg himself, but as Goeth analyzed Płaszów's inevitable demise before the advancing Russians, Chilowicz loomed as a potent threat. He knew too much, as did some of his relatives, including Moniek Ferber, who was Chilowicz's secretary.

For a time, his position granted Moniek—eleven years older than Roman—extraordinary latitude in, and resources for, protecting his family. (They had a sister in Płaszów, Hanka, who married Joseph Lipshutz, another *Schindlerjude,* after the war. They had two children and cared for the orphaned Willie S. until he was a teenager.)

"I was one of the privileged kids in Płaszów because of the Chilowicz connection," Roman Ferber acknowledges. "I was hiding when they knew there was a major selection. Chilowicz [who had no children] would take me. All I had to do was stay in his place. They wouldn't dare to come in there. It was a bungalow: a pretty large room and bedroom and bathroom, where he conducted his major business."

Chilowicz and a man named Mietek Finkelstein handled the camp's day-to-day administration. Moniek Ferber was charged with "maintaining the lists, allocating resources, expediting German requests," according to Roman. "He was the pen man. He placed most of our family on Schindler's list." Before the war, Moniek had attended Jagiellonian University. He was a Zionist and a disciple of the famous Dr. Ozjash Thon.

Roman Ferber doesn't think his brother or Chilowicz left the camp to work deals on the outside; they sent functionaries. He is certain that these expeditions "were missions for Goeth and Schindler." He saw both Nazis enter the bungalow from time to time, and he knew that Goeth often summoned Chilowicz to his villa or office. The boy knew exactly who Oskar Schindler was. "I saw him come and go from Chilowicz's place many times. He was a stunning man who looked almost like President Ford." And Goeth, for all his bestial ways, "was a gorgeous-looking man."

When Amon Goeth decided to launch one of his "hunting missions" for Jews, Chilowicz and Finkelstein accompanied him. So did Goeth's Great Dane, Ralph. "This is a strange way of putting it," says Roman Ferber, "but that dog saved more Jews. He was running ahead of Goeth, and we would get alerted and hide. The moment Goeth would come in, if he didn't like your looks, he would set the dog on you. The second dog [Alf] became the first dog's companion maybe three months later, and between the two of them, he would just let them rip people apart."

Roman and his contemporaries spent most of their days scrambling to stay one step ahead of trouble, seeking sanctuary in furnace flues, under floor-boards, and in the latrines. "We would come out when we heard the people walking around," he recalls. "There was a difference between the way Jews and Germans walked."

In a scene from *Schindler's List* that never fails to elicit gasps, a small boy—Alex Rosner in the script—pursued by SS guards lowers himself chest deep in a reservoir of human waste. Alex Rosner never hid in a latrine, but Roman Ferber did. "The pit was about twelve feet deep. You couldn't have jumped in it or you would have drowned. People would sit on boards with holes, and the stuff would fall inside. There were crossbars [under the boards], and this is where we used to hide, between the crossbars. I cannot describe the smell." But it was so repulsive that the guards wouldn't go near it . . . which was precisely the point.

Ferber relatives in the late 1920s: Front row (left to right): Hanka Ferber, Rena Ferber, Moniek Ferber. Center: Cyla Wiener. Standing: a nanny, Malia Ferber (Roman's mother), another nanny, Rose Ferber (Rena's mother).

"You realize that when somebody shoots at you and you are a moving target, it is difficult to hit. If there is *no* target, it is even more difficult to hit, so you hide. I always schlepped Willie along with me."

When the war was over, Roman Ferber gave depositions to war-crimes investigators about Amon Goeth and conditions at Płaszów, recounting scenes like the incessant butchery on the Chujowa Górka, the camp's hilltop mass grave site.

"I remember trucks of Russian soldiers, Greeks, whoever, [constantly coming in]. I was watching from a magazine [storehouse] where they were distributing clothing, and some of those prisoners started fighting the Germans and Ukrainians because they knew they had nothing left to lose. They got pushed into the ditches and shot with machine guns. You could hear and actually see it."

The Ferber clan had been a large one, close-knit and "upwardly mobile" before the war, according to Roman. Grandfather Aryeh Ferber and Grandmother Sara had eight sons and a daughter, most of whom lived in Kraków. Leon and Malia's apartment at 12 Waska Street in the Kazimierz "was an open house," with friends and relatives coming and going all the time.

"My father didn't have a mean bone in his body," says Roman. "He was very pious. He was a salesman, representing Pelikan, the German pen company. It was a new, modern building, third floor. We had a Polish maid and kept chickens and geese on the balcony off the kitchen."

On the Sabbath, everyone gathered at Grandfather Aryeh's house. "There were so many sons, they had their own *minyan*. We went to *shul* and the kids were running around. We used to go and pick up *cholent* [a hearty bean stew] placed at the bakery the night before. We spoke Polish in our house. The only time the Jewish language or German was used was so the kids could not understand what they were talking about."

His parents had discussed Hitler openly, and Roman says the family felt the effects of his hateful madness early on. "From my mother's side"—there were four sisters and two brothers—"portions of her family, the Goldfarbs, lived in Berlin. One of the kids in school said something against Hitler, and they were forced to pick themselves up that evening and get the child out of there. My father provided tickets for them to get out. They had a gourmet bakery in Berlin. I remember my father paying for the machinery, because they left and went to the United States and opened a bakery in Brooklyn. After the war, they sent for my mother and me.

"But everybody was saying that it was only temporary. People were always suggesting that they had dealt with tyrants before, and, deep inside, none of us could believe that anything of that nature could happen. We had a very nice life. My brother had a girlfriend. My sister had lots of boyfriends. We would go out all the time, to movies and cafés."

One uncle followed the Jewish migration east. "He was joking that he left Kraków hoping to come back in a week, and it lasted for six years in Siberia." But most of the family stayed put. "By the time we realized what was happening, it was much too late. The Germans did come back to blitz us, not only on the battlefield. Never would our parents leave us alone. The Germans used to come in and grab the Jews and beat the hell out of them." Certain Jews decided to protest these affronts. "They went to the German authorities. They figured that these are soldiers who were coming in as rogues. They never saw daylight again."

When Governor General Hans Frank decided to make Kraków *Judenfrei* (free of Jews), the Ferbers moved to the suburb of Borek Falenski. "At that time, it was a wasteland. A trolley went in, and then you would walk about five kilometers over a river, where we had a farmhouse. It was so bloody cold that we would go to sleep at night, then get up in the morning and couldn't get out because the snow was covering the door. We would open up the hatch, put on snowshoes, and get milk and bread. We'd buy it from the Poles.

"We were living with another family by the name of Horowitz—they are in Australia now. Two families together with kids, and we played. In the spring, we would run around the river and make fires. We used to dig up potatoes and get chestnuts off the trees and burn them on the fire. We played soccer with cans."

In the meantime, Poles appropriated their Kraków apartment, with everything in it. "We brought some clothes, silver, linens. No furniture, but photographs. We stayed about a year, at which time we were brought into the ghetto." It was March 1941, and Roman Ferber's childhood was over. "For me, for all practical purposes, the realization came that things were changing. We had to be cautious in terms of going out, because we were Jews."

The Ferbers shared small ghetto quarters with another family. "Generally, the sanitation depended on the people and how clean they kept the place. But there had been no inside bathrooms in Borek Falenski, so I was accustomed to outhouses."

Moniek Ferber was an operator in the ghetto, a skillful manipulator of the underground economy. For a short time, the sewers provided his conduit to the Kraków outside the ghetto walls. But the Germans caught on quickly, and those who emerged died in a shower of bullets. After that, Jews hid in the reeking tunnels. "The Germans would not go in there because it was a common sewer for Kraków. There were rats all over the place, and they were afraid to get contaminated."

Certainly, the Jews feared illness, too, but not enough to forsake the sewers as a refuge. "A human body is stronger than steel," says Roman Ferber, who works out at the gym five days a week, nearly two hours a day. "A human being has the ability to survive if he wants to." (His own week-long stay in a coronary unit in 1985 is a case in point. "I used to smoke three packs a day. You think you survive the Holocaust, you can survive anything. I smoked on my way to the hospital. But it changed my whole life.")

The Ferbers went to Płaszów on March 13, 1943, the day Amon Goeth liquidated the ghetto. Ferber says that his mother took two diamonds with her, drilled into her teeth. "I still have one, made into a ring, and one she swallowed. And I know I came through the concentration camp with an American one-hundred-dollar bill. We came with that bill to the United States. They always believed in America, so we had lots of dollars, gold, diamonds floating around. Many of us survived because of it." (That particular bill roved among Ferber family members. "It was on my mother and eventually it wound up on me. Many times I had it rolled up in plastic in my mouth. I had it rolled up in other places, too. I had it taped under my foot. They never looked at the bottom of your feet.")

Life for kids like Roman Ferber was bearable at Płaszów. "I think the reason they tolerated little kids is because they didn't know what to do with them at that moment—there were no facilities to get rid of them yet. They still didn't set off the kids from the adults, and I am not sure they knew how many kids were in the camp. They figured once they had them in one spot, they could do whatever they wanted to. I was too young to really understand what was happening. My mother was terrified, but my father was always downplaying things: 'God will take care of things.' "

One could debate God's role in the ultimate elimination of the Chilowicz family, but Amon Goeth's is indisputable. Few eyewitnesses remain alive, and most of them don't want to talk about it. But Thomas Keneally interviewed survivors in the early 1980s, and from these interviews describes the Chilowicz family assassination in *Schindler's List*:

> [*Amon Goeth*] *called Sowinski, an SS auxiliary . . . into his office for a conference. Sowinski was to approach Chilowicz and pretend to offer him an escape deal. Amon was sure that Chilowicz would be eager to negotiate.*

Sowinski went and did it well. He told Chilowicz he could get the whole clan out of the camp in one of the large fuel-burning trucks. You could sit half a dozen people in the wood furnace if you were running on gas. . . . Sowinski would of course need to deliver a note to friends on the outside, who would provide a vehicle. . . . Chilowicz was willing to pay in diamonds. But, said Chilowicz, as an earnest of their mutual trust, Sowinski must provide a weapon.

Amon Goeth gave Sowinski a .38-caliber pistol with the firing pin filed down (a condition unknown to Chilowicz). Sowinski briefed Chilowicz on the procedure: Load everyone up at the building-materials shop, head to the gate, exchange routine "formalities" with the guards there, then cruise on to freedom.

But that's not how it went. At the gate, Goeth and several henchmen stopped the vehicle.

> *They mimed surprise when they discovered the pitiable Chilowicz clan sardine-tight in the wood hole. As soon as Chilowicz had been dragged out, Amon "found" the illegal gun tucked into his boot. Chilowicz' pockets were laden with diamonds, bribes paid him by the desperate inmates of the camp.*

"That is fiction," says Roman Ferber, who goes to Poland almost every summer, researching his own book. "Those guys weren't that dumb. They buried all that stuff, and some of it was found after the war." What's not in contention is that Amon Goeth shot them all: Wilek Chilowicz and his wife, Marysia, Willie S.'s parents, Feiga and Chaim; and Moniek Ferber. He didn't get Roman, Leon, Malia, and Hanka Ferber because they were hiding.

Later that day, Płaszów's stunned and bewildered inhabitants paraded past the bodies. Even those who had despised the Chilowiczes had to wonder: If Amon Goeth could crush the mighty Chilowicz like a gnat, what hope was there for the ordinary prisoner? Signs on the corpses admonished: "THOSE WHO VIOLATE JUST LAWS CAN EXPECT A SIMILAR DEATH." The bodies were burned and tossed into a mass grave.

In the massacre's aftermath, Roman Ferber remembers "nothing but devastation. I remember my mother turning gray almost overnight. She lost a son, a brother, a sister-in-law, a sister, and a brother-in-law all in one day. She never recovered. She kept on fighting because there were still two kids around, and there was moral support from other members of the family. She survived Bergen-Belsen with my sister, and when my sister passed away from cancer in 1966, it was all downhill from that point. She became indifferent to life." Malia "Molly" Ferber Abramowitz died in New York in 1987.

Willie S.'s parents didn't die in the truck, but at the Madritsch uniform factory. "Willie's father worked as a supervisor of production making uniforms for the Germans, and Amon Goeth came in and asked him about something, and he shot him on the spot because he didn't like the answer. Willie's mother—who was my mother's sister—ran toward him, and he shot her. Willie happened to be there. He doesn't remember any of it. One of my cousins held him back, so that he wouldn't run toward his parents."

Roman Ferber calls that day "a turning point. Until then, things were reasonably well. Our spirits were that we will survive." Afterward, nothing seemed certain, except that Moniek had guaranteed his relatives spots on Schindler's list.

His memory served his family well. "My brother was a decent human being, and he must have done a lot of favors, and my father was second to none.

Everyone knew my entire family, and we did have the protection because there were other Ferbers there."

Roman believes that Moniek "was pulled into it by Chilowicz, because he was educated and easygoing. When you are in the position of power, when you say 'no' to somebody, you are no good. I learned that in government. In the process of this, I always tried to put especially my brother in perspective. I am totally convinced that he did no harm to anybody. Some people didn't think of him that way, because when they asked him to put them on Schindler's list, he didn't. If he had the ability, he would rather put his own family on than a stranger."

Long after the war, Roman Ferber turned for information to his aunt, Cyla Wiener, now eighty-four, who survived Płaszów but lost a toddler there. "She told me that this man [Chilowicz] saved many people, especially children. She started explaining how to me. She also explained some of the things that I don't care to discuss, that I was made aware of for the first time, some unsavory things on the part of our own Jewish population. She sort of refined the entire Schindler situation for me. It gave me a better understanding of my uncle, aunt, brother, and my own family."

He's also convinced that his brother cooperated with Płaszów's underground. "One reason my brother was killed was because he and Chilowicz knew what was coming. I know that my brother was involved in trying to get guns into the camp."

He's well aware of the other prisoners' conflicted feelings toward the "OD men": the Jewish police. "You could commit the atrocity or not commit the atrocity. For example, an OD had the ability to beat the hell out of you, but it was *how* he beat you. He might have been compelled to do it by somebody, and *how* he beat you was the difference between him being a good guy or a bad guy. Or, he [might] beat you to show [the Germans] that he is beating you; otherwise, you would have been shot by Goeth. Not too many people can balance this. There is a fine point between good and evil."

That point sharpened when the *Schindlerjuden* left Płaszów. "We went to Gröss-Rosen in cattle cars, then we walked about four kilometers to a town, under heavy guard. All the Germans were looking out the windows. After the war, the residents denied they were aware of a camp at Gröss-Rosen. It was one of the first camps the Nazis created for German murderers and political prisoners. These guys were well fed, big, devastating. They were killing people on the soccer field in the camp. They would push the people they didn't like and chase them with clubs. These murderers, the German *Kapos,* they were the worst."

From there, the men went to Brinnlitz. "I remember pulling into Brinnlitz and I remember Schindler, but . . . it was an anticlimax to me." Not long after they arrived, while Schindler happened to be away from the factory, the youngest boys and their fathers were rounded up and sent to Auschwitz. The group included Roman and Leon Ferber, Ryszard and Dolek Horowitz, Alexander and Henry Rosner, Willie S., and another boy . . . who was actually a girl.

"I think we found out she was a girl on the train. We were put on a passenger train, with one bodyguard with a rifle, in a private compartment. He was a decent guy—*Wehrmacht,* not SS. They could have taken us to the side and shot us, but that's the German mentality. We were sent to Auschwitz, stayed overnight, then marched to Birkenau. That is where I inherited this number: B14435.

"They came in and shaved us, gave us some kind of clothing, tattooed us, and we were screaming, because they used a sort of Rapidograph-type art pen. I remember my hand was infected for three weeks and when we cried, we were told by the workers that we just should consider ourselves very lucky because we have the numbers, and we had to live." Guards sent the girl to a gypsy barracks, and she died almost immediately, according to Roman Ferber.

Cold. Gray. Sodden. Birkenau was "absolutely a lot worse than Płaszów," he says. "This was a huge place with different barracks, all of them made out of bricks. There were no paved roads except for paved pools where they maintained water for fires: reservoirs. We were brought into barracks that were very dimly lit, with all kinds of hungry-looking people supervised by a *Kapo.* I was in a barracks with Greek prisoners of war." Willie S. shared his bunk.

"The burning of the dead. That smell I can never forget. Did you ever smell chicken feathers burning?"

As the Allies rumbled inexorably toward them, the Germans used the Auschwitz and Birkenau prisoners as cover. Roman recalls being driven from the barracks into the frigid night, to stand, like a scarecrow in a cornfield, against the bombers.

He soon figured out that in addition to maintaining the will to endure, a prisoner needed luck. "Yes, indeed, to be at the right place at the right time was very important. Those that survived with Schindler were protected by Schindler. He was there, and nobody touched them. But for us who were thrown into a different set of circumstances, I think we survived because we had the moxie to survive. When I heard the Germans were coming *here*, I was already *there*. You developed a sense."

In the waning months of 1944, as the Russians advanced, the Germans decided to clear out of Auschwitz and Birkenau. Everyone was assembled for what turned out to be a death march to Germany. "I was standing with my father, and I said, 'I am not going anyplace.' I grabbed Willie and snuck out to a closed barracks. We were on one side and the Germans were evacuating the other side. I didn't think I would make it if I left. It turns out I was probably wrong, because a friend of mine made it."

That friend, Joseph Klausner, told Roman Ferber what happened to his father. On the last day of the war, in a final, homicidal frenzy, German soldiers injected many of the death-march survivors with gasoline. Leon Ferber was among them.

In the meantime, Roman and Willie were dodging the camp's remaining guards, pillaging abandoned barracks, and hiding out in the electrical station between the two camps. Others have reported cannibalism among the camp's starving slaves in those last days. Ferber says he didn't see it, "but I do remember people just wandering about and dropping dead. I don't think it made an impact; I just looked out for myself and Willie. I had seen people like this throughout [my time at] Auschwitz, not only [on] the last days, and I just didn't think about it happening to me."

The Soviets liberated Auschwitz and Birkenau on January 27, 1945. "I saw the guy come in behind the tank, an officer on skis, one guy, and I touched the tank and the machine gun. That moment, I took Willie, and we started walking to Kraków. Many of the people that remained in Auschwitz died in

Auschwitz after the war. They opened up [food] magazines and ate themselves to death."

They hooked up with a Pole headed from Auschwitz to Kraków, who had a bicycle. "We are talking about maybe fifty kilometers. It took us a week. It was a terrible winter. Winter in that part of Poland ends about May fifteenth. The rivers were still frozen in April. I've made the trip by car in forty-five minutes."

Roman and Willie were among the first Jews returning to Kraków. They were, essentially, on their own. "Food was supplied through the United Nations Relief and Rehabilitation Administration, and [distributed] at a place called Dluga Street. We would get our food and stay overnight. All day long, I didn't hang around and reminisce with the others and wait for people to come; I just did my own thing."

He didn't know it at the time, but his mother and sister were at Bergen-Belsen. He figures someone took them off Schindler's list after the Chilowicz massacre. "My sister came to Poland with a friend, from [the Displaced Persons camp at] Linz. They took us out of Poland through Prague. We joined an American convoy, then from Germany took the train to Linz." He left Willie there with his sister, then tagged along with a British convoy to Belsen. Roman and his mother were reunited there in the late summer of 1945.

But before he saw her again, he spent about two months recuperating at Rabka, which had been a luxurious resort town before the war. Jewish relief agencies sent "maybe forty or fifty kids. They fed us very well, and we had a doctor on the premises. I had an enlarged heart. We used to play soccer. It was a nice environment, and we sort of continued with our childhood, to some extent.

Roman Ferber in a G.I. cap at the Bergen-Belsen displaced persons camp, 1946.

"But we didn't think about playing with toys; you thought about playing with women, even at that early age, because you were sort of open to all of this throughout the time [in camp]. All of a sudden, we were thrown into an environment with girls. There were no shrinks. There were people who were teachers, who went with us. This was not normal life either . . . eight, twelve, fourteen kids sleeping in one room, girls and boys together with adults. The normal times really returned when we were thrown into an environment with children where there was proper care for us, or when we joined with the surviving members of our family," some of whom knew, even in Brinnlitz, that Roman was alive.

"They heard me on the radio. There was a trial going on. I discovered one of the Auschwitz camp guards who tried to conceal the fact that he was a camp guard. In the [Kraków] Jewish community, he came for help. He maintained he was Jewish. Somebody saw him, and then they called me over, and I said, 'Yeah, I remember that guard.'

"We were cleaning up [garbage] at that job with the wagons, but we were cleaning up the remains of the crematory, too. We took the shoes away, and he was one of the guards over us. The trial was carried on radio and that was how my family found out that I was alive."

Bergen-Belsen had been a death camp. The Allies converted it into a Displaced Persons camp. Relief agencies "created yeshivas and trade schools there. I got my basic education at Bergen-Belsen," and a certificate of graduation from auto-mechanic school.

Roman and his mother stayed in the camp until 1949. "I traveled throughout Germany. I visited family and was basically on my own. My life sort of moved in different directions [from my mother's and sister's], only that we were put together when she decided we would come to the United States, and I had no option of doing anything else, since I was not of age."

Roman and his mother arrived in New York still clutching the American one-hundred-dollar bill that they'd safeguarded throughout the war. "We didn't do very well when we came to the United States. My mother was undergoing menopause, and she was quite sick. We wound up in Elizabeth, New Jersey, living in one room above a garage in [the home of the] very wealthy man who had sponsored us. She was working as a domestic, taking care of old people. This was a woman who was educated and dignified, working as a domestic."

Roman Ferber says that if his mother was alive, she would say, " 'I didn't raise him; he raised himself.' I went to work at Levy Brothers. It was then the largest department store [in Elizabeth], and I remember getting there for the Christmas season and I was wrapping packages. I was thrilled. I was putting in eighty hours a week of work, and had a few dollars in my pocket. When the season was over, I became a porter, then I became a shipping clerk and a receiving clerk.

"We tried to better ourselves. You listen to some of these people in some of these detention camps and how they are just staying there and sticking their hand out to get things—we didn't do that. Because we were in this tough time, I think it gave us an edge. You probably realize that many of [the survivors] did much better than the average person in the United States because we worked harder. We were accustomed to it."

In the meantime, Malia Ferber got married. "In 1951, we moved from Elizabeth to the Bronx. He was a survivor from Lodz . . . an intelligent man, educated, but not a very palatable man. I didn't get into it with him until I lived with them on Walton Avenue [in the Bronx] after they got married. I was going to Hunter College. He charged me fifty dollars per month for sleeping on the couch in their apartment. I saw his treatment toward my mother, who was very emotional, and I didn't like it."

Years later, after Malia Ferber entered a nursing home, an ugly tussle developed between her son and her husband over her assets: bank accounts and the co-op apartment in Queens that Roman had bought for her. He says the man got it all when she died in 1987, and then "took off to Israel and lived with some woman. I knew exactly where he was, but I just decided to hell with it. I paid all the expenses for my mother's funeral." He believes that the man, whose name was Abromowitz, has since died.

By then, Roman Ferber, married and a father of three, was a long-time fixture at City Hall. He'd had his share of postwar adventure, and had been captain of the Hunter College soccer team and president of its political science club. He earned his bachelor's degree from Hunter in 1958, followed by a master's and a doctorate from New York University. He says his thesis on the management of the New York City waterfront sold ten thousand copies.

He was also a Korean War–era veteran of the U.S. Army, in which he never got beyond the rank of private. "I was drafted and spent the war first at Camp Kilmer, New Jersey, then Aberdeen, Maryland, in ordnance. Then the army decided to send me to Atlanta to become a welder. At that point I got sick. I think it was psychological. I developed a severe case of dermatitis. We were graduating, and two days before the group was shipped to Seattle to go to Korea, I was put on a stretcher and shipped to Walter Reed Hospital. I was in Walter Reed when Eisenhower was being operated on.

"They didn't know what to do with me, and they finally brought in a group of consulting professors from all over. They tried all kinds of treatment. Nothing worked. Then a new doctor took over the dermatology department—a Jewish captain. He sat down with me and said he would like to try the new methods. He said, 'The first thing I want you to do is go home for four weeks and relax.' I was ninety percent better. While I was there, I won the U.S. table-tennis championship. They assigned me to Fort Totten in New York, and from there I started taking college courses. I was fortunate enough to get sick, because most of the people I trained with died in Korea."

After the army, Roman Ferber "tried to make up for lost time. I traveled all over the world. I was in Cuba for the revolution—four, five weeks in Havana just as Castro came in." He was also "looking for love," and he found it in the person of Maxine Singer from the Bronx, eight years his junior. A friend introduced them. "He said, 'I want you to meet Max.' I thought it was another guy."

"I was totally unimpressed," says Maxine, "but he drove us home, and I noticed there was something interesting about him. In his face, I saw there was something very deep. It was just something about him that was magnetic, and not like anyone I had ever met."

She sensed "kind of a sadness, and kind of closed doors. I thought, 'We're going to bring this person out of his shell and make him happy.' How long did it take? About twenty-five years. He wasn't easy, and he's still not easy."

He doesn't deny it. "I think trust comes with getting love. When people care for you, you develop a certain amount of trust, but that did not happen to the older generation [of survivors], unfortunately. I noticed when my mother remarried that it didn't happen with her. I have learned to accept certain things by being accepted."

Roman and Maxine married in 1960. They live in Monsey, New York, the Rockland County suburb largely populated by Hasidim ("We're on the other side of the tracks," says Roman). They share their split-level ranch house, on a sloping, thickly wooded lot, with a sofa-size Akita named Mikey, a cat named Ziggy, and their son Lenny, a personal trainer with a lair in the basement. Another son, Andy, who is also a personal trainer, lives in Boca Raton, Florida. Their daughter, Julie, a graphic artist, recently graduated from New York's Oswego University.

Maxine Ferber is a handsome woman in her early 50s with a crown of thick, dark curls, all tautness and sinews from relentless exercise. She manages a nail salon. "My mother was petrified around him," she says of her husband. "She didn't know how to act around him. He was so in charge in every situation. Aggressive. Strong-willed. He told me right away where he was from and what the situation was. He never had a problem discussing it, which I found very unusual because most survivors do. But it was always hard to break through that shield. He's not loose or spontaneous."

While he insists he does not "live the Holocaust," Roman Ferber is convinced that everyone who survived it still pays an emotional price for it, and always will.

"I am stuck with it, obviously. I've been branded. There is no way in the world you can forget. There is no way to describe visually, on film or anything else, what we went through, each one of us in a different way. When you see little babies being taken and thrown into hot lime, does that leave you with something for the rest of your life? Of course! I have forgiven, but I cannot forget.

"What it does is, out of nowhere, you get dreams, and when you get up in the morning and you look at your hands, it [the tattoo] is there. And I *want* it to be there. I could have it removed very easily today, but there is no reason for it.

[Camp life] made me impatient. I have no patience and no tolerance for the waste of food, even today. That is the one thing that stuck with me."

On the positive side, he says that in comparison, "everything that followed was relatively easy in life." But he found no reason to continue studying toward the rabbinate, as he'd planned before the war. "I just had to stop, look, and listen. Why were men like my father killed on the last day of the war? And why did some of the scum survive? There is no answer."

Maxine and Roman Ferber with their dog, Mikey. Monsey, New York, 1994.

Yet Roman Ferber does not hate. "I really believe that my success in adjusting to a normal life is that I said to myself a long time ago that you cannot hate. Hate destroys people. I have seen it with Holocaust survivors: they hate Germany and hate this and that. People say to me, 'Roman, I don't understand how you can go to Germany, and how you speak German. You still remember the language so well and now some of your friends are German.' I say to them that you can't blame the children for the sins of the fathers. Not every single German was a bad German. Not every single Jew hates the Arabs and not every single Arab hates the Jews. You must in some way give the people the benefit of the doubt unless it is proven differently.

"I think the key thing was I was able to turn over a new leaf. I said to myself, 'This is one phase of my life, and obviously it wasn't a very good one.' Through work, through education, and through looking at my mother—let her rest in peace—and the other generations, they have been so terribly involved in living the Holocaust day in and day out. I said to myself a long time ago, that is the surest way of going the wrong way. I have to live for today and for the future. I think all of the survivors live more for the day than they live for the future. We care about the future of our children, but all of us are more fatalistic. . . . I let my kids loose completely to do whatever they want. They have to live their own lives."

In any case, it's doubtful they'd try to follow in his professional footsteps: New York City Office of Business Development, Director of Manufacturing and Wholesaling (1984–1990); Office for Economic Development, Director of Business Development (1981–1984); Executive Director, Industrial and Commercial Incentive Board (1977–1981); Director of Financial Services (1975–1979). And that's just half of his work history, which dates back to 1963. Many of these agencies' officials, and the private-sector tycoons with whom they dealt, ended up entangled in scandals and behind bars. Prisoner B14435 caught the attention of the *New York Times* on occasion, but never that of a grand jury. And, at sixty-one, he's had just about enough.

"I started working at six," says Roman Ferber. "I want to retire. Pretty soon."

Murray Pantirer

From the way things have gone since 1949, you would think someone handed Murray Pantirer the blueprint to the American Dream. Despite an accent as thick as *cholent* and formal schooling aborted when he was fourteen, Murray Pantirer worked hard, prayed hard, played by the rules, and made a fortune. He raised and educated three children, who have stayed close to home and each other, geographically and emotionally. His nine grandchildren are more siblings than cousins. At sixty-nine, with his son and two sons-in-law running much of his business, he and his wife, Lucy, can escape the Northeast's nasty winters at their *pied-à-terre* in a fancy Miami Beach high-rise. He travels several times a year to Israel.

Murray Pantirer also has enjoyed the immeasurable satisfaction of witnessing Hollywood transform his private "angel," Oskar Schindler, into a public legend. No wonder he'll proclaim, "God bless America!" at the slightest provocation.

Murray is a little man, not much more than five feet tall, with an impish wit and a towering reputation among the *Schindlerjuden*. The New Jersey developer and philanthropist—with his childhood friend and business partner, Abraham Zuckerman, and his late uncle, Isaac Levenstein—helped support Oskar Schindler. He continues to help provide for the widow Emilie Schindler.

He was a founding member of the United States Holocaust Memorial Museum, and serves on the Holocaust Memorial Council (appointed by Ronald Reagan, then reappointed by George Bush until 1998). Commendations and tributes cover an entire wall of his den. He is president of the Keane College Holocaust Resource Center in New Jersey and serves on so many boards that it's impossible to list them all. But the survivors respect his humility and integrity as much as his generosity. He is wise, patient, and sensitive, a natural-born philosopher.

Murray Pantirer was a minor character in the Schindler saga—"a *schlepper* like I was," says another *Schindlerjude.* "He had no particular reason to be so good to Schindler." Yet in the world according to Murray, "no particular reason" is, perhaps, the best reason of all to do what's right. "He saved my life," he says, wondering why anyone might need a more complex explanation. "He was like an angel sent from heaven."

"I feel strongly that a Jewish person—or any person—cannot stay neutral," he says over a Passover-week lunch of matzoh and gefilte fish at the Hillside, New Jersey, home he built for his family. "Either you're in a position to help and you must, or you're in a position to need help and you ask for it. I strongly believe we are all God's children, and He created the poor man to test that the rich man deserves to have what he gets."

Mejzesz Puntierer—as he appears on Schindler's list, number 205—never saw his "angel" until August 1944. A transport was leaving Płaszów that day. The Germans had ordered Schindler to pare his workforce, and hundreds of Jews who'd worked at Emalia were sweltering and moaning inside locked cattle cars.

"Schindler came to see how his people were doing," recalls Murray, who worked in the Płaszów kitchen. "I saw him. And I saw his convertible full of cigarettes and whiskey and chocolate"—unconcealed bribes for Amon Goeth.

"He was dressed so elegantly, in a white suit. He got permission from Goeth, and he ordered some of us boys to stretch a hose to the cars and soak them with water. He himself was yelling, *'Mach schnell!'* You see it in the movie, with the hoses, except that we had garden hoses. To me it was unbelievable: a Nazi with the [party lapel] pin, but no gun or uniform. I said, 'Who is that man?' Later at Brinnlitz, I had to pinch myself that I am on his list." Fifty years later, he still has no idea how he got there.

Bella Pantirer, age 39.　　　　　　　*Lejzer Pantirer, age 40.*

Bella Levenstein Puntierer had a baby every other year between 1923 and 1935. Mejzesz, born in June 1925, followed Hershel as the second of seven. In 1937, after bringing Josef, Mordechai, Esther, Yisroel David, and Rachel into the world, she told her husband, Lejzer, that God didn't want her to have any more. She was thirty-six.

The family lived at 16 Josefa Street in Kazimierz, the old Jewish quarter. Lezur kept a small milk-and-egg store in the same building. His sons delivered orders to the better customers—toting heavy milk cans door to door. Others stopped by and bought what they needed. The family was "very religious," according to Murray, followers of the Belzer Rebbe. "My father had a beard, and all the boys had *payess* [side curls]."

Here's how he remembers life before the war: "I would get up before the sun, help my father in the store, go upstairs to the apartment, pray, have something to eat, and walk to *cheder*. You learned Hebrew and Talmud, then you went home at noon for the major meal. The family ate together, and no one got up till my father had his glass of tea."

Then it was back to school for an afternoon of secular classes, then more religious education. On the way, the boys stopped to buy an afternoon snack. "If you had five cents, you bought a roll and cheese. If you had ten cents, a roll and a piece of herring." If a girl stood behind the counter, he says, the boys had to order facing backward, so as not to gaze upon her with desire. "That's how fanatic I was."

After school, until nine o'clock, they went to the "prayer house," first to pray, then to study in a place with decent light. "It was impossible at home." Then it was off to bed. "We didn't have a radio. For us, that would be like the Hasidim in Borough Park [Brooklyn] having a television."

The coal-heated apartment had three rooms, with benches that pulled out and doubled as beds. The kids slept head to foot. "We didn't fight about turf because we didn't have any," says Murray. For recreation, they played dominoes and chess, and made soccer balls from rolled-up rags. Maurice Markheim, another *Schindlerjude*, remembers how often boys beat up little Murray "for dribbling too much."

He remembers clearly his bar mitzvah, celebrated a year before the war began. "In the morning, they called me to the Torah. I put on tefillin. We had sponge cake, vodka, and a bar mitzvah cigarette for the older guests. That was the custom in Poland in those days."

German soldiers occupied Kraków within a week after the September 1, 1939, invasion. "After that, we did not go into public places," Murray remembers. "I saw first the Germans on Rosh Hashanah pulling out Jews from the worship places, and with scissors or just ripping, cutting off the beards and *payess*. These were not SS, just regular *Wehrmacht*. I didn't like my *payess* anyway, so I cut them off at the beginning of the war. But my father kept his beard."

Between afternoon and evening services at *shul*, "the young people, twenty to forty, would always have arguments with the elderly that we had to do something. The elderly were saying, 'What are you talking about? In 1914, the Germans came in and were much better than the Russians.' But the argument was coming back: 'What about *Mein Kampf*? What about *Kristallnacht*?' The older ones would say, 'They chased out the Polish Jews because they took their jobs away. Hitler is crazy; the German people will never allow him to do that here.' The argument was going back and forth.

"The elderly always won: 'We have a gracious God, and God will help us.' But my father was worried that he had a family of seven and not much money and no place to go—no relatives in America, and there was no state of Israel then, and nobody wanted us."

Methodically, relentlessly, the Germans plodded from house to house, collecting the gold, the silver, the furs, and the jewelry. "I even remember some saying they got a little piece of paper from the Germans, like a receipt," Murray recalls. "In many cases, they were ripping and throwing out the *tallis* from

Murray Pantirer, age 15.

the windows. They put tables on the street, and right there they sent off to their families what they took from us.

"Then I said they were a bunch of robbers. Little did I know they would rob us of our lives."

Still, Lejzer managed to do business from the family apartment. "Me and my brother would go to Podgórze [on the other side of the Vistula from Kazimierz], meet farmers, and get eggs and live chickens, maybe some bread or wheat. And we gave them back material—textiles or shoes. We had blond hair, blue eyes and spoke Polish, so we got away with it."

He got caught once without his armband in February 1941. "They took me to the Gestapo, and I was very fortunate. They put me on a train taking people from Kraków to Biała Podlaska, in the east, near the new border. My family didn't know what happened. I wrote a letter that I was going to take the train and come back. They just dropped us. I stayed by some Jewish people. We were building an airfield for the Germans. But my father wrote back: 'Don't come. We have orders to pack.' "

By then it was March. The Germans had designated a sixteen-block area of Podgórze the new Jewish ghetto. Anyone permitted to live there needed a *Kennkarte,* a pass. "Mostly young people with trades got them," says Murray, "but not large families. We had to leave."

The family relocated to a town in eastern Poland called Międzyrec, not far from Biała Podlaska. On June 22, the Germans invaded the Soviet Union, occupying eastern Poland. Murray escaped rather than end up in a closed camp. For a brief time, the family was together, then Murray and Hershel headed west, bound for Kraków. Each stopped short of the city, but in different places. Lejzer went after them. In the meantime, Bella "put on peasant clothes and took all the children by train to Kraków, but she could not make it into the ghetto, so she went to the suburbs to a friend, and the friend rented us a single room by a farmer."

The family reunited in the fall of 1941: nine people in one room. "These were very rough times," Murray remembers. "My mother was cooking for seven children, but there was no food. We used to say, 'Ma, why don't you eat?' She said she wasn't hungry."

At the end of the year, the Germans issued bread ration cards, "but to get that, the order came out that my father had to go to work in a camp called Julag. To save our father, Hershel went. He was eighteen. Then, in 1942, February or March, again they came to take my father. This time, I volunteered to go. We made a deal with the *Judenrat.*"

Murray worked in a brick factory until September, "then we went to Płaszów. A few weeks later, Hershel came. Then at the end of forty-two, they gathered all the Jews from the outskirts [of Kraków] and shipped them to Treblinka. On November eighteenth, they got my father, my mother, and five children. Three escaped: Chaim, Mordechai, and Esther. They took the rest to Miechów."

At Miechów, soldiers directed the men to one line, the women and children to another. But Lejzer Puntierer defied them, according to his son. "He wouldn't leave my mother. The men went to Płaszów, the women and children were killed on the spot: my father holding one child, my mother holding the other. People who knew them came to Płaszów and told me the story. My father was like a hero to not give in to the Germans.

"These men felt so guilty. The irony of the story is: We the innocent felt guilty, and the murderers felt proud of it."

When Murray and Hershel heard about it, they "went to pieces. We were never the same again." They had tried hard to spare him, and could have easily escaped, but they said they would go after our families. We were no match for them."

The three escaped siblings remained at large in the ghetto through the final liquidation on March 13, 1943. "They had no papers, so they hid," Murray explains. And they almost made it. "A week later, they were hungry, and it was quiet, so they went out and one brother escaped. The other, with my sister, was coming down the wall on the free side, and a Polish policeman shot them. They brought the bodies to Płaszów."

Amon Goeth had taken over the command of Płaszów from *Lagercommandant* Müller in February. Müller, says Murray Pantirer, "was not so bad. We built barracks. There was no shooting. No hanging. Goeth came on a Friday morning, and the first thing he did was take everyone on the *Appellplatz* and shoot Katz the OD man, and Goldberg [another OD]. He took the hat full of blood, and put it on one of our friends, that he should be the successor. He said to him, 'You will be in command now.' It put a real scare in me."

Amon Goeth "couldn't have breakfast or lunch without seeing Jewish blood," says Murray Pantirer. "Every day, he would shoot somebody else at random, hunting like an animal in the jungle. He wore three hats: an officer's hat; a plain cap, like a soldier. When he put on his Tyrolean hat, we were in terrible danger. Regardless where I was working, I would always run to the latrine, because he never came in. He would come to the barracks and wouldn't leave till he shot a few people."

Schindler's List reenacts Goeth ordering the summary execution of an engineer named Diana Reiter, who argues that a barracks needs to be razed and rebuilt. Murray was nearby when it happened. "Two coworkers put her on a wheelbarrow and took her up to the Chujowa Górka," the hill that became a mass grave.

He had one more harrowing experience with Goeth. "It was August or September 1943. We were fifty boys, building a barracks. Goeth wanted to make a garden. They put a few Ukrainians and SS on a truck, and took me up there but did not take my brother. I threw my coat down to my uncle [Levenstein]. I said, 'You might as well have it.' I thought they were going to kill us all."

They almost did. "After the day's work, a boy escaped. They counted us. Goeth came on his white horse with his dog: 'Where is the fiftieth?' We acted like we didn't know. He called a few SS and shot every second guy. It took a tremendous toll on me."

Murray decided to try for a job in the camp kitchen, so even after a long day's labor, he'd show up there to make himself useful chopping wood and washing pots. "Mr. Meyer, a German Jew, was in charge. He liked me. He promised, 'If they enlarge the kitchen, I will give you a kettle.' And at the end of 1943, I started working in the kitchen. My brother [Hershel] was working another job. We saw each other at night."

After May 1944, they never saw each other again.

"We were all on the *Appellplatz*," Murray recalls. "It was a Sunday—Mother's Day, or a week before. Mengele came. He wrote the names of all the children. I was next to my brother, and they took his name. The following Sunday, the trucks came in, playing German music, and took them all to Auschwitz, [including] my brother, even though he was twenty-one, and my two cousins. We knew they were going there and they gassed them."

Murray's remaining brother, Mordechai, wasn't caught until October 1944, in Kraków. "With the boys, they pulled the pants down and saw that you were circumcised."

The kitchen job occasioned a chance reunion between Murray and one of his oldest friends: Abe Zuckerman. In his book *A Voice in the Chorus*, Zuckerman writes that he wandered into the Płaszów kitchen one day and, to his surprise, found "Moniek" Puntierer working there.

Zuckerman worked for Oskar Schindler at Emalia but didn't make it to Brinnlitz. In fact, he was among the crazed wretched cooking in the boxcars that Murray helped hose down in August 1944. (It seems like an act of mercy, but some who witnessed it said the water turned to steam in the cars, simmering those who'd been baking inside.)

Zuckerman writes that the transport, bound for Mauthausen, sat sidetracked in the throbbing summer sun for up to three days. The men, packed in so tightly that they couldn't sit, weren't fed. Many went out of their minds. "People began to suffocate," Zuckerman writes. "A lot of them became dehydrated, and a lot of them died of thirst and hunger. . . . A lot of people even drank their own urine. . . . The stench was unbearable. It was impossible to move the corpses."

Murray's uncle, Sam Levenstein, went with Zuckerman. Three months later, Murray and another uncle, Isaac Levenstein, were on their way to Brinnlitz. "But all of us," says Murray, "Abe, myself, and my uncles, owe our survival to Oskar Schindler. The strength they had left from Emalia sustained them in Mauthausen."

For the next seven months, Murray did odd jobs at Brinnlitz. He shined the German officers' boots until the women came from Auschwitz and claimed the task. The list calls him a metalworker, a craft of which he knew nothing.

Murray says that five days after the camp's May 9 liberation, he was back in Kraków. "I went to the apartment, and still everything was standing the way we left it. There was a woman with a few children there. I told her I was not looking for anything, just to leave a message that I survived and will be registered at the Jewish federation. If by any miracle one of my brothers survived, he will know I did."

The woman offered the bedraggled refugee "a glass tea," and as he enjoyed it, sent her son for the police. She wanted to make sure he didn't try to claim anything that she now "owned."

"I lost the feeling for my own apartment and the people of Poland at that moment. I was thinking I would be treated like a hero. The Czechs were feeding us like part of their own family, and if I had to take a train, they gave me a whole bench to lie down. They gave us a driver and a horse and wagon if the bridges were out of commission. When we came to Poland, where we spoke the language, always they wanted something from us."

Barry Tiger, Murray Pantirer, and Abe Zuckerman (left to right) at the Displaced Persons Camp, 1945.

He stayed a few weeks, "saw that nobody survived," and traveled back through Czechoslovakia to Linz, Austria. At Graz, he inquired about going to Palestine. "The British authorities looked at me like I was crazy. To go to Palestine, you needed a visa and money and someone to send for you and a trade. So I went back to Linz, and said, 'I'm going to America.'

"But the American representative told me the quota was very small for Polish citizens. To put more salt to the wound, they told me if you had a father or mother or close relative, you could come quicker, and I realized in this war, I became an orphan twice: once in November 1942, when they killed my father and mother, and once in May 1945. The Poles didn't want me. The British wouldn't let me go on to Palestine. The Americans had a short quota.

"I was a boy left without a country, and that's like a child without a father and mother."

But he wasn't alone for long. Who should he run into at Bindermichel, the huge Displaced Persons camp near Linz? Abe Zuckerman. Another refugee, Berl Teiger, became a good friend—he's now Barry Tiger, and he works for Murray and Abe—and he met Luška Lorber, the woman he would marry on January 5, 1947. A friend of Rena Ferber Finder, Luška lived nearby with her parents, who also had planned to go to Palestine, but were held back by the British.

Like many survivors, Murray Pantirer still chafes at the policies that trapped thousands of Holocaust survivors in Europe. "Being five years with the Germans and going through hell, that I had to sit another three and a half in a DP camp, with no place to go? The irony is that the Ukrainians and White Russians and some peoples who collaborated with the Germans could go to Canada and America and South America. When doors were opened up, they claimed [they were] anticommunist. The Cold War was a factor. They were older and had trades. But we Jews had to stay."

Toward the end of 1948, President Harry Truman bumped up the quota by two hundred thousand. This included the expectant parents, Murray and Luška, who is now called Lucy or Louise. They arrived in Boston on January 17, 1949, aboard the SS *Marine Flasher.* "I remember in Boston, by the pier, going to a tavern and ordering a beer," he says. "Everybody heard my English, and I told them I got off the ship, and somebody paid for my beer." Then they took a train to New York.

The Pantirers got a furnished room in the Bronx. His first American job, in a garment factory, netted Murray fifteen dollars a week. Then he got laid off. Soon after, he and Lucy went to dinner at the home of people she'd known in Europe. "Quite a few people, I asked them to find me a job," Murray remembers. "They all went to their pockets and tried to give me money. I started to cry. I told them, 'I don't need money; what I need is a job.'

"One was a union delegate [in the] garment center. He sent me to a dressmaker. He said, 'I understand your wife is expecting any day. This job pays twenty-five dollars, and that's not for you.' I felt I needed a job, so I told him, 'I'm not asking how much you pay me; just let me work a week, then you'll see.' "

He never spent an idle moment. Waiting for a rack of dresses, he'd grab a broom and sweep the floor. "We worked eight to four-thirty. I stayed till six." At the end of the week, he pocketed fifty dollars. "Then they said, if I wanted to come Saturday, they worked eight to two, so that was another ten dollars, and the boss ordered lunch."

Son Larry—named for his lost grandfathers, Lejzer Puntierer and Leib Lorber—entered the world that July. His dad "was very proud that another

Pantirer was born." A month later, Lucy's mother and sister arrived. They all lived together in a single room for several months.

In 1950, Murray Pantirer made a career switch. "I decided to be a builder. I had asked the American soldiers in Linz what they needed most when they got home. They said housing. So I said I was going to build housing for them in appreciation. In the meantime, profit came along. So who's not going to make a profit?" he says with a twinkle.

Murray Pantirer, Abraham Zuckerman, and the Levenstein uncles, Sam and Isaac, formed the Lepaz Corporation. They started small, but didn't stay that way for long.

"We bought a lot on Tillman Street in Hillside, New Jersey. The lot was fifty by one hundred. We built one house for a GI and sold it for twelve thousand dollars, no down payment. Most of the carpentry we did ourselves. We did not take out a single penny for wages. My uncle Sam worked in a clothing factory, and he was single. He netted forty-six dollars. I netted fifty-four dollars [at another factory]. We had a total of one hundred dollars for the four families."

Isaac and Abe began the day on the construction site. Sam and Murray joined them after they left their respective garment-factory jobs. "We took a train and a bus to Hillside, for more than an hour, and worked till dark. Then we went home [to Washington Heights], and had no strength to eat dinner. I would fall asleep. My wife would wake me up, but instead of eating, I would take a shower and go to bed, then get up at six and do it all over again."

They sold one house then bought two more lots, then twenty, and Murray quit his factory job. "In 1952, we bought forty-four lots in South Plainfield. I got up at five in the morning. I didn't own a car yet. I was on the site at seven, and worked till dark."

Murray Pantirer says he worked harder in the building business than he did in the concentration camp. "The moral is that when you work for yourself, you don't care if you're hungry or cold, but if somebody is holding a gun over your head, and you don't get nothing out of it, you don't perform."

In South Plainfield, Murray and his partners needed to build new streets through their subdivisions. "We decided to name one Schindler Drive. We told the town planning board, and they had to ask permission from the council and mayor. Normally, they named the roads after veterans and town fathers. When we explained the situation, we were never refused.

"Right now, in almost twenty towns in New Jersey and Pennsylvania, we have Schindler Drives. Our children in business with us know that whenever they build in a new town, they must name at least one street after Schindler."

In addition to subdivisions and garden apartments, the group built luxury homes on the estate in Livingston of the father of former New Jersey Governor Thomas Kean. Murray Pantirer built his current Hillside home in 1965. By then, two daughters had followed son Larry (in 1951 and 1957). The husbands of Betty Pantirer Schwartz and Elisa Pantirer Pine, joined the building firm, now called L.P.Z. Management Corp.

Murray says he played it safe during building recessions. "Whenever I start making a few dollars, one-third goes for living, one-third saved, one-third for speculation. In America, they would say I didn't put all my eggs in one basket. There are tough times, but if you're not greedy, you can make it. Everybody should know how much they can lift."

Just as his construction business started modestly, so did Murray Pantirer's charitable giving. "In 1949, Passover, I was *davening* [praying] at Young Israel in the Bronx. They had an appeal for UJA [United Jewish Appeal], for people who came to Israel. They said for ten thousand dollars, they could build an apartment, and there were many ten-thousand-dollar givers, and five-thousand-dollar givers. I stood up and said, 'I give two dollars,' and the entire *shul* turned around and looked at me: 'Who is that idiot? Who is the big spender?'

"The rabbi had a talk with me, and told the congregation that I was working in a shop making twenty-five dollars a week, and my wife was expecting, and I paid ten dollars a week for a furnished room. He met me later, and he said he was using that story on many occasions for campaigns."

It may not have amounted to much in terms of revenue, but it carried powerful symbolism for Murray Pantirer. "I felt very strongly that it was time for me to give and not to take. Thank God I am in a position now to give much more. But one thing that stayed with me all the years I have worked in [the Jewish Federation of Central New Jersey] was how lucky I was that a delegate in the Federation did not say to me: 'Murray Pantirer, we really didn't know what was going on in the war years and we really couldn't help you when you were in the DP camp, but now that you came to America, make up a list of how you want to live the rest of your life, and we will take care of you.'

"Thank God you didn't offer, and I didn't ask. . . . I took life like a gambler in Las Vegas and Atlantic City. When you shoot dice and the numbers come in and you win a few hundred dollars, you play better with your own winnings."

He thinks that Holocaust survivors had several options when it was all over: "After you found out nobody survived from your immediate family, to say, 'I don't have the strength to continue.' That would be a mistake."

An even greater one was to lose faith: "Some married out of the faith, and in certain instances didn't circumcise their sons. They say, 'Why should I bring up another generation so another Hitler would come and kill them?' This is playing into the hands of the Nazis, and, right now, plenty of Nazis survive. They say, 'We tried our best to kill all the Jews, and if the war had taken six more months, we would have killed them all. But . . . we put such a scare in them, now they kill themselves [by assimilating].'

"When my son was born, I made up my mind to bring him up Jewish and not to ask questions. There is no question that after I pass away I will ask a question of God himself: 'Why?' I know for sure there was a Holocaust; I saw it with my own eyes, and I don't understand what we did to deserve such a fate. I was under the Nazis for six Yom Kippurs, and where were the angels in heaven to speak for us? But I couldn't ask questions when I was building up a family."

As hard as he worked, Murray Pantirer was determined to participate in his children's lives. "Every time they graduated from kindergarten, or had something special, I used to take my suit and better shoes and go to work early, so I could be at the school to take part with my children. I managed my life to separate my priorities. I talked to them: 'I can understand a mistake, but stupidity I will never go for.' And I always tried to reason with them, to talk things out; I never left things where there was room for misunderstanding.

"And I never looked to win every battle and, God forbid, lose the war."

One battle he knew he had to win, because it *would* mean losing the war, was intermarriage. "It's like a Holocaust in America, and the worst part of it is, they kill you with a kiss, with 'I love you. I cannot live without you,' and, unfortunately, too many American Jewish children don't know how to say, 'If you cannot live without me, don't live without my heritage.'

"The European Jews who came [to America] in the beginning of the [century] did a marvelous job of giving their kids education and building themselves up for a higher standard of living, but their biggest mistake was to throw away the heritage of Judaism. So I strive to give my kids a good, modern Orthodox upbringing. Then, if they are going to get married and want to join a Conservative or even Reform [congregation], they will know for what reason, but not out of ignorance.

"I'm not trying to be harsh on those who came before us. In the new country, they felt they had to be Americanized. They tore off the yoke. But for us, it was ripped away. When things are taken away, you are determined not to give in." He's enormously proud that his children all keep kosher homes.

"I taught my kids never to use the word 'hate,' and to start off the morning with a smile on their faces and to say, 'I'm alive.' Everything that happened the day before was over; there was nothing to be mad about. If they didn't get something they wanted, they should remember that hundreds of thousands had it much worse off than them."

In addition to caring for his family, Murray Pantirer cared for Oskar Schindler. "I saw him in 1945, when Zuckerman and I went to Munich. We met Oskar and took him to Linz. There was a party in the DP camp. We lost contact when he went to Argentina and we went to America. The [American Jewish Joint Distribution Committee] bought him a farm in Argentina, but in a short time, he left his wife and came back to Germany. He started a cement factory and failed. He was a personality who could not live a normal day's life."

Murray Pantirer and his partners began contributing to Schindler's support in 1967. "Every time a partner went to Israel, we gave him some money, and every time he came here, we gave money and bought him four or five suits. He was very pleased with that. On one occasion in Israel, I was there with my wife and he was there with a girlfriend, and I gave him some money. She said, 'Herr Pantirer, don't give him so much; he'll get himself another girlfriend!' "

In 1968, Pantirer met Schindler in Tel Aviv. "We went to Mount Scopus,

Oskar Schindler attending Murray and Lucy Pantirer's twenty-fifth wedding anniversary,
Short Hills, New Jersey, 1972. Murray is at far right.

and visited the Truman Library. There we got the idea that Truman signed the quota, and Schindler saved our lives, so we raised money and years later dedicated a room at the Truman Library to Oskar Schindler."

In 1972, two years before he died, Schindler attended Murray and Lucy Pantirer's twenty-fifth wedding anniversary: a lavish soiree at a Short Hills, New Jersey, catering hall. The guests, many of them survivors, hoisted Oskar above their shoulders and paraded him around like a hero. A photograph of the event shows a man exploding with pleasure.

Schindler was no longer alive when, for the second time, he could have rallied to the cause of the *Schindlerjuden*. In 1978, Northwestern University Professor Arthur Butz published a book called *The Hoax of the Twentieth Century*. In it, he claimed that no more than 250,000 Jews died under German occupation.

It was more than Murray Pantirer and thousands of others survivors could bear.

"I was thinking there was some decency left in human beings. I am still alive, but wounded all the way through from losing my parents and four brothers and two sisters. I was thinking that they would let me go to my rest place without questioning what I went through. So we always have to be vigilant, and when a dictator comes along and says he's going to make the country better, and starts picking on the Jews, you got to—as they say in America—nip it in the bud. Don't say he's crazy. Believe him, even if he only has ten people with him, because you never know what can happen."

Murray Pantirer says he came to America sad, but not bitter. "Yes, it's true, we had a heavy rock pressing on our

Schindler with Murray and Lucy Pantirer at the anniversary party.

hearts, and that could never be removed unless you rip the heart out with it. When we make a *bris* [ritual circumcision], or a wedding, we are without a family—grandparents, uncles, aunts." He prays for them all, not just at the times prescribed by the ritual calendar, but on November 19, the day in 1942 his parents died at Miechów. "I keep it for the entire family," he says. "It's the least I can do."

Would it have honored his family if he'd taken revenge when revenge was possible? Murray Pantirer doesn't think so. "I had made myself a promise that after the war, I would kill some of them. And once I had a gun [in Germany]. I saw a kid—seven or eight, a girl—and I had the urge to kill her. But at the last second, I felt that would make me no better than the Nazis. Thank God I didn't pull the trigger."

And of course, he's grateful for one more thing: "That I am part of America. God bless America!"

BARRY TIGER

W hen Barry Tiger built a house for his wife and two sons in
Morris Plains, New Jersey, it was with all the care and ex-
pertise you'd expect from a construction project manager.
There's a big eat-in kitchen, a cozy den with a fireplace, four
bedrooms upstairs, and a two-car garage. This was more
than a house; it was home.

It was 1972, the year of his younger son's bar mitzvah. Barry Tiger had
lived in the United States for twenty-five years. He was working for Murray
Pantirer and Abe Zuckerman, his old friends from the camps. Things were going well, except for the nightmares.

"I was screaming a lot, and my wife used to wake me up. It was always the
same thing: running away, chasing me, choking me. Then I'd wake up, and I'm
in bed, soaking wet. Maybe that was part of the problem; we couldn't sleep together no more."

Barry Tiger came home from work one day in 1989 and found "the
problem" resolved (though hardly in a way he would have liked). Her note in
blue ballpoint on a single sheet of ruled yellow paper stated what the missing
living room furniture instantly made obvious.

Barry Tiger's wife of thirty-two years had skipped for Florida, with a
woman friend, and that was that. "What could I do?" he asks, clearly not

expecting an answer. "Everything was thrown around like somebody burglarized it."

The lime-green living room remains empty, save for the potted plants standing near the front picture window like expectant children. A Disney World coffee mug with "Mom" on it still sits on a kitchen windowsill. Dozens of high-heeled pumps still gather dust in an upstairs closet. Vintage NutriSystem meals still stock the pantry. He still has her books and magazines piled up.

To this day, he can't understand her leaving—"She had everything she wanted: kids, grandkids"—any more than he understood when the SS thundered into Grabowic in 1941, and shot or dragged off nearly every Jew who lived there.

"They were throwing everybody out of their houses and pushing to the marketplace. If anybody was found in the houses, they were shot on the spot. They took my grandfather, my aunts, my uncles, all on the truck, to be shot. They took us all to the Rymanow railway station. Where they went, nobody knows. I last saw them packing on the trains. They held back twenty of us. On the train, they were screaming. I was in a haze."

Berl Teiger was fifteen years old, the only son of Markus and Raisa Teiger. They also had five daughters: Blinka, Goldie, Rivka, Sarah, and Freida. His father was religious, but nowhere near as religious as some of his other relatives. His father's brother wouldn't sit at the same table if his father didn't have a beard. They were in a shtetl. I remember my father said he had to grow the beard to go there and see him. Then as soon as he came home, he cut if off."

The twenty able-bodied young men spared that day went to work for Siemens, the German industrial conglomerate. "They kept us in a building without food. Once a day they gave us soup, on the road. We were chopping stones, hauling stones. They built a road to invade Russia." On June 22, 1941, the Germans massacred thousands as they rampaged over eastern Poland.

Barry Tiger's crew was trucked to the Krosno ghetto, in western Galicia, and from there, to the nearby town of Rzeszów. "We were cleaning up all the houses from the Jews. A lot of people died there. They were shooting every day. We were there about six months. We could find some extra food, and some people found valuables. We were sorting them."

Barry met Abraham Zuckerman in Rzeszów. In his book *A Voice in the Chorus: Life as a Teenager in the Holocaust*, Zuckerman describes the situation: "Earlier, the Nazis had turned the area into a closed Jewish ghetto and then they liquidated the Jews who lived there. Then they converted it into a sort of camp. . . . It was not really a concentration camp or death camp—it was just an encircled section of the

David Werner, Jack Oling, Barry Tiger, Bindermichel Displaced Persons Camp, 1945.

town . . . for the purposes of gathering Jews for transit. . . . [Nazis] roamed the camp with . . . big Dalmatians. The Nazis loved their dogs."

Next stop for both men was the *Julag*, a labor camp at Płaszów. They repaired vehicles coming from the front for a company called Ostbahn. In contrast to Murray Pantirer, Barry Tiger thinks Commandant Müller, who ran the *Julag*, was as mean and ruthless as Amon Goeth. Periodically, the Jewish slave laborers would have to line up, and Müller would shoot every fifth man. "One time, I was picked as the fifth one. But an older man I worked for started to say, 'No, no! I need him! He's good!' So they took another man in my place."

The *Julag* was hell. "There was shooting every day. Do you believe it, I met my uncle David there, my mother's brother? He had typhus, and he died. After they liquidated the *Julag*, they took all of us to Płaszów." It was early 1943.

Abe Zuckerman found his childhood friend Murray Pantirer working in the camp kitchen at Płaszów. This was a bonanza for Barry Tiger and Zuckerman's other friends (including the late David Werner, Tiger's closest friend). "He went to the kitchen and brought us extra soup every day. Also, there was a high wall [around the camp]. We let down money with a rope and they [Poles

199

on the outside] tied the bread and we pulled it up. We sell it, got the money back, and had some for ourselves."

The OD men, the Jewish police, assigned the prisoners to work details. For a time, Barry Tiger excavated the Jewish cemeteries on which Camp Płaszów had been built. "We used to dig up the old graves, dig out the bodies, and take out the teeth. They gave us tools: You pull them out with pliers, just the gold. We were like [zombies]. We didn't know if we would survive the next day. . . . One day about forty or fifty of us are marching to work, but [we were really going] to the hill [Chujowa Górka] to be shot. My friend Dave and I, we had a feeling, and kept going back, back, to the end, and took off. That's the second time I survived."

Untersturmführer Amon Goeth took command of Camp Płaszów in February 1943. About that time, says Barry Tiger, the old Ostbahn crew, separated at Płaszów, got transferred to Oskar Schindler's Emalia. "They had a list," he says. "They didn't tell us where we were going, but some rich people tried to buy themselves in, so we knew it was a good deal. Then all of a sudden, some of us from *Julag* were off the list. I started screaming, 'I'm from *Julag!*' The Germans themselves look at the list. Finally, they put me back on the list.

"When we got into Emalia, it was like heaven. Everything changed. They were building a new factory. Steel was going up." Tiger worked the construction projects, made pots and pans, and cleaned up after Oskar Schindler's parties.

"They left a mess, but those were some good parties," he remembers, grinning and shaking his head. "There were bottles all over the place—they did a lot of boozing—and SS uniforms. And you could find some leftovers there too: cake and sandwiches. I saw [Schindler] with women. He was a lady-killer."

But Barry Tiger, Abe Zuckerman, and hundreds of others would not enjoy Schindler's "heaven" for long. They were sent to Mauthausen in the August 1944 transport—the one Murray Pantirer helped hose down with water, under Schindler's direction.

"The cattle trains were right there waiting for us," Barry Tiger remembers. "It was so hot, people were dying in the trains. There were people in the cars from other places, too. It was without food, without water. Everybody was cooking in there. All we knew was we were gonna go to a death camp. We passed a couple of railroad stations; they wanted to give us water, but they couldn't get near the trains. People were crying, 'This is the end!'

"Then they unloaded us and chased us like dogs. Everybody was thirsty and wanted a drink, so they gave us very salty cabbage soup, and everybody was running to the latrine, drinking themselves to death with that cabbage soup. But we didn't stay long there. We were the lucky ones."

Thousands died on Mauthausen's infamous 186 steps, carrying heavy rocks from the camp quarry (or pushed to their deaths by guards). And others died simply because they couldn't stand living anymore.

"You had to have a strong will to keep going," says Barry Tiger. "A lot of people threw themselves on the wire. I saw them! But as long as you got a piece of bread and soup, you waited [to see] what was gonna happen the next day. *Somebody* had to survive. But if that had gone on another few months, I wouldn't have."

Barry Tiger and Abe Zuckerman went with a work group to Gusen II, a Mauthausen satellite camp. The Gusen prisoners made warplanes for Messerschmitt. "We worked there till the end of the war. We had all nationalities: Italians, Germans, Poles. On Sundays, we didn't work. We cleaned ourselves, got haircuts. They gave us once in a while a piece of meat. There was a lot of beating, but mostly [people] died from the cold."

The factories were underground, in tunnels. "We had German engineers who watched us build the planes." One of them used to leave Barry Tiger half a sandwich each day in a certain corner of a plane. If not for that, and for his stay at Emalia, Tiger says he never would have made it to liberation.

"We got up at five in the morning and they gave us black water and a piece of bread. Off the trains, we ran into the factory right away, and at night, they brought us back. There were two in the cockpit doing the wiring. There were four doing the rivets. It was an assembly line." He was a riveter. "You have to be careful not to break the drill. You got beaten for that."

The barracks' latrines were outside. "You had to run in the cold. There were no showers. And on the coldest day of the year—it must have been way below zero—they took us out, and we had to stay there till the barracks were disinfected. Half of us didn't survive; only the strong ones. We had just the uniform. You could see bodies laying all over. They were doing the exterminating in the barracks. What they were exterminating was us."

American troops liberated Gusen II on May 5, 1945, four days before the Soviets reached Brinnlitz. By then, Barry Tiger weighed seventy-five pounds and couldn't walk. "The prisoners killed a lot of [the Germans] and a lot of the Polish *Kapos.* They were beaten to death. I didn't kill anybody; I wasn't strong enough." He says that without his friend Dave Werner, he would have died. Somehow, Werner managed to carry him to the nearest town.

"On the outskirts of Linz, we made a little camp. It was a big house, like an estate, called Hart. Whoever owned it escaped, but when things quieted down, they came back. Whatever was there, we took it. A real bed! It was heaven. We had baths. We had to make our own hot water, but we had baths. Women came in there, also like skeletons. It was like going to the mountains."

When the original owners reappeared, the freed prisoners moved to Bindermichel, a displaced persons camp at Linz. "We were starting right away to make a buck," he says. "I hung out a lot with the GIs, so we used to get food and chocolate and sell it to the others. I met Murray there. He came in like a lost soul."

Seven of them lived together in a three-bedroom apartment: Barry Tiger, Dave Werner, Murray Pantirer, Abe Zuckerman, Jack Oling, Henry Sperling, and Irving Rosenbaum (all but Werner are still living). One by one, they got married, which meant the bachelors had to double up. "We had a German lady cooking, and it was fun," he recalls of those recovery days. "We were good friends."

Sperling was the first to take a bride. "We went out to the country, we bought a calf, and my friends slaughtered it and we made a big feast. We invited a dozen GIs—Jewish boys. It was the first wedding in camp."

Barry Tiger asked one of the camp's American chaplains to search for his relatives in the United States: an uncle in California and an aunt in New York. He found both, and sailed to New York in April 1947.

His New York uncle owned a Jewish nightclub called the Rainbow Inn on East Fourth Street. His uncle put him to work taking reservations. "They had kosher-style food. There were chorus girls: two floor shows every night, and a lot of famous Jewish entertainers worked there. All kinds of union people came around, and my aunt was friendly with them." That connection later landed him a job doing electrical work at the three television networks.

"We did all the live shows: Sid Caesar, Ed Sullivan, Mitch Miller, Perry Como. They were all coming out of New York. Working in the studios, I learned English fast. I worked on *The Big Payoff* with Bess Myerson. They used to give away mink coats. And I worked on *Strike It Rich.* I used to put those numbers up on that show. You had to be very fast. My wife's brother-in-law worked there, and he introduced us."

He met many of early television's big stars: Milton Berle, Jackie Gleason, Ernie Kovacs. "I worked on *The Honeymooners* at DuMont Studios. That was a riot. There was more laughing backstage than out front. They were fooling around backstage with the girls. There was this saloon around the corner where we used to go in and eat. Gleason would sit together at the same table with us.

"See this watch?" He sticks out an arm. "One Christmas, the announcer from *The Big Payoff* gave everybody a Bulova. That was his sponsor. It's from the fifties, and it still works."

A two-year stint in the army preceded that phase of his life. "Everybody had to register, and they drafted me in 1949 for the Korean War. I was already in good shape." After basic training at Fort Gordon, Georgia, he was assigned to the 66th Battalion of the Signal Corps, a wiring company that installed switchboards. It was barracks and digging and lying in the dirt all over again. "But this time, I got to point the gun, only just at a target." Barry Tiger laughs.

The U.S. Army extracted the "e" from Barry Tiger's last name, which might have been an advantage. "They were looking for fights, those guys from Georgia and Alabama. I didn't look Jewish, and I didn't have a Jewish name, so they didn't bother me. But they went after a couple of guys from Brooklyn who had real Jewish faces. They just knew I was from Poland."

His military obligation completed, Barry Tiger returned to New York, where he met a young, American-born woman named Sandy. She had a clerical job with a publisher. "She was a good-looking girl!" he says. He flips open two photo albums, tracing two lifetimes of broken families: his father with his "temporary" beard, Murray's DP-camp wedding, and his own wedding in

Barry and Sandy Tiger's wedding, New York, 1956. Abe Zuckerman is at the far right and Murray Pantirer is second from left.

1956. "I bought that dress," he says, pointing to his beaming bride, layered in white lace. "I made the wedding at a hall on the Grand Concourse. In those days, it was nice up there."

In the beginning, he says, he and Sandy never talked about the Holocaust. "In those days, nobody talked about it, and she wasn't interested to ask me." He advances slowly through the decades, to the bar mitzvahs of his sons— Mark, born in 1957, and David, born in 1959. There is Sandy, in bouffants and brocades. "Didn't I take good care of her?" he asks. "A princess! Look at her!"

Then he gets to the pictures of his grandchildren, who live nearby. "They keep me going," he says. "I forget my problems with them. The little one reminds me of my younger sister."

In 1959, "the unions killed the [television studio] jobs and everybody went to California. The shows were on tape, so I was out of a job." He did

Barry Tiger (standing) and Murray Pantirer (seated) in the offices of L.P.Z. Management Group, New York, 1994.

maintenance work at RKO theaters until 1964, when his old pal Murray Pantirer called and asked him to join his construction outfit.

His line of work didn't make things easier at home. "I ran jobs. I was on the phone all night long with people calling me—masons, carpenters—getting set for the next day. When you're building, you work with rough people. You're using bad language. Maybe she got too lonely," he speculates. "You never can tell."

A friend who was a therapist suggested that Mrs. Tiger get a job. "And that's when the whole thing started. She was going out with women, all single, all divorcées. Little by little, she got involved with them. All night, she was talking to her friends on the phone in her room. You know how women talk; they never stop. Some of them. I don't say all."

The details are sad and sordid. Suffice it to say that Barry Tiger should not have been surprised to come home that day in 1989 and find an empty living-room. But he was, and nearly five years later, he still is. "I can show you birthday cards, anniversary cards—I still have them—with a lot of love in there."

Barry gets four hundred dollars a month in war reparations from the German government—a ludicrous amount, when you consider the 80 percent hearing loss in his right ear from beatings, the dizziness, the buzzing in his head that gets so bad he sometimes has to pull his car over, the chronic depression, the spinal problems, and the nightmares.

"I had one last night," he says. "When you have problems, it always comes back to you. All the bad things that happened in the camps, you think about it all the time. But what can I do?"

What he'd like to do is sell his house and move far away from those high-heeled pumps lurking in that upstairs closet. "This house," he says, "what do I need it for? I hate to sleep in a house by myself."

CANTOR MOSHE TAUBÉ

*I*t is the morning after the Academy Awards. *Schindler's List* has won Best Picture and Steven Spielberg has been named Best Director. One would think that as one of the *Schindlerjuden,* Cantor Moshe Taubé would be thrilled. Instead, he is furious. Yes, the awards were a good thing, he concedes, but how dare they allow Oscar host Whoopi Goldberg to make sex jokes? It was frivolous! Degrading! Didn't they realize that those awards belonged to six million martyrs?

He was so disgusted that he turned off the television well before the show ended. But he woke up mad. "Was this an X-rated movie?"

The musical/spiritual leader of Pittsburgh's Congregation Beth Shalom is a passionate man, so passionate that he has never seen *Schindler's List.* He fears he'd be traumatized to the point of physical illness. It's bad enough that fifty years later, vignettes far more ghastly than any Hollywood would dare show replay in his nightmares.

With Moshe Taubé, even ordinary conversation is drama. His tone and timbre career from whisper to bellow, from rumble to wail. When he's angry or indignant, he thunders. His cantorial style is equally elastic. It cries with anguish and yearning one moment, soars with hope and joy the next. His is a refined voice, sophisticated and operatic, yet rich with soul and emotion. It's one of the reasons Beth Shalom, founded in 1917, boasts 1,150 families. "I fashioned the service and choir in such a way that they are regarded as unmatched in the United States," he proudly declares.

He and Helen, his second wife, share a two-story home around the corner from the synagogue in Squirrel Hill, urban Pittsburgh's Jewish section. The house has a close, Old World feel to it. And there's an Old World formality about Taubé, who appears at the door in a dark blue, three-piece suit and a jaunty polka-dot tie that matches the lighter blue of his velvet yarmulke.

"I will tell you a different kind of story," he promises, with conspiratorial intensity. "I will tell you a spiritual story! I see God's hand in every movement and stage of my life."

The story begins with a boy who loves music, yet wants to become a businessman, just like his father—perhaps even his junior partner. It detours through the Nazi netherworld, where he loses all that's dear, except his father and his faith. Healed by the warmth of one woman, he finds his voice. Divorced after three decades of mutual disharmony, he finds an enduring love. Eighteen years his junior, she's a sturdy woman with dark, graying hair, a gentle manner, and a soothing voice. He calls her "Helusia," the Polish diminutive of her name, though she's about his height. He wears his love for her like an Olympic medal.

Moshe (Maksymilian, on Schindler's list) Taubé, born in 1927, was the son of Regina and Emanuel Taubé. His father owned a shirt factory in Kraków. He had one sister, Nina, three years his junior. "We lived a modest, traditional way of life [in a] beautiful apartment in the Jewish section. I went to fine schools, and I studied piano since the age of seven. I wrote my first composition at eight. I studied Torah intensively . . . . My mother took me to the opera. They were especially fond of Puccini. We had the radio playing all the time, with good

Moshe Taubé with his sister, Nina, in Kraków before the war.

music—classical music. There was always melody in the house."

Like most Kraków Jews, Emanuel Taubé saw no reason for alarm as the 1930s progressed. Unfortunately, my father was a businessman, and all businessmen had priorities. Business took priority over considerations of the future. We had a thriving business,

Moshe Taubé with his sister, Nina, and mother, Regina, both of whom were killed. The photo was taken in Kraków, 1940.

with so many clients all over Poland and Czechoslovakia, and shirts were being sold on consignment, so the debts were tremendous." His parents "were not focused on some implausible eventuality. They heard Hitler speak, but no one took him seriously. It never happened in the past that a nation like Germany, with its culture and history of poetical and musical giants, would turn into a genocidal entity."

Other relatives were more prescient. Two years before the German invasion, two cousins—"ardent Zionists who had premonitions"—left for Palestine, "because they saw the gathering storm." An uncle, Poldek Taubé, then in his late twenties, escaped to Rumania on a bicycle in 1939.

After the German invasion, Emanuel Taubé sent his family three hundred miles east, to Przemyśl, the town of his ancestors. "In case of war, he'd join us there, and he did. Then the Germans took it, and we went further east to Lwów.... Then the Russians came from the east and overtook us, and we went back to Przemyśl but because of concern about the business, he sent my mother and sister back to liquidate the factory. I joined them there in 1940. Then the Germans chased us out into the suburbs, where we rented a small room from a peasant.... Living in it felt like a straitjacket, but we still had hope that in spite of all the hardships, the situation will be ameliorated to help us reestablish our lives."

It wasn't. That year he remembers seeing religious Jews shorn of their beards in the streets, beaten up and otherwise harassed. "I was flabbergasted and depressed," he recalls. The following year his father returned, and the family moved into the ghetto. The synagogues were closed, as were the schools, but Moshe was bar mitzvahed nonetheless. "It was in a private house. My father was not present. It would have been a beautiful occasion, with a tremendous reception. . . . It was a watershed in my life. I became a man, but there was no spiritual elevation."

"We were seeing suffering and the beginning of the atrocities, when they took people out and nobody ever heard of them anymore. I was very religious, and I pointed to a portion [in the Torah] where curses and punishments are being enumerated, in the last chapter of Leviticus. I was telling my parents: 'Look at this; what is written here is happening to us.' I accepted it as a divine judgment."

They lived with two other families in a three-room apartment: a couple with a child and another with two grown daughters. There was a single kitchen and a single bathroom for all seven families on the floor. "Everybody had problems. The Germans took away this one and that, and every family was tragically affected. People were being herded into groups and sent away to Auschwitz for liquidation." Or to Belżec, which became the final destination of Nina and Regina Taubé, in 1942.

Moshe and his father were sent to Płaszów. "The first day, everybody was crying. After all, the ghetto was half-humane surroundings. There were still streets, houses, freedom of movement inside the walls. Here, it was a prison."

Still, according to Taubé, devout Jews managed to observe certain rituals. "In Płaszów, I had my own pair of tefillin [phylacteries]. I put it on every day. And we had a Sefer Torah, in the barracks. A man called Ritterman was the guardian of the small Sefer Torah, somehow smuggled into Płaszów. I think they buried the little Torah in Płaszów. Ritterman went to Mauthausen, I believe, and perished."

Father and son worked at the Madritsch uniform factory. "Eight or nine hours a day, I was on a machine that made buttonholes. Then, after work, we were schlepping stones in the quarry." Raimund Titsch, the factory manager, got them onto Schindler's list. The cantor believes it's because his father spoke excellent German, and the men became friendly. But first, there was Gröss-Rosen. "They took us in cattle cars, and it was extremely crowded. My father had a nervous breakdown in the cattle car. He couldn't take it anymore. There was a German SS man with us inside the car with a gun. Everybody else was sitting stacked on top of each other. The SS man had a seat, a chair, and he said, 'Whoever comes here to this chair where I sit will be shot.' He had like an invisible wall around him. Nobody dared to even approach him. . . . Fortunately, no one died, but people were exhausted and smelly. They were forced to defecate where they were sitting, and I was sitting on my father's lap. I couldn't sleep. But I was assured by my father that where we are going will be under the protection of Schindler. And this was a great plus. This will increase our chances of survival."

At Gröss-Rosen, "we showered and they changed our clothing. There was a thorough body search. They gave us so-called new clothing, with stripes and caps. On the run, we had to pick some shoes. My shoes were too small and I had to run back and beg them to change the shoes for me. Somebody helped me, but I got beaten up by a Polish guard because I went back."

At Brinnlitz, he shared a bunk with his father. A man named Janek Sternberg had the bunk below, with his son. The teenagers talked constantly about food. "We dreamed about it: challah, cake, and fish, and pieces of wonderful meat, and roasted ducks, and goose livers! There was a sensual satisfaction just speaking about it . . . . "But food was short from the very beginning, and because of it, I got infections on my body. I was very sick. Twice they operated on me without anesthesia. They opened my wounds, which were full of pus. They were on my feet, my belly, my legs, even my neck. I still have scars."

When they arrived, the factory wasn't complete, "so we schlepped chains, and put the machines in specially constructed concrete foundations. After the machinery was in place, my job was to put paint on the shell components so they wouldn't rust. My father was in the storage section, where they counted the shells and put them in wooden boxes." '

Schindler was on the factory floor every day, he recalls, chain-smoking. "He was in his white shirt, with bloodshot eyes, a red face, cologne, a gruff voice. And he would throw the inmates stubs so that they could smoke. I didn't smoke but my father did. A smoke was for some people more important than food. They sold their little piece of bread for a cigarette. . . . There were people in Brinnlitz who said a smoke is like an offering to God—I'm telling you! There was one extremely religious man who told me that."

Taubé also recalls that Schindler secured a single tefilla—the one worn on the forehead—for Mr. Jereth, the extremely religious and wealthy lumber dealer who sacrificed a gold tooth for Schindler's ring. "Every morning, there was a line of people standing to put on the tefilla and say one Sh'ma. It was in our quarters, Mr. Jereth oversaw it. It was his, but he gave it to everyone to say Sh'ma: 'Sh'ma. Okay, finish. Sh'ma. Next one.' It was a Sh'ma assembly line."

At Passover, he says, there were those who "put their lives on the line and didn't eat bread. They ate the roots of the grass." He struggled with this, "and in order to mark Passover, I fasted on seder night. At least one night, not to eat *hometz*. . . . We had to do everything possible in spite of ourselves to show that physical needs and deprivation would not annul the commitment to the Torah. . . . When you are committed to your way of life and the past of your people and the continuance of your people . . . your personal needs do not take precedence over the larger picture."

Of those who lost faith, he says this: "When God gave free hand to the destroyer, that destroyer does not differentiate between the righteous and the wicked. . . . Those who were to be destroyed had no choice. Some protested, some rebelled, but to stop believing or say that God is unmerciful, who are we to judge? We are like shadows, passing in the face of eternity, which, for the most part, is incomprehensible. I have questions and complaints, but that doesn't mean I should do things against God's commandments. I was convinced that no matter what happened to us, the nation of Israel would survive."

The last Russian offensive started on January 12, 1945. "We knew about it. All the Germans told us this is it. This was tremendous news, and it spread like wildfire in Brinnlitz. The same day, that night, I remember Leopold Rosner took his accordion and started playing so beautifully. Everybody was singing."

As the end of the war drew closer, "all of a sudden, some of the Nazis became so nice and so friendly. We saw the American bombers flying over and there was such joy, in spite of the fact that any minute the whole factory could go up in smoke. It was elation, but I was not able to rejoice because I was sick like a dog. I was skinny and very weak and my eyesight was very bad because of the malnutrition."

On the day before Schindler left, "everybody gathered inside the factory and he said, 'You will be remembered as *Schindlerjuden.*' He said it in his rusty voice. The Germans left the camp, and we were all by ourselves."

He remembers that the Russian soldier who rode up on a horse was Jewish, and spoke Yiddish. "He was mobbed. He was kissed from head to toe."

Like many of the *Schindlerjuden,* the Taubés headed back to Kraków. Along the way, the Czechs "were like angels. The goodness of their hearts is indescribable. They didn't have much, but they shared whatever they had with us: food, clothing. They are wonderful, warm people by nature. But the Slovaks were more like the Poles, the majority were hateful."

In Kraków, "there was nothing left. In June 1945 . . . my father told me that Uncle Poldek is in Craiova, Rumania, and we are going there. We stayed fourteen months, recuperating . . . I regained my equilibrium. It was an evolutionary process that had to do with the healing power of time. It was years since I sensed love, devotion, from anybody but my father.

"Being a spiritual man, I think God was good to me. He sent me a friend who brought me out of the emotional pits by making me understand that good people still lived in the world, and that the future could bring me happiness and beauty. I redeemed my sense of personal serenity. I started singing! I was singing for all the street to hear! I was singing at the top of my voice, off the balcony. It was a raw voice, but a strong, fine voice."

His father, Emanuel Taubé, returned to Kraków, to reestablish his shirt business. Emanuel met his second wife there, who also had been an inmate at Brinnlitz. "Her maiden name was Anna Schneeweis. I had seen her at Brinnlitz from afar." They had twin sons and moved to Israel in 1957. There's a framed photo on the wall of Moshe Taubé's dining room of a handsome, dark-haired man in an Israeli army captain's uniform. His name was Aryeh, one of Moshe's twin half-brothers. He was killed in the Yom Kippur War by a Syrian shell, on the Golan Heights, at the age of twenty-three. His death just about finished off Emanuel Taubé emotionally. He died in 1990 at the age of eighty-eight. Anna died in July 1994.

Moshe fought in the underground, the Haganah, which later became the Israeli army. "I was in the defense of Jerusalem. I wanted a quiet life, but the

Moshe Taubé and his father, Emanuel, after the war.

budding state needed my services in the army. Nobody asked me whether I wanted to or not. I was aspiring to a life of comfort, but it was not to be. I had to shoot at Arabs. I was terrified by the situation, by again war. Palestine was very unstable. I wanted to start my life there and work and be among Jews."

In 1948, he began studying voice. "In 1949, when I was released from the Israeli army, I was in terrible financial straits. I had a ridiculous government position in customs that I hated. I knew I had a voice and a knowledge of the chants, the knowledge and background to be a cantor. I was a God-fearing and religious man. Somehow, somebody referred me to a very small synagogue [in Haifa]. They grabbed me. The pay was almost nothing, but they loved me. I was there for one year, then I got a little bigger position in a German congregation. There I got a little more pay, but I was still very poor. My son was born in 1950, and I was in the army reserve. It was a life of hardship. I had to hustle."

Daughter Regina was born in 1954 in Jerusalem. "At that time, I was engaged as chief cantor at Rishon L'Zion. This was a God-sent opportunity to develop my dexterity in the cantorial arts, because they wanted more, more, more. They wanted me to sing nonstop. I was two years there, then I got a bigger position with a choir, at Bograshov Synagogue in Tel Aviv. All the time, wherever I could get a glimpse of any education in cantorial arts, I swallowed it up, from recordings, from other cantors at concerts, recitals. At the same time, I was singing in a professional Israeli radio choir."

But Taubé felt "confined" in Israel. "It was not in my milieu. I wanted to dedicate my life to music, and I hated every moment of government work. Sometimes I was sitting there and composing music at my desk. . . . Three days after my arrival in New York, I was engaged by one of the most famous U.S. congregations, Shaare Zedek. . . . There were famous cantors auditioning for that position, a cantor who taught me in Israel! To officiate in New York, with a fourteen-voice choir! What a jump! It was plush, with red velvet, the officers in high hats and cutaways. And nobody saw the choir; they just heard it."

But his real break came when he was admitted to the Juilliard School on scholarship. "I had to study for a whole year for entrance exams . . . but I had the best musical education you could get. It was thrilling and extremely demanding. I had to compose for every professor, in this medium and that, for this period and that. Not only music, but languages: Italian, French, English—German, I knew. I had to give a lecture on Gregorian chants and their resemblance to ancient Jewish music. At Juilliard, no less!"

He graduated in 1962. By then, he'd been teaching at the Jewish Theological Seminary's Cantorial Institute for a year. In 1965, he took his current job with Beth Shalom. "People in the synagogue recognized that I was sincere, not just performing. I was praying with my soul. They knew I meant it, and they appreciated it very much. . . . Each holiday brought back memories of holidays at home, in the old country, memories of the cantor, his dissolving in tears during the services. His name was Yussele Mandelbaum; [he] just died at the age of ninety in Brooklyn. I sang with him in Kraków."

Despite Moshe Taubé's professional success, which included seventeen years at Duquesne University, teaching sacred music, his home life was deteriorating. "In spite of all my efforts, there was no *sholom byet* [peace in the house]. It came to a head. Somebody expressed their admiration for me and I shared my feelings with her."

Helen Gontscharow was born in Austria. In 1979, she converted to Judaism. She holds a degree in library science from the University of Pittsburgh. Helen developed an interest in cantorial music, and came to hear Taubé's well-known service. They began to talk. Then she developed an interest in the cantor. "You can't separate the voice from the man," she says.

"She knew I was unhappy," he says, "but when I met her, I never contemplated a divorce. It was unthinkable that I should initiate it because of my family, my standing in the community." But his wife, Bertha, who subsequently moved to Israel, solved his dilemma by filing for a no-fault divorce. His daughters, Regina

Cantor Moshe Taubé in the sanctuary of his synagogue, Pittsburgh, 1994.

Berger and Nina Balas, also live in Israel. Regina's husband is American, Nina's is Yemenite. His son, Ben Zion Taubé, teaches Hebrew in Boston. A seventeenth Taubé grandchild was due in September.

"With Helusia, I became my natural self," he explains over chicken and vegetables at a kosher Chinese restaurant run by Lubavitchers in Squirrel Hill. "I had been unnaturally tense, irritable. There were slivers of happiness during the marriage, especially with my children and grandchildren, but on the whole, it was very unhappy for me. With Helusia, I felt younger, bouncier"— "Yes, bouncier!" she agrees—"and I was happy to share and have a communicative relationship. I had been closed within myself, and extremely lonely."

They were married in his backyard in August 1983. Looking exactly like the actor Eli Wallach, in a white dinner jacket, Moshe sang his favorite cantorial selections.

"Helen came into my life as a God-sent mate," he says. "She was like an angel. Yes! The Almighty said, 'Here he is; I set you down . . .' She is extremely emotional and understanding and warm and so forthcoming and tender. She cared so much."

He notes that she is eighteen years younger than he is, and that in Hebrew, the letters that make up the word *chai*, which means life, add up to eighteen.

"This," he says, "this is also not by chance!"

216

VICTOR LEWIS

There was something different about the fearsome *Aktion* of October 28, 1942. Victor Lewis knew it as soon as he thrust his *Arbeitsbescheinigung* toward the Gestapo officer, and the Gestapo officer tore it to pieces.

This was the same document, proving he worked for the German military as an auto mechanic, that had done the trick during the two June *Aktions*. He figured it would save his family and himself from deportation again. What had changed?

The June *Aktions* more than halved the original ghetto population of fifteen thousand: one thousand killed; seven thousand transported. But a certain perverse logic attended those sortings. Labor cards mattered. Ghetto passes mattered. Age and physical fitness mattered, to some degree.

What had changed was that the Nazi master plan to render Kraków *Judenrein* (cleansed of Jews) required less pretense. Fewer explanations. All Jews were ordered to Plac Zgody, with their belongings. *All* Jews.

Victor Lewis—then Wiktor Lezerkiewicz—was twenty-four years old. He was strong, tough, and physical. He knew exactly what the Nazis intended by the time his shredded work permit hit the ground, and he wanted no part of it. So as Abraham and Bertha Lezerkiewicz waited glumly on Plac Zgody with three of their five offspring—Greta, Leon, and Wiktor—Wiktor told his father

Victor Lewis before the war, Kraków.

he intended to escape. "If you can save yourself, go ahead," said Abraham Lezerkiewicz. "I am too old to run."

Jakob, the youngest son, called Kuba, was hiding with a Polish family. Lola, the oldest, had gone to Palestine in 1932 with a Zionist group, over her father's vehement objections. When she visited for Passover in 1939, she told her family, "I smell war," and urged them to leave with her. They didn't, but she got out during the summer, just in time. After mid-September, it was all but impossible.

The family lived at 1 Targowa Street. Abraham ran a retail fabric store. Victor was getting started in pharmacy—earning his own money at sixteen—but dutifully curtailed his chosen career when his father got sick and needed help at the store. He spent his youth playing soccer in the Maccabi leagues, and falling seriously in love with Ida and Israel Steiner's middle daughter, Regina. Israel was a furrier. "We weren't rich," says Regina Steiner Lewis, "but I had a beautiful coat." (Neither Regina's older sister, Teofila, nor her younger sister, Eugenia, survived the war.)

Regina and her beau belonged to Zionist youth organizations and "had a beautiful social life. We danced: the tango, fox-trots, waltzes." Now in their seventies, they have a two-story, brick row house in Flushing, Queens, decorated with the Oriental rugs and the framed needlepoint scenes so popular with many of the older *Schindlerjuden.* They have a summer cottage in the Catskills. Victor, born in August 1918, is a jaunty type, sporting a heavy gold bracelet, and his initials, in tiny diamonds, on one pinkie.

When the Gestapo issued ghetto residency passes called *Kennkarten* in March 1941, Victor and Leon were the only Lezerkiewiczes to get them. "I said I was an auto mechanic, but I lied. My brother was really a mechanic." His parents, with Greta and Jakob, moved to Niepolomice, a suburb. Victor and Leon went on

The Lezerkiewicz family (left to right): Brother Leon, mother Bertha, Victor, and brother Kuba vacationing in Jordanów, 1937.

Friday nights for *Shabbat,* and returned Saturday afternoons. In 1942, the family "couldn't stay anymore, so we brought them to the ghetto without *Kennkarten.*"

On June 6, 1942, the Gestapo imposed yet another layer of bureaucracy on the Jews: the *Blauschein,* the blue labor card. No longer was a *Kennkarten* good enough, even with the right kinds of official job-category stamps affixed to it. This new *Blauschein* legitimized the working ghetto dwellers. Those denied it became human surplus, carted away to death camps. Theoretically, an *Arbeitsbescheinigung* carried even more clout. It identified the bearer as crucial to the war effort.

But on October 28, Victor Lewis realized that none of them was crucial to anything, except as fodder for the ravenous Nazi death machine.

The order came to line up in fours. Thousands lumbered toward the Płaszów railway station, where cattle cars awaited. As they passed Wieliczka

Street, Victor tried to make his break. Someone caught him, and flung him back into line. "I was lucky I was not shot right there," he says.

Once inside the railroad car, Victor tried to stay by the window. "Adults and children were crying and screaming," he recalls. "There was no air, no water. People were ripping at their clothes, they were so hot."

In his boot, Victor Lewis carried a hacksaw blade, and not just for this occasion. He always carried one, just in case. He began sawing away at the four half-inch-thick steel bars across the small window. Others implored him not to. They feared that if a head count on the other end of the trip revealed anyone missing, they'd all be killed. "Do you believe you're going to work, or to die?" he retorted. "I believe we are all going to the gas chambers!"

By dusk, he was finished. As the train approached a forest, he and his brother Leon decided to make their break, mindful of the armed sentries on the car's roof. "My sister didn't want to jump," says Victor. "I begged her. She was two years older than me. I thought it was better to die by jumping than to be in the train and choke to death."

Abraham gave Victor his gold watch and his blessing. He and Leon leaped. The next thing Victor Lewis knew, it was dawn. He'd fallen on a parallel rail, smacking his head. And he couldn't find Leon. He didn't know that his brother already was headed back to the ghetto, as their parents and sister rolled on to certain death at Bełżec.

"I got my bearings and began walking along the tracks, hoping to meet my brother. At the station in Kluj, I boarded the train for Bochnia, where I thought I could locate him." Leon wasn't there, so Victor returned to Kraków.

Fifteen-year-old Kuba, who had been staying with Poles, "sneaked into the ghetto to see where was his family." Victor found him, and made arrangements for his safety: He bought him a job at Kabelwerke, the electrical-wire factory run by a German named Böhme, who treated his Jewish *Haftlinge* humanely.

"By sheer luck, somebody told me who was making the list to go to Kabel. I went to visit him, and I said, 'Put him on the list.' He said, 'OK, I maybe can do it, but you have to pay.' I sold this watch and gave this guy the money, and my brother went there."

A few days later, Victor heard that the Nazis were using Jews to build a work camp at Płaszów. "I was interested. I went and looked for a connection to *Barakenbau,* the barracks-construction detail. I went to that group. When we built the first two barracks, they didn't schlep us back and forth anymore [from the ghetto]."

For some months, the population lived in flux. During construction of the women's barracks, Victor recalls that "because there was a ghetto in progress, two girls went there and didn't come for the *Appell* the next morning. Goeth saw that people were missing, so he called on Leopold Goldberg and Katz [Jewish policemen] and they gave a report. He told them to kneel down. First Katz was shot, [then] Goldberg was shot. They found those two girls, and they were hanged. This was the first hanging in Płaszów. We had all to watch it."

The camp filled up after the March 13 liquidation. Regina Steiner was among the newcomers. "I saw her every day," says Victor. "I came up to her barracks. I really took chances. I told myself, 'I'm alone, and if I have to be killed, it's only gonna be from the back.' I didn't want to see the gun in front of me.

"We spent a half hour, an hour together. At the gate [to the women's quarters], if the Jewish policeman knew me, he let me in. I was assigned to be an electrician at Płaszów, but I didn't know how to put two wires together. So I was cleaning boots, even for the soldiers. That's how I had something to eat." Regina worked at the camp's fur factory, making warm winter coats for the Nazis.

They heard certain things about Oskar Schindler's pot-and-pan plant. "We knew that the people in Emalia had a good time there," says Victor, "and we in Płaszów were every minute in danger, not only because of Goeth, but the other SS and the Ukrainians." He and Regina often wondered why they hadn't gone there, considering her father's status in the community. (Israel Steiner was with his daughter at Płaszów, but he died later at one of the camps in the Mauthausen system.) On August 6, 1944, Regina Steiner went to Auschwitz, then to Oederan—"heaven, compared to Auschwitz, with clean straw and showers"—then to Theresienstadt. "By miracle, I am alive," she says. "I was in the transport to Stutthof [the Baltic Sea camp]. The whole boat went down. My aunt went, my cousins went. I was standing in the line. A girl in the line said, 'We must run away from this line!' I said, 'How could we run, with them with machine guns?' She said, 'You idiot, run! Whatever will happen, will happen!' I was always going with the straight line. My husband was a fighter; I was not."

This time, she ran. "We hid under the bunks. They ran to the barracks, but thank God not with the dogs. The fear was tremendous."

A cousin of Victor's did some running at Płaszów, and Victor took the punishment for it. "His name was Max Lezerkiewicz. He hid in a box, and they took it out. He went to the partisans, but they shot him. I was arrested in Płaszów. After two or three days, Goeth came to see the people in jail, with Chilowicz present. We had to step out, and he was looking. Goeth wanted to know, 'What he is locked up for?' Chilowicz said, 'Some Lezerkiewicz ran away, but he got nothing to do with it. He is from Kraków; the other is from Kalvaria.' I told him my father was Abraham and his was David. He said, 'Let him go.' This was next to the OD barracks. It was filthy."

By the time Regina left, Victor's brother Jakob had arrived. "In 1944, he came from Kabel to Płaszów, and from Płaszów, I hid him under my bunk." This was after Amon Goeth had been arrested and jailed. "My brother was supposed to go with a group to Mauthausen. I wanted to keep him with me." He couldn't. Jakob lived through the war, but died at Ebensee just after it ended. "He poisoned himself with a can of meat. Somebody who worked in the hospital told me he was dead."

Victor Lewis had been an energetic participant in Camp Płaszów's black-market economy. It almost got him killed. "I was trading in cigarettes with the SS," he explains. "I had an SS man, Franz Simonleiner—they locked him up in Austria after the war—I used to buy from him cigarettes."

Just days before the move to Brinnlitz, Simonleiner double-crossed his business partner. As usual, Victor handed over cash; Franz handed over cigarettes, and Victor tucked them under his shirt. Then Simonleiner grabbed Victor Lewis and marched him to the security office.

"There were three high-ranking SS officers. He said, 'I brought you a guy who is doing black market.' They asked me, 'What you have?' He [Franz] pulls up my shirt, and the cigarettes are falling down. Maybe ten packs. All of a sudden, I heard questions: 'Where did you get this from?' I pointed to him. 'From him.' I figured I was finished anyhow. He started to talk German, and I knew perfect German. He said it wasn't true. I said it was. They started to make a trial. He was selling to me two years! They started to beat on me till I couldn't stand up, and blood from my mouth came out."

In his stupor, Victor Lewis heard one officer tell another, " 'He's finished.' They called the OD: 'Come get one body and bring to Chujowa Górka.' I heard it. They took me in a wheelbarrow and wheeled me to the hill. They told me, 'Keep your mouth shut until we come up there.' They let me out, and I went underground. I went to the hospital and cleaned up a little bit." Among other injuries, he had a broken nose. "And I was all bumpy."

Victor Lewis says he doesn't know who put him on Schindler's list, but he considers it a miracle. He went, officially, as an electrician, though he knew virtually nothing about the trade. His name is on page two of the list, number 108.

"The only real electrician was a German foreman. He picked me to hook up a welding machine for one of my good friends. The wires were going outside: three wires. I didn't know how to put it. I went on a ladder. All of a sudden, I hit one wire on the other. I jumped off the ladder, and there was no light in the factory. The electricians ran into the shop and fixed it. The foreman yelled, 'You son of a gun!' He kicked me in my behind. He said, 'Go to my shop!' I said to myself, 'Why I'm gonna do that? I'm going to Schindler.' "

He did, and encountered Oskar's wife, Emilie. "I said to Mrs. Schindler, 'I have a bad experience, and I need some help. I blew up the electric and now my foreman is after me.' She started to talk to Oskar about it. He said, 'You go back to the shop; I'll be there.' The foreman wasn't there yet, because he was busy with the machine. All of a sudden the foreman came, and Schindler came, and said, 'I need an electrician.' He said, 'I want him,' and he pointed to me. The foreman said, 'He's not an electrician!' Schindler said, 'I want him.' This was how I got away from a beating, and worked for Schindler."

Oskar's workers were building an apartment for him—some *Schindlerjuden* call it a villa—at the nearby grain mill. "From this time, I was electrician in his apartment, doing nothing. I was putting oatmeal in my toolbox and my tool belt, and bringing it [to the Brinnlitz camp]. My friends were cooking it. That is how Schindler saved my life."

He says he was part of the effort to rescue others whom Schindler saved: the "frozen people" from Goleszów. "The train was in front of our factory. We took straw and burned it underneath the cars. We tried to melt the ice [immobilizing the locks and latches]. Schindler said to take old mattresses—'tomorrow you get new.' Mrs. Schindler was there to help. When this melted and they opened the cars, people were lying on the floor, frozen. Schindler made a room, and everyone got help. They had with them one German, a guard, who was later hanged. We hanged him on a pipe."

Once, Amon Goeth appeared at the plant. By then, he'd been jailed for black-market profiteering and disgraced as an officer. When the *Häftlinge* saw him sans epaulettes and sidearm, they went wild. "Everybody was screaming at him: 'What you think, you are in Płaszów?' He was yelling back, 'I'm gonna kill you guys!' Schindler was afraid about himself, so he gave him some money and said, 'Get out of here.' "

Someone recruited Victor Lewis into the Brinnlitz underground. The underground consisted of two factions: the *Budzyners*—burly political prisoners who came through Gröss-Rosen from Majdanek with Josef Liepold, the Brinnlitz camp commandant—and a core group from Płaszów. "We were thirty partisans. [Schindler] made sure that one group did not know about the other.

"Each unit [of the underground] had five men," Lewis explains. "We made contact with the Czech underground fighters. They supplied weapons. They said they would come to help us if we were under attack, but we must defend ourselves. They were sending cigarettes, guns, ammunition, and food. I had a gun under my jacket even in the *Appellplatz*: six-shot revolvers, German-made. Nobody was investigating you at Brinnlitz; the *Appell* was inside. The count was made by Jews and sent to Liepold."

The groups knew little about each other, and even those asked to recommend new members never found out if, in fact, they were recruited. Lewis recommended Joe Lipshutz and Joe Jonas. Lipshutz married Roman Ferber's sister after the war, and now lives in Cape Coral, Florida. Jonas married Helena Sternlicht, who'd been one of Amon Goeth's maids at Płaszów. (After Jonas's death, she remarried, and is now Helen Rosenzweig of Colt's Neck, New Jersey.)

"They wanted somebody mentally tough," Victor Lewis explains. "If they were caught, they would not give up the others. They talked to you, checking you out. Nobody knew the chairman till the end of the war. One delegate from the group of five was the liaison. I was with strangers." Schindler made sure that no one in the underground was hungry. "And the worst time we were hungry, Schindler went and brought a dead horse," which the whole camp ate.

As Soviet troops rolled into the Sudetenland, the Czechs told the inside group what to do: "We had the order from the outside partisans to start [armed resistance], then they would come and help us out. Schindler took ten rifles and put them against the wall. These went to the underground people, and we took care of the other people." When the camp guards bailed out, it was up to the inside underground to make sure no one left the Brinnlitz confines. "Germans were still around," still looking to kill Jews.

"Nobody got out in twenty-four hours—only Marcel Goldberg, who went through a window. When the first Russian came on the horse, we opened the door. Mrs. Wohlfeiler ran out and gave him a big hug and a kiss."

Lewis says the Czech partisans made sure that in addition to what the fleeing Oskar bequeathed the *Schindlerjuden*—fabric, leather, scissors, and other trade items—there was enough food to go around.

Lewis learned that his brother Leon was at Theresienstadt, deathly ill, and headed there immediately. He didn't know that Regina Steiner was there too. "The Russians closed [the camp] up because there was typhus," says Victor. "But I always had some tools with me, so I cut a few wires and we went through. I met a guy from Kraków. I asked him, 'Did you see my brother?' He says, 'Sure, I bring you to your brother, but before I do that'—he knew we were dating—he says, 'I gonna bring you to someone else.'"

Regina picks up the story. "I was sitting with a few girls from Kraków, and they knew we were dating before the war. I said, 'Oh, at least if Victor was here alive!' I knew that nobody from my family was. And you know, the minute I finished [saying] it, somebody called, 'Rega, somebody is asking for you.' I got to the gate and who do I see? Victor and two or three people! I just could not believe it! What am I, a witch? My wish was [for him to come], and he came! Not just that freedom came, but some happiness. I was really shocked, like he was sent from God. I still feel it."

Regina Lewis in a Displaced Persons camp after liberation, with "Willie S."

But Victor Lewis didn't have time for romance. "He was looking for his brother, because he was very sick," Regina explains. "People were lying on the ground, dying. He was maybe thirty kilos [about sixty pounds]. He was right that he wanted to grab his brother." She knows that now, but at the time, Regina was heartbroken.

"My pride was hurt. As a girl, being in love, and finally we find each other! Then he leaves, and we could get lost in this whole mess again!"

Victor reassured her he meant for them to reunite, but first he had to save Leon. He took him back to Brinnlitz. "He left me there!" says Regina. "But he said something: 'Give me your little suitcase. You will follow me after a week.'" The Brinnlitz doctors told Victor to take Leon to Kraków for better treatment. So with a group that included Joe Jonas, Joe Lipshutz, and the Sternlicht sisters, he did just that. Doctors there told him his brother needed a richer diet than what was available. "They said, 'You gotta get him milk and butter.' Where I'm going to get it? I went 'shopping.' I went into the woods and got eggs, milk, butter. I was begging. Slowly, he got better."

And slowly Regina Steiner came to her senses. "I had my aunt, she was a pusher. She said, 'Go to Poland.' He was sending letters, I should come right away. He even had the certificates of permission to leave Kraków and go to Romania, then to Ebensee. But I didn't leave for two months. I was upset. I was insecure. I was young. 'Is it true, he really wants to be with me?' I couldn't read him at this moment. But I went."

Victor's group from Brinnlitz hitched a ride with some American soldiers to Ebensee, where he learned that his brother Jakob had died right after liberation. "There was no grave," he says. "So we built a cemetery for those people who died in Ebensee, near the concentration camp. They moved it up the hill

Displaced Persons camp soccer team, around 1946. Victor, with mustache, is standing at the center, next to the man with the hat.

later, where it was harder to find. The Austrians were worse sometimes than the Germans."

From Kraków, the group of ten separated. "We stayed six months. We didn't do anything productive. We needed the rest. And like one family, it helped us recover from the sorrow and hunger and horror."

Rabbi Menashe Lewartow, the *Schindlerjude* who performed several marriages among the group after the war, married Victor and Regina in July 1945 in Kraków. "He was living on Dietal, the same street I was living, at number 21, before the war. He was at number 19," Regina remembers. "I had a beautiful blue dress, but it was far away from a wedding gown." She still wears the ring Victor gave her that day: gold, but thin as wire. "A few friends were there. We came to the court in Kraków to get a marriage license. The judge said, 'You cannot put Jewish where it says religion.' He said, 'You have to put "no religion." ' I said, 'Then I'm not going to get it.' In 1946, we got our civil wedding [in Austria]."

They moved to the Bad Ischl Displaced Persons camp near Ebensee. Victor became commander of the camp police, and Regina—much to her surprise—got pregnant. "At the end of the war, I couldn't wait to have children and a family— to be able to build something new, and emotionally I was OK, but I didn't believe my body could do it. I became very thin. It was too early for me to try."

227

In any case, a doctor had told her there was no chance for the time being. When she proved him wrong, Regina wanted an abortion. Victor had other opinions. "Never in my life are you going to have abortion!" he told her. Then he paid the doctor a visit. "I said, 'If you ever will try to do something without my knowledge, I'll put you away.' "

"He was really rough with him," Regina acknowledges. She gave birth to a daughter, Ida. "She was the princess. She was one of the first children in the camp, and she was like everybody's baby."

From the camp they moved to Linz, then Vienna, where they spent about a year and Victor played soccer. The Red Cross located some Lezerkiewicz/Lewis relatives in New York. "I had an uncle who didn't change the name. He was a very old man in Woodmere [Long Island]. He said, 'You come, the house will be yours.' But the waiting period for the Polish quota was five years. We came in forty-nine; he was dead and the house was sold."

Lewis brought a document to the United States "from the Russians, that I was a hero, which got me a place to live in Kraków. But then I come to the U.S. and it's the McCarthy era, so I lit it and burned it. I was very afraid to be searched and [have them] think we were Russian spies!"

Victor got a job mixing dough at the Streit's matzoh factory, and then worked at a plastics factory. His brother Leon was also in New York, working as a toolmaker. "Slowly, slowly I was making a good living," says Victor. He went to work for Signalstat, a company in Brooklyn. "The owner was a Jewish guy. We made auto parts. Everything was patented. He told me his ideas, I made them." The company's turn signals are still in use.

When Signalstat was sold, Victor opened his own machine shop. "I rented a little room in the Bronx and bought two machines. Then my brother joined me." (Leon's wife died when she was twenty-nine. They had two children. Leon still has a machine shop and lives in Westchester, New York.)

VR Precision Corporation made airplane parts. "I was president and Regina was vice president. Thank God, I was there until I retired in 1989. Here, I say, 'God Bless America!' I paid plenty taxes, and I never took a penny from nobody."

Ida Lewis lives in Israel. She is single. Son Alvin Lewis, an environmental engineer, lives in Queens. He and his wife have a daughter. The Lewises say

Victor and Regina Lewis, Queens, New York, 1994.

they raised their children "very traditionally," as Jews. "We never hid the past from the children," says Regina. "My daughter wanted to know everything about our life during the wartime, and Daddy's escape from the train. She used to come to our bedroom Sunday morning: 'Tell me more, Daddy!' But my son was different. When we would be at the table, I could see the child slowly disappear from the kitchen and go to the living room. So I saw it was not good, and we limited it to when he was not present."

When Ida—a former San Francisco flower child—went to Poland seeking the family's roots, Alvin was not ready to go. Several years later, he not only went, but secretly photographed parts of the death camps that were off-limits.

"We were gentle to them," says Victor. "There was no use of pressure. We didn't come out [of the camps] neurotic. We came like normal people. Looking for our future, looking to build a new life. I had the opportunity to get Austrian citizenship in a minute, because I was playing [soccer]. I had a few friends in Vienna who became multimillionaires."

The Lewises preferred to become American citizens, which they did in 1955, even if it meant that for years Victor barely saw his kids: "up at six in the morning, home at ten at night. I didn't mind. I loved America; every minute of it!"

In 1965, several Holocaust survivors in Flushing, including Victor Lewis, Sam Wertheim, and Roman Gunz—"all the Kraków people used to live here," according to Victor—founded the New Cracow Friendship Society. The first meeting drew three hundred. The membership stands at seven hundred today, with an active and growing "second generation" chapter. The organization helps support the few remaining Jews of Kraków—ninety families, according to Lewis—and social-welfare projects in Israel.

The Society never supported Oskar Schindler, though many individual members did. Lewis says that during Schindler's 1972 visit to New York, Murray Pantirer and Abraham Zuckerman wanted to bring him before the Society board, but some members objected. "They said he was a Nazi. These were people who didn't get into Brinnlitz at the end. This was only jealousy. Sour grapes."

Victor Lewis calls Oskar Schindler "a genius. Probably, in the beginning of the war, he didn't want to go to the front. What kind of a chance he had there? Schindler liked money, girls, alcohol. He saw a different life for himself, when he discovered the factory of [Abraham] Bankier. Here is the point: Schindler risked his life and his fortune in order to save the people under his power, building up for himself a powerful postwar alibi."

During a visit to Israel shortly after Schindler's death in 1974, Victor and Regina went looking for Schindler's grave. It's become a popular tourist attraction since the film, but back then, it took hours to find. "We had an Arab taxi driver who took us to the cemetery," Victor remembers. "I tell him I give him a good tip if he bring us to Schindler. He never heard of it. An old Arab came, and he says, 'These people are looking for somebody named Schindler who save their lives.' [The old man] said, 'We have somebody here by that name.'"

He let them in, "and right there, maybe fifty steps, is the grave of Schindler. I put a stone on it, and my wife too. I was very happy I saw it."

IGOR KLING

"You son-of-a-bitches; what the hell are *you* doing here?"

With that, the "big shots from Kraków" welcomed Igor Kling and a friend to Brinnlitz. It was an ungracious though not altogether unreasonable question, under the circumstances. Kling had spent only four months at Płaszów. He had never worked at Emalia. He neither hailed from the capital nor had connections among the influential. In the Płaszów social hierarchy, that made him a nobody, and certainly unworthy of a spot on Schindler's list.

The "big shots," on the other hand, had friends and relatives who had worked for Oskar Schindler since the ghetto, people who attempted to ransom their own lives with diamonds and still didn't make it. "They were angry!" Kling remembers. "But my friend—he did not lose his sense of humor—he said, 'I tell you what you do: Why don't you send us back to Płaszów?' I'll never forget it."

Kling has a small chuckle over this. He is stretched out in a chair—barefoot and in shorts—seventeen floors above the Intracoastal Waterway, in a luxury complex a few miles north of downtown Miami. He and his wife, Lena, spend most of the year here. Their other home is in the Catskills.

"We wouldn't *dare* to answer like this in Płaszów. They would take two, three *kapos* and beat us to death, without German interference! But we realized they already lost their clout. We were not afraid of them anymore."

Kling—then called Ignacy Klinghofer—knew nothing about Oskar Schindler when he found himself at Brinnlitz. He'd heard that "someone was good to people" at the Lipowa Street enamelware factory, but he'd never even heard the man's name. The best he could figure, he had got on the list because he'd worked at Płaszów's auto repair shop, and his *Autoschlosser* job title accurately described his abilities under the hood—unlike so many of the Brinnlitz "metalworkers," "masons," and "electricians," who could no more work steel, lay brick, or run wire than they could fly.

Igor Kling hadn't intended to become an auto mechanic; it wasn't the kind of work a wealthy bank director's son did. But the Germans needed laborers of all kinds—to dig sewers, build roads, fix cars—and it happened that he was assigned to the garage complex on the outskirts of Borysław, his hometown in eastern Galicia. "So then I actually learned, and when it came time to register [for working papers], I put 'mechanic.' Did I like it? Anything that got you through the day, you liked."

Borysław was the capital of Poland's petroleum industry. Jews accounted for nearly a third of its population before 1941. "We had visiting theater, opera, libraries, and movies," recalls Kling, who was born there in 1925. "To this day, I remember seeing *Treasure Island*, with Wallace Beery, and cowboy movies: Tom Mix, Ken Maynard, John Wayne. The last movie I saw there—the last American movie—was *I Am a Nazi Spy*, in 1939. Can you believe it?"

When Igor was a boy, the family lived well: French nannies, summer vacations at mountain resorts, ski trips, tennis, a fine Bösendorfer piano, and one of the city's few private telephones. Igor cherishes his copy of the three-page 1935 Borysław phone book, listing the Klinghofers, that he got from a friend.

In addition to his bank position, Igor's father, Arnold, was CEO of a drilling equipment company, and owned oil wells. Igor's older sister, Helena, went to medical school in Vienna. (Polish medical schools admitted few Jews, so those who could afford it went out of the country.) Dorothea, his mother, ran the household. As a schoolboy, Igor wanted to become an engineer.

But on September 28, 1939, less than a month after the invasion, the Germans and Soviets split Poland down the middle. Everything west of the river Bug came under German control. The Soviets occupied the east. Immediately they nationalized all private industry, and seized bank accounts, real estate, insurance policies, and other sources of individual wealth. Arnold Klinghofer lost his businesses and went to work at the agency established to run what was now the state-controlled petroleum industry.

"Once the Russians came in, life was not normal, but it was tolerable," says Igor Kling, who was fourteen at the time. "They instituted schools, so I went to school. We took three families to live, so they let us stay in our own house. They didn't snatch people's possessions, but they would come late at night to certain homes and snatch people, for political reasons."

But even that small degree of normality didn't last. On June 22, 1941, the German Army invaded the Soviet Union from the west, claiming all of Poland. During the next three years, transports and *Aktions* decimated Boryslaw's Jewish community of fourteen thousand.

Arnold Klinghofer was among the few Jews permitted to stay on in the offices of the petroleum agency's Boryslaw headquarters. Reduced to a clerk's status, he nonetheless was better off than colleagues forced back into the field as manual laborers. His boss was a man named Berthold Beitz, "German, of course," but a decent sort.

In August 1942, seventy-six thousand Jews were transported from eastern Galicia to the Belżec death camp. Dorothea Klinghofer was among them. Igor Kling says his sister, Helena, would have gone with her had it not been for Berthold Beitz.

"I was working in the auto depot and my father was in the office. We were still living in our house—they made the ghetto two months later. They took away my mother and sister and put them in a freight car, with the wife and daughter of Engelberg, another Jewish engineer who worked with my father. My father found out they were taken away. He prevailed on Beitz—begged him—with this Engelberg. Beitz said, 'I'll see what I can do.' He got into the car, drove to the railroad station, and went track to track, car to car, and he yelled, 'Klinghofer! Engelberg! Klinghofer! Engelberg!' just

The only existing photo of Igor Kling's father.

like you see in the movie, when Schindler runs around and plucks out this guy Stern from the train. Exactly the same thing!

"In one car, my mother and sister were there. He told them to open the car, and pulled out my sister, but they wouldn't let my mother go. Then he went to the next car, and the next car, and found this Mila Engelberg—the daughter—and took them both out. The Jewish *kapos* escorted them back to the house. That was the last I saw of my mother."

Helena, who died in New York about fifteen years ago, felt guilty the rest of her life. "She tried to stay, but my mother pushed her out. We didn't talk about it much, because it was too painful for her and for me. That evening, we had like an evening of wake, but the danger was not over for us—we didn't know what was going to happen the next day—so we couldn't brood too much over it."

As for Beitz, "He survived the war, and became CEO of Krups [the huge German industrial firm]. He's still alive, not quite eighty. He came to New York and gave a testimonial, and a few people from Borysław were there, and everybody went to see him."

The Borysław Jewish ghetto consisted of a few streets of what had been private homes. Finally forced out of theirs, the Klinghofers moved into a house

Igor Kling with the Polish women now living in his prewar family home, Boryslaw, Poland, 1993.

owned by Helena's husband, a doctor. A local militia occupied what had been Igor Kling's childhood home.

The new conditions were cramped, he says, "but we still had more than one shirt and some jewelry. The peasants would come from the western part of Poland, and we would trade them clothes or jewelry for food."

Helena's husband was spared deportation because he was a physician. As his assistant, she also was spared. Igor and Arnold were protected for some time by small, R-shaped lapel pins, which stood for *Ruestung*, or armament workers.

In 1943, the Germans closed the Borysław Ghetto, cramming all remaining Jews into a World War One-era military barracks called the *koszary*. Still, the auto depot workers, who marched nearly four miles from town to their jobs every day, maintained access to the outside world through the Poles who worked with them. Together, Kling recalls, they watched the most dreadful crime committed by the Germans against the Jews of Borysław.

"They took three hundred people to a slaughterhouse and killed them. Some of the Poles had binoculars, and we saw movement there, the trucks, and heard shots. We were getting fewer and fewer, so we knew everybody."

In a subsequent *Aktion*, soldiers came to the auto depot and rounded up the Jews who worked there. Igor managed to escape. "At the last minute, another fellow and I ran into a building and we slid down into a furnace. The next morning, we were hungry and thirsty, so we climbed out. We were all black with soot. I see cars and trucks, and life is normal, but there are no Jews. We tried to crawl and walk to the garage where we worked, and it was like nothing ever happened. No one was looking for us by name, so that same evening, we walked back. It was like after the rain, there is sunshine, and you're not wet anymore. That's the way it was when these things happened."

This was in the spring of 1944, not long before one final transport emptied Borysław of Jews. On a June day, to their surprise, the *koszary* residents found themselves face to face with a man named Walek Eisenstein, who had been transported six weeks earlier to Płaszów with his son. Eisenstein, head of the Borysław Jewish police, "was a bastard," says Kling, "a terrible guy." Now here he was, with a shaved head, SS guards in tow. He told the Jews of Borysław they were going to Płaszów, a work camp. "They brought him in order to pacify us, that everything was going to be all right." Kling thinks Eisenstein and his son were killed at Płaszów.

Clutching their remaining odds and ends, the Klinghofers climbed into freight cars for the trip. Igor recalls that it took less than two days, and that it wasn't so bad. "We had water, and on certain stops they let us get off."

The Chilowiczes, Płaszów's Jewish leaders, were waiting to "greet" the latest arrivals. "Chilowicz and his wife, they started cursing us right away. Using such profanity! The women were shocked. I remember he was wearing riding breeches and boots—all shined up—and a white silk shirt. He had a whip in his hand, a full head of hair. We didn't know who the hell he was, but we found out in about five minutes." (Amon Goeth later killed the Chilowiczes and most of their relatives at Płaszów.)

Igor Kling didn't know it then, but his first few days at Płaszów would be his last with his father. "He was taken to Wieliczka, the salt mines, and I didn't see him again. I understand he subsequently was transferred to Mauthausen—somebody said they saw him there. I was very distraught. Everything was so strange. There was no such thing as goodbye."

Not long after that, Helena disappeared. "She went from Płaszów to Auschwitz, Birkenau, then Stutthof, and Bergen-Belsen too. I don't know how she survived, but she did." Manci Rosner was the head of her barracks at Płaszów, and later Helena would remark that Manci had been very kind to her.

As an *Autoschlosser*, Kling was assigned to the Płaszów garage. "We used to repair the vehicles of all those [German] big shots in the camp." He was summoned once to Amon Goeth's villa. "There was a little problem with his car. We came in there, and Helen [Sternlicht Rosenzweig] was there with those two tremendous dogs. Tolek [Manskleid], my friend who's next to me on the list, and I, we were dreading those dogs. She put them away, and we were trying to work out what was wrong with the car." (Manskleid now lives in Israel.)

Kling stayed at Płaszów just long enough to draw the most horrendous assignment imaginable: exhuming and burning thousands of bodies. The Germans didn't want advancing Soviet troops to find proof of the carnage that had soaked Płaszów's ground with Jewish blood.

Kling and another friend—Marion Speicher, who lives seven floors below him in the Florida building—paired up on the night shift. "There were special digging commandos, working at night with bare hands. It was very cold, so at night they used to bring soup that was somewhat thicker than the normal during the day, because they wanted us to be able to work. These bodies were buried in sand, so it was not difficult to dig them up, but they were decomposed. I'll tell you a gruesome story: My friend and I, we were picking up a body—he had it by the hands, I by the legs—and in the middle of the way, the body falls down. I'm standing with two legs and he with two hands."

Kling shakes his head. "In the movie, they were putting them on a wagon and carrying them to the fires. There was nothing—no wagons! We just schlepped them. What did you think about? You thought about just how long it will be to twelve o'clock and you'll get soup. You didn't feel anything anymore. But you realized one thing: 'Since they're liquidating, they'll kill us at the end.' We knew already about the ovens and the gas chambers."

What Kling didn't know was that he, as an *Autoschlosser*, had been added to Schindler's list. He found out at Gröss-Rosen.

"What a terrible camp! They stripped us naked. It was cold like hell. Then we went to take a shower; they had a barrel with disinfectant that they put on us; then they made us bend down to see that we didn't have anything hidden inside. They chased us to the barrack. I would say it was at least a mile from where we took those cold showers. They herded us into a recreation room, and they said, 'Here, you're going to spend the night.' We were one on top of the other. God forbid somebody had to get up."

He also can't forget what happened when some of the Płaszów men tossed away pieces of stale bread. "We had enough bread in Płaszów. There was wheeling and dealing. A delicacy was raw bacon, white bread, American cigarettes. But we were three days on the way to Gröss-Rosen, and when we got there, we thought, 'What the hell do we need this old bread for?' These guys at Gröss-Rosen, they threw themselves on it. They yelled to us: 'Boys, boys, don't throw it away! How could you do it? You're going to starve here!' "

They would have, had not he and Tolek—classified as an auto mechanic's helper—been summoned from their barracks after perhaps a week, leaving Marion Speicher behind.

"They called us by name, so we didn't think they were going to shoot us. They shoot you, they don't ask for a name. I asked Tolek, 'Did you steal anything?' There are two basic things you learn in camp: Never volunteer for anything, and if there is a transport, you never try to go. Wherever you are, if you're alive, it's possibly better than where they transport you. They put us in the transport. We didn't know where we were going, but on the train we saw all the big shots from Płaszów."

This was further cause for speculation. "What were they going to do with us: kill us or save us? There was nothing in between. It was always extremes, so we didn't know if it was good or bad."

As it turned out, the transport was headed for Brinnlitz. "Right away, we saw a big difference in the SS. The viciousness from their faces had disappeared. The behavior we saw was completely different than in Płaszów. They were middle-aged, the leftovers."

Kling didn't want one of the "cushy" factory jobs, and was pleased with his outside work: building fences "which they never got around to electrifying. We used to steal potatoes from the fields. We had to make a fire for the SS who were guarding us. We would dig a little hole, cover it up with a little sheet of tin, and on top, put some old wood, and have baked potatoes."

He remembers with a certain fondness how the men spent their evenings at Brinnlitz. "We sang and told jokes. I remember the Rosners playing music—Leopold and Wilhelm. Tolek and I had a bunk next to them, so we had a front-row seat." The Rosners had a friend named Willie Krantz, who told jokes. "He was a great stand-up comic."

After liberation, Igor Kling went east, toward Borysław, the opposite direction from most of the *Schindlerjuden*. "We were walking, schlepping, in a freight car with German prisoners of war." Near the city of Przemyśl, about sixty miles from Borysław, Soviet soldiers caught Kling and his friend and brought them to a detention camp already holding many of the men who had fought under the traitorous General Vlasov.

"We were ready to commit suicide. We were thrown in with a few thousand of the Russians who were fighting with the German Army. A lot of them were guards at Płaszów. They took a lot of collaborators as prisoners of war, and they threw us in too. We tried to talk to somebody, but they were immune. They [had] lost all their families, and millions of Russians. [To] one of the officers in charge, we said, 'We just came from a concentration camp,' and he said, 'Concentration camp? Who told you to go there? Why didn't you go to the partisans?' He was very cold.

"So we thought now we may be suffering more than during the war. We got an idea. We registered by a different name. I had my hand in a sling, and didn't shave for three, four days so they didn't recognize us. They put us together with a group of six Poles and let us out. From there, we came west to Kraków. That was in the end of May, beginning of June."

Kling had long ago given up hope for his parents, but had gotten "conflicting reports" about his sister, Helena. The mystery was solved one summer day on the streets of Kraków. "There was a little place where the Jews used to gather. All of a sudden I saw her, with her hair cropped short. She wasn't beaten, but she was in bad shape. She wasn't sure about me being alive either. That was something wonderful."

The two stayed around Kraków for a few weeks. Then Igor got a chauffeur job, near Katowice, with a Borysław woman who had married a prominent communist official. "She gave us a room in the old stable, but I saw there was no future, so I left." Tolek Manskleid, meanwhile, had fallen in love, and decided to stay. After "a big cry," Igor Kling headed west with a group, aiming for the part of Germany under U.S. control. "On the way, we went to Salzburg and were supposed to stay there for two days and be transported to Germany. I liked the city so much that I stayed for four years."

Helena went to look for her husband; she had heard he was in a Munich Displaced Persons' camp. When she found him, he was involved with someone else, and they split up. She rejoined her brother in Austria. Igor studied medicine for a year in Vienna, then dropped out so that he could support his sister while she resumed her medical studies.

In 1946, Igor and Helena began searching for relatives in the United States. "I had a friend who spoke English, and we went to some kind of American mission. They had telephone books, and I found about three or four Klinghofers between Manhattan and Brooklyn. I wrote letters to all of them. I told them who I am, I come from Poland, my mother's name, my father's, and I would like to know, perhaps we are related.

"[From] two I didn't get any replies. Two said we were not related, and the fifth one writes that he looked it over through all the genealogical tree, and we're definitely not related, but due to the fact that he sees I was in concentration camp, I shouldn't be insulted, he sends me a package."

And what a package it was. "Chocolate! Cigarettes! Oh, what it was worth at that time!" Igor wrote and thanked the man, but didn't stay in touch. He's sorry about that to this day. In 1985, Palestinian terrorists hijacked a cruise ship called the *Achille Lauro*. In an act of cynical cruelty worthy of Amon Goeth, they pushed a Jewish tourist from Brooklyn overboard, in his wheelchair. His name was Leon Klinghofer.

"That was this Klinghofer who sent me that package. I was heartbroken."

Igor and Lena Kling at a dinner honoring Emilie Schindler, 1994.

Igor and Helena came to the United States in May 1949. A month later, Igor found himself busing tables at a Catskills resort, the Lake Plaza Hotel, in Parksville, New York. "It was very good for me: the air, the food, the young girls. Then I worked for a while in an automotive shop, repairing clutches."

His next job introduced him to the business in which he still works. "A friend of mine told me that a certain costume jewelry firm needed a salesman. My English wasn't so great, but I got the job. I went to school—English for foreigners—for two sessions. But it was for morons. I was told before I came to America, to get good English, read *The New York Times.* So I bought two newspapers every day: *The Herald Tribune* and *The New York Times.* I would read them completely, from the first to the last page. I also watched a lot of television and listened to the radio."

He met the woman who would become his wife in 1951. Her name was Lena Rybak, and she had survived the war with her parents and sister in labor camps and in hiding. They were liberated by Russians in 1944, in Boryslaw. "We are from towns five miles apart"—she from Drohobycz—"but we didn't know each other. But her father knew my father. He was a textile merchant. That last few months in Boryslaw, in the *koszary,* he was there."

They married in 1954. Two years later, they had a daughter, and two years after that, a son. Today, the daughter, Dorothy Kling Weinstein, is a New Rochelle silver wholesaler and mother of two. The son, Arnold Kling, is a Manhattan lawyer. Igor and a partner started their own company, Deming Jewelry, Inc., and the Klings began a socioeconomic progression familiar to many immigrant Jews: from Queens to Long Island—East Williston—to South Florida.

Thanks to their son, the Klings may have been the first people in Florida to see *Schindler's List.* Arnold Kling and Steven Spielberg's sister are close friends. Yet Igor was omitted from the group of *Schindlerjuden* filmed at Oskar Schindler's grave.

Igor says, "She told her brother: 'Imagine this; there is the father of my friend, and he was not interviewed or invited to Israel!' Steven says: 'What can I do for him? I'll arrange a private showing before the movie opens.' One day I'm sitting here and the phone rings: 'This is Amblin Entertainment.' I say,

'Yeah, yeah.' She says, 'How would you like to have a private showing of *Schindler's List*? You can bring anybody you want; we have a whole theater for you."

The Klings are among the most Americanized of the Schindler couples. They ski and play tennis. They contribute to Jewish causes, but don't participate. In fact, the most visible South Florida *Schindlerjuden* didn't know Igor was around until he surfaced in May 1994 at a Miami Beach tribute to Emilie Schindler, in a well-tailored, cream-colored suit that perfectly offset his tropical tan.

Little about the Klings' life today hints at their past, but, says Igor Kling, "You never recover. When the children came, we had discussions regarding the future, and we both decided you cannot bear a grudge and hate all your life. You become obsessed, and it's the only thing you can talk about: revenge and pain. We decided to let them know, but we wanted them—and ourselves—to lead a normal life. It didn't mean we should forget what happened, but on the other hand, we shouldn't think about it twenty-four hours a day. We know people who do."

Sol Urbach

There he is, literally front and center, number 31 on Oskar Schindler's list: Dawid Urbach, born on February 18, 1896. Could this man have been his father? Could Dawid Urbach actually have survived the ghetto liquidation? Could they have breathed the same Czechoslovakian air for seven months and never once glimpsed each other?

Sol Urbach probably will never know. Though one of the busiest public speakers among the *Schindlerjuden,* Urbach hadn't seen a copy of the list until early 1994. Before he even had the chance to locate himself—page ten, number 569—there was his father's name, leaping off the first page. Granted, he didn't know precisely when his father was born, but 1896 certainly fell within range. This man would have been thirty-two in 1928, when Bertha Urbach, wife of Dawid the tailor-cantor, gave birth to her third child: a son they called Salomon.

The list that Schindler compiled in April 1945 included men from Płaszów, Emalia, the Budzyners, and the frozen transport from Goleszów. "So it's possible that he came from Kraków together with me by way of Płaszów by way of Gröss-Rosen," Sol speculates.

Possible, but not likely. "I mean, if I knew there was a Dawid Urbach there, or a Dawid Urbach knew that there was a Salomon Urbach, we would have looked at one another at least. It wasn't a very common name, not like Smith, but there were a few Urbachs." Still, Oskar Schindler's Brinnlitz factory camp was a big place, housing about eleven hundred Jews. And as Sol Urbach himself notes, "You've got to remember that in a concentration-camp setting, you didn't have a mess hall where you met to eat. . . . And you also were going about your business; you were not over there when you were supposed to be over here."

Then factor in what he learned on a trip to the Auschwitz records room in 1973. "I gave them the names Dawid [pronounced David] Urbach, Bertha Urbach, all my seven family members. They had absolutely nothing on them. I was on my way out, and an idea came into my head. I went back, and I didn't tell her who I am. I simply asked, 'Do you have anything on a Salomon Urbach?' She went back to the filing cabinet and brought out a card: Salomon Urbach worked at the enamelworks factory for Schindler. He was in the ghetto. He went to Kraków-Płaszów, and to Gröss-Rosen, and he should have survived."

Sol Urbach was amazed. He told the records clerk the whole story, and asked why so much information existed on him, yet not a word about the rest of his family. "She explained that the Germans felt obligated to keep track of people that crossed borders. If they took Polish people like myself from Poland and crossed into Czechoslovakia, that was a triggering device that they had to keep track. But if somebody was born in Poland and died in Poland, then there is no record."

Presumably, his father died on March 13, 1943, when German troops mowed down the remaining Jews of the Kraków Ghetto like so much overgrown grass. Sol was safe at Oskar Schindler's enamelware factory that day, but always assumed that his parents and siblings—Chana, Rivka, Samuel, Simon, and Haskel—were murdered.

Still, the semiretired builder from Flemington, New Jersey, can't let it go. What about the list? "This list doesn't lie," he declares. But in fact it does, over and over, by omission, commission, and typo, to protect both the innocent and the guilty, and simply through carelessness.

Sol Urbach was indeed born in Poland, but spent much of his later childhood in Romania. A maternal uncle had done well there in business, and urged his

The Urbach family. Parents: Dawid and Bertha; Girl, back row: Rivka; Boy, back row: Samuel;
Front row: Chana, Simon, Haskel, Sol.

sister and brother-in-law to join him. The family moved to Sadagura, a small
town just across the River Prut from the big city of Czernowitz.

When he was twelve, Romanian authorities kicked out the Polish Jews
who'd never become citizens. "Soldiers came and picked us up as a family, and
drove us over to the Polish border, which was not very far, and set us free to
walk over into Poland. We had just what we could carry."

Their first stop on the Polish side: jail. "I remember a high window where
I was trying to climb up and see out of it, but we weren't there long—two, three
nights at most. And from my understanding, the Jewish community quickly
mounted an effort to get the family out of jail."

The Urbachs settled in the Kraków suburb of Borek Falenski. Sol remembers a public school right across the street, but because the Urbach kids

didn't speak "comfortable" Polish, "and we were afraid of anti-Semitism," they walked an hour each way to a Jewish school in the center of Kraków. "I remember on these walks to school, non-Jewish kids would throw stones at us."

All eight Urbachs occupied two rooms. "And also my father worked out of the same room as a tailor, but it seems to me they were large rooms, like twelve-by-sixteen. We had in the backyard a well where you dumped the pail in to get the water out. We kept food on the kitchen balcony."

His family was quite religious, says Sol, but not as devout as his mother's family in Kalwaria. "I remember when I would spend a week with [his maternal] grandfather, I would return home totally unfit to be with the other children. Even my own family was not good enough. In one or two weeks, they converted me totally. My grandfather [Akiva Boldinger] stood and listened to my prayers at the temple. He was deeply involved in his own prayers, but he didn't miss one word. To mumble was not good enough. He would stop me and tell me that I prayed like a goy. I know that my grandfather or my uncle would not come to visit us because they couldn't have as much as a glass of water in our house." They couldn't be sure it would be kosher enough.

By 1939, the Polish government's propagandists had done such a good job of lulling the populace into a false sense of security—based on wildly inflated claims of Polish military might—that when the Germans marched into Kraków that September, few Jews seemed alarmed. ("Hitler was back-page news," says Sol Urbach.)

"There was already a shortage of food, and the German soldiers from the trucks would pass out some soup to us at the very beginning of the war." But soon enough, "mass confusion" took hold. The Urbachs left Borek Falenski and moved in with relatives in Podgórze. Jewish kids couldn't go to school anymore, so Sol began hanging out at a furniture shop in their building.

"I would go down and watch how they built furniture. I had nothing else to do but to go and stand on bread lines, sometimes the whole night. I watched long enough until this man said, 'Pull the saw and work.' His name was Kaminski."

When the order came to move to the ghetto, the Urbachs refused. Kaminski, who wasn't Jewish, suggested that his young protégé move into the workshop. "Later on it became very difficult, because the neighbors would tell my mother and father that they could no longer keep quiet about them not reporting to the ghetto. So the family reported, with the understanding that I would stay behind in that workshop."

What seemed like a good idea in theory didn't work in practice. "I remember at night, trying to sleep with the moon shining against the windows, and a kitten going up on the ledge convinced me that somebody was trying to break in and kill me. This was the first time in my life I was alone in a totally strange environment. The fear drove me absolutely out of my mind. I stood this for seven days, then I pleaded with [Kaminski] to let me go and report to the ghetto."

Eight Urbachs lived in a single basement room. Still, says Sol, "I distinctly remember now feeling we were safe amongst Jewish people. I remember the feeling that we could breathe now. We had nobody to report us, and this was a good thing."

No matter that getting a decent night's sleep was impossible because of the crowding. "People by and large began to live, and show a little happiness, and there was a social life that went on. We were downgraded, but it sort of felt like maybe this was the worst, and we could live with it."

Now and then, a forced-labor detail would snare an Urbach or two, but even that seemed tolerable. "My older brother worked mostly cleaning streets, also unloading some cars at the railroad station, but they always returned."

Then one day in the summer of 1942, someone snared Sol. "Two small trucks of Germans came into the ghetto and simply rounded up one hundred people from the streets. Those days, you didn't know where you were being taken or for how long. As it happens, these small trucks delivered us to a factory backyard. When we arrived, there was a tall, handsome guy working on a machine outside, which was sitting under some kind of a shed roof. He was wearing one of those leather aprons.

"They put us into a formation so we would be presentable to this fellow, who turned out to be Oskar Schindler. That's when he said, 'I don't want these kids.' He meant me and a fellow named Guthertz," who now lives in Israel. The guard retorted, " 'You keep who we bring you.' " Sol was fifteen years old.

In time, the young enamelworker began to learn more about his employer. "What I heard was that Schindler was given this factory but could not operate it because he could not deal with the Poles. He didn't speak Polish and the Poles didn't trust the Germans. So he invented this idea: If he got the former owners and managers to help him run his business, they would set him up in the back, and the Polish customers would come in and do business through Abraham Bankier [the plant's Jewish former owner]."

For a time, small groups of workers marched under guard to and from the Lipowa Street factory. Then the regulations changed. The SS refused to escort groups of fewer than one hundred workers. "So Schindler said, 'Okay, I step up to one hundred.' The SS escorts would take us to the ghetto whether it was a night shift or morning shift. They would take us back to the ghetto and we would stay with our families."

By the beginning of 1943, Sol remembers that "the situation had changed from the jovial mood and hope to fear. You were told where you go and when you go. We already had no other alternative but to follow orders, or we would otherwise endanger our lives."

On March 12 of that year, a Friday, Schindler detained his workers at Emalia. "He went around the factory and talked to everybody in groups, or individually. He told us we couldn't go back in the ghetto because there was an *Aktion*. I don't remember him using the word [for] liquidation, but *Aktion*, that the Jews were being shipped out or whatever. That scared me horribly, to a point where I was actually unable to eat whatever was provided. For a number of days I was eating less than I was given because of not knowing what was happening." He remembers staying several days at the factory, then being taken to Płaszów. He never saw his parents, brothers, or sisters again.

"Distinctly, it felt that we arrived in hell. It was a gruesome scene to enter. You could almost tell it was some kind of a killing machine. You saw the gallows as you came in. You could see the [Chujowa Górka] from almost anyplace in the camp. You knew that that's where people were being killed. You heard the popping of the gunshots."

Survivors of the liquidation staggered into Płaszów, reporting that the ghetto "looked like a huge, outdoor morgue. The truckloads of bodies arrived in the Kraków-Płaszów camp, and I am convinced that what went through my mind is what went through the minds of everybody else: our family was arriving."

He heard that his oldest brother had been selected for a work group, not for extermination. "But this fellow who knew my brother told me that he saw when my brother tried to cross the street to join my family, and he got shot."

Płaszów was indeed its own hell. The few rules of civilized behavior that the Nazis exercised over the ghetto vaporized on the business side of the camp gates. Soon after arriving, young Sol Urbach thought he'd met his end.

"An SS man came into the barrack at night and yelled out, 'Urbach!' As it happens, two of us stuck our heads out. The other was a fellow named Orbach. The guard took us down to the guard station . . . and as soon as the two of us came in, one officer took this fellow Orbach into the other room and began to beat the hell out of him. They hanged him by his hands tied behind his back and pulled him up. They dropped him on the floor and dumped some water on him. This went on for a good while. I was sitting in the other room, where I could see all this through an open door."

Sol Urbach figured he was next, but before they got to him, the SS guards simply left the building. "The two of us made our way back to our barrack. There was a rumor that somebody referred to him as the 'Red Orbach.' He had red hair, but red meant communist."

Until Schindler built his subcamp at Emalia, his workers lived in the Płaszów barracks. Urbach says the SS who escorted them back and forth to Lipowa Street resented their "special treatment" at the factory. Just to make life unpleasant, they required each Emalia worker to carry a heavy rock from the barracks to the camp gate on the way out, and retrieve it on the way in.

The group moved to the subcamp in 1943. At its peak, it would house one thousand Emalia workers, and hundreds more from another factory called NKF (which Schindler didn't own). Sol Urbach became a carpenter whose chief task was to maintain the pot-and-pan factory's blackout shades.

In August 1944, Schindler got an order to reduce his workforce by seven hundred. Everyone lined up for selection. "What went through my mind was that somehow I was in the wrong group," Urbach recalls. "As we were standing

Sol Urbach's wooden cover autograph book from the last days of Brinnlitz.

there, I was horribly anxious. By that time, I was already totally convinced that if there was a future, you had to stay close to Schindler. At one point, Schindler passed in front of me. I stepped up to him—risking my life, because the SS were there, too. I yelled out to him, 'Herr Schindler, there are no carpenters left!' What would this have meant to him, I have no idea, but I had to say something. Schindler recognized me evidently, and he put me into the group which remained: three hundred of us." Most of the three hundred would make it to Brinnlitz.

Urbach remembers the short, intermediate stopover at Gröss-Rosen as a whirlwind of violence. Ukrainian guards delighted in kicking prisoners "until they curled up on the ground in a fetal position," and spitting on the Jews' half-shaved heads. He also recalls that the men were "stunned" the day they were lined up and called by *name*, to a certain assembly place. They'd been numbers for so long that this had to be a good sign.

It was. They boarded cattle cars for Brinnlitz, where Schindler awaited, jaunty and reassuring in his Tyrolean hat.

The Brinnlitz factory looked busy but accomplished little. Sol, the carpenter, spent much of his time working on Schindler's private office. "I remember putting up the paneling on walls. We had no materials to finish it—like paint or varnish—so we went around with a butane torch and burned it, so it turned brown."

His job enabled Sol to leave the factory. "Sometimes at night, I would go out and look for some lumber. There would be truckloads of something, and I would be able to steal some of whatever it was. I could jump on the truck while no one was watching me. I would take these things and give them away.

"[Once,] I came back from Schindler's villa, which was inside the [grain] mill, with oatmeal or something else. My friend Max and I noticed that we didn't see anyone guarding the door to the women's barracks. We ran in and dropped off what we had, but when we came out, there was a woman SS. Evidently, she wrote up a report, and that night we gathered in the *Appell*, and [camp commandant] Liepold yells in German, 'Who were the two guys who went into the women's quarters?' We were wondering what do we do now. But this was toward the end of the war, and the fear wasn't that great anymore, so we made the decision to step up. All he wanted to know was which of the SS guards let us in."

Sol and others who worked at Schindler's villa sometimes had a chance to hear radio broadcasts. "This SS guy guarding us fell asleep, with his rifle between his legs. We would work our way behind that radio and fiddle with it until we got the BBC." They knew that the end of the war was at hand.

Max Blasenstein, his friend, made Sol Urbach a gift that he still has: an autograph book with the date May 7, 1945, carved into the wooden cover. In the days of their liberation, he went around to friends like Rena Finder, Helen Beck, and Halina Silber, who inscribed messages: "Let us rejoice, be happy as loved ones should be. The fresh grass didn't grow yet, still we are thankful. Our faces are jubilant. My heart, your heart, is happy. The beauty of youth, the beauty of happiness is outstanding. They didn't disappear too far. Our whole life we shall reach for love. We shall rejoice and sink in eternal happiness."

Sol left Brinnlitz with a group of seventeen men and women bound for Kraków. "In those days, you could round up horses roaming the fields. The same things with wagons. We didn't have a great deal of respect for somebody else's private property. We arrived in Kraków and the toughest moment in my life began. Most of them found distant relatives, close relatives, but I didn't find anybody. All of a sudden, everybody was for himself, and before you know it, I was practically on my own."

He moved into a dorm for refugees, and found Adam Mondel, a buddy from Płaszów who had survived Mauthausen. They began a brisk trade across the Polish border. "In Czechoslovakia, they had a lot of things like towels, ropes, and linen, which in Poland there was a short [supply]. So we smuggled these things. This became our way of making a living" until they realized they were vulnerable to the draft in Poland.

"This was the fall of forty-five, and we went to Czechoslovakia thinking we would settle there, but we couldn't stay there very long because we realized that this was communism also."

They slid over the borders to Germany, settling in Bamberg, Bavaria. He and Adam "lived like brothers, but in 1947, an aunt and uncle of his showed up from Munich. They said, 'Adam, you belong in school.' They yanked him out. This was the second time I went through losing somebody I was attached to."

Polish Jews began to arrive from captivity in Siberia, and among them was Ada Birnbaum and her family. They struck up a romance that crossed the Atlantic. Sol Urbach arrived in Boston on March 13, 1949, six years to the day after his family fell in the Kraków ghetto. Ada followed in June. He made her a June bride the next year in New York, where he had relatives on his mother's side.

"It was extremely difficult to get jobs in 1949 because all the boys were coming home from the war," he recalls. "I did get eventually a job as a furniture maker in Paterson [New Jersey]. Another job I got, oddly enough, was at a place where they did enamel works. I don't remember if it was pots and pans, but they did something similar to Emalia, where you would stamp out the things from metal, dip them in enamel and take them over to the hot oven."

He remembers going to dinner once at a "fancy" Manhattan restaurant. "We're eating, and this guy is on stage playing the violin. I said to my brother-in-law, 'This guy could have me fooled. He's playing Spanish music and looks Spanish, but he also looks like Henry Rosner.' Sure enough, it was Rosner." The "fancy" restaurant was Polonnaise. "The first thing that came out of my mouth was, 'Where is that son of yours that was taken away from Brinnlitz to

Sol and Ada Urbach, Flemington, NJ, 1994.

Auschwitz?' He pulled out a picture and showed me this tall, muscular guy in a U.S. Navy uniform." That, of course, was little Olek.

In 1951, Sol and Ada moved to Flemington, New Jersey, a quaint, Revolutionary War–era town where Ada's parents had bought a farm (it became something of a mecca for Jewish war refugees). The Lindbergh baby kidnapping trial had put Flemington on the map. According to Sol, "Walter Winchell set up headquarters here, where he broadcast to the whole world." Today, Flemington is famous for its scores of outlet stores.

Sol found a partner and got into the building business. His partner contributed a wheelbarrow, a pick, and a shovel. Sol Urbach put up his savings: $125. They started digging ditches and repairing roofs. When the partners split up six years later, Sol was a major Hunterdon County developer and property owner—"lord of the manor," he jokes.

On a clear day, he and Ada can relax on the back patio of the hillside house he built thirty years ago on three wooded acres, and gaze past the Wachtung Mountain east to the Verrazano Narrows bridge, thirty-five miles away.

In the 1970s, the Hunterdon County Historical Society invited Urbach to speak. Its members wanted to learn more about the Jewish refugees who had come to populate the area. "I talked about my experience in the war, in the concentration camps, and I talked about Oskar Schindler. I never had any problems in talking about what happened to me. As a matter of fact, it would almost seem like I enjoyed it, because that was the only thing I could do about what happened to me. So if anybody wanted to listen to me, I talked. My kids knew from day one, as soon as they were able to understand, exactly what my story was."

Born in 1952, son David is a cardiologist on Cape Cod. Daughter Barbara Urbach-Lissner, a lawyer, lives in Cresskill, New Jersey. Between them, they have five children. Son Henry, thirty and single, is working toward a doctorate at Princeton University.

Since the release of *Schindler's List*, Sol Urbach has been everywhere: on nationally syndicated talk shows, at colleges, in the newspapers, on the radio. In addition to telling his own story, he tries to convey certain messages: "how the brutality in this film and the brutality in the Holocaust have nothing to do with one another," and how anyone inclined to believe the Holocaust deniers should listen to survivors like himself. "And they don't even have to rely on that—they should talk to some of the GIs who found these concentration camps and who found these mass burial sites, and went into shock entering these camps."

Sol Urbach hasn't yet directly confronted a Holocaust denier, but if that happens, he says, "it would be a very short conversation. I don't imagine that anyone could convince them. They have a vested interest in what they do. I am not so much worried about them as I am interested in the rest of the population knowing the truth: what happened, how it happened, and how, when hate groups spring up, those who stand by and don't do anything are really helping spread the hate."

RENA AND LEWIS FAGEN

Before it devolved into grotesquery and peril, the German incursion into Poland actually thrilled teenagers like Rena Schönthal and Ludwik Feigenbaum, now Rena and Lewis Fagen. An invigorating scent of menace spiked the Krakovian air. And the exploding ordnance? *Son et lumière.* Their parents didn't seem unduly alarmed, so why should they be?

"When there was talk about the outbreak of the war, and we were taping the windows against the bombs, I said to my parents, 'Don't be angry, but, you know, I would like to see for two or three days what war looks like.' In the beginning, there was excitement over the bombs," Rena Fagen admits.

"I was appointed a runner," remembers her husband. "In the building they appointed a warden [and] a deputy warden, and I was running with different messages. And for me this was the greatest adventure," until the Germans came stomping through Kraków, barging into private homes and carting off whatever appealed to them, slapping and smacking Jews as if they were pesky insects—and rounding them up in a cheese wagon.

"I want to tell you an interesting story," says Lew Fagen, silver-haired and fit at about seventy. "As soon as the Germans came into the city of Kraków, probably three or four weeks later, there was a van—like Kraft would have to distribute cheeses to the grocery stores—which had signs from some kind of a cheese company in Germany. It must have been requisitioned by the German army and brought to Poland. This van was coming to the Jewish section of town to catch people to work. We used to call it the *Käsewagen:* the cheese van. And soon as the word spread that the cheese wagon was in the vicinity, everybody ran. You could walk down the street and be caught to work. For several days, mind you, you'd disappear. This was the period where we had to do forced labor. During the winter, we were used for shoveling snow."

Marauding German soldiers raided Jewish homes without warning. "They knocked on your door and four or five of them walked in and upset the whole apartment looking for valuables—furs and other things—and beating up people."

Rena Schonthal Fagen with her brother, Paul, and her parents, Bella and Aaron. Kraków, 1930s.

The conquerors soon closed the schools. With lingering embarrassment, Lew Fagen remembers the exact day. "I was playing hooky. I didn't even know the school was closed. We wore school uniforms. They looked like army uniforms: navy blue with light blue. I was walking on one of the main streets of Kraków, and I was stopped by a civilian, who was a Ukrainian. He asked me for my papers, and I showed him that I was a student. We went to a private Jewish academy. He said, 'Oh, you're a student? You don't have to go to school.' He put me on top of a truck where there were a dozen other people, and they took us to a fire department. At the fire department, they had trucks with hoists, and we were going from lamppost to lamppost hanging up Nazi flags for the arrival of Governor General Hans Frank.

"My mother was dying a thousand deaths because I didn't return home at the time I was supposed to. She was absolutely out of her mind. And finally, one of the firemen, who knew my father, recognized me. I told him, 'Can't you see to it that I go home?' And he said, 'OK, get off the truck and go home. I'll cover for you.' After four or five hours of this kind of work, I came home. This was my first encounter with forced labor."

After that, students "were going clandestinely to teachers' homes in groups of three or four and having classes there."

The Fagens of Boca Raton, Florida, grew up together in Kraków. "We belonged to the same group of boys and girls, going to parks, going to picnics together. We were good friends," says Lew. And neighbors. Rena was born in October 1925, the younger of Bella and Aaron Schönthal's two children. Her brother, Paul, is five years older. Aaron imported fruit and nuts from all over the world. The family had an apartment at 85 Dietla Street in Kraków in a building owned by Rena's grandmother, Amalia Schönthal. Amalia lived on another floor with her daughter, son-in-law, and another grandchild, Pola. The Feigenbaums lived at Number 77.

Rena's family were "traditional" Jews. But the Feigenbaums were "progressive," says Lew. "My father kept his business open on Saturdays. He was the nationwide sales representative for Kaminski, a major Polish bicycle manufacturer. And he also had an interest in a factory that manufactured bicycle parts. I had a custom-made bike, and in Poland that was a big deal." An even bigger deal: "We had a company car, a Citroën."

Jakub Feigenbaum joined the mass migration east of Jewish men in the fall of 1939, leaving his wife, Natalja, son Ludwik—called Lutek—and daughter Janina, or "Janka," behind. "As you know, at the beginning of the war [September 28], they had an agreement: The Russians came from the east, the Germans came from the west. So I was with my mother and sisters. We had difficulties supporting ourselves and my mother was selling her jewelry."

The Schönthal men left Poland. "My father had a business passport and my brother had a student visa, and we figured that nothing would happen to women," says Rena. "The men they would take to forced labor. They left, and we wanted to follow two months later. We had all the papers, but [the Germans] wouldn't let us out. They went to Italy thinking the war would last a few months and they'd come back. Nobody expected. Nobody imagined."

And then it was too late. "They were in Trieste, then they went to North Africa to Tangier, and finally they came to the Unites States. Then my brother volunteered for the Royal Air Force in England. He wanted to fight for his mother and sister."

Relaxing on a smart, ivory-colored sofa in the couple's home, surrounded by Oriental rugs and her own artwork, Rena Fagen smiles at the irony. "The whole idea was that when my father and brother left, we would stay to take care of our possessions, [so] nothing would happen to them. Every apartment building had a cellar with coal in it, so we took the silver and we hid it under the coal in the cellar."

"Everybody did it," adds Lewis, whose father returned from Lvov in March 1940. There were other places to hide valuables. "The doors in those apartments were very thick, heavy wood, I would say probably two or three inches. We employed a Jewish carpenter who took the doors off the hinges. At the bottom of the door, he created a cavity where some jewelry could be hidden, and coins and other things. The cavity was covered with a little piece of wood and two screws right on the bottom. Every time you wanted to get to it you had to take the door off the hinges."

"And we also had another method," Rena continues. "We had a nanny, a woman who had come to our house since I was six months old. She did every-thing. She was like my second mother. She was a Ukrainian, but she was an ex-tremely devoted and trustworthy person. Her name was Tekla. She was an 'old maid.'

"My mother had quite beautiful jewelry. She took a corset, and she had the jewelry sewn into it. This nanny would put it on, and every time there was a search, she would walk out under any pretext from the apartment. She saved it all for us, and eventually my mother got it all back, and the photographs."

Tekla Wozniak was so loyal that when the Schönthals moved to the Kraków ghetto, she stayed behind at the Dietla Street apartment. "She thought she would take care of it for us until after the war. But some German family was assigned to the apartment, and she started telling them, 'My lady was doing things this way' and 'My lady was cooking that way.' They threw her out."

Treuhänders appropriated Jewish businesses. They were Germans, as well as *Volksdeutsch* (ethnic Germans) and Ukrainian collaborators, rewarded with the war's earliest spoils for service to the Reich. Oskar Schindler, who was so help-ful to the *Abwehr*, got Abraham Bankier's Rekord plant, which made enameled pots and pans. He renamed it Deutsche Emailwaren Fabrik.

Bella Schönthal and Abraham Bankier were related through his late first wife. After the war, he married Rega Peller, a sister of Sally Peller Huppert.

"He was very good to my mother and me during the war," says Rena. "He helped us out financially, saying always, if we all survived the war, he wouldn't have to worry because my father would pay him back every penny. And he did."

Lewis Fagen managed to secure a job with a German firm that imported Italian accordions. For a time, this exempted him from hard labor. "I was ship-ping and packing and so on at the business of my father's friend [a Ukrainian]. He had a son my age, and we became very good friends. He joined a special unit of the German army, and walked around in a uniform, until they sent him to the invasion of Norway. I've never seen him since. But to walk with him on the street, I felt I had armor, I could go to places where I [normally] couldn't go."

In March 1941, Kraków's Jews learned that they'd have to move into a ghetto if they were issued a permit. Rena and Bella didn't get one, "So we went to a small town called Wolbrom. An uncle of my mother was there, and we thought we might as well be close to somebody that we knew. We lived in one room with kitchen privileges."

Rena Fagen pauses. "I tell you, there is something about being young. It just so happened that when we were packing to move, my mother was sick in bed with an infection in her leg, and I was the one in charge of packing and deciding. She saw that I was packing bathing suits, and she said, 'Where do you think we are going?' I said, 'Don't worry; there will be some kind of a pond or a lake—we will need it.' And it turned out that there *was* a pond! On one side, the cows and the horses were taking a dip, and, on the other, I was swimming. When one is young, everything seems not exactly fun, but you experience new things."

She doesn't remember her mother being quite so enthusiastic. "I guess she

got depressed, but she didn't show it. She wanted to keep my spirits up. But she was without her husband. She was in charge. And this was a woman who was always very protected by her husband."

They stayed about nine months. "Then we got the permit, and Bankier sent a truck for us and brought us to Kraków. It wasn't important how many rooms there were because each window was assigned to three people. So if a room had three windows, there were nine people. There was one room, so we had one window. My aunt, my cousin, and my grandmother [Adele and Pola Gerner, and Amalia Schönthal] had another window, and there was a pharmacist and his wife. The partitions were made with hanging sheets."

Rena and Bella got jobs at the Optima Uniform Factory. "I was working

Rena with her nanny, Tekla Wozniak, Kraków, 1930s.

on a sewing machine. I learned on a machine that was making buttonholes."
And Tekla—"every once in a blue moon"—would try to bring them some extra food. "That was the advantage of people who were from Kraków, because
there were many people from other cities."

It can be said that this "old maid" Ukrainian nanny was the first "righteous gentile" in Rena Fagen's life. "I have to tell you a story about Tekla," she
says. "On one of those *Aktions* of resettlement—where they were sending people to extermination camps—we were going out from the ghetto to Optima.
We never knew which [group] was going out to work and which was going to
a transport. We were coming out of the gates of the ghetto, and here, next to
us, was standing Tekla with an armband in her hand. Had she seen us going
with the transport, she told us, 'I was going to put it on and go with you.' She
had no family. We were everything to her. Today, when I talk about it, I get
goose pimples. I can never forget that moment."

After the Optima factory closed, Rena, her mother, and the rest of her female relatives were transferred to Emalia. "As far as I was concerned, Bankier
was the one who got us to his factory. I still call it his factory. We knew Oskar
Schindler was *Herr Direktor*, but [Bankier] was the head of it. We were in awe of
Schindler. We knew there was no need to be afraid of him. We looked at him
with respect and with admiration. He was an extremely good-looking man. He
was so accessible when he did talk to people."

Rena got the "KL" (*Konzentrationslager*) tattoo at Emalia. "But after we
were tattooed, we all started sucking [out the ink], and the letters started fading. I wouldn't even find a spot where it was now." By that time, probably in late
1942, she and her family were living at Płaszów.

Work began on Camp Płaszów in October 1942. As barracks went up, Jews moved
in. Work groups relocated en masse. The ghetto liquidation on March 13, 1943,
completed the process. Rena recalls that she, her mother, and her grandmother,
had moved well before that date.

"It was bad," says Rena Fagen. "There were barracks with wooden plat-
forms: a lower level, middle level, and upper level. I was on the middle level with
my mother, and I think my aunt and cousin and my grandmother were on the

bottom. We could take only what we could carry with us. A platform filled with straw was what you slept on. I think we managed to carry with us a pillow. My grandmother was in the barracks, and all of a sudden she started praying in Yiddish: 'Dear God, if you don't want to help all the Jews, help at least me.' Everybody remembered that."

Lewis already had spent time at the camp, if briefly. "I was sent to Płaszów when they were building Płaszów. I was brought back to the ghetto under the pretext that I was sick and spent two or three days in the hospital. Then I was assigned to a group called Steyer-Daimler. It was an automobile and motorcycle works where they were repairing [vehicles] coming back from the front. I went there on the pretext that I was an experienced motorcycle repairman. I knew absolutely nothing. I knew a lot about bicycles but not about motorcycles. Milton Hirschfeld was there, too.

"A Polish foreman got a whiff that I knew nothing about it. In order to get me killed, he told me, 'Here is a motorcycle. Take it apart, clean up the parts, replace the parts that are worn, and put it together.' And I struggled tremendously with it. I could take it apart because I was mechanically inclined. But when I was trying to put it together, I went crazy."

Fortunately, another Jewish mechanic gave him a hand. "Finally, the thing came together, but when they started that motorcycle, it exploded. I was called [before] the head of the Steyer works, who was a German who picked up people [suspected of sabotage] for the Gestapo. And at that moment, I thought, 'Aha, I am finished. That's the end of me.' However, the Jewish mechanic, who was really the one and only Jewish mechanic in the place who knew what he was doing and who was needed in those days, went to the director. He knew me and my father from before the war. And he pleaded with him that under his eye, I would work out well. And they let me go."

Between the September 1939 invasion and the March 1943 Kraków ghetto liquidation, the German governors inundated the city's Jews with orders, regulations, and edicts. For a time, they seemed to follow some pattern or order—the Star of David armbands, the labor cards, asset confiscations—nerve-racking and humiliating, but predictable. But a bewildering series of seemingly arbitrary and ever-changing directives followed. Some in a family got ghetto passes; others didn't. Some got the latest required work stamp; others couldn't. One day your factory hummed along; the next, it was deemed nonessential.

That's what happened at Steyer-Daimler. "There was an *Aktion* in the ghetto," says Lew Fagen. "Groups that were important for work, they let out of the ghetto into their work. [Then] another group would present itself at the gate, and the German standing there would say, 'No, this group, we don't need anymore.' It so happened that they declared they didn't need my group anymore. So my parents, who worked for Madritsch already, and my sister walked out, and I was stopped at the gate with my group." The Madritsch uniform factory had been owned by a Jew before the war. By this time, Julius Madritsch, a Viennese *Treuhänder*, ran it.

"They sent whoever remained in the ghetto to report at an assembly place called Plac Zgody, and they'd be resettled. The fact is, they sent them to Belżec. So I went home. I was left all alone. I put on the best boots I had. I packed a few things into a bag and I left the apartment. I met two friends of mine and I said, 'Why don't we keep together?'

"As we were getting close to the square, [we saw] a Jewish policeman who was very active in a student organization, like a fraternity, to which I belonged before the war. It was called Bar Kadimah. It was very Germanized, like a fencing society. As we came close to the square, he took a whip out of his boots and he started beating us and chasing us away from the square. A German stopped and asked him, 'What are you doing?' And he said, 'They don't belong here. They belong to *that* group!' And he chased us into the group coming out of the gate. And we walked out instead of going with the transport. We knew exactly what he was doing. He saved our lives, because nobody survived from that transport."

Lew Fagen joined a new work group making ventilating equipment for the German navy. "That factory was called Wachs. It belonged to a friend of my father's before the war. When there was the liquidation of the ghetto, I was still with that group. And when I went to Płaszów, we were coming out and marching to that factory every single day, on Limanowksa Street. Then when they stopped that group, they didn't let us out anymore."

Jakub Feigenbaum approached his boss, Julius Madritsch. "He told him, 'You know, my son is an expert sewing-machine mechanic,' and they brought me to the factory on the night shift. They closed me in a room with about forty or fifty sewing machines and they said, 'Fix them.'" It could have been the exploding motorcycle all over again, "but, you know, within three days I learned how to fix sewing machines," says Lew Fagen.

Jakub became one of Madritsch's "right-hand men," according to Lew. "In fact, whatever my father had left in jewels, Mr. Raimund Titsch, who was Madritsch's deputy, took with him to Vienna. After the war, my father went to Vienna with the father of Cantor Taubé, who also had things with Titsch, and he returned everything." The two men were later declared Righteous Gentiles.

Because of Julius Madritsch, Lew Fagen had a personal encounter with Amon Goeth. He'll never forget it. "Madritsch sent me to the villa with Goeth's uniform. On the way, I wondered, 'Am I going to get out of there alive or not?' And I kept walking slower and slower and slower. But finally I got to the door, and I had to ring the bell. I was hoping that the little boy [the servant Lisiek] or Helen [the maid] would open the door. Goeth opened the door himself, like you have seen him in the movie. He wore an undershirt [and had] a huge belly. I got jelly legs. I was literally shaking. But he grabbed the uniform from my hand and slammed the door in my face. This was the happiest moment in my life."

Rena never got that close, but soon learned the sickening rhythm of Goeth's murderous routine. "Every time we were going out from Płaszów to Optima, we were marching five in a row. And when we were entering the gates of Płaszów, the first question was, 'What's the score? How many were killed? How many were shot or hung?'"

Here Lew breaks in, repeating the assessment of so many *Schindlerjuden*. "Whatever you have seen as far as Płaszów was concerned [in *Schindler's List*] was way underplayed. They didn't show the hangings. They didn't show the mass shootings of people, which I watched one day. They brought a group in [from a Kraków workshop]. My uncle Nathan Frenk was in the group. He was a little, thin man. All his life he was a bank officer. I found out that they took them to Chujowa Górka. One of our friends who was taking care of the cattle in the camp had a little room, and that room had a view of the hill. I went there to see whether my uncle was among the people, about one hundred forty in that group—among them, some young fellows that I knew from school, with their mothers.

"I had to watch this whole horrible scene. They stripped them when they put them facedown against the hill. The Latvian and SS guards were firing with machine guns all around that hill and shooting people, but my uncle was not in that group. He had been living in a factory building that was guarded by the Germans. Instinctively, during the *Aktion* he jumped out a window. "Two days later, somebody told us that my uncle was in Płaszów. He went to a Polish woman who worked in the bank with him, she kept him overnight, and the next day he went by himself over to where the camp was in Płaszów. Groups were coming back [into the camp] and to his luck, somebody escaped from one of the groups, and they substituted him. He's still alive, in La Jolla, California."

To that point, young Lewis Fagen had never seen anything as dreadful as that hilltop execution. "I'll tell you the truth: When I saw what was going on, with all the blood flowing, I couldn't watch, and I closed my eyes and I ran out of there."

But the worst was yet to come. "What they showed in the movie [about the children] is close, but not exact. We had to report every day to an assembly place in Płaszów, the *Appellplatz*, and from there, in groups, we were going to our work. When we came to the assembly place [that day], they kept us there and they wouldn't let us go.

"All of a sudden, we saw that they were setting up machine guns all around us. You know, Płaszów was hilly. The *Appellplatz* was sort of in a valley. We figured this was the end of it; they were going to shoot us all. We stood like this for a couple of hours. And all of a sudden, the first truck came in with the children, and there was such an outcry, and everybody started running. They started shooting over our heads. Then an order came over the loudspeaker system: 'Everybody lie down.' They were playing music, by the way.

"Everybody lay down. But this was truck after truck after truck. They were shooting overhead. You can imagine how I felt, and I can't forget how the mothers felt. Some ran after the trucks, and they were grabbed by the guards."

Some children managed to run away and hide. "My cousin was one of the little girls who jumped into the latrine," says Lew. "After the whole thing was over, a woman came over to my mother to tell her, 'Your cousin's daughter is there in the latrine.' My mother ran over and took her out. She now lives in New Jersey."

The Fagens explain that people reacted in various ways to horrific losses, but gradually most became inured to all feeling. "Of course, there were lamentations. But it was such a daily occurrence that people wore an armor," says Lew. "Different people reacted differently," adds Rena. "There were some that were very close to each other and became almost like family. I was with my mother, so I really had no need to be very close with somebody. Besides, there was an aunt and cousin and grandmother. My mother and I were extremely close. But do you think we are able now to record exactly our feelings and our sensations?"

"You're talking to people who tried to forget everything, and never talked about it for thirty-five years," Lew adds.

Julius Madritsch and Raimund Titsch made sure that the Feigenbaums got on Schindler's list. Abraham Bankier secured spots for the Schönthal women. Lew remembers that before the stopover at Gröss-Rosen, his father had taped a gold coin into the arch of his foot, and brought it to Brinnlitz. He relinquished it there, when Schindler needed cash to buy special food for the frozen Goleszów people.

The Schindler women were hardly prepared for their reception at Auschwitz: the shaved heads and mismatched clothing. "We looked like a circus," Rena remembers. "We burst out laughing when we looked at each other. But what was scary was that during one of the selections, before it was known that the list was [secure], they put my mother aside. I became frantic, and she heard me screaming, and she managed to work her way back into our group."

Lew remembers "great worry" among the men at Brinnlitz when the women failed to arrive. "The rumor mill was working. Every day another story, that Schindler sent somebody, he didn't send someone. It was great joy when we finally saw them."

Lew worked in the Brinnlitz machine-tool room with Milton Hirschfeld and Leon Leyson. Rena worked nights, distributing hand tools to factory workers. She spent a few days at the camp infirmary, where nineteen-year-old Janka Feigenbaum lay terminally ill. Lewis Fagen says no one is really sure what made his sister so sick. "Over three years, she had a back problem, which could have been sciatica. She started developing it in the ghetto, and progressively it got worse. By the time she came to Brinnlitz, she was bent in half. She couldn't walk. She was in tremendous pain." She also developed excruciating bedsores.

Lewis tried to visit with her most days, and talked to Emilie Schindler about providing her with extra nourishment. She did this, bringing apples and bowls of farina to the dying teenager. Emilie Schindler also replaced Lew's eyeglasses.

"I broke them, and I had another pair with a Polish family in Kraków that had some of our things. I stopped her in the factory and told her, 'I broke my glasses and can't see.' The next day on the floor, I handed over a piece of paper with the address. A week later, I had them." (Emilie Schindler doesn't remember. Lew Fagen reminded her of the incident when they met in Jerusalem, where

Janka and Ludwik Feigenbaum, about 1930.

Schindler's List's final scenes were filmed, and then later at a testimonial dinner. "I showed her my glasses," says Fagen, "but she still didn't remember.")

Jakub and Natalja Feigenbaum believed that if their daughter could hold out through the end of the war, they'd secure the best medical care the West had to offer, and she'd live. They never got the chance to find out if they were right. "Dr. [Chaim] Hilfstein gave her an injection two weeks before the end of the war," says Lewis, referring to the camp's well-known physician. "We didn't know he was going to give the shot. We found out from another doctor. My mother was not the same after that. She never got over it." He goes on, "I'm not a great fan of Dr. Hilfstein. I am reluctant to admit that the school I went to in Kraków bore his name."

He and his father buried Janka themselves, contrary to the standing German order to cremate all prisoner corpses, but with Schindler's complicity. "We counted the steps from the road and memorized different points, to know where we buried her, and, sure enough, after the war, we exhumed her. While I was in Feldafing [a Displaced Persons camp], my parents left Poland with a Mexican visa. She is buried today in a Jewish cemetery in Prague, the same one as Kafka. They brought her body by train in the original box in 1946."

Lewis Fagen became part of the Brinnlitz underground. Richard Rechen, Schindler's auto mechanic, recruited him. They'd attended the same school in Kraków. The underground stored weapons under huge bales of wire in an electrical transformer station. Fagen's job was to make sure the German supervisor didn't find them. "Rechen was very influential with Schindler, and he asked him to put me there. The German lived at the transformer with his wife and child. Every time he got near those bales, my heart stopped."

Fagen and others in the underground carried weapons after the Germans left, but he, for one, didn't learn how to shoot until Leopold Page taught him after liberation. Winston Churchill's victory speech, which was piped into the factory, heralded the wondrous event. Lewis Fagen had taken English lessons with a tutor and understood the basics. "To me, this was inconceivable that still under German supervision, we could listen to Churchill."

His family stayed several days at the factory before heading back to Kraków in a group that included Rabbi Menasha Lewertow. (In *Schindler's List*, he's the character who makes a hinge for Amon Goeth. Goeth tries to shoot him, but his gun jams. After the war—in real life—Lewertow became Chief Rabbi of Kraków. He died in New York in the 1960s. A car ran him over one Friday night as he left a synagogue.)

"We stopped one night in the Czech woods. One of the fellows went out to look around. He came back and said he found a German army car full of rations. Rabbi Lewertow wouldn't touch it! We were all starved. We lit a fire and he was looking at us. We apologized to him. . . . We came to the city of Olmuntz. The new mayor was one of the communist underground. He found out we were there because we wore the striped suits. He advised his helpers: 'Take them to the best hotel.' They provided food for us. The next morning, he gave us a wagon with a horse, and we rode that horse until it practically dropped."

Things changed almost as soon as the traveling party crossed the Polish border at Zebrzydowice. "We stood in line in a Red Cross queue for soup, and we heard all those epithets from the Poles: 'Look at all those Jews that survived. Hitler didn't do a good job.'

"We took a train to Kraków. We came at night after curfew, so we had to sit at the railroad station. Early in the morning, I ran to our house and woke up the janitor. The same one! He was really happy to see me. I told him we wanted to get into the apartment. He said, 'Forget about the apartment; a communist official is there and before that, a German.' So I went back to the station, and on the way there I met a man who said, 'Aren't you Lutek Feigenbaum?' "

The man told Lew that a childhood friend named Adam had become a top official of the militia. He was Jewish but had survived by having Aryan papers.

"I went to the police station. My friend took my mother and myself home. He provided a suit for me. We stayed overnight. The next morning, he secured an apartment for us in the same building [77 Dietla Street], only much smaller. Soon after, my father came back. He had a little interest there in a factory manufacturing bike parts. I went to work managing the factory, which was located in Podgórze."

But any hope the family harbored of resuming life in Kraków vanished one Saturday in August 1945. Lewis was walking home from the factory after it closed at noon. Crossing the bridge over the Vistula River, he encountered a young woman pushing a baby carriage.

"She kept looking at me and looking at me. I said, 'Excuse me. Why are you looking at me?' She said, 'I'm very sorry; are you Jewish?' She said that down the street they were beating up Jews. I couldn't understand. This was *after* the war! But sure enough, there was a prewar dormitory for Jewish students. This was a home for refugees. I heard people yelling 'Kill the Jews!' I got home—this was the big meal, Saturday noon, and my father had invited one of his friends who also survived [under] Schindler, and they were pale because they heard it. I closed the window. Two minutes later, somebody knocked on the door."

Four police officers and a civilian were at the door. They demanded to know who had been shooting out the window. "I told them we didn't have a gun. They took us out of the apartment into the street. Within minutes, we were surrounded by one hundred people: 'Kill the Jews! Beat the Jews!' It was such a moment of total fear. I was sure we were going to be lynched."

Just at that moment, a militiaman rode by on a horse. Lewis yelled to him that he was a friend of Adam, the militia official. The police—ready seconds earlier to feed the Feigenbaum family to the mob—feigned ignorance of the situation. The militiaman warned the police to make sure they were safe. In the meantime, "someone yelled that they'd caught a Jew on the next block," and the mob took off. "So I said to my father, 'Start walking; we'll meet at Millers'.' This was a family that had converted after the war. We didn't come back home for two nights. Right there and then, I decided I was leaving Poland."

He and a friend left that December, first crossing the border into Czechoslovakia. "We had an address to go to of the head of the Jewish community in the city of Theresien. We came there on a Friday, and on a Sunday the [man's] daughters invited several young people to a dance party in the house. A man in a Czech captain's uniform walked in. I recognized him. He was from Kraków—from our school—but had served with the Czech partisans. I said to him, 'Is there any way you can help me get to Prague?' It was very dangerous, because they asked for papers all the time. It was already a communist society, and we didn't have any papers.

"He said, 'I tell you what. Tuesday, the Minister of Foreign Affairs is going through the city from Warsaw to Prague. I'm going to put you on the wagon on which he travels. Nobody is going to ask you for papers.' We went on a sleeper overnight with this captain."

Lewis and his friend wanted to cross the border into Germany. The captain told them to get to the city of Ash "on the border of Bavaria, which was sort of a German ethnic city, but in Czechoslovakia. He walked over to the corner where there was a taxi stand. [The captain] talked to one of the taxi drivers and came back and said, 'I made a deal with him. I told him you were American, and you're going to Ash. He's going to drive you.' But he said, 'Don't talk Polish; don't talk German.' So I was throwing out English words on the trip.

"When we came to Ash, [the taxi driver] took us to the best hotel in town, and I heard him say in Czech that we were Americans and we were going to Germany. In this communist country! They gave us a room. As soon as they left, I went down into the basement. I noticed a wooden trapdoor. I forced the door open. I went out. I called to my friend, who took our valises. We went into the basement, we walked out of the trapdoor, and we started walking on the streets of Ash, not knowing where to go."

They walked for about an hour. There was a ten o'clock curfew, and it was already eight. A boy of no more than sixteen passed them, and said clearly, "*Am Hu,*" which means "from the nation" in Hebrew. They knew it was a code. They told the boy they wanted to go to Germany. He took them to a house where they found about a dozen people in the basement. "It was a way station of the Bricha. The man in charge asked the boy why he'd brought these people. He said, 'We don't take smugglers.' Because we were so well dressed, they thought we were smugglers. Luckily, I had a letter on me that I was active in Kraków in the Zionist movement."

They crossed the border on New Year's Eve 1945, in snow up to their knees. "And you know who was the leader? That boy! We walked like this for maybe an hour and a half. All of a sudden he said to us, 'You are in Germany.' We walked over to a railroad station and bought tickets to Munich."

There was a big Displaced Persons camp near Munich: Feldafing, temporary home to twenty thousand Jews. "I got a job right away, in charge of HIAS (Hebrew Immigrant Aid Society) emigration applications. I was taking [applications] every Wednesday to the American consulate. Eventually I became the head of immigration in the DP camp, and I emigrated myself pretty fast."

Jakub and Natalja arrived at the end of August 1946. They got their visas just before the High Holy Days. "My mother was talking all along: 'When we come to America, all I want is a little house, and I want to sit in the garden and read.'"

They arrived in New York at the end of 1946. "As I was leaving the pier," says Lew Fagen, "I met Dr. [Stanley] Robbin. I knew him before the war. I asked, 'Who is here from our people?' He said, 'Rena is here.'"

Rena Schönthal and her mother spent their first postliberation year in Rotterdam living in a home for repatriates. "I took advantage of the museums, and took classes in history of the arts, French, English," she says. "In Holland, I could peek through the window and see a person in an easy chair with a lamp, reading. That's all I wanted for myself."

Her brother Paul, a bombardier, came to visit in his Royal Air Force uniform. "It was extremely emotional for all of us," she recalls.

Rena and Bella came to New York on a freighter. "There were six passengers on that boat. It was in December 1946. The trip lasted twenty-one days and we were seasick for twenty. When we disembarked, we walked out on the pier and we saw a very tall man coming. My mother told me, 'This is Daddy, you know?' It was a long time. Not that I didn't recognize him, but it seemed very strange." She had last seen her father in 1940. Then, he was a successful international businessman. Six years later, he was a night-shift cafeteria cashier.

For weeks, Bella and Rena told Aaron Schönthal about the part of their lives he'd not only missed but couldn't seem to grasp. "He looked at us, and he said, 'If you were not my wife and daughter, I would never believe you.' He said, 'I don't understand it; if my wife and daughter are hungry, I will go out and get bread!' It just wouldn't penetrate."

For a time, she recalls, "he made a resolution that he was not going to refuse us anything." But Rena got a job within ten days. Neither she nor her father would permit her mother to work ever again. "This," she says, "was beneath us. I did handpainting on silk, metal, glass. I could start in Brooklyn at nine in the morning and come home six, seven at night from the Bronx. I bought a newspaper and looked for ads for places offering better pay, and I would go there. Many of those places, they paid by the brush stroke. If I painted a rose, and it had fifteen or eighteen petals, I was paid for each petal. There was a time I couldn't look at roses!"

Rena and Lewis got to spend exactly one day together. "My father's stepbrother sent for us," says Lew. "When we came to Chicago station, my uncle and cousin were waiting. My cousin already owned a twelve-cylinder Lincoln, a 1946, with pushbutton doors! I remember like it was today. It was the height of luxury. He had a big cigar in his mouth."

The American relatives took the newcomers home. "We had lunch. My cousin was showing me different things. He thought I came from hick town: 'This is called *ba-na-na.*' When I went to answer him, my father was kicking me under the table. He said, 'Say banana.' I said, '*Ba-na-na.*' To me it was a big joke. Then he took me to the alley to show me his car, and said, 'This is called *au-to-mo-bile.*' Then his wife called him to the telephone, so I got in it and drove around the block."

Lew Fagen roars. "When I came back, the whole family was there. He said, 'How come you drove?' I said, 'I have an international driving license. Don't worry about it.' He ran to the telephone and called some friends who also had some family from Europe, and he said, 'Our greener knows how to drive!' "

The Feigenbaums didn't intend to change their names, but their relatives insisted. "My uncle, who was a very nice man and wanted to make things easy for us, took us for our first papers. He said, 'Who is going to spell Feigenbaum and pronounce it?' He never read Dickens, so he gave us Fagen. Then he said, 'What is Ludwik?' so he gave me Lewis. My father he gave Jack, and my mother was Natalja, so he gave Natalie, at least. When I wanted to change it back, I went to HIAS. They said, 'Why do you have to rock the boat? Leave it alone.' But I'm not happy about it."

The Chicago relatives owned a chain of plumbing and heating-supply stores. They gave the "greeners" an apartment over one of them and put Lewis to work. "I had told [my cousin] I would like to finish my studies, but [he] took me outside and he said, 'In this country, you don't need education. You stay with us long enough at the store, you'll be making one hundred dollars a week.' I came on a Friday. Monday morning I was working in the warehouse, loading and unloading railroad cars with bathtubs, pipes, boilers. I became a schlepper. I was getting twenty-two-fifty salary—seventeen-fifty clear—working until seven or eight in the evening."

A few months later, he quit and went to a competitor. "Right away my salary doubled. I was assistant manager. The assistant manager was in the basement, cutting and threading the pipes to order."

As a boy, Jakub Feigenbaum was apprenticed to a jeweler in Kraków, and figured that's what he'd do in America. "We set up a bench in the apartment," says Lew. "Every evening I was going to three stores getting rings to size. My father used to cut and put the pieces in, I was filing, and my mother was polishing, until one or two in the morning. Before Christmas, we were working all night long."

Lew Fagen aborted his career in plumbing supplies and went into the jewelry business. "I got a little room in someone's office on Wabash Avenue. I was a dapper dresser, so once we started getting a lot of work and making money, I went to the Sulka store, where I got myself a coat, some shirts, a hat. I spent all my money on it."

Appearances, of course, can be deceiving. "One day, I decide I'm going to visit Rena. The train used to leave at four in the afternoon and arrive early in the morning. My uncle was courting a lady in New York, too, so the first trip I made with him, we came to Grand Central, and, at that time, they had people standing at the station yelling out hotels. So we gave the luggage to this guy and he took us to the Biltmore. We walked in and I said, 'This is a mistake. We can't afford this.' They gave us a room. I went downstairs and said, 'I just got a call; they want me in Washington and we cannot stay.' So they gave us a porter who took us back to Grand Central to a Washington train! After he left us at the tracks, we took the luggage and we started schlepping." They ended up with friends in Queens.

Lew Fagen started selling a line of rings made in New York, but they were expensive, so he decided to bypass the middleman and deal directly with the manufacturer. "I told him, 'I am a refugee trying to make it, but the prices are much too high. If you would give me two thousand dollars' credit, I assure you, in no time I pay you back.'" He not only paid it back but got the man to extend further credit. Soon, the Fagens moved to New York. Childhood friends Lewis and Rena got married in 1949.

"I would go out every night with him when he came [from Chicago], and my mother smelled something brewing," says Rena. "One night I came home and she asked me, 'How was it? What's doing?' I said, 'Don't ask.' She said, 'He kissed you!' I said, 'Worse. He proposed!'" The ring salesman had no engagement ring hiding in his pocket. "He wasn't sure I was going to say yes!"

After she did, he established Rena Jewelers on Sixth Avenue. Then there was a Forty-seventh Street store, and then a company called Fagen & Stahl with offices on Fifth Avenue. He started manufacturing in Italy, going twice a year to Paris for designs. Their son Arthur, who is a New York orchestra conductor, was born in 1951, followed in 1954 by Lester, who is a lawyer in Newton, Massachusetts. At one time, he had thought of becoming a rabbi and attended the Jewish Theological Seminary. A sixth grandchild was due in September 1994, three for each son.

Rena and Lewis Fagen know how lucky they are, and how far beyond the obvious this luck extends—to their own emotional recoveries and to the way they were able to raise their sons. "There was a big difference," says Rena Fagen. "We had our parents. Our contemporaries had children, and when they asked about their grandparents, they had to tell the whole story. Ours had their grandpas and grandmas. We tried not to throw at [the boys] the con-

Rena and Lewis Fagen's wedding, New York, 1949.

centration camps. We had a lot of American friends. But the kids still made fun of us for being too European. For instance, we didn't believe in sleepover dates. If a kid lived two houses away, I didn't see any reason why he had to sleep in my house. I am sorry today for it."

Lew Fagen's lost sister, Janka, had been a wonderful pianist. And Bella Schönthal had a lovely voice. Arthur Fagen inherited their talent. "He was always listening to classical music," says Rena. "It is the love of his life." Arthur was "discovered" at the age of fifteen noodling around on a ski-lodge piano in Lake Placid, New York, by Laszlo Halasz, who was then the music director of New York's City Center Opera. After graduating from Philadelphia's Curtis Institute of Music, and Connecticut Wesleyan University, Arthur Fagen became the assistant conductor of the Frankfurt Opera's orchestra. He's now the music director of the Queens Symphony Orchestra. He has also been a guest conductor of orchestras all over the world, from New Orleans to Bejing.

The family moved to Long Island's Five Towns in 1956, then to Long Beach. Soon after, the senior Fagens and the Schönthals bought a two-family house together in the neighborhood, and lived there to the end of their lives. The children and grandchildren alternated Friday-night dinners: one week with the Schönthals, the next with the Fagens.

Aaron Schönthal died first, in 1977, followed by Jack Fagen in 1983. By then, Natalie had withdrawn deeper into the sorrows of her past. "She always talked about my dead sister," says Lew. "And she would never dance again, because of the loss of her daughter." She died of Alzheimer's disease in 1994. She was ninety-five. Bella Schönthal died in 1984. The previous year, she'd gone with the senior Fagens to Washington for the Gathering of Holocaust Survivors. Three days after returning, she was window-shopping in Long Beach when a car backed into her. She was in the hospital for months. Despite the pain, she managed to walk again, with a walker, and, according to Rena, "it looked like she was going to make it." But she developed a stomach ulcer and died. "Even today, there is a void," says Rena Fagen. "She was the last link to everything the family was before the war. We were always close, but what we had to go through together, under the most terrible conditions, made us even closer. Then, after all that, to watch her suffer so. I don't have the words to explain what it felt like."

They all lived long enough to see Oskar Schindler again. When he came to New York in 1957, the Fagens gave a garden party in his honor at their Woodmere home. Leopold and Mila Page came east from California. "We were discussing establishing a fund for Schindler, and, believe it or not, nothing came of it," says Lew Fagen. "It took several years to realize what he had done."

The Fagens would see Schindler twice a year in Frankfurt, when they visited Arthur. Schindler lived in a third-floor walk-up across from the railroad station. "He was very nicely dressed, but he had no money," says Lew. "I talked to some successful Jewish businessmen in Frankfurt, and they didn't do anything. The Israeli government gave him a little office in public relations for the Hebrew University."

During those visits, Schindler liked to talk about who was still alive and

Oskar Schindler visiting survivors on Long Island, 1957: (left to right) George Scheck, Adele Gerner, Dave Fishman (rear), Bella Schönthal, Oskar, Rena Fagen, Lewis Fagen (kneeling), Pola Yogev, Henry Rosner.

how people were doing. "He used to throw a lot of Yiddish words around," recalls Lew. "He was involved in everyone's life in Israel." But these were not easy visits. "We had an image of him as an enterprising person," says Lew, "and all of a sudden, we see a helpless Schindler who cannot cope in normal circumstances. We were very embarrassed because of this, and I'm sure he knew it."

Over the years, the Fagens, like all the *Schindlerjuden*, have given much thought to Oskar Schindler's motives. Here is Lew's analysis:

"He was an entrepreneur who went into a venture where he employed slave labor. It started with a greed for money: All of a sudden, here was this opportunity to become a big man. And he *became* a big man. Then, in those surroundings, he became a savior. He got caught up in this scam of saving his workers. And it became with him probably an obsession or a challenge to beat the system. I cannot say whether it was stupidity or guts, but he took chances. He was a gambler. If he hadn't been what he was, he wouldn't have done what he did.

Rena and Lewis Fagen, 1994.

"But with all that, he was a man who basically was good-hearted. He was a man who loved women, he loved wine, he loved parties, and he loved life. He probably couldn't identify with all the killings that were going on."

Several times, Lewis Fagen asked Oskar Schindler the same question those intrigued by his legend are still asking: "Why did you do it?"

Sometimes, when Schindler got drunk, he'd tell the story about the rabbi who lived next door to him when he was growing up who had a son his age. "Whenever [Schindler] had an argument with his own father, he used to go to the rabbi, and the rabbi used to quiet him down.

"But really," says Lewis Fagen, "I never got a clear answer. I almost think that with him, this was a sport, an adventure, to defy the Final Solution of Nazi Germany, in his small way. Whatever his reasons were, without his devotion to our survival, we wouldn't be here to tell this story."

POLA GERNER YOGEV

It's hard to imagine anyone less adaptable to the privation, degradation, and rigor of concentration-camp life than Pola Yogev. She's a Schönthal on her mother's side, a Gerner on her father's. By the 1940s, it's safe to say that no one—man or woman—on either side had performed manual labor in a generation. "I must tell you quite frankly," says Pola, a wry and savvy woman, widowed once, now remarried, "we were quite privileged."

She describes herself as "the pampered only child of well-to-do people." The Schönthals and Gerners owned property and commercial enterprises not just in Kraków, where they lived, but in several Polish cities. Her father, Ignazy Gerner, had a wholesale fruit business that took him all over Europe. His wife, Adele Schönthal Gerner, generally traveled with him. "I was brought up by the help," says Pola. "Maids and nannies."

Her maternal grandmother, Amalia Schönthal, had been widowed young. She never remarried, and lived with her daughter's family in a building she owned. Pola sketches an imperious, Victorian matriarch—"tall, handsome, elegant, cold as ice"—who expected "everyone else to dance to her tune," the kind of person "who made an appointment with her attorney at eleven, showed up at four, then was furious that he hadn't waited for her.

"It was all very formal. I kissed her hand, but I never kissed her."

Pola Gerner Yogev, age 2, Kraków.

Amalia Schönthal was born in Poland during the administration of James Buchanan, the fifteenth president of the United States. She was about eighty-five when she died in the fall of 1944. America's thirty-second president, Franklin Delano Roosevelt, outlived her by only six months. The oldest person on Schindler's list by at least twenty years, Amalia probably would have survived the Holocaust if not for a beating at Auschwitz. Her family went to extraordinary lengths to keep her alive in the ghetto and at Płaszów. Most Jews older than fifty never made it out of the ghettos, but bribery and influence got Amalia as far as Auschwitz. Then Pola took over. "Whenever we went for *Appell* and selection, I had to go out three times, because I was covering for her."

This is how selection worked, according to Pola: The women stood five deep, dozens across. Guards would scan the first row, then send that row to the back. The women in the second row stepped forward, becoming the new first row, and the rotation repeated. "I was in the first line, then I would go to the back. Each time, on the way back, I switched with my grandmother so she never got to the front."

In the end, of course, it didn't matter. An SS guard beat Amalia so severely that she was taken to the *Krankenstube* (infirmary). Neither her daughter nor granddaughters—Rena Schönthal Fagen is Pola's first cousin—ever saw her again. "Somebody said she died in bed there," says Pola. "She had an infection in her face. She was not gassed. At least that's what we were told after the war."

Pola Gerner was born in January 1921. Her family had a spacious apartment at 85 Dietla Street. Rena Fagen, whose father, Aaron Schönthal, was Adele's brother, grew up in the same building. "Believe me," says Pola, "I wouldn't mind having that apartment here." The Gerners were not particularly devout.

"We were kosher at home, but when we got to the Polish border, my mother used to ask me, 'Would you like a ham sandwich?'"

When the war broke out, Pola was eighteen and had just graduated from high school. "There were fights at home," she recalls. "I should have gotten married, according to my parents, and I wanted to go to school to become a physician." The invasion rendered the argument moot.

Ignazy Gerner left Poland in February 1940 with Aaron Schönthal and several other men in the family. They went to Italy, to Tangier, and then to the United States. "He arrived the day before Pearl Harbor. We decided the war is already a few months old, what can happen? If they do something, they do it to the men. Nothing will happen to the women." In any case, Amalia Schönthal certainly wasn't about to uproot. "My grandmother said, 'What will I do? Where will I have it so comfortable?'"

Pola's paternal grandmother had died before the war. Her father's father, Ozjasz Gerner, and his four sisters came from Lvov, and probably died in camps. Two Gerner cousins survived: They were blonds and held fake Aryan papers.

Surprisingly, Pola, Adele, and Amalia adjusted fairly well to their deteriorating circumstances. "The Nazis were very smart," she says. "They must have had terrific psychologists. It went step by step down. They took the silver; what's the big deal? Tomorrow they take the fur coats; what's the big deal? And that's how it went."

Sometime in 1940, the occupying Germans forced the Polish headquarters of the American Jewish Joint Distribution Committee, known as the Joint, out of Warsaw to Kraków, the Government General's capital. The Joint established offices at 85 Dietla Street. "We had this house and one floor was empty, so my mother gave them rooms," Pola explains.

Until Japan's December 1941 attack on the American base at Pearl Harbor, which brought the United States into the war, the Joint was able to distribute resources from the United States to Poland's Jews. Pola did office work for the Joint, and, after its offices closed, for the Yiddish Society, its Red Cross–affiliated successor in the ghetto.

She met her future husband, a mechanical engineer named Jerzy Scheck, while working for the Joint. Marek Biberstein, his maternal uncle, was presi-

Jerzy "George" Scheck, at the end of the war.

dent of Kraków's *Judenrat*. When the Germans jailed Biberstein, "the Joint decided to help his wife," says Pola, "but they couldn't do it directly, so they gave the money to [Jerzy]. He would come to the office, and we kept on meeting accidentally. The ghetto was not very big." Neither was the ghetto apartment that Pola, her mother, and grandmother occupied: "Very small quarters in a nice apartment, with lots of people," Pola recalls. For the move, they had stuffed their personal items into Adele Gerner's fine leather suitcases bearing her "AG" monogram. "Guess who got them?" asks Pola, her sneer telegraphing the answer: Amon Goeth. "Someone saw them at Płaszów."

From their ghetto quarters, Pola and Adele Gerner went to work at the Optima Uniform Factory. On March 13, 1943, they left the ghetto early with Amalia, avoiding Goeth's festival of carnage. "You get very selfish in a situation like that," Pola says. She remembers their exit well. George took a hammer to the cast on his recently broken leg rather than hike to the camp with such an obvious disability.

Over the years, Pola Yogev has spent a good deal of time pondering the forces that whipsawed the Jewish conscience during the Holocaust. She has reached certain conclusions, and refuses to apologize for any of them. "Everybody tried to save themselves and their families. Some did it by 'ethical' means, some by unethical means. My grandmother was in her eighties, and you might tell me it's not 'ethical' that somebody younger didn't get on Schindler's list. You protected your own. It cost a fortune to keep her alive, but we didn't miss the money, and it would have gone to Germans anyway." They relinquished the last of their jewelry at Płaszów: "amber beads from my father's mother. An OD man [at Płaszów] said, 'You have to give them up,' and he put them in his pocket."

Pola and Adele continued working for Optima for a while, marching to and from Płaszów. Amalia went with them. They soon joined the ranks of the *Schindlerjuden* at Emalia. There, says Pola, "you didn't live in this constant fear. He was very protective of us."

The months at Emalia passed uneventfully, but the Schindler women's first night in Auschwitz profoundly impressed her. "I said to myself that if I ever survive this, I'll be glad I was here, because otherwise I wouldn't believe it.

"I will never forget, as long as I live, that as we were walking into the barracks they assigned to us, they were emptying the barracks of the women who were in there. One little girl walked by me—I think she was Greek—and she said, 'Take my sweater, because where I'm going, I won't need it.' She said it in Jewish. Did I understand what she meant? Of course. We saw the chimneys." Pola gave the sweater to her grandmother, who vanished into the *Krankenstube* soon after.

Even at that point, Amalia Schönthal's family thought she would join them for the trip to Brinnlitz. "When the list was made and we were already leaving Auschwitz, a man came by on a motor bicycle with a tommy gun, and I said, 'Some of the women are still in the *Krankenstube.*' That was Mengele. Did I know? He said, 'Let me check.' What an idiot I was! It was absolutely ridiculous."

Pola, her cousin Rena Schönthal, their mothers, and Pola's future sister-in-law, Irene Scheck Hirschfeld, remained together at Brinnlitz. Jerzy Scheck and Lutek Feigenbaum—Rena's future husband, now Lewis Fagen—were never far away.

"We had easy jobs," says Pola. "Schindler used to say, 'Scheck will work, and you will live after the war.'" She says Schindler joked about how Jerzy—called George in the United States—would have his own factory, and they'd all work there together. As it had at Emalia, Pola's life at Brinnlitz passed without incident. Her strongest memory seems to be of watching a dog running one day outside the camp's barbed-wire perimeter and thinking enviously, "That dog is free and I'm not."

After liberation, Pola and her mother went first to Prague, then to Holland, with Rena and her mother. George accompanied Irene and her husband, Mil-

Pola Yogev, mid-1940s.

ton, to Paris. "We had a fight and we separated," says Pola. But it didn't last long. "He came to Holland and we stayed three-quarters of a year. I didn't think of marrying because my father was here [in the United States] and I couldn't do it without my father. I got to the States in July 1946. We had preference visas because my father was here."

They located Ignazy Gerner through an uncle, Bernard Schönthal, part of the group that had left Poland in 1940. Pola says the last letter they got from Bernard that year contained the address of a Red Cross office in New York. Fortunately, it was an easy address to remember—99 Hudson Street—and it was the only way they could think of to search for family.

As Pola and her relatives made their way to Holland, where the family had business connections, they stopped in Pilsen, at an Allied military base. "A big general was due there that day," Pola recalls. "His name was Patton. I started talking to a Jewish soldier who was with him, and asked him to please write to my uncle that we were still alive.

"The man said, 'I'm not going to write any letters unless you take some money from me.' I have till today, in the vault, a few English pounds and a couple of American dollars he gave us. He wrote to [Bernard]—he was the one who lost his wife and three children. It was very sad. [Bernard] misunderstood: [He thought] that *his* family had survived. When we got to Holland, we got in touch with a business acquaintance and he sent another letter."

The first letter had arrived on the day that Ignazy Gerner was scheduled to undergo ulcer surgery at New York's Mount Sinai Hospital. He later told his daughter that he'd said to himself, " 'If I lived this long and they are alive, I'm not going in,' so he turned back. He had the surgery two years later. He always believed we were alive. He wouldn't let it enter his mind that we weren't. That probably kept him going."

Apparently, he also always believed his American hiatus wouldn't last long. So instead of entrenching in a new business, this wealthy, sophisticated man—as warm as his wife was chilly—became a cafeteria cashier.

Having survived the war, Adele Gerner decided that she wasn't about to risk air travel. So they took a ship from Holland bound for Galveston, Texas. "Can you imagine," says Pola, "in July, in a woolen dress and coat! When we got to Cuba, I said, 'Mother, I have had enough!' The mosquitoes were that size"—she indicates the length of a housecat with her hands—" 'So let's go to the American consulate and see what we can do.' "

They got permission to enter through Miami and cabled relatives in New York. "We got back to the ship. We were standing at the railing, and we saw a man walking on the pier who looked so familiar. It was one of my mother's brothers! He came to pick us up. We finally flew to Miami and took a train to New York."

A vignette from their short stay in Miami is etched in Pola's memory: "I saw a sign on a washroom: 'For Whites Only.' You could have knocked me over the head." To that time, Pola had seen only one black person in her life—a dancer. But she still understood what the sign meant.

Pola Gerner and George Scheck married in February 1947. He was, by all accounts, an extraordinary man: a talented painter and sportsman who was well read, witty, bright, and handsome. "A half hour before the wedding, I was lying on the couch reading a book," Pola remembers. "My mother said, 'Are you crazy?' I said, 'I made the decision long ago; what's the big deal?' I don't have to tell you it wasn't a wedding with all the trimmings. It was in the rabbi's study. I wore a fifteen-dollar suit from Gimbel's Basement and a one-dollar pair of shoes from Fourteenth Street. This I remember! Rena's mother made me a bouquet of artificial flowers. We went to a rented room in Washington Heights, then we got a bigger apartment, then this house [in Long Beach, Long Island]. I've been here thirty-eight years."

Their son, Lawrence, born in 1949, is a cardiologist in Poughkeepsie,

New York. Their daughter, Karen Sussman, is married and lives in Westchester County. Karen has one son, and Lawrence has two.

George Scheck worked most of his life for Welbilt, an appliance manufacturer. He eventually became vice president of production, and his job offered attractive perks. "Once a year, there was a trip for the top salesman, and because George was a corporate officer, we always got to go: Italy, Spain, Majorca. And on our own, we traveled a lot, too: Rio, Tahiti."

They told their children next to nothing about their war years. "My kids knew we spoke with an accent, but that's about all," says Pola. "My parents finally told them. Then they were angry with us for not telling them."

The Holocaust left Pola Yogev with an enduring aversion to violence. "I cannot stand violence on television. My husband laughs about it, but when I see somebody fighting or shooting, I can't watch it. But I must tell you, right after the war, they lynched a guy [at Brinnlitz, a *Kapo*] and we got our first good soup at the same time, and, believe me, my spoon didn't stop for one minute."

George Scheck died in 1976, after two years of desperate sickness. "He's written up in all the medical books," says Pola, ruefully. "He had C.A. [cancer] of the heart."

In 1984, Pola Gerner Scheck married Samuel Yogev. They'd attended the same high school in Kraków, but didn't know each other. Sam had gone to Palestine in 1935, and eventually became assistant commissioner of the Israeli prison system. He was in charge of security for the Adolf Eichmann trial in 1961, and later taught at the university level in Israel.

Pola says she did such a thorough job of submerging her Holocaust memories that when someone she knew took the stand during the Eichmann trial and began talking about Birkenau, she couldn't quite place it. "I thought, 'Birkenau: That sounds familiar.'"

Pola and Sam went back to Poland in 1990, revisiting scenes of their youth. "We went to Auschwitz. It was a beautiful May day. The spirit of Auschwitz was not there. People were eating ice cream. We went to the apartment building that belonged to my mother and two aunts, in Gdynia, next to Danzig. I went to the door and said who I was. The man said he was the son of our chauffeur. He was

Adele and Ignazy Gerner, New York City, 1950s.

so happy to see me. He showed me some papers signed by my father. He told me because of the papers, he was permitted to stay there and be the super."

But the apartment at 85 Dietla Street in Kraków looked shabby and neglected. "It was all divided up, and four families were living there. There was no sign of our things. But one woman was very nice. I wanted to see my room, but it wasn't my room anymore."

Incredibly, Pola was able to relate all this to her mother. Adele Gerner died in 1992, five days after her ninety-ninth birthday, in her own home in Long Beach, a few blocks from her daughter's. By then, she was a widow. Ignazy Gerner had died at the age of eighty-four. He not only survived ulcer surgery, but lived for twenty years after a lung-cancer operation. He spent his later years playing the stock market, and, according to his daughter, "did very well."

In the winter of 1993, Pola intended to decline an invitation to a preview of *Schindler's List,* but her children wanted to go, "So I was trapped." She ducked in

Irene and Milton Hirschfeld with Pola Yogev (right), Long Island, New York, 1994.

and out of the New York theater, avoiding several *Schindlerjuden* she hadn't seen in decades. "Two weeks later, my daughter called and said, 'Mom, I'm going to see *Schindler's List.'* I said, 'What for? You saw it already.' She said, 'To tell you the truth, all through the movie, I didn't look at the screen—I looked at you.'"

Pola Yogev says she does not believe in "higher powers." She has asked the question every Holocaust survivor has asked, time and again: "Why did I survive?" At this point, she doesn't really care. But ask her to pinpoint her happiest moment in America and she doesn't hesitate: "My son's bar mitzvah. It was wonderful that my parents lived to see it. That is, thanks to Schindler."

MILTON AND IRENE HIRSCHFELD

Schindler's List permits itself a few moments of comic relief, just as the *Schindlerjuden,* on occasion, found reason to smile.

In one of the film's more obvious play for laughs, a couple, summarily evicted from their sumptuous, modern apartment, surveys their new ghetto "home." It's a single, dingy room in a flat, several flights up, already occupied by a family with a squalling infant. Sophisticated urbanites in fur-trimmed coats, they are appalled. The wife, eager to put the best face on it, ventures, "It could be worse." Her husband, nearly apoplectic, screeches, "How on earth could it *possibly* be worse?" Right then—as his outrage still vibrates in the air—a prodigious Hasidic family trundles in, one long, black coat after another. "Good day. Good day," they greet their mortified housemates.

Variations on this scene repeated hundreds of times in the Kraków Ghetto. Circumstance forced strangers—often with nothing in common but their religion—into uneasy cohabitation at intimate range. It was bound to produce a certain amount of what, in retrospect, seems like sitcom humor.

Irene Scheck Hirschfeld tells a story about an energetic couple who lived for a while on the other side of a flimsy partition in the room she shared with her brother, Jerzy "George" Scheck. The man was older and had money. The woman was younger and didn't. He supported her. She obliged him.

"We had to listen every night to their sexual practices that consisted of [him] beating her but good. I remember one night, my brother had a fever, and they were going at it like nothing had happened. Finally, I got a little bit of courage and said, 'Please be quiet, because my brother is sick!' and that stopped them. This was part of daily living in ghetto," says Irene Scheck Hirschfeld, her lips pursed in a sarcastic smirk.

You just never knew who'd end up on the far side of the armoire, or the blanket-draped clothesline, or whatever illusory barrier bisected your allotted space. The lucky ones managed to encamp with friends and relatives.

For a time, Irene and Milton occupied the same apartment: she with her brother, he with his sister. The future spouses met right after the war began in 1939 at the Kraków Jewish center where they both worked. Their lives had run on similar tracks before then, and would seldom diverge from then on.

Irka Scheck, as she was then called, was born in 1921, the same year as Milton's sister, Polda. Milton Hirschfeld, born in 1919, was two years younger than Irene's brother, George. Irene's father, Leopold, died when she was twelve. She and George lost their mother in the ghetto the same year that Milton and Polda lost their parents.

In the good days, both families had enjoyed the middle-class comforts of Kraków: spacious homes and domestic help. Irene's father was an engineer; Milton's was a property manager and diamond broker. The Hirschfelds were more religious than the Schecks.

When Irene Hirschfeld talks about her childhood—her pet spaniels and shepherds, the sun-drenched, plant-filled salon of her family's apartment on Rejtana Street—it's with profound sadness and longing. But these bereavements hardly rival the loss of her brother. They were so close that she feels guilty to this day about his death from cancer at age fifty-nine. After all, she had cancer, too, but she's still here. "I'll never forgive myself that I lived and he died," she says tearfully.

Brother and sister had to separate for a while after the Nazi Government General declared the formation of the Kraków ghetto in March 1941, not in Kazimierz, the old Jewish quarter, but in Podgórze, on the south side of the

Vistula. Displaced Podgórze gentiles took apartments vacated by Jews who, if granted the ghetto passes called *Kennkarten*, relocated to the ghetto. Those denied *Kennkarten* had to hide in the ghetto, or leave.

George, who was an engineer like his late father, got a pass and stayed. The rest of the Schecks and Hirschfelds went to the suburb of Borek Falenski: Irene and her mother, Sidonia; Polda, Milton, and their parents, Rosalia and Markus. "We had to close up the apartment, and a Polish family moved in," Irene recalls. "We took two beds and some clothes." They moved to a peasant's house.

In late 1941, the Nazis' philosopher-bureaucrats switched gears, ordering Jews from the outlying areas into the ghetto, or to collection points for transport. Irene and Sidonia moved into a "cubicle" on Limanowskiego Street, with an uncle and an aunt. "We had my mother's bed, and I had a folding one under hers, pushed in during the day," so that her uncle, Dr. Alexander Biberstein, could maintain his medical practice. Part of their living quarters became his waiting room. (His brother, Marek Biberstein, was co-leader of the Jewish Community Council. The Germans arrested and jailed Marek on trumped-up bribery charges. "By arresting him, they told the rest of us: 'Beware. If we can do that to him, we can do it to anybody,'" says Irene. "Later on, [Alexander] was a doctor in Płaszów. They made a list of people to leave the next day to other camps. [Marek] was on it. When [Alexander] found out, he gave him an injection. He wanted to spare him.")

Before the war, Milton Hirschfeld wanted to become a doctor. "I passed my exams with flying colors, but there was no way to get in [to medical school]," he explains. "There was a quota. They used to admit ten percent Jews of one hundred twenty at the University of Kraków. This was the percentage of the population. By 1937, when I was supposed to start, they admitted only three Jews"—all doctors' sons. "I started chemistry. It was too expensive to study out of the country, and I thought that after two years, I could get in. But then it was too late.

"In 1939, they started anti-Semitic riots at the university. Once I was arrested [on grounds] that I wanted to hit somebody during the riots. It went to court. I said I was defending myself, and I was freed." Anti-Semitism already permeated the university's academic atmosphere. "They told you to sit on the end on the left side. You were not supposed to take a seat wherever you want. This everybody took for granted."

The Hirschfelds' first ghetto accommodations on Rinkafka Street weren't so bad: two rooms and a kitchen. Polda got a job at Optima, the uniform factory, as did Sidonia Scheck. Milton went to work at Steyer-Daimler, the automotive factory.

The year 1942 was tragic for both families. In June, Rosalia and Markus Hirschfeld disappeared on a transport bound for Treblinka. "They were taken during the day," Milton remembers, "because in the morning, we had to go to assemble. Whoever had a card to go somewhere else they let out, and the other people were transported at the end of the day. They called it a relocation. They said they would send us a letter. It didn't look as bad as it was. We didn't believe it." Still, his parents' departure depressed him so much that he spent two days in bed.

"We were not masters of our own thinking," adds his sister, now Polda Brenes of Queens, a twenty-seven-year fixture on the sales staff of New York's Bergdorf Goodman (where she used to dress Ingrid Bergman and Gloria Swanson, and continues to serve a cast of the rich and famous whom she's too discreet to name).

"We sat still, waiting for some kind of sign of life from our parents. We had friends and neighbors who had relatives taken on the same transport who kept coming to us, wanting to know if we had heard from our parents. Our father was very resourceful, and they thought if we didn't hear from him, nobody would hear from anyone."

Things hadn't been easy for Leopold Scheck's family since his death, and they were about to get measurably worse. "The impact of his death was tremendous," Irene recalls. "I thought that I was worth less because I didn't have a father."

Sidonia Scheck died in the fall of 1942. "I had been working to unload coal, and I finally got a small job in a bindery," Irene remembers. "My mother was at Optima. One day, I was coming home, and on the way, my brother met me. He said she took very ill. It was a stroke. She never regained consciousness."

The last traditional funeral the Nazi Government General allowed Kraków's ghetto-bound Jews was Sidonia Scheck's. After all, countless of the Reich's battlefield "heroes" simply rotted where they fell; why should dead Jews merit such ceremony? From then on, says Irene, only immediate family members could go to the gravesite.

Sidonia Scheck was buried in the "new" Jewish cemetery, next to her husband. "Whoever wanted to attend got a pass," says Irene. "She was very well liked, so a lot of people came out." A horse cart carried the casket. The mourners walked. Within months, Jews whose ancestors lay under that holy ground—and at the adjacent "old" Jewish cemetery—would be forced to uproot and smash the headstones and monuments to pave the road to Camp Płaszów, soon to be the Schecks' and Hirschfelds' new home.

Milton Hirschfeld worked at Steyer-Daimler until the summer of 1943. By then, his work group had been living at Płaszów for half a year. "We walked every day to Steyer, in the middle of the city, with four Ukrainians. We were counted on the way in and on the way out. We didn't wear any armband. You put on a uniform. You could buy food."

He entrusted his remaining valuables—cash and jewelry—to a Pole who'd been a secretary at the university. "From time to time, he should have been able to give me some. The first time I asked, he became evasive, then he sent me to the German soldier who was the supervisor of the shop. He said, 'He didn't want to tell you, but somebody came in his house and they took everything out.' That was baloney, because later on another Pole told me he was a drunkard and he started drinking and he used the money."

He remembers the day the ghetto was liquidated. "In the evening, they started bringing people into Płaszów. Everybody said they were shooting and killing. The Optima people came in a group to Płaszów that morning. . . . We spent three months at Steyer after the liquidation." Then the Germans told Steyer it could no longer use Jewish labor. "On the last day, we bought a few things: chocolate, bread, whatever we could bring."

On his last day at Steyer, Milton Hirschfeld had his first—and only—personal encounter with Amon Goeth. "He was coming out of the camp in his car. He had a Jewish chauffeur. He said, 'What do you have in the packages? What are you doing here?' I was the one who had to talk. I told him that we were going out every day [to Steyer] and today was the last day. We could not go out anymore, so we took all our tools and uniforms. I put my hand on the bag and he said, 'Don't move it.' He thought I had a gun. He said, 'What do you have there?' I said it was my notebook. He said to take it out. He looked at it, and he gave me a slap twice in the face, a kick in the back, and then went back to the car. This saved everybody.

"Inside [the camp], all the people knew already that Goeth caught us on the outside. Irene was all excited." And with good reason. Not many Jews lived to tell about close calls with Amon Goeth. She'd had one herself. "I remember sitting morning till night on the ground, breaking up stones with a hammer for a road. One day Amon Goeth came out and decided we didn't do enough, and they were supposed to kill every tenth one. I don't know why, but they changed [the order to] physical punishment. They prepared tables. We had to undress, and you had to count to twenty-five in German, and start over from the beginning if you missed one.

"Goeth was looking row after row, [to see] if someone turned their head away. I looked right into his face. He didn't pick me."

Irene had lived on Manci Rosner's block for about six weeks before going to the Emalia subcamp, where "life wasn't so hopeless and miserable. We still had a little bit of dignity." She even recalls a night when the Emalia women organized a conga line, and "imitated a choo-choo train" through the barracks. Irene got the KL tattoo at Emalia. It's still visible on her thin left wrist.

Soon after Oskar Schindler built his subcamp, many of those who would comprise an extended family after the war went to live and work there: Milton and Polda Hirschfeld; George and Irene Scheck; Pola Gerner—later George's wife—her mother, grandmother, aunt, and first cousin, Rena Schönthal, who would marry Lewis Fagen.

The group had connections with two influential figures: Marcel Goldberg and Abraham Bankier. Goldberg was the powerful Jewish policeman. His wife, Louise, who now lives in Argentina, was a first cousin of Milton and Polda. Bankier had owned the enamelware factory before Schindler took it over. His first wife, who was lost in the ghetto, was Rena Schönthal's maternal aunt.

Irene's first job at Emalia was to carry pots on heavy boards, which she dropped with regularity. "One of the Polish supervisors came to me and cursed me: 'From now on, you are going to sweep the floor all night!' So I was going with the broom."

Irene was well dressed for a broom jockey. "I had a sheet and pillowcase at Emalia. I made the pillowcase into a sheet and dyed the sheet navy and made it into a uniform. We had our own shoes, and I had an old leather bag. A shoemaker made me a pair of sandals out of it, even a little bit fancy: He cut little round [shapes] in them. I felt so dressed up, you have no idea!"

After all, she had a man to impress—actually, by then, a husband. They'd had a clandestine Jewish wedding in the ghetto, after they'd lost their parents. "In Emalia, Milton and I saw each other in the factory, and afterward, we had a yard where we could hold hands and walk. This I have to say we should thank Schindler for. The towers were full of German soldiers with machine guns, but they never used them."

As a romantic gesture, Milton made a metal comb and a signet ring at Emalia for Irene. She managed to sneak the ring through Auschwitz in a chunk of soap, but lost it later.

"I was in the tool room," says Milton. "We made machine tools. The advantage was, I never worked at night. However, many times they woke you up at night because a tool broke, and every hour counted."

In general, the subcamp's residents escaped most of the terror that daily confronted the Płaszów camp inmates. But Irene remembers that Schindler had to send a representative to the main camp whenever there were hangings. "There was a fellow, not completely mentally grown up, and this is the one who went. And when he went, everybody was hugging him and crying. I guess [Schindler's] thinking was he might not get as upset as someone else.

"Schindler always used to walk through [the camp] and ask people, 'How are you doing?' This guy used to say, 'For you, it is better.' Maybe he wasn't that stupid after all."

Milton Hirschfeld remembers only one incident at Emalia during which Schindler played the tough guy (or pretended to). "One evening, he called all the people in to the bottom of the stairs. He said, 'We need better production,' and [implied that] if it did not increase, he would have to send us all back to Płaszów."

Schindler came to know Irene and her brother, George, well. He always called him "Scheck." Irene says that "Scheck" knew more about Schindler than most of the *Schindlerjuden* alive today, "because he was in charge of the part that

Photograph of the Refugee Center in the Ardèche region of France, summer 1946. Irene Hirschfeld is seated third from the right. Milton is standing in the row behind, fourth from the right.

was supposedly making the ammunition at Brinnlitz, but there was never anything that went out."

Oskar Schindler was "a big mixture of everything, but we only saw the good side of him," she says. "He was always kind. He always had a smile. Nobody opened the door to our barracks when he walked through with [officers] from Płaszów. He never hit anybody."

During the family's "exile" to Borek Falenski, Irene had learned something of the seamstress's art. She already knew how to knit. This came in handy at Auschwitz, of all places. "One day, one of the block women asked, 'Who knows how to knit?' I said I did. They gave me needles made from wires—they cut my fingers—and I was making mittens for the SS women! Because of this, I didn't have to get up in the middle of the night when they threw us outside to count people.

"I was so inventive then; I don't know whether it was the willpower to survive. But I don't have it today. There were women in that group who were professional knitters who didn't say a word."

Her sister-in-law, Polda, got a job in the Brinnlitz kitchen that prepared

296

meals for the Germans. "We salvaged food," Polda remembers. "They had carp, and we got the heads. So we could bring extra food to our men. I cannot say I suffered there. I gave my brother my portion of bread. But then there was friction in the barracks and we were thrown out. After that, I was still cleaning for the Germans and doing their laundry. One of the German engineers would say, 'Before you throw away from the wastebasket, you might want to look inside.' He would leave two slices of bread with jam."

Milton, on the list as Samuel, says that he and those close to him "were in relatively good shape. Everybody from Schindler was. We knew that the war was coming to an end, and that somehow we would be free."

Milton Hirschfeld and his sister, Polda Brenes, Paris, 1947.

Milton, Irene, and Polda spent the immediate postwar years in France. Polda began a pen-pal romance with a refugee named Joachim Brenes, who'd been an accountant and lawyer from the city of Turka, in east Poland, and had survived in Siberia with his mother. He was then living in Australia. She followed Milton and Irene to the United States, where she and Joachim married. They have a son.

"Paris for me was marvelous," says Irene. "It was colorful and lively, and we could walk on the sidewalks, not in the gutter. We even got free rides in the metro, for a while." They ate well, drank well, frequented the opera and the races, and spent two glorious summer months at a convalescent camp for refugees in the mountains.

"I have beautiful memories of this time," says Milton. "They gave us a double food card: four bottles of wine a week each." It took them a while to understand that they didn't need to hoard food. "When we came to Paris, we had our arms full of baguettes" from the train trip through Switzerland. "That was the concentration-camp mentality."

They were put up initially at "a very fancy hotel that the German officers used to live in during the war. It was very elegant, but of course no one was changing the sheets. And every time we went in and out, an American MP would be there and would pump DDT into our clothes."

They stayed in Paris for four years. "Milton started to finish his chemistry," says Irene. "I wanted to be a dentist—I had crooked teeth. If I had known we would wait so long, I would have done it. So I worked at a dentist's office."

Milton got a job at the Helena Rubenstein cosmetics factory near Paris, and worked as an administrator for the *Organisation pour Enfants Juifs,* founded by a Polish Jew named Lena Kuchler. "She saved one hundred children," says Milton. "She brought them to Israel through Paris. These were children who were left alone after the war. They were starving, and had no one to care for them."

Schindler visited them in Paris, Irene recalls. "His first question was, 'Where is Scheck?' We met in a sidewalk café. We lived in a dormitory, for free. There was one kitchen where you could get bread and coffee in the morning and soup at night. From our window, you could see Sacre Coeur."

They had a civil wedding in Paris. Irene remembers painting her legs with makeup for the ceremony, because she couldn't buy stockings.

The Hirschfelds arrived in New York in May 1949 on affidavits of support arranged by "Scheck," through an uncle. For a time, the couple had a one-bedroom apartment in Jackson Heights, Queens. Says Irene, "This is where I came home with my babies," whom she wasn't sure she ever could bear.

"I had a doctor [who] said, 'It won't be so easy for you to have a baby,' and I was very upset. I said, 'Why did I have to come out alive from Auschwitz if I can't have a baby?' Pola [Scheck Yogev] was pregnant when I came, and they had a little jalopy, and we went to Jones Beach. I covered her in the water so she wouldn't get hit by the waves, then two days later, I found out I was pregnant."

Son Michael was born in March 1950; daughter Audrey followed in March 1956. Both Michael Hirschfeld and Audrey Hirschfeld Fass are lawyers in New York; both are married to lawyers. Irene and Milton have three grandchildren.

"When I became pregnant," says Irene, "I thought this baby would replace the ones who were lost, and I was so happy. Of course, this is impossible. But I remember saying to myself that when I have my own child, my feeling of loss for my mother will be compensated. I will transfer the love I had for my mother to my child."

For the first few months of the pregnancy, Milton worked the night shift at a chocolate factory. "We had one small bed," Irene recalls. "I don't know if you've ever experienced the smell of chocolate [up close], but it was killing me! I don't exaggerate! He was mixing it in big vats. I told him he could not sleep in the same bed with me."

They both got jobs at the Helena Rubinstein factory in Long Island City. Irene closed face-cream jars until her seventh month. Still, it was evident to her doctor that she and Milton had no money. "This doctor put two and two together. I had no insurance, and I had reserved a semiprivate room. There was none available, only a private room. In those days, you were in bed for a week. When I finally went home and tried to pay, the [hospital] told me, 'Your doctor paid it for you.'

"I'm ready to cry now," says Irene Hirschfeld. And she does.

Milton's next job was with Holzer, a Manhattan-based Swiss watch importer. He has worked there for more than forty years.

When Michael was in the second grade, the family moved to Oceanside, Long Island, a few minutes away from the Long Beach home of "Scheck," Pola, and their children. As a small child, Michael had severe asthma. "It was a nightmare," says Irene. "I thought, 'How will I decide to have another child, when he needs my attention so much?' But I decided when he was five. My brother had a boy and a girl, so we had to catch up."

The strain took its toll on her. "My nerves were coming out, and I was short of temper," she admits. "But my kids were always the best dressed and cleanest on the block, and they both skipped two grades. I set certain rules: They had to do homework first before playing, [and Michael rebelled] a little bit. When kids came and asked, 'Is Mike there?' I used to tell them, 'If you come to my house, you address me as Mrs. Hirschfeld.' Maybe these are the old European customs, but that's the way I was."

In addition to the house in Oceanside, the Hirschfelds also have a winter condo in Delray Beach, Florida. Irene would gladly spend the entire year there, except that Milton is president of the New York–based New Cracow Friendship Society, he won't retire from his job, and the grandchildren live in New York.

British director Jonathan Blair featured Irene Hirschfeld in *Schindler*, his 198300 BBC documentary. That was the last time she spoke publicly about the Holocaust. She wasn't pleased with that experience, nor is she particularly thrilled with the current Schindler phenomenon. In fact, she hasn't seen the film all the way through. Certainly, she says, Oskar Schindler deserves recognition. What she doesn't like—and she's quite direct about it—is that others have "distorted" reality for commercial reasons. (In any case, her brother used to ask, " 'Why do you want to undress yourself for Hitler again?' " by talking about it, so she stopped.)

For example, she says that the following incident may not be as "sellable" as the story of a Nazi who saved Jews, but it's the kind of thing that happened far more frequently.

"There was one *Aktion* in the ghetto. Almost all the Optima people were out and safe. But I was so scared that instead of going with the group out of the gates, I kept going backward. Finally, I decided to go through the German selection, and I noticed an OD man from Podgórze: Poldek Goldberg [no relation to Marcel Goldberg]. I knew him. I said, 'Poldek, please help me,' so when the German soldier turned around, he pushed me on the good side. *He* saved my life, not Schindler. And look what happened to him: Amon Goeth shot him. He was one of the first."

LOLA FELDMAN ORZECH

Before Oskar Schindler, the sympathetic Nazi, there was Herman Feldman, the loving brother. And had it not been for the latter's chutzpah, Lola Orzech knows she never would have enjoyed the former's protection.

"When my brother took us out from Wieliczka," she says, "he was the first one to save my life."

Near the end of 1941, Jews living outside the Kraków ghetto were ordered to assemble at Wieliczka, the salt-mines town. The Feldman family complied. Unwilling to move into the ghetto earlier that year, they'd rented space from a farmer in suburban Kocmyrzów. Only Herman stayed behind.

"He was not afraid," says Lola Orzech. "He 'made things' with the Germans"—that's code for black-market trading and bribery—"and could go out from the ghetto. He helped us financially that way."

As they dutifully followed the evacuation directive, asking the farmer to help them truck clothing and some furniture to the assembly point, the Feldmans didn't know that the Germans intended to transport the assembling Jews to a death camp.

Herman materialized on the third day of their wait. "He said, 'Don't ask any questions. Quick! Come with me.' He had a tip that the transport [from Wieliczka] was going east, to Treblinka, so he was going crazy. He took a whole truck and [pretended] to pick up people for work at the airport [near Kraków]." He bribed a German soldier to drive the truck. "By the time he found us, it was already full with people [who] were pushing into his hands money and diamonds. My brother had to take me and throw me on the people like a sack of potatoes. I lost my shoes. That same German had to beat him up a little to cover up for him."

Lola's father didn't understand the gravity of the situation. "He started to cry, 'What will be with our things?' My older sister, Regina, said she would stay behind to look after them. Just to quiet down my mother, my brother said there would be another truck." Regina probably died at Treblinka.

Leon and Matilda Feldman Markheim had six children when the war began: Regina, born in 1914, Herman, Erna, Lola, Dora, and Marilka, all with the last name Feldman. Another daughter, Hanka, died in infancy. "My name should really be Markheim," explains Lola, who was born in August 1925, "but before the war, my parents had the Jewish wedding but they didn't have

the civil wedding, so I was going to school as Feldman, after my mother. That was the law. I remember before the war, my parents were talking: 'We have to go and take care of that.'"

After the war, Lola Feldman married Stanley Orzech, also of Kraków. They live in North Hollywood, California, a few miles from Lola's first cousin

The Feldman family at the resort town of Cherna, near Kraków, around 1938: (left to right) Herman, Lola, Regina, Marilka, Leon, Dora, and Matilda.

Maurice Markheim, another *Schindlerjude*. Her father, Leon, and Maurice's father, Solomon, were brothers.

Leon Markheim had a fish store, which was open to the public on Thursday and part of Friday for Sabbath preparations. "In the middle of the week, he was going around to the fish farms, for carp, trout, salmon," Lola explains. "People liked the fish still alive." Before major holidays, she would skip school to help pack fish.

The family had "a nice, traditional home in Kazimierz," the old Jewish quarter, at 37 Krakówska Street. The girls shared beds, and a maid slept in the kitchen. Lola was "the quiet one"; Dora was her closest sibling rival. Sisters Regina and Erna already had social lives; they were old enough to go to tea dances.

Lola says her parents knew that conditions for Poland's Jews would degenerate, "but who wanted to leave everything?" So life went on. Erna married "and right away became pregnant"; then Regina married. (Her husband's family had been among the German Jews of Polish origin deported in 1938.) Erna Feldman Lebler gave birth to a daughter, Helen, in 1940.

Leon Markheim supported his family in Kocmyrzów by smuggling. "He took the train as a gentile person. He took an afghan and put it over his armband, so if they caught him, he was wearing it, but it was covered up." He brought trade items back to Kocmyrzów, where he would barter underwear, socks, shoes, and fabric for flour, butter, poultry, and eggs. "That's the way we lived. Then came the order that everybody from the outskirts had to go to Wieliczka."

After the daring rescue, Herman sneaked the family into Kraków and found a place for them in Ghetto B, which housed the children, the elderly, and anyone lacking a work permit. "We had to get work, because we had no papers," Lola explains. "My father found a job on the outskirts, taking care of horses. My brother was in Ghetto A legally. Erna found a different place [to live], with her baby, but she was bringing her every day to my mother, because we got up every morning at five to go to the work-placement center in the ghetto. I was waking Dora, but she would say, 'Leave me alone; I'm not going to work for Germans.'"

The labor office placed Erna at Kabelwerk, an electrical wiring factory. And they sent Lola to a place called Deutsche Emailwaren Fabrik. "I was one of the first seven girls working for Schindler, with Edzia Liebgold [Edith Wertheim], Lola Krumholz, and her mother-in-law."

They marched to and from the ghetto every day for their shifts. In the meantime, Jewish slave laborers were building Camp Płaszów, Stanley Orzech among them. Lola would meet him in Kraków when the war ended, after he'd survived Mauthausen, Gusen I, and Gusen II.

In the fall of 1942, German soldiers surrounded the ghetto, culling thousands of Jews for transport, including Matilda, Dora, and Marilka Feldman. Leon and Herman learned the previous day that something was afoot. "I had a night shift, probably three in the afternoon to eleven or midnight," Lola recalls. "My father and brother came, and they told me, 'Make sure to go to work.' They chased me out. I didn't want to leave. My mother said, 'Please don't cry.' She wanted me to go. At the factory, Schindler gave us a room. . . . I was sitting crying all night. I didn't know who survived."

The next day, the Emalia workers returned to the ghetto. Lola went to her family's apartment and found it empty. Hysterical, she wandered the streets. "Then all of a sudden, I saw my brother, and I fainted." Erna, who'd been at Kabelwerk, survived, as did Leon, who'd been at his job. Herman Feldman knew full well what had happened to his mother, but he didn't let on.

"I remember going with my sister to the bathroom [in an outhouse], with the candle, and it was winter," says Lola. "We were thinking, 'I hope Mother is not cold.' We were thinking she was going someplace to work. She was taken to Treblinka."

The toddler Helen also disappeared. Herman arranged to spirit her out of the ghetto, through the barbed-wire fence, to a waiting Christian couple. "It was a problem at the end of the war, but we got her back," says Lola. "They were taking her to church. She was almost five." (Helen Lebler Matthews lives in Camarillo, California. Her mother, widowed once, is now Erna de Michelle of Los Angeles.)

The Germans further compressed the ghetto, squeezing those who remained into even closer quarters. "We got a different place to live, right on Plac Zgody. It was one room. My brother used to come drunk almost every day with Maurice's older brother, David, and they were crying, because they knew [what lay ahead]."

Lola moved into the Emalia complex. "I was living there, schlepping boards at the factory. A gentile guy, a Pole, was standing and painting all those pots, and my job was to pick up those pots to bring to the drier. We had to bring back the boards, and when I took a minute too long, he was yelling, 'Lolka! Where are you?' He knew my name, but he called me Lolka."

The Poles came to work ready and willing to sell the confined Jews extra food. Herman made sure his sister always had a few złotys in her pocket to buy bread, even after he moved into the Płaszów camp.

At Emalia, Lola shared a bunk with two young women: Herta Nussbaum and Pearl Lezerkiewicz. They ate together, cried together, and became close friends. Herta spoke fluent German. Oskar Schindler was attracted to her. "She had a beautiful face," Lola Orzech remembers. "She was blond, zaftig, busty, but she had good legs. Schindler used to come up and flirt with her. She wanted him to bring her husband from Kabel, and he did."

A brisk commerce in goods and information operated between the various Płaszów-based installations—Emalia, Kabel, the Madritsch uniform factory—and the main camp, which supplied food and provisions.

"Once in a while, I heard news that my father and sister and brother were OK," says Lola. "I had a boyfriend, too, at NKF [a factory at the Emalia sub-camp that Schindler didn't own]. I could spend maybe a half hour with him after work. I was not hungry, but I was dead tired. Smooching—that's as far as I went. Then I went to bed. I should say, to hay."

Lola swears the boy, who later died at Mauthausen, looked just like Tom Cruise. Stanley jokes, "That's why before we got married, I said to her, 'You sure you want to marry an ugly guy like me?' I knew this guy."

When Amon Goeth liquidated the Kraków ghetto in March 1943, Stanley Orzech was among those dispatched from Płaszów to mop up the mess. Piloting a flatbed handcart through the swamp of gore, he found his father's body. "I was crying," says Orzech, now a retired liquor-store owner. "Suddenly, while I was walking, a German with three stars asked me why I was crying. I didn't give an [honest] answer, but I said, 'You can see yourself why.' The blood was running from the [cart] platform. He went in his pocket and gave me two packs of German cigarettes. He said, 'Don't worry; keep yourself. The war will be over soon.' Can you believe it?"

Lola, Herman, and Erna lost their maternal grandmother in the liquidation. During a raid on the ghetto's Jewish hospital, where she lay ill, someone threw her out a third-story window.

For a brief time before they left for Brinnlitz or other, less reassuring, destinations, the Emalia subcamp workers moved back to Płaszów. The night before the move, says Lola, someone got hold of some vodka, and a whole group drank themselves silly. In the process, Lola created a novel hiding place for a five-hundred-złoty note that Herman had sent over.

"I rolled it up in my hair. At that time, I got drunk, because we didn't know what was going to happen to us. There was a *gurale*, like a mountaineer, on the five-hundred-złoty note. I remember saying, 'Here I have my *gurale* in my hair.' I was crying about my mother. We were all kissing and emotional. After the war in Germany, my friends made up to get me drunk again, and guess what? I cried and cried."

Herman secured a job for his sister at the Płaszów laundry, ironing shirts for SS officers. "I was a good girl, always obeying, but I had a bad incident in the laundry: I burned the collar of a shirt for one German. The Jewish policeman bawled me out, and my brother had a big fight with him."

Lola and Erna expected to complete the journey to Brinnlitz together, but were separated at Auschwitz. "My sister was supposed to be on the list, but she went from Auschwitz to Lichtenburg, and she went through hell there. I was yelling her name and waving, and she was calling mine. She didn't know where I was going and I didn't know where she was going."

At Auschwitz, Lola was determined to keep her hair and her boots. "I was next to my [future] sister-in-law. We messed up our hair, so they wouldn't cut it, and they didn't. I had high shoes with laces, so I took off the laces and stepped on the heels of the shoes, and they didn't take them away."

Elsa Ritterman married Herman Feldman after the war. Lola and Elsa bunked together at Brinnlitz, where Elsa made a deal for extra food. "We were knitting some sweaters for one of the *Budzyners,* and he was giving us more bread. I was sitting all night knitting." A balcony partition, easily breached, separated the men and women in the Brinnlitz barracks, which was actually the factory's top floor. "He would give [Elsa] the yarn, and he wanted a kiss for this. One day she said, 'I'm going to sleep; when they call for me, you go to the wires to him.' I said, 'Oh no; I can sit all night and knit, but I'm not going to that old stinker that he wants a kiss from me . . . or something else.' She was called, and I said, 'Please tell whoever it is that she is sleeping already,' and I did not go. She was furious, and my brother got mad at me."

Brinnlitz offered Herman Feldman his first real taste of hardship. His eyes, says Lola, "were getting wild from hunger. When I had the soup, I was digging out the meat and slicing the bread and making sandwiches for the whole day. But do you think I could sit and swallow, while he was hungry? So I gave him mine, and so did Elsa. He was yelling that he didn't want to take it, but we made him."

After the war, "we didn't have much either," says Lola. "My sister-in-law came from a very rich family before the war. They had two buildings, at Forty-one Wwrzynca and one on Bochna Larza. In one, the janitor was still living. When we got back to Kraków, she let us in and we slept, all three of us, in the kitchen on the floor. . . . I remember going to the Jewish center for something to eat. We had no money, no clothes, no nothing."

They also went back to the apartment at 37 Krakówska, by then occupied by Poles. When the janitor saw Lola, she was incredulous: " 'You're the one who lived through? You were the most quiet of all of them!' We were still hoping someone was alive, but all that came was my older sister Regina's husband. After that, if we had to go someplace where we had to pass the house, I couldn't make myself go. I had to go round and round."

In Kraków, Herman discovered their father's fate, but he didn't tell Lola. "He was taken from Płaszów to Mauthausen, and he was OK there. Then maybe four weeks to liberation, he got sick with typhus. My brother's friend slept next to him. He couldn't go to work. In the barracks, they couldn't take the smell, so the *Blochalteste* stood on a board on his throat, after everybody went to work.

"After the war, we went to a movie. My brother ran into [his friend]. He was talking and talking. When we came home, I said, 'Who is that person?' He said, 'Oh, nothing.' Later on, my sister-in-law told me that was the time he found out about my father. Can you imagine?"

The group moved to an apartment in the Rittermans' building on Bochna Larza. There, Lola Feldman met Stanley Orzech. "He and my cousin David, Maurice's brother, were in camp together and saved each other's lives. My brother was so good-hearted, whoever came and didn't have somewhere to stay, he gave a place to sleep. You slept on the floor, but you had a roof over your head. Sometimes in the one-bedroom apartment, we had maybe twenty-five people. That's how I met him." They married on May 19, 1946.

"They started to have pogroms. Stan wanted to leave, but I didn't want to because my brother was staying. That's the first time he got mad at me. He blew his top. He said, 'If you don't go with me, I go by myself.' "

They left together, with a single suitcase, sneaking across borders to Linz and the big Displaced Persons camp at Bindermichel. There, says Lola, Stan "started to make a little business. When he left for one 'tour,' he got stuck in Germany, in Regensburg. They didn't want to let him go because he played very good soccer. . . . I got a letter to get all our things together, and they would send a car for me. I didn't know if I was doing the right thing or wrong thing."

Two American intelligence officers came to take her to her husband. "We came to the border, and one said to me, 'Take off your hat. We will do all the talking,' like they got themselves a chick. A Jewish fellow!"

The Orzechs stayed in Regensburg for three years. Stanley did what many of the Jewish refugees did for a living: He smuggled. Lola gave birth to the first of two daughters in January 1949: Matilda Fela Orzech, known as Marty. Eleven months later, the family arrived in New York.

"When I was in Germany, I had a maid and a nurse. It was very cheap. The maid was with me to the last minute, and she took us to the train. I was crying. I cried for whatever was waiting and how good I had it. I knew I wouldn't have it anymore. . . . I tried not to get pregnant. I was scared to death, knowing that I had to travel, and what kind of future was waiting for me here, in the United States, with no family, not knowing the language."

A Jewish relief organization sent the Orzechs to Omaha, Nebraska. They

Lola and Stanley Orzech after their wedding, 1946.

went by train, through Chicago. Lola remembers how disappointing the landscape looked. "I thought, 'This is the United States?' It was all wilderness and farms."

Omaha had a sizable Jewish community, "and very nice people. A family took us. They gave us an apartment and a mattress with a hole in it. They found Stan a job with a veterinary medicine company, in a plant that made medication for chickens in the incubators. He brought home thirty-nine dollars a week, and we saved ten. On Saturday, he worked at the Omaha potato market."

Erna, having retrieved her daughter, was living in California. "My husband was working to go on vacation there," says Lola. "I went to see her in Ventura County. My older daughter was three. The weather was so wonderful. My brother-in-law started to talk to us, that there were not so many of us [in the family] left, that we should stay together. I never went back to Omaha."

Stan went to work at a fruit grower's laboratory, testing soil. The Orzechs had a second daughter, Dorothy. (Marty and Dorothy married cousins named Spector. They both live in Southern California and have five children between them.)

After a stint as a supermarket produce manager, Stanley Orzech bought a liquor store on Melrose Avenue in Los Angeles. By the time he retired in 1987, he owned three. "Those stores were getting rough to handle," he says. "I thought, 'Let's not jeopardize our luck.' We were lucky for so many years. We got robbed, but we never got in trouble. I had a policy: They want money, give it to them, and keep extra on the side, to give them more. Don't fight. Keep your hands on the counter."

The Orzechs have lived for twenty years in a split-level ranch house on a quiet street. The 1994 earthquake put a noticeable dent in Lola's Lalique and Lladro collections, but the structure held. It certainly didn't help Lola's nerves, which, she says, have always been fragile.

"It's even a miracle that we survivors wound up the way we are, from what we were going through, but we were very young." She laughs at a remark her daughter Dorothy once made, when the senior Orzechs applied for restitution from the Germans.

"They sent me to a German psychiatrist. My daughter was twelve. I said to her, 'I am very nervous today; tomorrow I have to go to the German doctor.' She said, 'Mother, there is nothing to worry about; just be yourself.'"

Lola and Stanley Orzech, Los Angeles, 1994.

Lola Orzech, flawlessly coiffed, with perfect red nails, says that for years, the girls "didn't want to hear anything" about the Holocaust. "In the evenings, I was making lunch for them for school. This they didn't want to eat, that they didn't want to eat. I used to say, 'Oh boy, would I be happy if I had had that.' They would say, 'Mother, don't tell me; I'm not interested.'"

The 1978 television miniseries *Holocaust* got their attention to some extent. Then Marty's book club read *Schindler's List.* "She called me ten thousand times: *'That's* what you did?' It opened their eyes. [Watching] the movie, to tell you the truth, I had no more tears. But they were crying.

"Those things never really get out of my mind. I think about it every day. You see the picture of my mother and father? I have it on my nightstand, and not one time I look at it, it doesn't bring memories. But what can I do? Shoot myself?"

MAURICE MARKHEIM

*I*t was December 1939, and the Germans had been in Kraków for three months. To them, a Jew on the street—no matter the age, gender, or social status—was nothing more than slave labor on the hoof. One minute you were walking home, and the next someone was pitching you into the back of a work truck like a hunk of cordwood. This is how sixteen-year-old Maurice Markheim found himself at a labor camp far from home: alone and frightened.

"I remember like it was today," says Markheim, who was born on Valentine's Day in 1923. "I was at the main square in Kraków. They surrounded it, and I saw what was going on. Someone grabbed me and threw me on a truck. They took us to a forest—Pustków. We started to feel what the Germans were. That was the first beating I got. And no food. The ground was very hard already, and we were digging and building barracks." (A full-scale labor camp opened on the site in September 1942.) Maurice Markheim discovered a principle that would save his life more than once during the Holocaust: "It's not what you know, it's who you know."

In this case, *what* he knew was that his mother came from nearby Tarnów. The *who* was an uncle still living there. So when Jewish day-workers from Tarnów returned to the city at night, he asked them to spread the word that he was there. "That was the way we started to get connections. . . . My mother took right away a train, with my sister, and went to Tarnów to try to get me out of there."

His uncle knew people on the *Judenrat*. Arrangements were made, cash changed hands, a plan was hatched. "For five hundred złotys, which was a lot of money, the SS man promised my uncle, 'I will bring the boy to your house.' The next day I got a loaf of bread, so I wasn't hungry. Then the man said, 'In a couple of days, you'll go with us to Tarnów, so that day, don't go to work. Try to play sick.' But a half hour before I'm supposed to meet that guy, they caught me to unload a truck full of potatoes. I saw the SS man. He came on the truck and he started to beat me: 'Get out of here; you don't know how to work!' So I knew what was going on. I ran off the truck [to] where I was pointed to go, and he picked me up and drove me out."

His mother got hysterical when she saw him. "I was already looking very bad: skinny, beat up."

In 1939, the Markheim family lived on the edge of Kazimierz, at 9 Pieskarska Street. Maurice had six siblings: Rena, Nathan, Amalia, John, Michael, and David. Rena, married to a jeweler, had a son. Nathan was in the textile business. John was a customs officer. Michael worked for a brush company, and David helped his mother, Esther, in the family fish business. Maurice and Amalia attended school. Maurice recalls that his father, Solomon, who'd once had a leather business, was working at the city's Jewish hospital when the war broke out.

The Markheims were not a religious family—"my father was completely assimilated"—though Esther kept a kosher home. "Once in a while on Friday night, she would say to Nathan, 'Take the kids and go to a *shul*.' So to give her the enjoyment—he was a wonderful guy—he'd say, 'All right, boys, let's go together.' Once we left the apartment, everybody went in different directions. And he set a time [when] we would get together. I went to my friends. My brothers went to their girlfriends. At a certain hour, we met right at the door; we walked in and said, 'Good Shabbos,' and my mother was happy.

"We went to *shul* [as a family] twice a year. On Yom Kippur, my mother was sitting all day, and everybody had to show up at a certain hour and visit her: Bingo! and out. At night, everybody showed up to go home together."

Maurice didn't like to go to *cheder.* "I never went. I was there the first day. My mother signed me up and paid for the month. After a month, she came to find out how I was progressing. But the rabbi said, 'Who's he?' What did she do? I got beat up! But I was bar mitzvahed. Six weeks before, a man came to the house and taught me all the prayers." All young Maurice wanted to do was play soccer, basketball, hockey, and water polo at the Maccabi sports club. Leopold Page was his high-school gym teacher.

Tall and rugged, Markheim still walks four miles a day. He underwent heart bypass surgery in late 1984 and likes to keep in shape. He lives in a duplex apartment a couple of blocks from the Los Angeles–Beverly Hills border with his second wife, Regina. Blond and blue-eyed, she survived the war with forged Aryan papers. They belong to the 1939 Club, a Los Angeles–based survivor organization, and socialize almost exclusively with other survivors.

When planning the Final Solution, the Nazis decided to demoralize Poland's Jews by dislocating their families. What befell the Markheims was typical. As the ghetto formed in early 1941, Nathan, Rena, Michael, and Maurice couldn't get passes (*Kennkarten*). They went to Niepolomice, a suburb, where Maurice worked on a chicken farm. Solomon, Esther, David, and Amalia stayed in the ghetto. John was drafted into the Polish army.

Rena "was very well off," says Maurice. "My brother-in-law worked for a man named Holzer." (Milton Hirschfeld, another *Schindlerjude,* still works for the Holzer company.) He had a Chevy convertible and a Packard. They were Omega watch representatives for all of Poland, and my brother-in-law made the cases." His name was Samek Schnur. Maurice Markheim holds out his arm, displaying a well-worn Omega wristwatch. "You know how old this is? Old as you are! Another one, a gold one I got for my bar mitzvah, the maid kept. I have it today, in the safe."

His brother Michael was "so tough, you could put him on a fire, he wouldn't burn." Denied a *Kennkarte,* he moved to Bochnia with his wife and child.

At the end of 1941, Jews from many small towns around Kraków were ordered into the ghetto, or to Wieliczka, a salt-mines town near Kraków. We sent "my sister and her baby to Kraków. Later, for money, my father bought her papers, that she is an Argentine citizen. Nathan and I went to Wieliczka. We thought, 'What can happen? We're young.'

"What was going on was incredible. They called everybody into a big field. Then they pulled back with the trucks, and old ladies and babies were thrown on the trucks like a sack of potatoes, one after the other. They picked up thousands of people," among them his cousin Regina Feldman. The rest of her family, including Lola Feldman Orzech, who today lives in North Hollywood, California, escaped.

Maurice and Nathan were assigned to the cleanup crew. "What was cleaning up? Picking up the dead bodies. They were shooting [people] left and right. I was thinking, 'If there is a God looking, where is the God? How can he look down on us—innocent people, babies, old people—and see what is happening?'"

Maurice and Nathan decided to work opposite shifts: "When he was in the barracks, I went to work. When I came, he went. I was at night covering the bodies, and the other group was bringing the bodies. Thousands! But it was bad the way we did it. One day, an SS man said, 'We need one hundred volunteers.' Everybody was afraid. Volunteers for what? I knew a little bit of German. I asked a German—a nice guy—he said it was a good commando job, and I should go. I was looking for my brother; he was the only one I had. They had an order to employ one hundred people at Kabelwerk. That was a *Julag*—an *Arbeitslager* [labor camp]. Płaszów was the main camp." (Nathan missed the chance. He was sent to the Stalowa Wola labor camp, escaped to the Bochnia ghetto, was transported to Płaszów, and died at Mauthausen.)

The director of Kabelwerk, where wire, switches, and other electrical components were made, was a man named Böhme. To hear Maurice Markheim tell it, he was a decent man who tried to make life more bearable for his workers.

"I think certain things he was doing, Schindler was copying from him," says Markheim in his unmistakable gruff, rumbly voice. "He was a party man, one hundred percent German Nazi, but a human being. . . . He was treating us very well. But conditions were very bad in the *Julag*, especially the sanitation. The commander was Müller. He was a very bad guy. The soup was awful, and it was very hard to work that way. So Böhme gave us permission to eat from the Polish kitchen in the factory."

Still, his workers complained so bitterly that *Herr Direktor* went to Gestapo headquarters on Pomorska Street and said, " 'Look, these are qualified people, I need them, and I want those people out [of the *Julag*]. So they put us in the ghetto under special permission. The *Judenrat* had to provide us with everything. So being in the ghetto, I was home."

Barracks were under construction at Płaszów. As soon as the first ones were ready, Markheim's group was moved out of the ghetto and into Płaszów. "In our spare time, we were building barracks. We were under the Ukrainians, but the director wouldn't allow beating.

"At Kabel, it was safe, and we were not hungry. Once in a while I had a piece of bread with butter. Some of the gentile girls liked me. I told one of them, 'You go see my mother [in the ghetto]. You want a nice pocketbook? She gonna give you a nice, beautiful pocketbook.' So she went there and got a gorgeous pocketbook—believe you me!—and she was bringing me food."

He also got to know the head of his department. "They got so tough that they were checking how much food [the Poles] brought in. They were not allowed more than one sandwich for lunch. That gentile fellow was hungry the whole day, and he gave me the sandwich, because he knew he would go home and have something to eat; when I went home, I didn't. But [he didn't do it] for nothing, believe you me!"

Markheim compared Böhme with Oskar Schindler: "Schindler was a womanizer. Schindler was a drunkard. Schindler was black-marketer. Schindler was a Nazi. Before Schindler, there was Böhme! Why don't they start with him? In my opinion, Schindler copied Böhme. He was like an aristocrat. He was a big, handsome guy in his forties. There were some Jews in the office! His main bookkeeper was a Jew! But there was no hanky-panky there. No black market. He had character! He was a better class of German: educated. He didn't send nobody to die. Nobody! If we stayed to the end of the war with him, we wouldn't lose a hair."

His only injury at Kabel was to his right pinkie: a machine "grabbed" it, permanently twisting it out of shape.

In February 1943, Amon Goeth took command of Camp Płaszów, "and started the agony, the brutality, the real thing," says Maurice Markheim. By then, his parents were gone; his mother transported to Bełżec, his father shot on Plac Zgody. "I didn't find out for *twenty years,* from Lola Orzech's brother, my cousin! He said my father was lucky: He got shot in the ghetto. My sister [Amalia] went with my mother."

As for Rena and her baby, Roman: "Eventually they caught up with all those people with [forged] papers and sent them to Bergen-Belsen." Her husband had already committed suicide in Lvov. Rena initially had gone east with him, but left their child in Kraków with Esther. "If she hadn't come back for the baby, she would have survived the war," Maurice believes. Samek Schnur "was so desperate that before she came back, he went upstairs on the third or fourth floor and jumped—and he was in good hands, with the Russians."

Under Amon Goeth, conditions at Płaszów degenerated from rotten to unspeakable. "We went to Böhme and complained: 'We don't know if we come tomorrow to work or if he's gonna shoot us.' He went to Pomorska, to the Gestapo. He said, 'I want to build the barracks on the factory.' And after that, we lived in the [factory's] barracks. I think this is where Schindler got the idea to build barracks on the premises and keep his people there.

"But no matter, we were the property of the SS. We were surrounded by wire and patrols. We had to get food and rations from the main camp, so three or four prisoners dragged a wagon up to the camp, loaded up, and came back. One fine day, I wanted to see my brother Nathan." Maurice got to be the "horse" pulling the wagon.

"We came to the main camp and they wouldn't let us in. What was going on? If Goeth caught us there, he'd take out the gun. But the SS man said, 'No, don't worry.' Two big trucks had to go by before we could enter the camp. What was in the two trucks? The Polish intelligentsia, kneeling, tied up by the hands to the sides of the trucks. They were yelling, 'You idiot Polacks; don't take advantage of the Jews! The [Germans will] start on the Jews and finish on us!' And they were singing the Polish national anthem. A minute later, those two trucks headed straight for Chujowa Górka, and a minute later: Bam-bam-bam!"

For a short time, three Markheim brothers were at Płaszów. After

Michael's wife and child were killed in Bochnia, he came to the camp on a transport. "Every time a transport came in, Goeth and Chilowicz were there. Marysia Chilowicz was going to school with me before the war. Oh, what a bitch! And she was so stupid—you have no idea. Chilowicz owed Michael money he had borrowed before the war. This is what he said to Michael: 'I need you here like a hole in my head. I'll talk to you later.' Later, he asked my brother, 'What did you come here for?' Michael said, 'What do I have to lose? My wife and baby are dead.' "

In the fall of 1944, the Germans ordered all the Płaszów subcamps closed, including Emalia and Kabel. "We were three hundred people," Maurice recalls. "At the same time, there was a transport to Mauthausen. The director didn't know what to do; he had to cut his personnel in half. He didn't need the women, only the men. What for? To carry big machinery.

"So we had an *Appell,* and he said, 'I feel very sorry, but all the women got to go back to Płaszów.' Ninety percent of the men had a girlfriend or a wife. So they started to scream and cry. I remember like it was yesterday, so help me God! Böhme went on the side and talked with the SS. Then he said, 'OK. This is what we're gonna do, and that's final. The men who're gonna liquidate the factory have the right to take a girl with them, or their wife." Schindler never did that!

"I was the second name he called out to stay. I had two brothers at Płaszów [Nathan and Michael], and I never had the opportunity to join them, and now seemed like the time. I was ready to cross the line. I said to myself: 'No. What happens if, at the same time, there is a transport? And that happened! The people who went back to Płaszów from Kabelwerk didn't go to the barracks; they went straight to the cars and they all went to Mauthausen."

Chilowicz got Michael assigned to a job outside the camp, and he escaped back to Bochnia. Somehow, he managed to get an SS uniform, "and with 'Heil Hitler!' a briefcase, and a revolver, he went all the way to Budapest," and from there to Palestine. He died in 1961 in the United States.

John deserted the Polish army. He, too, made his way to Palestine, where he joined the Haganah. He and Michael were reunited after they bumped into each other on the street.

Michael (left) and John Markheim in Palestine, late 1940s. They escaped Poland during the war.

When the remaining Kabel workers finished at the factory, "we had no choice. We went back to Płaszów. That's the first time I started to feel hungry, at the end of 1944. At that time, Goeth was behind bars, and there was another guy who wasn't too bad. They were not allowed to shoot anymore. But they had a commando at the quarry: You worked there one day, you never came back."

Maurice Markheim got the only job that was worse: "They sent me to the hill [Chujowa Górka] after Kabel, digging bodies. It was already close to winter. The ground was frozen. You had to work with an ax. You hit the head, and the brains spilled all over you, or you couldn't get the ax out, and you were pulling the legs, the arms. You didn't know how the body lay. Once you discovered a little bit of the body—this was the order from the SS—you had to clean it by hand, just to get to the face; the rest they didn't care about. When you discovered the face, you had to holler. A man came down with a pair of pliers, opened the mouth and pulled the gold teeth. You could recognize one thing: a child. [You could tell] a woman from a man by the hair only."

He remembers that the men on the detail—barehanded, without even a kerchief to cover their faces—had to eat among the corpses. "They were bringing down the soup, but we were zombies! You didn't think. People didn't smell it anymore. The fire was burning twenty-four hours. About two or three months later in Brinnlitz, my body was still smelling like the dead bodies, because the smell got under your skin. You came back [from the detail], you were dead yourself. You didn't wash; you lay down. I was lucky: I was working at night, so the smell wasn't so bad."

Markheim doesn't know how he got on Schindler's list. His brother Nathan knew Marcel Goldberg, but he didn't. And, in any case, Nathan was already at Mauthausen with David.

"One fine day, we were coming to the barracks. We were working from seven at night to seven in the morning. But instead of going to the barracks, they said, 'The Schindler group is going, and the transport goes away today.' All of a sudden, my cousin went by—Herman Feldman, Lola Orzech's brother, who knew some bigshots—and maybe about ten minutes later, they called my name. How did I get there? If there is a God, only God knows who put me on the list. I had no protection anymore: no diamonds, nothing!"

At Brinnlitz, Maurice worked on a lathe. He remembers making coffins for the "frozen people," the men from Goleszów, a cement plant at Auschwitz III, who'd been locked, unclaimed, in the cattle cars.

Once he was "in contact" with Emilie Schindler. "She got a whole truck of bread from somewhere on the black market. They called me to unload it. She was talking to the SS, and [because of] the way she turned around and talked, I could slip a loaf under my shirt. I saw that she did this on purpose. A loaf of break at that point was gold!

"There is an old expression: 'Behind the man, there is the woman,' and I believe *she* was the great human being."

After liberation, Maurice went straight to Kraków. "I stopped at the Jewish community center, and they gave me a few złotys and some food and told me to come back if I couldn't find a place to stay. I went to our house. The janitor was still there. She couldn't believe it. She almost fainted. She said, 'You're my son! You're not going nowhere. You're gonna live with me. I'll give you everything.' Whatever we had, I said, 'You can have it.' She deserved everything. Her

Maurice Markheim after the war.

name was Jednejowa Bartyzel. Her son was killed by the Germans in Auschwitz. She was a widow. I stayed a few months. Then people found me, they taught me to black-market a little bit, and I started to earn my living."

David, starving, was liberated from Mauthausen. "He was much better when he came to Kraków. At least I knew he was alive. All through the war, I had been most of the time by myself. I was thankful for anything. At least I had somebody."

Maurice sailed to New York in December 1949. "My ambitions in America were just to support myself. I had no possibility to go to school, so when I came to America, it was on a fixed contract through the Joint [Distribution Committee], as a truck driver. I never drove a truck. It was all a bluff, just to get me out. We stayed at the Hotel Emerson, and we had to go to One hundred third Street to eat."

His first job was in a plastics factory owned by a man who'd been a general engineer at Kabel before the war. "Then, as time went by, people said, 'Listen, you go to the Catskill Mountains to work as a busboy. You're not gonna make a lot of money, but the main thing is, a lot of people get together there, and you can make a lot of tips and connections. You can probably save a thousand dollars.' The fare to go there by bus to Brown's Hotel cost seven-eighty."

Maurice didn't become a busboy; he washed dishes and mopped the kitchen floor. "After a week, Mr. Brown gave me fifteen dollars' pay. He docked me for room and board. Where did I live? In the barn! The cows were there!

Then he said to me, 'Hmm, I gotta call up the agency, send me a few more *greeners*. They're good workers—not the same *greeners* that used to come here.' I could have killed that son of a bitch! He should turn over in the grave! He called me a *greener!*"

The highlight of his brief employment at Brown's was the chance to play Ping-Pong one day with Jerry Lewis. "He spoke Yiddish to me. And it's true about the food: I ate nothing but the best!"

After leaving Brown's, he got a room in the Bronx and a series of jobs, including work in a lace factory. He then started making freezer showcases. His boss, a man named Kraus, took him under his wing. "He said, 'You have to get yourself together and learn English.' He advanced me the money to join the Sheetmetal Workers Union. He asked if I had clothes: 'I want you to look a little bit American,' because I was looking like a greenhorn! He brought me a couple of his own jackets and shoes. They were like new! But they didn't fit me.

"The first few dollars I put away. I dressed myself: a double-breasted suit, navy blue, a white shirt, a pair of shoes. A tie I had already. So, until I opened my mouth, I looked American. . . . I was making thirty-five dollars a week. I was a bigshot! My shoulder blew up; everybody knocked my shoulder and said, 'You're gonna make good in America!' "

And the women? "They were a little bit after me." One of them caught him. Her name was Marlene. "It was a big, formal wedding, but there was no one there from my side, just my best man, who was a friend. But her mother was against me. She was making trouble the night before the wedding."

It should have been an omen. Maurice and Marlene moved to California, where the four living Markheim brothers—Maurice, John, Michael, and David—spent a few years together. (Michael died in 1961, David in 1964, and John in 1975.) Their son, Stephen, was born in 1957, followed thirteen months later by daughter Rena. Today, Stephen Markheim manages real estate in Minneapolis and has one daughter. Rena Markheim teaches school in Truckee, California, near Lake Tahoe. She is single. "All she can meet there is a cowboy!" her father complains. "There are no Jewish people there. But she says, 'I love nature.' " He shrugs.

"I was a partner with my brother John in construction. I had some property. Thank God I was successful, and I am retired now. My brother got sick in 1975 with bone cancer. He had no children. I was laying by the bed on the floor, watching him, and in the morning, I went to work. At that critical moment of my life, my wife asked for a divorce, and till today, I don't know the reason why."

He says the combined effect of his brother's illness and the divorce pushed him over the edge. "I was missing my children. I had adjusted to American life, but I had a hang-up from Europe. I had [a flashback] to the war right away: 'Oh my God, I'm gonna lose them.' I was so *farblonget* [mixed-up]. I locked myself up and drank a whole bottle of vodka and took tranquilizers."

At the time, he was designing stainless-steel fixtures. His boss prescribed a novel remedy: "He said, 'Every morning when you get up, I want you to say four-letter words to yourself.' I did it. One day I just got up, and I was better. I got better by being with normal people, and started to live an honest life. I admit it: I was a zombie."

In 1976, Maurice Markheim married Regina Litmanowitz Rose, who'd been a widow for twelve years. "She is very brave," he says, hugging her close. "All by herself, she raised a son who is a very good fellow, a successful lawyer. She lost her parents, two brothers, and two sisters. In Warsaw, she was on the other side of the wall when the ghetto was burning, on Aryan papers, and, believe you me, it was harder to be on the outside. You never knew who you could run into, and death looked into your eyes every minute."

Maurice Markheim is not a man to mince words, certainly as they apply to his feelings about the Germans. He remembers going on a bus tour of the West and stopping at the Grand Canyon. "Another bus pulled in. They were all Germans. I had had a couple of glasses of wine, and when I looked at those faces, I could see this one's father or grandfather, he was a murderer. It started to boil in me. How much hate was in me!"

He has no sympathy for Jews still living in Germany and Austria who endure anti-Semitism. "They stayed because they had nothing on their minds, just to black-market and make money. Today even, if something happens like

Maurice Markheim, Los Angeles, 1994.

[the Holocaust], I wouldn't feel sorry for them for five cents! They have no right to be there. I've been back to Poland three times, but Germany? My foot never stepped on that soil and never will!"

On his last trip, Maurice Markheim's stepson, Jack Rose, accompanied him. But he wants to return once more, alone. "I want to go to my birthplace, and spend some time quietly by myself: how I was, how I grew up, and I could go to Płaszów. Hopefully, this year, for the good memories and bad memories."

And for the slim chance that he'll be able to find something precious. There had been a place called the Eagle Pharmacy, which was run by a sympathetic non-Jew. Part of his store—"the last stop before Plac Zgody"—faced the ghetto.

"He was taking pictures of the people going to Plac Zgody. They made a museum of that place, and maybe, by luck, I can find there a picture of my father."

SALLY PELLER HUPPERT

J ackson Heights, Queens, is a working-class mix of ethnic whites and peoples of various colors. Squat, red-brick apartment buildings share blocks with modest private homes, many in need of repair. Sally Huppert, a widow, lives alone in one of the brick apartments. To find her two-bedroom flat, a guest just has to follow the scent of fresh-baked mandelbread lingering in the corridor. It leads directly to a plate of the crunchy, halfmoon-shaped cookies in Sally Huppert's narrow kitchen.

Anyone who believes that time can heal all wounds should sit for a few hours in that kitchen and talk to Sally Huppert. A Nazi murdered her mother and youngest sister fifty-three years ago, but for all she still suffers, it might as well have been last week. She cannot stem the tide of tears. "I couldn't help them, and I was the one they counted on!"

There's no use pointing out that, collectively, more than three million Polish Jews couldn't save themselves, so for any individual to feel guilty about failing to prevent another's demise makes no sense. But the Nazis annihilated logic and reason long before they murdered the first Jew, so Sally Huppert remains inconsolable.

She was born in 1910, the oldest of Pinchas Peller and Marie Geller Peller's five daughters, two of whom survived the war. (On Schindler's list, she is Sara

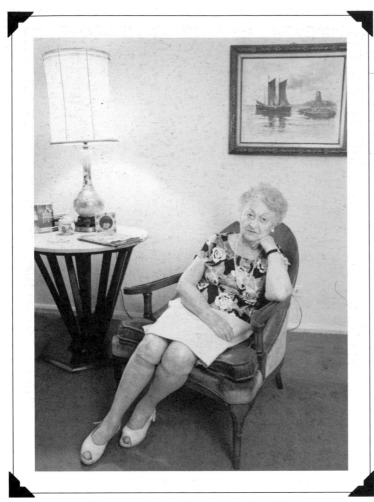

Sally Huppert, Jackson Heights, New York, 1994.

Peller, number 188, born in 1918.) The family moved from the city of Strosze to the resort town of Rabka when she was fifteen, because one of her sisters was sick, and doctors recommended Rabka's pure mountain air. It was a beautiful place then, with a year-round season. Sally says there was always music in the air.

She has only fond memories of her childhood. "One grand-mother had forty-two grandchil-dren and five great-grandchildren." The other had six children. "So many cousins and uncles! The wed-dings would be three or four days. The people were all around the house, and everybody ate and ate."

Pinchas Peller suffered shrap-nel wounds in World War I, fight-ing in Italy, and received a disability pension from the Polish army. It wasn't enough to support his family, so as soon as she was able, Sally got a job. At age fourteen, she became a secretary, first for a lawyer, then at a petroleum company. "I was working, traveling, giving my mother my money. I was very independent. In the daytime, I was working. At night, I was going to school to learn bookkeeping."

But in her twenties, she made a career switch: "I learned to be a corsetiere," the only one in Rabka. "There were no factories—I had to make everything to order: corsets, brassieres, slips. I had a room, and I had my shop there. I was working for actresses. They came in the summertime with their children."

After Sally came Rega, who married Abraham Bankier after the war; Necha—"I don't know where she is; they killed her"; Blanka, a student nurse

A Geller family wedding, early 1930s.

who died of a blood disease in 1936; and Hilda, the baby, who was only sixteen when she was killed.

Rabka's Nazi overseer was Wilhelm Rosenbaum, a twisted killer who couldn't tolerate any Jew sharing his name. Sally knew a family he slaughtered for that reason.

"In Rabka, you couldn't get a lot of things. A man used to come and bring packages from Kraków. I gave him an order, and he bought everything for me. His name was Rosenbaum, and he had a wife and two children, a boy and a girl. One Friday evening, [the commandant] sent for Rosenbaum and his wife and daughter. The son was working. When he came home, they were waiting for him. He was maybe eleven. He said, 'Please, let me light the candles for my parents.' They took him to the Gestapo and killed them all."

Rosenbaum almost got her, too. "I was working for the German women, making corsets and brassieres. Once I went to a German—Tante Lola, a kindergarten teacher. She said, 'Take off your armband. The children will see and ask.' She had to try on a royal blue slip. It was Christmas Day, and she needed it for a party. All of a sudden, Rosenbaum came." Apparently, a young woman who worked with Tante Lola was his mistress. When he saw the Jewish corset-maker without her armband, he chased her out of the building. "He wanted to kill me," she says. "I hid under the steps, and he didn't see me."

Rosenbaum was among the handful of Nazi brass actually captured and brought to some semblance of justice after the war, and Sally Peller Huppert helped. "I was in court to say that he killed!" she crows. "I testified in Germany in 1968!" Excitedly, she riffles through a stack of papers for a yellowed *New York Times* clipping, dateline Bonn, August 15, 1968:

"A former SS officer was sentenced to hard labor for life by a court in Hamburg, which convicted him on charges that he killed one hundred forty-eight Jews in wartime Poland. Concluding thirty-five court sessions, the presiding judge said that Wilhelm Rosenbaum, the fifty-three-year-old defendant, committed his crimes out of racial hatred, a particularly lowly motive. Rosenbaum, who worked as a Gestapo official in the Cracow [sic] district, shot at least ten persons, including children, and ordered several mass executions, the judge said."

Obviously, he killed many more. Rosenbaum liquidated the Rabka ghetto in the fall of 1942. The Peller family had to split up. "We were afraid to go together, all of us. . . . A lot of days, they were looking, the soldiers, because they were thinking the whole family was together." Her father went to a sister in Strosze. He later died in the Bobowa shtetl with this sister and her children.

"Hilda went with my mother to a friend, a woman who was bringing us milk and butter. She had a house and she was alone. One of my customers said, 'Sally, come to my house. I'm going to keep you there, and at the end of the war you can go.' But it was not so easy."

She stayed until things settled down a bit, then set out to find her mother and sister. She went to the place where they'd been staying. She knocked on the window. The woman of the house said, " 'Oh. The Jew is here.' " But Marie and Hilda were not. "She said they were gone. She let me sleep there where my mother was sleeping—on the straw full of flies. And they bit me. My poor mother was there with [my little sister]! [The woman] threw them out, because [the Germans] said whoever hid a Jew in the house would be killed. So my poor mother went with her daughter to a different woman who she knew, but nobody wanted to keep her."

Nonetheless, Sally was determined to find them, even though she had no idea where to look and nowhere to stay herself. "So I had to go to the forest. I was sitting at night under the trees, all alone, and it was raining. And the owls!" She throws up her hands.

From time to time, a sympathetic Polish boy brought her bread and coffee, and she grabbed potatoes left behind by peasants harvesting nearby. She remained in the forest for six cold, miserable weeks. "In the meantime, a man came. He cut the trees. The man brought me raspberries to eat, and said, 'In the

Sally Huppert, shortly after liberation.

evening, I will come and pick you up and you will stay in my barn.' But the boy who was bringing me the coffee said, 'Be careful, because he is going to bring you to the Gestapo. For a pair of old pants, he brings people to the Gestapo and they kill them.'

"When I heard this, I told the man, 'In the evening, I will come to you.' But in the meantime, I left. I had holes [in my skin] from the dirt, and I was limping. I had infections. I had terrible cuts, and I couldn't wash myself or do nothing. I was very sick." Then, as if an explanation were necessary, she implores, "I couldn't help it; I had to give up!"

Later, she found out what happened. "My mother sent my sister to our landlord for bread, and he took my sister to the Gestapo. My mother was left all alone. She didn't know what had happened to her child. [My sister] was tall, beautiful! The Gestapo took her to the office, and she had to sign a paper that she was a Russian spy. She couldn't help it! I would have done the same. They took her and they killed her. Later, my mother went to the landlord to look for her, and he brought her to the Gestapo. They killed my mother, too."

Somehow, Sally made it to Kraków by train. "The Ukrainian soldiers were looking for Jews, and I don't know how they didn't see me," she says. She

Abraham Bankier and Rega Peller Bankier, after the war.

didn't know it then, but her sister Rega was already there. "When I came, I met a man from our building. He said, 'Are you going to your sister? Come, I go with you.' She was with friends in the ghetto."

That's where Rega met Abraham Bankier, by then a widower and former owner of what became Deutsche Emailwaren Fabrik—Emalia, for short—the enamelware factory at 4 Lipowa Street taken over by Oskar Schindler. Bankier was a wealthy, influential, and respected man in Kraków's Jewish community. He was "short, fat, and smart, and a shrewd businessman," according to Sally Huppert. "He was twenty years older [than Rega] and very *frum* [religiously observant]. What she saw in him, I don't know. But he was a decent man."

Schindler's List casts Bankier in little more than an inference, transferring much of what he actually did to the Itzhak Stern character, the accountant. Bankier appears as the grizzled old man who argues about the factory's value with Schindler in Oskar's car, and later delivers the fledgling tycoon's start-up capital in a cash-stuffed briefcase. In fact, says Sally Huppert, Bankier was the real brains behind Emalia. "He had to tell Schindler everything to do. He was paying the bills."

He made sure that she and Rega got jobs at Emalia—Rega in the office, Sally on a machine—and, later, spots on Schindler's list. But there were tragedies neither he nor any other powerful Jew could prevent, which still stalk Sally Huppert.

Relatives entrusted her and Rega with the care of two small cousins in the ghetto: a nine-year-old boy and a seven-year-old girl. The boy contracted scarlet fever. The sisters took him to the ghetto hospital. The next morning, they learned that all the pediatric patients had been killed.

When Sally moved into Płaszów, she tried to bring the little girl through the gates. "Goeth was standing there with the two dogs," she remembers. "He said, 'Don't take the child.' But I couldn't leave her! I already had lost one child! So I put her under my coat. The girls crowded around me." It didn't work. Wilek Chilowicz, the head of Płaszów's Jewish police, took the girl away.

They lost Bankier's protection one more time: in Auschwitz. But Sally still tried to safeguard her sister. In the clothing distribution, "I got this little dress with short sleeves. Rega got a black dress. I grabbed a wool kerchief. I got hit, but I didn't care; she should put it on her bottom. Someone got a ballgown! It was a horror. We were laughing and crying like crazy people!"

Max Huppert, early 1960s.

After liberation from Brinnlitz, Sally went to Prague with a friend. Rega went to Kraków with Abraham Bankier. "The Czechs gave us rooms [in a convent] with girls from Holland. They were nurses. You should have seen how they treated us, like princesses! They gave me a clean bed and a warm bath, and five times a day I had food. It was like I was back from the dead."

She gathered enough strength to return to Kraków, where she found out, finally, what happened to her mother and youngest sister. She also met and married Max Huppert. He had been a forest ranger before the war, and had managed to escape to the Soviet Union.

"He had a big story to tell—not like me. He was in the forest, on horses, just like a *goy*. He was helping to give ammunition to the Warsaw ghetto. He was a wonderful man, really! Strong." His first wife died in the Warsaw ghetto. "They were thinking he was her boyfriend. He was bringing her food there."

Sally Peller married Max Huppert in Kraków. Rabbi Lewertow performed the ceremony.

Abraham Bankier died of a heart attack in Vienna in 1956. Sally Huppert says he didn't live long enough to collect reparations, and left his widow without means. "After the war, they thought they were going to have millions, and they got nothing. . . . He was in Warsaw, and he was a big man for

Sally Huppert and her daughter Mary Ann, arriving at Ellis Island, 1948.

the Jews, but then they ran away [to Vienna] because of the Polish [anti-Semitism]. He had no business anymore."

The Hupperts spent three years in Constance, a German city near the Swiss border, where Max worked as a chemist. They came to the United States in 1948. Max became a baker, working at night, sleeping during the day. By then, they had a little girl. "I had to take the child from the house because she was crying. And the whole day I was on the street with the child. I lived downtown in a third-floor apartment that rented for eighteen dollars a month. The mice were running [all over]! And I had to schlep with the baby and the carriage up and down the stairs. When she was two, I went to work."

Her first job was selling bras and girdles on Pitkin Avenue in Brooklyn, for thirty-five dollars a week. After four years, the family moved to Jackson Heights, into an apartment across the street from an old-age home. Little Mary Ann Huppert would gaze out the window at the old people and ask,

"'Mommy, where is *babbe?* We have a grandma? A grandpa?' I said, 'There. There.' So she used to go with bananas or cookies and would give them to an old lady, and she would say, 'This is my *babbe.*'"

In 1966, the family moved to the apartment where Sally still lives. By then, Max owned a laundry. "He got headaches. He got dizzy and nauseous." It was a brain tumor. He died in 1967. Sally says she withstood it. "I never say, 'Why is this happening?'"

What hurt the most was her daughter's loss of a father. "She was twenty when he died. He was crazy about her. She was his sun. He took her to dancing school, bought her a piano. He wanted everything for her, that she should be somebody." Today, she is Mary Ann Lisnitzer of Queens, mother of two, stepmother of one.

The sixties were an agonizing time for Sally Huppert, and not just because her husband died. "I worked like a slave: work, work, work. I *ran* to work. I had to! My daughter—we both wanted she should go to college." (She went to business school.) Sally had resumed her old trade: custom-made bras and corsets. She worked for Bergdorf Goodman on Fifth Avenue. Her clients included most of the Kennedy women, including the late Jacqueline Kennedy Onassis. "Ethel I know. Rose I know. And every actress called me."

Then there was the sociopolitical climate of the times. Mary Ann was a good girl, but the era's reigning parental paranoia gripped her mother. "I was very upset, very worried about her all the time. Nervous. She called me *meshuggener.* I was always calling, always standing by the subway to see if she was going to the office."

Sally Huppert would get up early in the morning and hide at the subway station from which her daughter left for work. "I would wait till I saw her, that she was alive," then she would go back home. "I was completely crazy," she acknowledges. "I didn't tell her things and I was wrong. I tried to cover up everything. She knew what was going on. . . . She always asked me: 'Please, tell me, for my children!' but I couldn't tell her. I didn't have nothing else—only my daughter. I *died* with this, with my family!"

She says she lacked both the courage and resources to see a therapist. Now, she says, "I worry about the grandchildren."

MOSES GOLDBERG

Most of Oskar Schindler's workers came from Kraków or through its ghetto. Many had known each other for years. Some were related. But a few, drawn into his orbit from towns and villages elsewhere in Poland, never so much as glimpsed a familiar face in the crowd of *Schindlerjuden*.

So it was for Moses Goldberg, possibly the only resident of Stary Sącz—a town about forty-five miles southeast of Kraków—to work for Schindler. Known as Moniek or Murray, Goldberg is a modest, devout man in his late sixties. He prays each morning and evening at an Orthodox synagogue near his home in Brooklyn's Flatbush section. Retired from the garment industry, he helps out his wife, a former kindergarten teacher, at Shirts Plus, her menswear store on Coney Island Avenue. Businesses near Shirts Plus have names like Paper Maven, Shimon Goldman's Glatt Kosher Meat and Poultry, and Avodah Employment ("We Speak English and Polish"), though there's a storefront Pentecostal church a few doors down. In addition to sweaters, slacks, jackets, Italian silk ties, and a few loud Hawaiian shirts—"Even some of the Jews buy them," he marvels—they do a brisk trade in forty-dollars-and-up, all-cotton shirts.

Until now, Goldberg never spoke publicly about his Holocaust experiences.

The youngest of eight children, Moses Goldberg had four sisters—Sara, Lotti, Chara,, and Mala—and three brothers—Samuel, Baruch, and Benek. Their father, Zelig, ran a shoemakers' supply store in Stary Sącz. Their mother, Cyla, had died in 1938 of complications from gallstones. Only Moses and Sara and her family, who'd been sent to Siberia, survived the war. Sixty-five-year-old Zelig would be gunned down outside his own home as Mala watched. The rest of the family, living in the industrial town of Bielsko, would be killed later.

In May 1942, when he was seventeen, Moses was among one hundred men and boys rounded up and taken to the town of Rabka, a resort before the war, then under the control of *Untersturmführer* Wilhelm Rosenbaum. Goldberg calls him a sadist. "Whoever he found with his name, he shot. There was a guy who came in our group whose name was Rosenbaum, and he was the first one to be shot." For a year, the group hacked a firing range from a hillside at Tereska, a nearby SS training school for Ukrainians. They used picks, shovels, and their bare hands. "It was a hell camp," says Goldberg. There were hangings and beatings. The inmates' heads were shaved. One of the Stary Sącz prisoners was shot in the grave he'd been digging because he wasn't agile enough to hop out.

Despite the horror, it was an open camp with a certain amount of freedom. The men formed a minyan (group of ten) every day for prayers. Each week until the August 1942 liquidation of Stary Sącz, ten to fifteen inmates were

Moses Goldberg (center) as a boy at a family wedding, mid-1930s. The others (left to right) are his sister Sara; his father, Zelig; his brother Samuel; the bride, his sister Chana; his brother Benek; his sister Lotti; and his brother Baruch.

permitted overnight visits home. The men could return with bread, butter, eggs, and other supplements to their work-camp diets. And they always returned. "You knew if you didn't come back, they would take your family."

Goldberg was still among friends. "We tried to stay together. My sister had a friend whose husband took care of me. He was a *Kapo*, but he was an OK guy and gave me very easy work to do, not the heavy work. I wasn't built so strong."

Two weeks after one of his weekend visits, Moses received a heartbreaking letter from Mala: " 'I have very bad news for you; we lost our father. He was shot and didn't suffer too much.' The story was, once a week, all the Jews had to come to a plaza and be counted, and they took them to all kinds of work. This was the day. There was a lame man who was going to the plaza, and they told him to stop. He ran into our house. He hid in the closet. Right away the Germans came in and said, 'Where's the *Jude*?' 'Where's the Jew?' My father said, 'I don't know.' They opened the closet, took my father out with the man, and the man's wife and my sister had to look out the window. They tell him to lay down on the ground and shoot him. This my sister told me because she witnessed it." Goldberg never saw Mala again. She was taken to the Nowy Sącz ghetto, then sent to Belżec.

In June 1943, the Tereska group was sent to Płaszów. To the young Moses Goldberg, the new camp looked tremendous, "like a big city. You see people all dressed the same way." His group had no idea the move was imminent. They were taken from a work detail one day and loaded onto trucks bound for an unknown destination. They left all their belongings behind, including Moses' tefillin. It was the last time he was able to say morning prayers properly until he was liberated.

His group was targeted for special punishment at Płaszów, because they had "come from a resort." They were put to work in the camp's rock quarry, "right under the windows of Amon Goeth, and they really worked us hard. I worked with people I didn't know. The old group was dispersed." Goldberg's worst punishment came at the hands of another Jew. "One day, a Jewish *Kapo* gave me another ticket for the meal. Lunch time, we went into the mess with the pot that they put some soup in. He had an extra, so he gave me one. You couldn't get [both portions] together; you had to go once, eat up and stay in the line again. So I ran in first, ate the soup, and stood in line again. There was standing a Jewish policeman, Green. He saw my face was red, maybe because I ate before. He said, 'Show me your spoon!' and I said, 'I have a ticket.' He saw the spoon was wet, and he gave me such a *zetz* in my head, I fell down and thought I would never be able to get up."

Goldberg joined the *Schindlerjuden* as a night-shift bricklayer at Emalia. He knew nothing about laying bricks but enough about survival to learn quickly. There, he had his only personal encounter with Amon Goeth: "One day I was walking from the factory to the barracks and I met Goeth. I always used to stay away when one of those Germans came, but I couldn't move. He was wearing high boots, and the ground was wet, and he got dirty. He said, 'Clean my shoes,' in German, so I took my finger and went around the boots. I was hoping he wouldn't do anything bad to me, but he was with Schindler, so he couldn't. If he was alone, it would have been my end."

When Emalia closed and its workers were sent back to Płaszów—where Schindler could no longer influence their fate—Goldberg found himself assigned to exhume and burn corpses. "I knew if I go to that job, I would be finished. I had still one thousand złotys, sewn in my clothes somewhere. I gave them to the Polish *Kapo* and said, 'See what you can do.' So he said, 'OK, you don't have to come back to this group anymore,' and that saved me. This was the most horrible job, and they didn't keep you afterward. They got rid of you, too."

Goldberg didn't think he'd made the cut for Brinnlitz. "We were standing on the *Apellplatz,* and they were calling names. We knew if we go to Brinnlitz and Schindler, we will be OK. If we stay in the camp, we would go to Dachau or Theresienstadt and we would be finished. I was almost one of the last to be called. They took people who had influence and put them on the list, and took out people like me. I was single, I didn't know too many people. I think God was watching over me."

Arriving at Brinnlitz, they found Oskar Schindler—and little else. "Nothing was prepared for us. First we slept on straw. Only the older people got bunks." The rest slept under the bunks, sliding into a space perhaps a foot high.

"There was no room even to turn over. Until they built a third [tier], there was nothing."

Goldberg was assigned to the building-supply warehouse, close to the food storehouse, where he could get a bit of extra nourishment. "When it came Pesach [Passover], Rabbi Le-wertow and Mr. Bankier didn't eat any *hometz* [food forbidden on Passover], and I was cook-ing for them some rice. It wasn't kosher [for Passover], but it was better than bread. We had an oven with a double bottom in the warehouse, heating the room. Schindler knew about it. He would ask, 'What's cooking?' "

After liberation on May 9, 1945, Gold-berg went to Stary Sącz, Nowy Sącz, and Kraków, looking for relatives. He found none. He and friends decided to go to Palestine, and were spirited across the Czech, Hungarian, and Aus-trian borders in the Bricha, the underground Zionist operation smuggling Jews out of the

Moses Goldberg in his Brinnlitz stripes, two months after liberation from the factory, Kraków.

occupied zones. It took three months, from June to August 1945. They got as far as Italy and decided to stay, because the British were shipping Jews trying to enter Palestine illegally to detention camps in Cyprus.

From a United Nations refugee camp in Cremona, he wrote to a Pol-ish neighbor whose children had been his childhood playmates. His sister Sara, who had returned to Poland from Siberia, also wrote to the neighbor, who reunited the two by mail. It made Moses Goldberg "feel like a king. I'm not alone."

During the two months they spent in Poland after liberation, Goldberg and his friends didn't think much about practicing their faith. "We were walk-ing around without a hat," he admits. "But as the years went on and you started to go back to normal life, you started to be religious again. It's in you. It's your upbringing and feeling. . . . I was always praying. I felt like someone was watching me. My mother, she was dead already, I was feeling she prays for me that I should survive."

Life was easy in Italy. Goldberg was single, with no responsibilities or worries. He learned English and Italian, did office work while he waited for papers to emigrate, and learned to love pasta. In 1950, he arrived in New York. At first he picked up odd jobs, then settled down for a quarter century in the office of a company called Mavest, which made men's sports jackets. His boss offered to help him get rid of the KL tattoo. "I was walking around with short sleeves. He was a German Jew and he noticed it, and said he would pay for me to go to a doctor and have it taken off. I told him, 'I didn't get it so easy, I'm going to keep it.'"

He met Tonia "Toby" Englander in 1953. Also a Polish survivor, she had endured the Holocaust in hiding, with her parents. (Her mother, now in her mid-nineties, lives with the Goldbergs.) Toby was visiting from Israel, and Moses courted her for seven weeks. "My boss asked me, 'What are you rushing?' but [Toby] was on papers and was going to have to go back. We liked each other very much and had the same language, and our backgrounds were similar. And"—he chuckles—"we lived happily ever after."

The Goldbergs have two sons: Harry, born in 1955, and Elie Dov, three years younger. Both work in computer research in New York. Between them, they have eight children. Moses and Toby didn't talk to their sons much about the Holocaust. Moses says he has survivor friends "who became so nervous, their kids got nervous. I have other friends whose kids say to them: 'You still live with the concentration camp. You still didn't come out.'"

But it wasn't always easy. "When the children were small, I was afraid for everything. I used to get up at night and go see if they were all right. When they went to school, I used to call my wife: 'Are they home?' I was very anxious. I had nightmares, waking up and screaming about the camps."

Harry, who is Hasidic, remembers those nights, and remembers that he got the message not to ask too many questions. But what he recalls far more clearly is that each year, on the night before Yom Kippur, his father would gather his children to him and, with tears and great emotion, ask for blessings upon them. "He imparts so much of what he is. It was always a special time, and that transferred over to me." He says his father is the kind of man who "never says no to anybody," including a lonely fellow survivor who used to show up at their home after dinner, night after night, and want to talk. "My father used to say, 'He has nobody, and I can be there for him.'"

"I have *naches* [pleasure and pride]," Moses Goldberg says about his life today. He looks back on what was and sees nothing short of a miracle. "That we built a new life and family—that's all that matters to us. I would give away all I have for my kids, everything I own to my kids, if need be. We knew that life meant nothing."

Moses Goldberg in his wife's clothing store, Flatbush, Brooklyn, 1994.

He and Toby travel often to Israel and Italy. Just once, he says, he'd like to go to Poland, "for a day, maybe, to my hometown, to see if there is a grave of our people murdered in the forest, and to say Kaddish."

HENRY SLAMOVICH

On Washington's Birthday in 1978, Henry and Miriam Slamovich and their youngest son, Elliott, spent the day hiking on Mount Tamalpais, the wooded peak crowning Muir Woods National Monument, just north of San Francisco. It was a lovely day, Henry recalls, so warm that they opened the windows when they got home that evening. The family lived on a quiet cul-de-sac in the city's Sunset District, a "nice" neighborhood, so safe in those days that Henry thought nothing of leaving the garage door open all night. "There was never any crime," he says. "Nobody bothered us."

After dinner, while Miriam washed the dishes and Elliott did his homework, Henry went off to putter in the basement. Suddenly, he heard what sounded like an explosion. He galloped up the stairs and burst into the kitchen, where he found Miriam lying in a pool of blood. "A black man came in to rob the house," he says, inhaling deeply, his voice quavering, "and he shot my wife." When the intruder turned the gun on him, Henry bolted out the door, screaming for help. The man was gone by the time police arrived. Fingerprints on the windowsill offered the only clue to his identity.

Even though the shot had pierced her jugular vein, Miriam Slamovich reached the hospital alive. Doctors predicted she would survive unless she developed a blood clot in the brain. For three weeks, everything seemed to go her

Henry Slamovich, San Francisco, 1994.

way. She went home, where her husband of twenty-five years tended her day and night. But exactly what doctors feared came to pass: Rushed into surgery, she never regained consciousness.

Miriam Glat Slamovich, who had survived Bergen-Belsen and the state of Israel's violent birth pangs, died at the hands of an American teenager with a gun. She left two sons, one daughter, and a husband whose parents and four siblings had perished in the Nazi death camps. She was forty-six.

After the shooting, Henry Slamovich moved to Golden Gate Heights. The house, high up on one of San Francisco's famous hills, has wraparound windows that offer a head-spinning view of Ocean Beach, the Seal Rocks, and the south end of the Golden Gate Bridge. Since 1982, he has shared it with his second wife, the former Bella Kurant Fox. "Thank God, my children love her," says Henry. "She is very generous to me and to them." He and Miriam had known Bella and her husband for many years. A survivor of five concentration camps, Bella bears the tattoo A15522 on her arm. (A photo of her arm, along with hundreds of others, is part of an exhibit at the United States Holocaust Memorial in Washington, D.C.) Her late husband, Paul Fox, was a Dachau survivor. Together, they ran Fox's Delicatessen, near the Moscone Center. She is a fabulous cook.

From behind a bird's-eye-maple-and-granite counter in the spacious, open kitchen, Bella Slamovich answers the unspoken question: "Don't forget, he had three kids to take care of and to love."

After Miriam's death, Henry chose to go on living, just as he had after the Holocaust. "We cannot give up," he says. "We have to fight. You want to regain your respect, more than you had before. He [Hitler] wanted me to be destroyed to nothing, mentally and physically. He wanted us to give up and disappear. You want to show him, 'I'm here. I didn't give up.' "

There's a notable absence of rage in his tone and in his cornflower-blue eyes, and a notable presence of resignation. Like an ocean laying down sediment, fate seems to have layered sadness upon sadness over this man.

"I had five uncles from my father's side, and only one cousin is alive. The rest is wiped out. I had five from my mother's side, and I have two people left. I don't know what you can call it—fate, or luck—that I am here. I wasn't strong. I wasn't smart. We were just in a wave, and wherever it took you, you landed. At the same time I went to Schindler, many people went to Auschwitz or to the gallows."

Henry Slamovich was born Chaim Wolf Szlamowicz in September 1927, the son of Josef and Blima Szlamowicz (he changed the spelling when he came to the United States). His parents had lost a son before Henry was born. In keeping with a custom of the time and place, Henry was given a name—his grandfather's—preceded by Chaim, which means "life."

"It looks like it helped," says Slamovich. "I survived."

His father dealt in meat and hides, and ran a grocery store in Działoszyce, where Jews had lived since 1729. There were ten thousand Jews in Działoszyce before the war, 90 percent of the town's population. Only one store was open on Saturday: a liquor store run by a Pole. There was a Jewish library and the whole political spectrum of Zionist groups.

Henry had an older brother, Elias; a younger brother, Berek; an older sister, Rachel; and a younger sister, Feigel. Elias was in business with Josef. Rachel was married and had a baby.

One day in September 1940, Henry's mother sent him to the market for vegetables. Out of nowhere, German troops roared up in trucks and blocked off the marketplace. They grabbed forty young men and boys, including Henry, and took them to a Kraków labor camp. He never saw any member of his family again, except Elias, briefly, in Płaszów. His only prewar photo is of the Zionist youth group to which he belonged. A man he met at a bar mitzvah in New Jersey gave it to him.

Działoszyce was liquidated two years later. Most of its Jewish residents were sent to Treblinka or Bełżec, but some were shot on the spot. "In Poland," says Henry Slamovich, "every little forest is a graveyard for Jews."

The group of forty was pressed into the service of a German company called Rischard Strauch, which built sewers, bridges, and river-management systems. The workers lived together in a big house on Kobierzynska Street in Kraków. They slept on cots and ate from a central kitchen. "You could not run away, otherwise they would punish your family. But I got word to them through Poles, an older couple who lived across the street. They sometimes shared whatever they could with me, whatever little they had. . . . We were working hard—seven days a week—but we didn't get beaten at that stage. They needed us to work."

The next stage was Płaszów. Strauch workers helped to build the camp. "In Płaszów, they were beating you up for no reason. There were hangings right away to scare the people. You had to fight for every minute of your life. In no one's imagination could they perceive what they could do to human beings in Płaszów. When the Germans occupied Poland during the First World War, people had a very good experience. No one could imagine that they would commit hideous crimes." Marching under SS guard to a work detail in the Kraków ghetto, Slamovich witnessed the murder of a newborn. A soldier grabbed the child away from its mother, swung it by its feet, and slammed it into the pavement. "The brains spilled out all over, and the mother started screaming, so [the SS guard] took out his gun and shot her."

Dealing with death became a way of life for Henry. Once, on a sewer-building detail, the man working next to him simply fell over dead. "We didn't know where the bullet came from. Some soldier went by. He was just going around with a gun, for fun. When it happened, you just froze. Somebody fell, and you just picked him up. You saw so much of it."

But never as much as in the aftermath of the liquidation of the Kraków ghetto on March 13, 1943. "They were bringing up from the ghetto hundreds. Thousands. We were digging graves a block long and ten feet wide, and filling them up with people. Sometimes the earth was moving; the people were not even dead."

The work proceeded, whatever the weather. "You worked sometimes in the rain or snow. Your prisoner suit was wet, and you were sleeping two to three hundred in one barracks. Sometimes a drunken soldier came in in the middle of the night and everybody had to get out. He wanted to count us. You ran outside—you didn't even put your shoes on—then about fifteen minutes later, he counted and you went back in. He did it just to make life miserable."

There seems no end to the madness he witnessed at Płaszów. "We were repairing the railroad tracks—fifty boys. In the morning, the SS had to sign for fifty. While we're working, one boy ran away. On the way back, they counted and had only forty-nine. Goeth came out with his whip, and he lined us up in fives, and he touched every fifth boy's nose with the handle, and he took out these boys, and pow, pow, pow!"

One evening, a little girl of about ten staggered into the barracks, an escaped survivor of a mass grave. "She was shot in the arm. The next day, when we went out to work, whoever remained in the barracks, they took them out and killed them including the child." Through a mist of tears, he describes what happened to a group of young girls brought up from the ghetto. "[The Germans] had a special barracks, and they raped them all night. In the morning, there was snow outside. They let them run out naked, and [shot them] with a gun: pow, pow, pow. We had to go back later and pick them up to bury them. . . . A human life was nothing, especially after they bring up from the ghetto tens of thousands. You wanted to live as much as you could, but you could not resist. You resisted, you right away got shot. We were angry all the time, but helpless."

A certain kind of garden-variety abuse became so routine that even those subjected to it didn't react. A crease in Henry Slamovich's scalp bears witness to one such incident. "In Płaszów, they assigned everybody about ten feet [apart] to build the sewer. They gave you a shovel and a pick. There was one older man from our hometown—he never had a shovel in his hands. I had my topsoil already fairly well taken off, and I was digging deep, and the poor guy didn't get anywhere. So I told him, 'Avrom, why don't you move over to my place?' The SS noticed it later and took a two-by-four and hit me over the head. There were no bandages. You just used your cap for the blood. And you know what we used for an antiseptic? Urine. It has some kind of acid in it. It was better than nothing."

The Nazis were as unpredictable as they were vicious. One evening, as it was getting dark, a high-ranking SS officer came to the barracks area, selected twenty people, lined them up, and marched them up to Amon Goeth's villa.

"We were sure we were going to get wiped out," Henry says. "We're going up all the way, and we could hear music playing, and dancing. We're going up to the second floor, where Goeth's bedroom is. We had to dismantle the beds and take everything out to the basement, so when Goeth comes back with his girlfriend, it would be empty. It was a joke."

For a short time in 1942, Henry's spirits lifted. During the liquidation of Działoszyce, certain people had been selected to join the slave-labor force at Płaszów. Elias Slamovich and his father-in-law were among them. The brothers were in different work crews, but got to see each other in the evenings. They could talk a bit, sharing the fantasy that at least some in the family had made it. Then Henry was sent to a new locale.

"We were working as a group, digging and building barracks. They surrounded [our] group, and we thought for sure that was it. They loaded us on trucks and brought us out to Emalia. Emalia was entirely different circumstances. Schindler was always kind. He was never screaming on anybody.... Usually when the SS came for inspection, Schindler wined them and dined them and later took them for inspection, but they never bothered to hit anybody."

At Emalia, Henry made a lifelong friend: Moses Goldberg. "In fact, we looked alike. Our *Kapo*, he called him Slamovich and me Goldberg." But Henry also received some terrible news. "The man who delivered our food from Płaszów knew my brother [Elias]. He said, 'Chaim, if they pray here, you can say Kaddish for your brother.' They accused him [of] trying to form a group to run away, and they hanged him by his arms and tortured him to death. In Mr. Bankier's barracks, they were praying, so I went in and I said Kaddish," the prayer for the dead.

Slamovich doesn't know why he was put on Schindler's list. "Usually, the people from Kraków got on it because they had a lot of pull. All those bigshots from the camp—the [Jewish] police—were from Kraków. I didn't have money or connections." But at Brinnlitz, he did have a connection, and it served him well.

"One man from my town was in charge of the stable. They had horses and cows there, dogs, chickens. He said, 'Why don't you come work for me?' His name was Abe Balicki. He was dealing with cattle before the war. So I cleaned the cows, the horses, and raised little chicks. I was getting canned meat for Mrs. Schindler's dog—at that time, a German shepherd. It was regular meat from the soldiers' rations. And we had potatoes to feed the pigs, and milk from the cows. It was very good. . . . I worked in the warehouse, too. Once you were there, you had a free hand to roam around. In the factory, you had to be at the machine."

On Passover, he was able to get potatoes for a deeply religious friend (Josl Ryba, who now lives in New York) who didn't want to eat bread. But Henry Slamovich did not observe holidays or rituals during his enslavement. He'd witnessed too much treachery in the war's early days. "You saw what was going on and you lost faith. The most pious Jews were taken out in the market, and they cut their beards and put on their tallith [prayer shawl] and their tefillin and [the Germans would] ask them, 'Where is your God? Why doesn't he help you now?'"

On May 9, 1945, Russian soldiers liberated Brinnlitz. Slamovich and two cousins immediately headed for home. Along the way, sympathetic Czechs "opened up their homes and gave us food and clothing and bicycles—whatever they could. . . . But at the border, the Russians took away our bicycles. And we had papers that we were going home from a concentration camp. They told us, 'Either you give up the bicycles, or we kill you like dogs.' "

That was just the beginning. "There were several boys and girls who already were liberated. They lived in a two-story Jewish house in our town. I came to the place where I lived, the hello was: 'Are you still alive? What are you doing here?' They didn't even tell me, 'Come on, have a glass of water.' Even the people who knew us! I was there maybe ten days, then one night, they surrounded [the two-story house] with a gun and they start killing us. One father and son by the name Piechas had survived [the camps]. The father was killed instantly. Four brothers by the name Urista had survived [the camps], and one was killed instantly, and one was wounded.

"We all ran away to a larger town: Miechów. Then we ran later to Kraków, but they did it systematically: a month later in Kraków. Then we ran to Bavaria, illegally. We crossed the borders at night and risked our lives."

Slamovich has never forgotten this betrayal. "It hurts more after the war what the Poles did even than what the Germans did. After coming home, to get such a greeting, this was devastating."

He ended up in the Displaced Persons camp in Deggendorf, where he stayed for four years. "The camp was mostly German Jews from Theresienstadt, mostly professionals, very well organized, some actors and directors. In fact, they formed a group that performed operettas, and opened up a coffee shop and had musicians coming in in the evening, and you could listen to music. You had to work to get 'scrip.' For that, you could go into the coffee shop and get coffee and listen to music."

He took classes in radio repair and traded currency, but passed up chances to indulge in serious illegal activity out of respect for his parents. "You wouldn't do anything wrong because you wouldn't do it to the memory of your parents, you were also thinking of your reputation. There were very many occasions you could do all kinds of criminal things, very rewarding, but you'd never do that."

It was in the town of Deggendorf that Slamovich and some friends spotted *Untersturmführer* Josef Liepold, the Brinnlitz commandant. "Before Christmas, they had like a fair, and we looked around to buy or sell something. And here at once we see Liepold. We surrounded him, about four, five boys."

On one side of the square stood a U.S. military police officer (MP). On the other stood a member of the Central Intelligence Corps (CIC). According to Slamovich, most CIC agents were Jews.

"We went to the MP because he was closer and told him, 'We have here an SS. He was a commandant in our camp.' They came with a jeep. Liepold takes an ID out: completely different name. So the American—an easygoing guy—says, 'Different name. We cannot do a thing.' So we run over to the CIC, who used to come pray with us in the DP camp on the holidays, and he arrested him. He told us that whoever was in [Brinnlitz], to come over to the DP camp. So we took a bus and everybody came to the jail, and they made a lineup of about fifteen prisoners. Everybody recognized him. They sent him back to Poland and they hanged him.

"I was a witness to Amon Goeth, too. They made an announcement in the camp that they needed witnesses, so we chartered a bus from Deggendorf to Dachau. Everybody went in, and there was Goeth. He was a big man, and his uniform was too small. It wasn't a court; we testified in front of a panel that took depositions. It was eerie to be in the same room with him."

He also saw Schindler in Germany. "He was a very handsome guy, always dressed in a long coat with a fur collar and a hat with a little feather. We brought him several cartons of cigarettes. We made a little party for him. He enjoyed it."

Henry Slamovich came to the United States two years after the Truman administration's 1948 quota expansion, which permitted entry to two hundred thousand refugees. "I came to Stockton [California]. I didn't know where it was, even. But the people were very nice, and the second day, I got a job as a stockboy at Berg's, a clothing store. I worked there eight years, and I left as the highest-paid man in the store. I learned how to sell. In August, we used to have layaway topcoats, when it's very hot in Stockton. You used to get ten

Henry Slamovich and his late wife, Miriam, in San Francisco, 1976.

percent off. So Christmas came, and that greenhorn had laid away maybe fifty, sixty topcoats. . . . The Americans are wonderful customers. The best in the world!"

The Bergs were Polish Jews whose families had left Europe before World War I. Slamovich developed a close relationship with them. At his wedding, they stood in for his parents. "I worked just as hard for them as I did for myself," he says. "They were very generous to me. At Christmastime, they used to give me a thousand-dollar bonus. They had a summer home in Santa Cruz, and he used to give me the keys: 'Henry—go for your vacation.' Mrs. Berg, she found out our first child was sick. She came in, she said, 'Miriam, go to sleep.' She washed the diapers, she made the bottles."

Miriam, a veteran of the Israeli army, had two sisters in San Francisco. Henry was friendly with them, and got to know her during a 1953 visit. She stayed, and they married that year. By 1961, they had three children. Rochelle Slamovich Blumenfeld, who lives in El Cerrito, California, is an optometrist. Joseph Slamovich is a chemical engineer with Bay Area Pollution Control. Elliott Slamovich teaches materials science at Purdue University. Henry has four grandchildren.

In 1958, the family moved to a rented house in San Francisco's Sunset District. Henry bought a grocery store with his brother-in-law. It was called the City Hall Market, and the two ran it for a decade. They also operated coin laundries.

Henry is a true believer in the American dream. Not even the "unfortunate luck with my wife" put a dent in it—a bit ironic, considering how reluctant he'd been to come here, even after the disastrous welcome at Działoszyce. "It was still home. Who knew about America? You didn't want to go to America. You were rooted for so many generations."

But the kindness of strangers, Jew and gentile, quickly won him over. "About the United States, I cannot complain. Nobody called me a dirty Jew, I worked very hard, I accomplished. With Schindler, I had a good education. If you're willing to work hard and be honest with people, you have nothing to worry about. Where else can a newcomer come, and you want to open a grocery store, and you're willing to work ten days a week, go ahead! In Poland, you could never do that."

In the 1960s, with San Francisco at the epicenter of cataclysmic social change, some of what he heard from his hippie patrons bothered him terribly. "So I talk to them and I say, 'How lucky you are to be in a country like this.' They were talking about Russia. I said, 'Why don't you take a one-way ticket there and make the way back?' I saw what communism was and what Naziism was. . . . I felt sorry for the parents of the flower children. There used to be a young man from New York who had long, red hair—Jewish. I used to cash his father's checks for him. He didn't want anything to do with his father, but I said, 'Now, before the holidays, you better call.' He listened to me."

He sold the grocery in 1968, turned to running the laundries, and bought property. He became active in his synagogue, and Miriam did volunteer work. At the time of her death, she was a museum docent, and was tutoring disadvantaged children in reading. In her memory, Henry established a lecture series at two San Francisco synagogues. Martin Gilbert, the Holocaust scholar, was its first speaker.

Her assailant was apprehended six years later, the first person arrested through California's new computerized fingerprint matching system. Expert defense witnesses sought to blame the childhood trauma he suffered at the hands of a drunken father for turning him into a seventeen-year-old killer. Convicted of second-degree murder in July 1985, he received the maximum sentence allowed under the law: seven years in prison, with an additional two for using a gun in the commission of a crime. He served fifty-six months, two fewer than Henry Slamovich spent enslaved to the Third Reich.

It's not impossible that some day Henry Slamovich might bump into this man on the street. "What would I do?" he asks, gazing out over the city, this day subdued by fog. "What *could* I do? We live in a country of laws."

BRONIA GUNZ

*I*f Romeo and Juliet had been named Roman and Betty, if they had lived in Poland during the 1940s instead of Italy in the 1500s, this could have been their story.

Betty Gross was a stunning, shapely brunette from a family of deeply religious Jews. They kept the Sabbath in the traditional way, which meant that their high-spirited daughter, who bore a passing resemblance to Greta Garbo, had to sit home, fuming about what she was missing. "I rebelled," she admits. "God blessed me with a pretty face, and the boys were running after me. When they leave you alone, you don't think about it, but I was anxious to go with them and have a little fun."

Roman Gunz was the handsome, well-to-do son of a businessman. At twenty-two, he was already a wounded veteran of the Polish army. Yes, he was Jewish, but his family was the worldly kind, completely assimilated.

They met in Kraków, where her father ran a delicatessen and his father had an auto-paint shop. She was smitten with another, but Roman Gunz would not give up. He wooed her and won her heart. He was so sweet, so good, how could she refuse? Besides, "I was grateful to him that he was taking me out of this stupid way I was brought up. He showed me if you eat nonkosher, you don't die!"

When she brought Roman home to the family's apartment at 1 Skaleczna

357

Roman and Bronia "Betty" Gunz.

Street in the Kazimierz—the same building where Poldek Pfefferberg lived—her father, Meyer Gross, refused to talk to him. "My mama spoke to Roman, but when he left, she said, 'Nu, what's wrong with Dr. Spiegel? He loves you! You'll have a good life!' I said, 'But Mama, I love Roman!' My mother came from rabbis. She said, 'What kind of name is Roman? You call him Avrom!' Then I said, 'What don't you like about him?' She said, 'He is so *gorgeous*, but what I don't like is his parents have the shop open on Shabbat!'"

Betty Gunz laughs with such gusto that it's tempting to forget, for a moment, the cataclysm rending Polish Jewry in 1942. This should have been her biggest problem.

Even if Meyer and Hudel Gross had approved of the romance, Adolf Hitler had no intention of letting Betty and Roman Gunz live happily ever after. Three months after the wedding, which Meyer boycotted, it seemed sure that Roman had no hope of living at all.

"He was taken with seventy beautiful young men from Kraków," says Betty, a warm, effusive woman in her mid-seventies, who sparkles with European charm. "They came at night to the apartment. We did not know where they were going. Two weeks later, I received a letter from the Gestapo to come pick up his ashes, because he died. My mother said, 'They will kill you if you go up there,' and I did not go. They sent him to Auschwitz, but I thought he was dead. He was twenty-three."

Neither of them knew it at the time, but Betty was pregnant, a sure death sentence for mother and child. "I went to my uncle, Abraham Gross, and he took me to the Jewish hospital, where I had an abortion. I was four months. It could have been a little boy. I was suffering very much that I lost [my child], but otherwise, they would shoot me."

Betty, the presumed widow, arrived at Płaszów during the March 13, 1943, ghetto liquidation. She'd already lost her mother and oldest sister, Lusia, in a transport from the ghetto to the city of Bochnia. "We never saw them again. They came with trucks on the streets. Three, four soldiers ran from apartment to apartment: 'Out! Out!' They were all pushed to the trucks.

Betty (left) with her friend Esther Englander, ogled by admirers in Kraków, 1936.

"I was hidden in a cellar. I always had a mild disposition and was very positive. My mother said I would survive the war." She did, with her father and her sister Pola, on Schindler's list. A third sister, Fela, went with Betty and Pola to Płaszów. She was three years younger that Betty, and, early on, decided to escape.

"She didn't tell me anything. She didn't think that I might be killed for her. She met a group of Polish young women, and they were sent to Berlin to work in the fields. She was there three and a half years. One woman approached her, a few months prior to the end of the war, and said she knew she was Jewish." But the woman didn't give her away. Fela Gross Machauf lives today in Manhattan.

"They prepared eight of us to be shot as punishment," says Betty, who still shivers with fear at the memory. "I went to one of the Jewish policemen,

Sperling, and asked him to help me. He took me out." (On Schindler's list, she appears as Bronia Gunz-Sperling. She thinks someone involved with composing the list did it out of spite.)

Betty worked for a time at Płaszów's paper envelope factory, then went to Emalia, and the safety of the subcamp, with Pola. Before she got there, she ran afoul of Amon Goeth. She survived the encounter, but paid a substantial price.

"We were on the *Appellplatz*. My friend was next to me—a very religious girl from my street, eighteen, from Hasidic parents: Schandl Müller. And she was smiling! She was stupid! Jews were not allowed to smile! Goeth was on his horse, with his two dogs. We stood like soldiers. And suddenly, he took a gun and shot her! She was falling down, and I wanted to go to her. I made a movement toward her. It was a subconscious thing: the fear that I was next, and I was losing her.

"One young soldier had this whip, and he hit me so bad here"—she indicates her side. "I didn't know what happened to me, but I felt it. Then another soldier came and really hit me in the back. I was in such pain! They damaged the kidney, and right after the war it had to be removed. But I couldn't be sick because I had to go to work the next morning. I didn't want them to shoot me."

Manci Rosner, who was the head of Betty's barracks, made sure she got an extra blanket. That was about all the care she could offer, not exactly the payback she imagined for a favor Betty once did for her.

The two had met in the Kraków ghetto shortly before its liquidation. Manci, already the mother of one child, had gotten pregnant with her second. Like Betty, she had an abortion. Betty remembers Marysia Rosner calling her. "She said, 'In the hospital is my sister-in-law. They will kill her unless she will have some food. They don't feed them there.' She said I should please cook for her. So I made a pot of chicken soup and a chicken, and I went to hospital. But who was Manci? How did she look? Marysia told me, 'She is a pretty woman with black hair.' *Everybody* was a pretty woman with black hair!

"I was looking for Mrs. Rosner through the rooms: 'Manci Rosner! Manci Rosner!' Suddenly, a very pretty woman with black hair said, 'I am Manci Rosner.' I brought to her the soup, and she burst out crying. She said, 'God, you are so beautiful, let me hug you! How will I ever thank you? If we survive the war, I will remember that.' I kissed and hugged her. I was afraid, because I wanted to cry so much. When I got out, I cried hysterically, because I didn't know if I would ever see her or they would shoot her there. Today it seems funny, but to her it meant so much." (After Roman died in 1979, the Rosners "adopted" her, says Betty. "We went to Vienna to Manci's mother's grave, and to Ryszard's [Horowitz's] father's. I was very happy I could do that.")

Betty Gunz was indeed blessed with a pretty face. Unfortunately, that meant as much unwanted attention as any she might desire. Marcel Goldberg, the "OD man," was one of her admirers. "He was big and ugly, but he had a sweet wife. He was like a wild animal, wanting to sleep with young girls in Płaszów. Twice he was running after me. Once he grabbed my hair. Another time, we were coming from *Appellplatz*. Two girls were walking, and one said to another, 'Look at this animal. He should be killed.' The night before, he made a girl sleep with him. He overheard it. He walked after her, turned her around, and, with his shoe, kicked her in the stomach."

But it was also at Płaszów that Betty Gunz's life took a Shakespearean turn for the second time. Gasping in all the right places, she tells how she got some startling news.

"Auschwitz sent to Płaszów for twenty men—carpenters. They were there a month. When they came back, one of the gentlemen, Immergluck, said, 'Could you please tell me, who is Betty Gunz?' I looked at him—I didn't know this gentleman. I said, 'I am Betty Gunz.' He said, 'I have to talk to you. I have here a handkerchief. Your husband, Roman, wrote his name, and he begged me to find you and give it to you.'

"I thought this was the end of me!" She swoons, sinking back against a soft cushion, hand pressed to her heart. "It was his handwriting, absolutely! I was *hysterical*. This man said to me that my Roman said, 'Tell her I love her.'"

She was overcome with joy and relief. Then reality set in. She had not lacked for male companionship at Płaszów. Now what? "So I said, 'He's alive; who the hell knows if *I* will be alive . . .' We were looking for companionship, to feel a boy next to you, to have some emotional support: walking, talking, crying together. We were going to work, coming back dead tired, having a slice of bread, some soup. We had to be in the barracks after six, and we were talking about boys and love."

After that shock, came yet another. "A group from Płaszów went to Auschwitz and brought barrels, and on one barrel in big letters was 'ROMAN GUNZ. I love you. I hope we will be together soon.' Well, I was going out with somebody else . . . but there was every month less and less emotion. It came to point when we were not interested in who was alive, who was dead. I didn't even want to know who was shot. We just wanted to survive."

Betty is sure she would not have survived, but for Oskar Schindler.

"We were in Płaszów, and they were choosing very young-looking girls. They said, 'Go to the right,' [to me and] my sister. I was asking, 'God, are you choosing me?' No one knew anything about Schindler. It was just heaven to get out of Płaszów. The trust [in him] came later on, when we saw how good he was to us."

At Emalia, she and Pola dipped pots in enamel. "At night, when we went to the barracks, we didn't care about the world of people. We would just talk about the war, or our families: 'Is my mother in heaven? Would I meet her there?' The world was dead for us. We spoke about the past." (Hudel and Lusia died in Auschwitz. Betty learned after the war that everyone on that transport to Bochnia was gassed.)

Betty Gunz may have been the only woman on Schindler's list who actually was looking forward to the Auschwitz stopover, because she knew Roman was there. "I was *dreaming* about it, if he aged, if he still loved me." But they never met. Roman had been sent to another part of the vast extermination complex before the women arrived.

But he did rendezvous with the small group of Schindler men and boys consigned to Auschwitz after their brief Brinnlitz stay. Roman Gunz—"an old-timer"—was waiting for them. "Roman did not believe he could help the children," says Betty. "It's not pretty what I'm saying, but it's the truth. He said to Henry Rosner, 'Listen, if you want to be alive, try to save yourself, because about children, I don't know.' But I know he took the children and put them in a bunker the Germans had prepared for themselves, and took care of them. They blessed him after the war. He gave them emotional support."

Betty, Pola, and Meyer were safely at Brinnlitz. "Then Schindler received the order that he had to close the factory and execute all of us, that we had lived absolutely too long. To deceive the Nazis, Schindler told us to dig graves. Oh boy, was I digging for two days! I thought I would die. We were thinking, 'All right, this is the end. He left for Germany, and after a few days returned with some documents—I remember the red seal. He came into the factory and said, 'Children, you are safe. You are going to make it. The war will not be forever.' "

And it wasn't. She recalls waking up early on the morning of May 9, 1945, and hearing the strangest sound: silence. "It was so quiet. I said, 'Something is happening here.' We didn't see guards. Schindler said that the war was over. We didn't believe we were safe. Slowly, we started to put our heads out from the barracks. We started to cry and kiss each other. But then we were thinking, 'Where do we go? What do we do?' "

Then the Soviet soldiers came, "one on the horse, and twenty, thirty of those animals after him. They were only looking to rape us. They raped my girlfriend three times. My sister and I were so lucky, you have no idea. They wanted food and . . ."

The film *Schindler's List* takes substantial liberties with Oskar's actual departure. He was not surrounded by hundreds of teary, worshipful survivors. When he left in the middle of the night with his wife, a mistress, and eight Jewish inmates, it was without ceremony. But this doesn't mean that many who remained weren't profoundly moved.

"We were hysterical when he left," says Betty Gunz. "He was like a father! One friend of mine said, 'Schindler is an angel dressed as a man . . .' Very often we had discussions after the war, and asked this question: 'Why did he do it?' My opinion is that in the beginning, he didn't know the Jews exist. He was a Nazi. But when he took us to Emalia, he started to speak to us and started to see some intelligence in us. He started to feel sorry for us when he saw Goeth shooting us. He saw we were nice, hard-working people, and they were killing us only because we were born Jewish. He had a change of heart."

Someone else took off, running for his life: Marcel Goldberg. Betty Gunz would see him one more time. "There was a bunch of young boys who wanted to kill him. He ran to Buenos Aires and settled about eighty miles away. One day, my Roman and I went on vacation to Curaçao with another couple, also survivors. It was the end of the sixties, maybe the early seventies. Whoever is in Curaçao is anxious to buy tablecloths, so we walked into a shop, and there I stood frozen."

Marcel Goldberg, leaning on a counter, was idly watching his wife browse among the linens. "Imagine what happened to me when I saw him! For a minute I said, 'Oh my God, what do I do? Tell my husband? He will kill him!' I took my husband out, and my friend called me from the shop, 'Betty—come come!' My husband said, 'What are you doing?' He was getting mad. I looked back at Marcel Goldberg and red, like blood, was in his face. He must have been very grateful to me."

Almost immediately, she realized she'd made a serious mistake. "The guilt! I couldn't eat. I couldn't sleep. How *dare* I didn't do anything?" It gnawed at her for months. Then she accompanied Roman on a business trip to Argentina. They stayed with the same couple who'd vacationed with them in Curaçao. "I said, 'Adolfo, I have to tell you that this and this happened.' He said, 'Betty, you did a wrong thing.'" Then Adolfo Smolarz swung into action. "'I'm not going to let him go,'" he told Betty. "[Adolfo] looked for him and he found that Goldberg had a factory where one hundred twenty people worked for him. His wife also [helped him] in the office. And they all loved him. He paid a very good salary.

"Adolfo, who is a very wealthy man, went to the Jewish organizations and to the [Argentine] government. He asked me to get signatures from New York. I got sixty-five, about what Marcel Goldberg did in the war. Adolfo went to the authorities, and they told him, 'He is an Argentine citizen. He gives bread and butter to one hundred families. His behavior is excellent. We don't give up a person like that!'

"Then we heard he had a heart attack and died. They should have cut him up in little pieces! Hung him! Most of the *Kapos* ran to Germany, and better stay there."

Roman, liberated from Auschwitz in January 1945, immediately returned to Kraków. He reclaimed his father's auto-paint shop—his father had died at Mauthausen—and settled into a routine. "He reclaimed one beautiful apartment from one of his father's buildings," Betty remembers. "A very well-known

German who killed many Jews lived in our apartment."

But the wife Roman Gunz hadn't seen in three years was a mess, mentally and physically, when she joined him in May 1945. She told him about the abortion, and she says he "cried like a baby" that she had suffered such trauma.

"When I came back home, I wore the Dutch shoes, and a dress that covered only one breast, and he saw me in all that, and he didn't know how to react. He was already four months a human being. He looked beautiful. He dressed beautiful. I was the little *nebbish*, but he did love me dearly.... There were moments I felt I was a stranger. So many years had gone by. So many

Roman Gunz at liberation from Auschwitz.

things had happened. Your mind starts wandering. I wanted twice to run away and not stay with him. My emotions were sick. I needed time to relax, by myself."

She also needed major surgery. "I went to see a doctor, and he said the kidney had to come out. He was Professor Glatzel, and he was a Pole, four years in prison by the Germans for aiding Jews. He didn't operate for a long time. But he operated on me in 1945, and I thought, 'He's going to kill me!' because he was crying. Two days after surgery, two old nurses were in the room— Poles. I heard them talking: 'This young woman, the Jew, he just removed her kidney,' and I fainted! I didn't know what he did."

The operation alleviated her physical pain, but it did nothing for her state of mind. A friend named Tadek "Tadziu" Kalfus intervened. He was the brother of Natalie Sterngast, whose husband, Joe, was on Schindler's list. (The Sterngasts live in Canada.)

"Tadziu survived with Roman in Auschwitz. He said to Roman, 'What happened to her? I'm taking her away for one month. I am taking Natalie and Betty, and she will be a new person. She needs help.' My Roman was in heaven.

"Tadzia had a job in the suburbs of Kraków at a concentration camp for German people. He took us in a motorcycle: Natalie sat on the back; I sat in the sidecar. He gave us a room like for a queen—two beautiful beds—and a German woman came in and cleaned, washed up after us, made the beds. Every morning for breakfast, she brought strawberries and sour cream. We were treated like two queens from Sheba! She cooked for us such delicious meals! [At] six o'clock, a table was [set] with a white tablecloth, and she walked in [wearing] a little white uniform. We were kissing and hugging each other, and somehow I started to feel, slowly, life. Natalie and I, we've talked for forty-five years about this."

When the month was over, Betty returned to "her" Roman, looking and feeling a lot more like the woman he married. "I was myself again," she says. "I said to him, 'Look, I am going to have one child. If I am not going to have one child, I am going to commit suicide.' He said, 'Are you crazy? Who needs children? Look at the war we just finished! I want you! You will not be able to, with one kidney.' I said, 'Leave it to me.' Then, for seven months, I was deathly ill. They wanted to take out the child from me."

Betty Gunz refused to bear her child in Poland. " 'She will never be called Polack!' " she swore. So two months before her due date, she wrote to Count Folke Bernadotte, the Swedish official who had saved 423 Danish Jews from Theresienstadt.

"I told him the situation and he gave me a visa to come to Sweden, also for my husband. I went by myself to Stockholm, by plane for the first time, with a little valise and two thousand dollars. During the trip the storm was so bad the plane turned to the left and I fell, and my feet were up, and my baby turned in my stomach completely. I went to the hotel, I went to take a bath, and I was bleeding."

She went right to the hospital. "I couldn't give birth to this baby. I was in such pain! I went to the window and wanted to throw myself down. 'I don't want a child!' I was yelling. I was running almost naked in the corridor.

"In Sweden there was a law, when you were healthy and young, you must give birth without cesarean. So four days and nights they tortured me, in this cultured country."

Finally, a visiting doctor from the United States performed the C-section. "So they cut me and took out the baby. She was coming out with the face up. The skin was hanging. I said, 'Take her away from me!' I didn't want to see her."

Roman Gunz arrived to find his wife a wreck once again. "My legs were paralyzed. I was in the hospital for two weeks, then he took me to a convalescent home; he was taking care of me. It took me six weeks to recover."

By then, Meyer Gross was living in Israel, where his brothers owned an appliance factory. He never remarried, and died there at the age of sixty-three.

Before leaving Kraków, Roman sold the family business to the Pole who'd been running it during his absence. Instead of money, he accepted a painting by the sixteenth-century French artist Jean-Baptiste Greuze. Allegedly, it was worth a fortune.

"When we came to the United States, we went to Sotheby's, and they told him it was a fake," says Betty. "I kept it on my wall for sentiment, then I gave it to my niece. It was by one of his students, one of six copies he permitted, worth one or two thousand dollars."

Betty and Roman and their daughter, Alice, waited one year to emigrate. In 1948, the best they could do was a twenty-seven-day visa for the United States. So they went to Cuba instead. "It was dirty, filthy, hot," she remembers. But they made the best of it. "Roman bought an old car for one hundred dollars, filled it with textiles, and drove from six in the morning till night. But I had food, and I had money to pay for the room. After a year, he even got me help. Then in March 1951, we got the visa and came here."

In New York City at the time, "if you had a million dollars, you couldn't get an apartment, so we got a room. My first job was packing stockings in plastic envelopes. I had to deliver ten dozen daily, and I made twenty dollars a week. Roman went as a partner to a lingerie shop. Then he opened Romphil International Corporation. We were importing Japanese watches to Latin America, and every summer, we were traveling there."

She worked briefly as a prenatal nurses' aide. It was as close as she'd come to her prewar dream of a career in medicine. "I dreamed about it since I was a little girl. I still read medical books."

Betty says that in the early years they didn't think much about how they would adjust to life in the United States. They'd already adjusted to conditions the average American couldn't begin to grasp.

"We were so poor, and there was so little time to worry about the problems we had because right away, there had to be a job, had to be a little room. [Being busy] helps you. When you work all day, you are exhausted, and you have to go to sleep because in the morning, you have to get up at six o'clock and go to work again. So being busy didn't permit you to suffer too much."

In addition to their own daughter, the Gunzes cared several years for Betty's teenage niece, now Nancy Wheatley of Cleveland. Nancy's mother, Pola Gross Neuwirth, died of cancer at the age of forty-four. Alice Gunz Sydney is a divorced mother of four who owns a New Age gift shop/yoga studio in Raanan, Israel.

Roman Gunz had his first heart attack at the age of fifty-one. Betty blames it—and the one that later killed him—on the abuse he suffered at Auschwitz. "We had a beautiful life. He was very successful. Everything was going for us. He was such an ambitious man, always struggling to give us the best. He was definitely an 'A' personality."

In 1978, the Gunzes bought an apartment in a luxury high-rise on Miami Beach, just across Collins Avenue from the tony Bal Harbour Shops. Roman got to enjoy it for a single season. He suffered a fatal heart attack in April 1979. He was sixty-two.

"It was a tremendous shock," says Betty. "When somebody is sick for a while, you get used to it, but when they get sick and die in a day or two, shock is added to the grief. The first time I lost him, I was too young and too silly. Not this time. Suddenly, it is like I am half a person, not a whole person."

After his death, Betty quickly discovered the role Roman Gunz had played in other people's lives. "He was always ready to help, to the day he died, and he helped many of our people in America. Young people were always coming to him for advice. When he died, the calls I got! 'Would you give me one hundred dollars a month like Roman did?' I thought it would kill me."

Betty, who had worked with her husband, closed his office and ran the business for five years out of her apartment in Forest Hills in Queens, New York. She also was active in the New Cracow Friendship Society, a survivor group formed in the mid-1960s to help Jews in Poland and Israel and each other. And she became part of a core group that supported Oskar Schindler until his death from complications of alcoholism in 1974. "We bought him an apartment in Buenos Aires. In each city of our people, we were gathering money. I will always be very grateful to him that I am alive," she says.

She was thrilled when Steven Spielberg's film opened. A week after seeing it, in December 1993, Betty Gunz talked about how she had braced herself to watch it.

Bronia "Betty" Gunz at home in Queens, under a portrait of her daughter, 1994.

"By now, I am a very strong woman because I went through a lot. I talk to myself—it helps me. I was saying, 'Look, Betty, you went through hell, then you lost a beautiful, gorgeous husband. What can happen? I can cry? I relive it? You sit in a movie, probably you'll hear many people crying. So what? How about those beautiful people with me who did not survive?' Even today, I am asking God, 'What did I do? I am the one who lives, even with one kidney.' "

Betty Gunz mentions God a lot, which seems odd, since she claims to have stopped believing during the Holocaust. "I lost my faith completely. How can I believe? Where was He? And what's going on in Israel now: He might just wipe out four million, like Hitler wiped out six million. On the other hand, I am alive, and I live nicely. I feel like a chosen person. But I have a tremendous feeling of guilt that I am robbed of this belief. As I grow older, I have even more guilt about it."

Other survivors were angry at Betty Gunz when she talked publicly about these feelings during interviews keyed to the film. "Some of my friends said, 'If you don't believe in God, keep it to yourself.' But I can't help it. So if there is a God, please God, forgive me. I am sorry."

HENRY SILVER

When the Brinnlitz factory gates swung open on May 9, 1945, Henry Silver had one mission: to retrieve his son. Of course, he hoped his wife would surface, too, but little Yehaskel was first in his thoughts.

Two years earlier, the Reich's list makers had routed Edith Silver in one direction and Henry in another.

Edith became *Haftling* A26567 at Auschwitz. Henry became *Haftling* 375 on Schindler's list. (He appears on the list as Hersch Silberschlag, born on April 7, 1912—though he was actually born in 1913 and called Henryk Zylberszlak in Polish.) Neither of them knew it then, but their son had become someone else, too: He was baptized by the Catholic Church as Henry's Zdunkowski.

"Whoever was gonna be alive and survive, was gonna meet where this child was." That was the deal, as Edith tells it nearly fifty years later. So Henry went back home to Radom, searching for his son. Six months and an emotional court battle later, he reclaimed his boy . . . who had no idea why this strange man was taking him from the only parents he knew.

Edith Neumann Silver realized that getting pregnant in the Radom ghetto in 1942 was a serious mistake. "I tried to get an abortion. I felt awful. But I come from an Orthodox family, and my mother said, 'A small tree, you don't cut it down. . . .' Today, you do what's good for you. At the time, I make my mother a

Henry and Edith Silver's "miracle child," who they gave to Christians in 1943 and fought to reclaim after the war. He is now Dr. Charles Silver of Dallas, Texas.

promise: I would never do anything to destroy this child"—directly, at least. "I did the most crazy things to see if something would happen anyhow—I was jumping steps . . . I was poisoning myself—because I was looking that something should happen to me in a 'normal' way. If it happened, I would be delighted."

What did happen was that on December 2, 1942, during a typhus epidemic, she delivered a perfectly healthy boy in the ghetto hospital. An hour later, she dropped him. Then, for much of the next nine months, she pumped him full of mother's milk and sedatives. Marched to forced labor, she had to make sure he wouldn't cry when left alone all day. Under the circumstances, she can be forgiven hyperbole: "This is a miracle child!"

It's probably a blessing that Dr. Charles Silver, a fifty-one-year-old Dallas surgeon, recalls "absolutely nothing" about any of this.

With full knowledge that their marriage—and their lives—might end the next day, or week, or month, Henry and Edith wed on January 12, 1941. He was twenty-seven, she was twenty. Members of Hashomer Haza'ir, a left-wing, Zionist youth movement, they'd known each other for years.

"He pinched my cheeks," Edith recalls of their youth. "He told me, 'Hurry up and grow up; I'll marry you.' But in those days, when you had an older sister, you couldn't marry first. He asked my parents if we could get married, and I said, 'Get married? You have to marry my sister.'"

In addition to Edith, Samuel and Frymet Neumann had a son, Moses, and two daughters, Lusia and Guta. Henry was the third of Leib and Huma Zylberslak's eleven children: five girls and six boys. Edith's father was a sales representative for a leather company; Henry's father was a wholesaler of Czechoslovakian china. At the beginning of the war, Henry was in the china business for himself.

He was completely assimilated, going to synagogue on major holidays only to placate his mother.

"My whole education was in the youth movement," he explains. "You learned Hebrew, Jewish history. You went to different working places from six to eighteen, training on a kibbutz [in Poland]. I was to go to Palestine when I was eighteen, but the English mandate stopped it. When the war broke out in 1939 . . . it was a disaster. They took the Jewish stores and warehouses. They sold them or sent [inventories] to Germany."

"Everyone was on the run," Edith says. "The main motive was not to be alone. Before the war, he was very well situated. He had no thought to get married." She'd been helping in his business because "I had equal to three years of college, I spoke French and German, and you could tell immediately he was Jewish by his accent." Better she should talk to customers and suppliers.

Edith Silver is doing most of the talking on this day too. Henry apologizes. "I got older. My English got worse." He is squinting badly, recovering from eye surgery. "In Majdanek, I got so beaten—my eyes," he explains. "After the war, you haven't got time to take care of yourself. I started to get worse and worse; now it's a little bit too late."

The Silvers also were recovering from the January 1994 earthquake in Southern California. It hurled a small fortune in china, crystal, and porcelain to the floor of their Encino apartment, just a few miles from the epicenter. Figurines, lamps, the good dinner service, the stemware—some of it still lay in a heap behind the padded bar three months later. The china hutch, with its few remaining plates, looked like a yawning, gap-toothed mouth.

But five generations of Silvers were back up on the living-room wall, behind the tapestry sofas: a gilt-framed genealogy dating back to his grandfather. "The hell with it," he says, "as long as we're alive."

Radom had twenty-five thousand Jews before the war, "eighty percent poor," says Henry. In 1941, the Germans killed or transported most of them. "They left a small percentage," Henry explains. "They took them out and made an *Arbeitslager* [work camp]. Later, they made it a branch of Majdanek." Edith's parents were transported to Treblinka. The elder Zylberslaks died in the

Henry Silver (left) with his brother Bernard, who was in the Polish army, about 1938.

Radom ghetto. Henry's youngest brother died trying to escape it. Another brother, shoveling thousands of bodies into mass graves, buried their father. Another, Bernard, survived, hidden by a Gentile woman. As for the rest, Henry says he can't recall the details. "You get so tense. You get mixed up."

Henry and Edith survived the selections. She was working for a uniform factory; he did whatever he was assigned. Their biggest problem was concealing their son: He was one of four children still in hiding. "Every day, you would gather before you went to work in the morning. . . . The four mothers put the children to sleep. All of a sudden, while we [were being counted], a child started crying. I was sure it was my child," says Edith.

The commandant bellowed, " 'Where is the mother who would hide a child?' I stood next to Henry, and naturally I wanted to tell them this was my child. He wouldn't let me. But I picked myself up, broke loose, and came up. The commandant, *Oberscharführer* Rocike, said, 'Is this your child?' I said, *'Jawohl!'* He said, 'Do you think you have a possibility under such circumstances to raise a child?' It was one moment he was humane—he was so bloodthirsty. He told me that the child must disappear, and this was what led us to put him in hiding."

Henry and Bernard developed a plan: Bernard's Polish girlfriend, Marysia, would deliver the baby to a teacher friend who—they all hoped—would keep him until the end of the war. The Silvers had declined to have Yehaskel circumcised, as Jewish law required; this was the one sure giveaway of a Jewish male. They tucked a note in with him, pushing his date of birth ahead by ten days to help obscure his origins. It said his parents were abandoning him because they had marital problems.

"The same evening, we brought him out. My brother-in-law got in touch with his girlfriend, to put my child on the doorstep of this teacher, and try to convince her to take [him]. This was the right moment to make this move. This was the only chance for him to survive: to give him away."

Henry had consulted with "a good German." The Jews who worked with him called him "Moishe Hussid." He told the man, " 'We got the feeling that something's gonna happen tomorrow.' He said, 'This child must be put in hiding.' They brought us once a week to the public bath, with the ODs," Henry continues. "I smuggled him out in a rucksack. Edith was watching from far away."

But things went awry. The teacher was afraid. "You kept a Jewish child, they killed you," says Henry. "She called the police, and they took our child to an orphanage. He spent a few months, then a couple of peasants adopted him legally."

A few days later, Henry and Edith Silver learned they were to be transported from Radom. Edith had to have a last look at her child. She bribed a ghetto guard with her wedding band, removed her armband, dressed as a peasant, and brought candy for the orphans. When she got there, a doctor was checking the children and she couldn't get near her son.

"But from far away, I took a peek, and made myself satisfied. He was in a crib. I was very heartbroken, but I was at peace about it." He was nine months old. Edith says the decision nearly destroyed her. But in retrospect, she knows she did the right thing. "I do believe something controls our destiny. The way we survived, and the way this child survived, that this didn't affect his brain, and he could utilize what God gave him. If you don't believe in those things, I guess your life is empty." (Marysia still lives in Poland. The Silvers send her fifty dollars a month. "I feel this is an obligation till I die," says Edith.)

The Silvers, along with "the whole small ghetto," went to Majdanek. Edith says that when they arrived, the *Kapos*—Poles—said, " 'What you need clothes for? You're going to the crematorium anyway.' "

"You saw them cut up a piece of human flesh to eat in Majdanek," says Henry. "You wished yourself two plates of soup and then to die. We wanted to throw ourselves on the wire."

But one thing kept Edith going. "The Nazis broke you physically and morally. They took away the doctors, the lawyers, the leaders, put you in a position where you were defenseless and you stopped fighting for life and gave in to any situation, except when you had a purpose like I did. Because of a mother's instinct, I felt if I wouldn't be alive, he wouldn't be alive."

Yet she suffered terribly from guilt. "We get to Płaszów, and two or three days later I see a tremendous difference in the way parents are treated, and I started to feel guilty again. Why was my child not here? Then they killed the mothers and kids, and I didn't feel so bad."

They arrived at Płaszów in early 1944, witnesses to unending slaughter. "To keep discipline, every morning, they picked up three, four, five Jews," Henry recalls. "They shot them or hanged them for no reason. One time, they were going to hang a guy. He said, 'I was a German [military] officer.' They said, 'Now you are a dirty Jew.' "

Henry and Edith saw each other frequently at the camp. "The women's *lager* was on top, and when they came back from work, they came through the men's *lager*, and we met almost every day," he recalls. "We used to talk: If we were gonna be alive, where we were gonna meet. We made plans—you couldn't help it. We fantasized. We were gonna meet where our child was."

Leopold Page was Henry's *Blochalteste*, though Henry didn't live on the block all the time. "I made him a striped suit, by candlelight, and that brought him luck," Edith explains. "He got himself a good position with an *Oberscharführer*, a female, who was fooling around a lot with officers. He was presentable. She picked him as a lookout, that she shouldn't be caught. He used to have good food, cognac, and everything."

Henry also cared for Amon Goeth's killer canines . . . not that he knew the first thing about dogs. "They said they needed a dog handler, you raised your hand. They needed an electrician, you raised your hand. Dog handler, I thought: 'This is gonna be a lot of meat!' I didn't know this was going to be Goeth's place."

Then he was assigned to the tear-down operation at the Wieliczka salt mines, courtesy of OD man Marcel Goldberg. "What a son of a bitch!" says Henry Silver. "Oh, he was a bandit! He needed some people to go to Wieliczka. It was terrible there! The worst thing was lice. They ate you up alive!" The *Budzyner* group was working there too. By a fortunate accident, Silver got into the group.

"Later on, they were going to liquidate, so they brought our group back to Płaszów. They put together the Emalia people. Marcel Goldberg, at the last minute, took out the *Budzyn* leader, Stockman, and put himself on the list. Everybody was so mad, they could kill him! I thought after the war they would. Oh, I couldn't look at this Goldberg!

"[Still] in a way, he done good for me. This was the way I got on Schindler's list." (Liepold, the salt-mines commandant, became commandant of the Brinnlitz camp. He took the *Budzyners* with him.)

When the Schindler people left for Brinnlitz in the fall of 1944, Edith didn't make the list. "At the last minute, she saw what was happening," says Henry. "She dressed herself as a man, and she slipped in this transport. I said, 'You know what would happen when you go to shower?' So she went back to camp."

She arrived at Auschwitz two days ahead of the Schindler women. "I was so humiliated," she remembers. "They cut my hair. I looked like hell. They tattooed the following day. Your arm was swollen up two or three days. But I met my sisters at Auschwitz! I nearly dropped dead. I was two days there, and they were shipped to Bergen-Belsen." They both survived the war.

Her brother probably had died at Auschwitz several years earlier. "They were looking for a Neumann who was a communist, with the same name, and they took him instead. He was fourteen. It was horrible."

By the time Edith Silver got to Auschwitz, "these were already the good days. I was sorting the clothes from the transports, day after day. Then we went to Ravensbrück after they liquidated Auschwitz. It was not so bad. Much cleaner. The fear wasn't so tremendous."

Henry, meanwhile, was at Brinnlitz, where he shared a bunk for a while with Bill Rosner. By the time he walked out, a free man, Edith was in Sweden.

"Count [Folke] Bernadotte, the Swedish diplomat, had an exchange for the POWs, six weeks before the end of the war. I went with the sick ones. I was like a vegetable. A skeleton. . . . I sent a wire through the Red Cross, and from twenty-five hundred survivors, I was the first one to get back a wire that my husband and two sisters were alive, and that he was in the process of taking back our son."

Henry Silver had help. Bernard and Marysia had managed to keep track of the little boy. Henry found him in the town of Pionki. "I knocked on the door and told them the story: 'I am the father of this child,' and I had to start with the whole *megillah.* They slammed the door in my face and ran away to another city. They were hiding him. I had to go with a gun, because they were killing [Jews]. They wouldn't part with him."

The custody battle ended up in court. After blood tests proved him to be the father, Henry Silver reclaimed his son. But he had to compensate the Polish couple. Henry still had the goods Oskar Schindler bequeathed to his departing workers—fabric, notions, and the like. He sold them to raise money. "Schindler's things helped to pay for my son," he says.

Henry also went to the Poles in Radom who had appropriated his family's home and belongings. He asked the man, " 'Just give me enough for five thousand złotys.' [The man] said, 'You still alive? It's a shame Hitler didn't kill you.' " He gave Henry nothing.

Edith wanted to stay in Sweden. "Jews and not Jews opened up so much heart to us. But my husband wouldn't come to Sweden. I tried to convince my husband I wouldn't set foot back in Poland." But she returned, only to find a son who told her, " 'You're not my mother.' He was kind of confused. In time, he got used to us. When I came back, he was already built up, [having spent] quite a few months with my Henry and my sister. He was really sick when they took him back. He was looking like a little *goy.*"

The family spent four years in Europe in Łódź and in Germany. Henry traded everything from hides to industrial diamonds on the black market and prospered. In 1949, the Silvers had a daughter, Florence. (Now a divorced mother of two, Florence lives in Tarzana, California, not far from her parents. She sells real estate and is the administrator of several weight-loss clinics.) The family immigrated to Baltimore, where Edith had relatives, six months after Florence's birth.

Henry went to work in an umbrella factory for fifty cents an hour. "I came home so tired," he remembers. "I made eighteen dollars a week." But he said to one of Edith's aunts: " 'A year from now, people gonna work for me.' She said, 'Have a good dream,' and a year later, I got twelve butchers working for me."

He had managed to save and borrow eighteen thousand dollars, and bought a grocery store in 1951, in a black neighborhood. "The guy said, 'You got a lot of competition, and if they find out you're a greenhorn, they're gonna kill you. But I'm going away for three months. When I come back, if you're not going to be able to handle the business, we'll give you back the money.' We worked our tails off.

"It was very important to treat them nice," Henry says of his customers. "When they asked for a pound of bologna, you gave them a pound and threw in two more slices. We used to make friends with them, and our business increased four times. We were so successful, I had six stores later on." All were called Chester's Market.

The Silvers faced a big decision about their son. "Charles survived be-

Henry Silver with a portrait of his mother, 1994.

cause he wasn't circumcised," says Henry. "Edith said, 'We're not going to circumcise here; you never know what's gonna happen.' Finally, we sent him to the finest school in Baltimore, the Talmud Academy. He went for maybe a year or two. It was bothering me. I told the rabbi, 'Charles is a half Jew; he's not circumcised.' The rabbi said, 'What? A brilliant boy like this?' I told him why. He said, 'I'm gonna bring tomorrow a *mohel* [ritual circumciser]!'"

Charles Silver was fourteen years old. Henry says he realized "you could not make a *bris* at home. You had to go to the hospital. We brought the *mohel*, but they said you had to have a surgeon! They said they were gonna do it in the operating room, with an anesthesiologist. They compromised with the rabbi. He said, 'You've got to have a *minyan!* So they brought ten doctors! Everybody put on yarmulkes, the rabbi said the *bruchas* [blessings] with the surgeons. We brought whiskey and cake." It made the newspapers.

In 1960, the Silvers moved to California. Henry couldn't tolerate the Baltimore climate, and Edith wanted to be near her sisters. Henry went into real estate, then construction. Charles, the "miracle baby," studied violin at the Peabody Conservatory, graduated Phi Beta Kappa from UCLA, served in the Vietnam War as a captain in the army medical corps, married, and had three children, one of whom is a nationally ranked tennis player. He says he's been healthy all his life.

"Hitler would have killed him because he was a Jew, and look at what he contributed," says Edith Silver.

Charles Silver doesn't want to talk about how his experience as both a "hidden" child and a child of survivors affected him and his parents. He says such things are "very personal." He does say that when growing up, the Holocaust was "part of [my] life, with positive and negative effects. The persecuted sometimes passed on things that were not all that wholesome. I've gotten a mixed bag." He says his father never told him he'd been on Schindler's list until the movie came out.

In the early 1980s, Henry Silver got a call from his old *Blochalteste*, Leopold "Poldek" Page. "He said, 'I have a writer here who is interested in writing about Schindler.' This was Keneally. I used to be president of the Congress of Survivors of Nazi Concentration Camps [in Southern California]. I told him, 'Let me discuss it with my friends.'"

He turned down Page's request. "I think of it this way: A Nazi is a Nazi. Schindler did nothing wrong by me—he did good for me. He passed by in the factory, he threw down a cigarette so I could have it. But he was dead already by this time, and I thought, 'I've been through so much, to me the best German is a dead German.'"

Henry Silver says he might have made a different decision if he'd known the Schindler story was destined to become "a big *megillah*. A big *spiel*. Who knew Schindler? Who knew Brinnlitz? Who knew Poldek . . . ? I was bitter, not because of what happened to me, but because nothing happened in [forty] years [to eliminate anti-Semitism]. I'm not gonna take a German and put him on a pedestal."

Edith Silver, who can still work up an impressive head of steam about how Franklin Roosevelt and American Jewry abandoned the doomed Jews of Europe, is equally candid. "The *Los Angeles Times* interviewed us, and [the reporters] said Schindler was like Noah's Ark. How can they glorify people like this? In our estimation, Schindler was not a hero; *Spielberg* is a hero. He woke people up after fifty years. As Henry says, 'Once a Nazi, always a Nazi.'"

Sam and Edith Wertheim

From the minute they met, when he spied her trudging barefoot, skinny, and bedraggled in the road, Sam Wertheim wanted to take care of Etka Pewzner Liebgold, and for the better part of a half-century, that's just what he has done.

By late 1939, Etka was the (presumably) widowed mother of an infant son named Leo. Her husband, Max Liebgold, had headed east, to the Russians, as soon as the war started, and he never came back. They were practically newlyweds, so it wasn't a shattering blow like the one that would follow.

"I almost didn't get used to him. I didn't know what hit me. I get married, I get pregnant, he's gone," she says.

Then came Sam Wertheim, riding his bicycle from the Kraków ghetto to the small town of Skala, where his parents and grandparents were living. He was, by trade, a smuggler, carrying yards of soft leather wrapped around his torso as he pedaled.

"I see a girl walking with shoes in her hand, stopped on a hill. I ask, 'Would you like a ride?' I took her on the frame of the bike. We were going maybe a half hour, and we got acquainted. I was about eighteen, and she was maybe twenty-three. After that, we started to date."

Her mother was Sonia; her father, Leo, was a violinist. There were four sons—all musicians—and four daughters. Only one survived the war besides

Etka, now called Edith: a brother, who died four years ago in Israel. Edith was the youngest, twenty years younger than the first child. "I was born in my mother's change of life. I was not wanted. I felt that since I was a little girl. My sisters took care of me."

Why had Sam Wertheim found her in such a state that day in 1942? There had been a selection. Edith was taken on a transport, aboard a horse-drawn cart headed who knows where. "The guy taking care of the wagon—a peasant from the village—he was sorry for me," says Edith. "He said, 'One part of that mountain, I will slow down for a while, and you jump. He pushed me, and I fell down from a big mountain. I was afraid, because the Germans jumped out and started to shoot. I fell in the bushes hidden, and I was hurt all around.

"When the evening started to get dark, I saw light from a little house. I saw a woman cooking on a fire and a man. I said, 'Please help me. I am so bad hurt.' She knew right away I was Jewish. Who would be begging for help? She let me stay there all night; she says I have to go before the sun comes out. I put some *shmattes* [rags] around my knees, and started to walk to ghetto." That's when Sam spotted her. He was smitten in an instant. "She had long black hair, very attractive. She was always in good humor, and, I may add, very sexy."

Edith Wertheim is a character: Carol Channing meets Zsa Zsa. In public speaking appearances, she never fails to rhapsodize over Oskar Schindler, how she found him so alluring. After the New York preview of *Schindler's List*, Steven Spielberg hosted the survivors at a party at the Essex House hotel. Liam Neeson, the film's star, gave Edith Wertheim a big hug and a kiss, "European style, on both cheeks. I said, 'You know what? You are gorgeous, but you're still not Oskar Schindler!' I always speak out. He was laughing."

Edith is—as they say—of indeterminate age. She claims she was twenty-one when the war started. On the list she is Etka Liebgold, born in 1914. But whatever . . . she takes wonderful care of herself.

"I pamper myself in America. I was always hungry in the war. So I eat when I'm hungry. I go to the beauty parlor to [get] my hair and my nails [done]—[they] were terrible during the war. Three weeks every year at a spa in Italy. Sam likes the Alps, and I love it there. We have dances, dinners, a very good social life." She spent most of the spring and summer of 1994 nursing a wrist injury caused by a fall—at Saks Fifth Avenue.

"My husband promised me he will make my life easier. Like Schindler, he kept his promise. If I want to go to Europe, he sends me. He never says no, which I admire in him. I don't ask for the impossible. I want in my late age, things a little easier, which I couldn't have when I was young. I just want to be not always thinking: 'I don't have tomorrow what to eat, or I don't have money for rent.' I am secure now, because I never believed I will have what to eat, where to sleep."

Sam is a "seventy-five percent retired" builder, not 100 percent, "because I want to get up in the morning and have something to do." They have luxury apartments in Fort Lee, New Jersey, and on Miami Beach. (One overlooks the Hudson, the other, the Atlantic.)

Sam and Edith Wertheim, Fort Lee, New Jersey, 1994.

Edith was one of the first women to work at Emalia. "I started to go to the [ghetto] employment office for work. Every day, Germans used to come and pick girls to work. A man came in and looked us over. He chose six of us: 'You are going with me to work.' We didn't know where. He took us to Emalia. We didn't know what we were doing there. Then I saw a tall, handsome, *gorgeous* man—I really was struck by how beautiful he was. I saw a good face, smiling at us. I was not scared. He said, 'Children, don't worry. Who works for me, lives through the war.'"

She did, but her son did not. According to Edith, her husband, Max

Liebgold, wrote once, "like a good-bye letter. He was sick, and he was begging me to take care of the baby. But who could fight the Nazis?"

She lost her son during the ghetto liquidation fifty-one years ago, and it still sears. "How can a mother live with a memory like that?" Edith Wertheim asks. "A child gets sick, goes to the hospital, you can't help it. But they were just grabbing him, grabbing him away from me. After that, nothing was normal. Emotional changes? I went through. Believe me, I went through. I didn't want to take care of myself. I had long black hair, and I didn't want to wash it. I thought it was the end of me."

But Sam wouldn't hear of such things. "He helped me a lot then," she says. Then she helped him.

"When I was in Płaszów," Sam explains, "she was working for Schindler. The beating, the killing, the hanging went on every day. Every day was like, 'This is my last day.' My father was with me. I sent a letter to her: 'Is there anything you can do to get me out of this camp?' She went to Schindler's office. Believe it or not, a few days later, an OD came over and called out my name: 'You are going to Emalia.' I felt like God sent an angel to bring me from hell to heaven. There was enough food, and I didn't mind to work."

But he had to leave his father in Płaszów. Telling the story, he weeps. "I hesitated to leave him. When I was called to go to Emalia, I was emotionally broken. I just couldn't separate with him. I felt terrible, but I had to go ... I spoke to someone who saw him alive three days before the end of the war. I never knew what happened to him, where he is buried, or if he is buried."

At least they had each other, and Edith had her sense of humor. "Humor kept me going," she says. "What can you do, when every day somebody else dies? Is beaten? But you have to have in yourself something to keep you going. They will tell you, I used to walk in the evenings and sing. I had a nice voice. My girlfriends remind me, in Israel, after fifty years: 'Are you still singing *Ave Maria?*' I used to love it, and I used to sing it so beautiful.

"So I went to the barracks. The girls were relaxing and sleeping. I said, 'Girls, today is the hour! We will sing!' That was my sense of humor. People in the camps wanted to get away from other things, so they did crazy things. All the girls were always sad. This way, I cheer them up."

But why choose *Ave Maria*, practically the anthem of Catholicism? Edith explains. "When I was eleven, in Kraków, they chose me from school for a Christmas performance in church: the one Jewish girl singing in the church, singing the solo. The acoustics were beautiful." She has loved it ever since.

When they were together at Emalia, Sam played the harmonica and Edith sang. "They gathered around us," Edith remembers. "But *Ave Maria* didn't come out so good on the harmonica!"

Sam worked on a lathe at the subcamp's ammunition factory. Edith carried pots to the ovens, "like a waitress," on twelve-hour shifts.

"Even in camp, there was black market going on. It was a trade situation: bread for cigarettes or the other way around, or socks, or a shirt."

Edith made the list. Nearly eleven hundred others made the list, but Sam Wertheim did not. He went to Mauthausen, on the August 1944 transport. Before he left, he divested all his valuables.

"I had a pile of Polish money that I gave to [Leopold] Page to give to Edith [for her to] give to my father. He gave her every single penny."

"That was the most beautiful thing he did, and I love him for it," says Edith. "He's my good friend. I put [the money] in a bread and kept it under the straw. We were in Płaszów, waiting to be called to Brinnlitz. The same day, Sam went to Gröss-Rosen. He kissed me. He said, 'I don't know where I am going and where you are, but let's hope we will meet again after the war.' He liked me very much.

"That day, they took us to Auschwitz. You can imagine how scared we were. We knew we were not in Brinnlitz: We were in that hell. They took us to a shower. We thought we were going already to the gas. We had to undress, and they pushed [us] in naked. We thought it was the last moment of our lives. Like a miracle, we felt water coming. So we started to yell to each other: 'I think we are safe!' I couldn't watch that in the movie. I left and went outside. I missed a lot of the picture. Two times, I didn't see it."

Sam didn't have an easy time of it from then on. "We were working at the Hermann Goeringwerke, making big guns, on the night shift. One evening, I was extremely hungry. It was really cold. Not further than twenty-five feet was a big pot of soup for the SS, smelling so good. I was dreaming how to get hold of a little.

When no one was looking, I ran to it and took a scoop in my little pot and ran back. A guard was watching. They took me down, hung me on chains, and I had the beating of my life. I was waiting just for a bullet, but it was time to go, so my friend took me under his arm. They were dragging me and put me on a bed."

Of course, he had to show up for work the next day, no matter how badly injured he was. "I ask myself many times: How was it possible to get up? But I would have been shot if I didn't. The human body is built in such a miracle way. When we were young and had the will of life and strength, you could get up and work again."

As they had planned, the lovers met after the war. "I was liberated in Linz, and I walked on the streets and met her girlfriend," Sam recalls. "I said, 'My God, you are alive! Edith is alive!' I rushed to Kraków, and we got together. I said I would not stay in Poland one more day. Hate was not even the word I had for them. My mother and brother were shot because of one of the Poles who pointed out where they were hiding, in Skala, in a stable and covered with hay. . . . There were some very few [Poles] who saved Jews, but most were very anti-Semitic and very happy what happened to us."

They went to Regensburg, Germany. "Quite a few of our people [were] there. We decided to stay and wait for immigration to the United States. Schindler came with someone and found my wife. She said we were getting married, and he said, 'I would love to come to your wedding.'"

They married in February 1946. Edith wore a borrowed floor-length white gown with a veil. Oskar Schindler not only attended, but "gave away" the bride. "He kissed me. He blessed me: 'This is my children!' He was crying like a baby." Sam says Schindler "made a very emotional speech."

Sam Wertheim believes that Schindler didn't intend to save any Jews at first. "He came to Kraków for a purpose: He knew he could have slave labor, and he had the opportunity to make a lot of money, which he did. But doing that, he realized these atrocities could not go on forever, and someday it would end. He had a feeling. He was a human. He never hit or killed anyone. His intentions were 'Germany would take over the world. I would be a rich man and live happily ever after.' He was disappointed when that didn't happen.

Sam and Edith Wertheim, after the war.

"I did ask him once, when we were together, 'What made you do it?' He changed the subject and never gave me an answer."

The Wertheims came to the United States in March 1947. Sam says he and Edith were "very poor, not knowing friends or relatives. It was very tough to start life from scratch. I worked anything and everything you can think of: sheet-metal factory, sales, the garment center, upholstery. I started a small business in Forest Hills [Queens] in the late fifties: a stationery store."

"My nervous system was shocked," says Edith. "The memories made me sick. I was crying without a stop. We had nobody. We were alone. But I never looked for a psychiatrist's help; we don't believe in it. My husband saw that I was very depressed, crying and thinking. He used to talk to me. 'You have to go on. We are free in the most wonderful country in the world. We are still young.' I didn't need a psychiatrist to tell me what happened to me. I had chronic depression."

And yet, she always seems so cheerful. "I am all the time smiling. I don't want anyone to pity me. I want them to say, 'Edith, thank God you are smiling.'"

Sam says that for years they felt the less said about the Holocaust the better. "With American-born people, questions used to come up: 'How did you survive?' I actually refused to talk to anyone about my experiences, because I wanted to first try to put my life together. I would sit and cry, or be home and not want to do anything. I lived with it for many years."

When she got pregnant, Edith Wertheim didn't believe it. Neither did her doctor. "The doctor told me I had a tumor. That was a lousy doctor! As time was going on, the tumor was growing. I felt I was pregnant. My husband was working in a factory. Our dream was to have a baby in the United States, but I didn't know if I could, because at Auschwitz they took my blood out. Sam's boss sent me to a Park Avenue gynecologist. He said, 'Don't worry how much it costs; I take care.' The doctor was laughing! 'In six months, you gonna have a nice, gorgeous tumor.' God gave me a boy! He answered my prayers."

They named him Elliot, for Sam's father, Eliezar. Elliot Wertheim, of Roslyn, Long Island, is in advertising. He and his wife have one son.

It was impossible not to see her lost boy when she looked at her son, but Edith Wertheim says she never mentioned him to Elliot until "much later, when he would ask me. I would say, 'You don't have grandparents, aunts, uncles. You would have a brother, but this, they took away."

In 1965, Sam helped found the New Cracow Friendship Society. It began with thirteen friends and now has 370 members. "In the beginning, we felt we needed to organize to help each other in case of need," he explains. "People were struggling. Then it became bigger and bigger." The Society bought a big cemetery plot on Long Island, where it built a monument to loved ones lost in the Holocaust. Each society member gets one gravesite free, and can purchase a second.

"We were more comfortable with survivors. They love to be together, because our past puts us together in memory, and most people like to be there."

In the 1960s, he also got into the building business, as a project superintendent. "I worked myself up to be an equal partner, then we were acquired by a public company on the New York Stock Exchange . . . then they went into Chapter 11, and all the money I made, mostly I lost. In 1973, I started all over again, from scratch."

Now it was Edith's turn to support and rally, just as she'd done for the women in her barracks. "I said, 'What are you worried? You lived through hell. You are going to be all right. I always was believing God will help, and I tried to keep him going because he was very depressed. I felt sorry for him, and for me, because I loved him."

"Somebody else in my place would have jumped from the twentieth floor," Sam continues. "But I said, 'I went through the camps and I survived, so I will survive this.'

"I was very lucky to have a wife like Edith to help me get through. Thank God, I succeed."

HENRY WIENER

*I*n his youth, nothing—*nothing*—meant more to Henry Wiener than sports. He loved the fun and excitement of it, and in a Polish city with a 3 percent Jewish population, athletic prowess assured acceptance, even for an ethnic outcast.

"I won the table-tennis championship in the whole school, so even though I was the only Jew in the class, I was *it,*" says Wiener, who grew up in Chorzów.

Of course, this didn't stop Polish kids from ambushing the Jewish boys leaving their Thursday-night Maccabi sport-club meetings—"they knew where we would be"—or from making it perfectly clear, as soon as the Germans invaded Poland, exactly where their sympathies lay.

Chorzów, in Upper Silesia, "was the first Polish town on the southwest border with Germany," Wiener explains. "It was a coal center, the smallest and richest state of Poland—still is. When you leave Germany and you put a foot in Poland, you are right there. So on September first [1939], a bomb came down on our town. They came the first hour, and everybody was *'Heil Hitler!'* The whole population, right away, all the friends I went to school with."

These were the same boys who had been helping him get around a rabbinical restriction on secular classwork. "By us, you went to school Saturdays, too," Wiener explains. "We went to the rabbi. The deal was this: 'You can go

Henry Wiener (far right) in his school uniform with his family: brother Maniek, sister Emilia, and parents, Sara and Jakub. Chorzów, mid-1930s.

to school because you need it, but you're not allowed to write. You make arrangements with your *goyishe* friends [to get the notes].' "

Henry Wiener was born on January 12, 1921, in Jurków, two years before his brother, Maniek. Sister Emilia followed in August 1928, shortly after the family moved to Chorzów. His father, Jakub, was a men's clothier and a World War I veteran.

The Wiener boys attended public school, then *cheder* in the afternoon. They also belonged to Maccabi teams, part of the European Jewish sports league. Henry may have been *it* to his classmates, but his parents had other priorities.

"Before the war, you had to pay [tuition to attend] high school. Every time I was doing well in sports, my grades went down." Henry literally came to blows with his parents at a crucial time: tryouts for the league's national table-tennis finals at one of the Thursday-night meetings.

"My mother said ten was curfew time, not only for my mother, but for the school. So I went [home] and put 'civilian' clothes on, because we had [school] uniforms. The top three players got to go to the national championships. I had to play for the third [spot]. And I made it. I came home after ten, and the door closed. I stepped in, and somebody hit me, 'Whack!' I was whacked both ways. My father said, 'Where is the racquet?' He broke it. He said, 'I don't care if the world comes to an end; tomorrow you have exams, and, for my money, you're playing around?' "

Money really wasn't the issue (at least for a time). Jakub made a good living. But things began to deteriorate as the thirties wore on. "Anti-Semitism was very big," notes Henry, "and they advertised, 'Don't buy by Jews.' "

After high school, Henry went to the nearby city of Katowice. The Adolf Kapelner i Brat bicycle factory soccer team drafted him. He worked at the factory and played on the company squad. "That company had a representative at the [1939 New York] World's Fair," he recalls. "I talked to my boss, [saying] I wanted to come to America. The government wanted to get from me ten thousand dollars, like a bond that I would come back. I said, 'I didn't know I was so valuable!' It wasn't even a figure to think about."

The company "vanished," according to Henry. "After the war, nobody knows what happened to them. The younger brother's son was sent to Sweden [as an apprentice] in a bicycle factory, so he survived."

In August 1939, Jakub and Sara Wiener sent their daughter Emilia to Malka and Israel Kleinberger, an aunt and uncle in Klaj, in the south of Poland, "because the smell of war was in the air. And a week before the war, we sent my mother and brother also. My father and I were going by train . . . and the train got bombed. We ran away and went on foot for two days, to my aunt. My sister was there, but my mother and brother were not. We didn't know for about two months what had happened."

Maniek and Sara's train was bombed, too, and they never got to Klaj. They'd walked back to Chorzów, but there was no mail, and no one was traveling south. They couldn't convey their whereabouts.

Henry and his uncle decided to head for the Russian border on bicycles. "My father said, 'I don't care what happens; I'm old. I don't have the strength to run. I might die on the way. You're young, so you want to go, you go.'"

They got as far as Janów, in eastern Poland, but turned back after confronting a cordon of German troops. "The Polish soldiers confiscated my bicycle," Henry remembers, "and with the constant shooting, my uncle and I lost contact with each other."

Henry arrived back in Klaj on the day before Rosh Hashanah. Uncle Israel materialized two days later. He'd stopped in a town rather than travel on the holy day. The whole family was soon reunited in Klaj. "One day in December [1939], a truck came, and my mother and brother were on the truck. The Germans were making Chorzów *Judenrein* [clean of Jews] and they were sending all the young people to the Russian border and forcing them to cross. This was actually a blessing in disguise. Those people are alive."

A month later, the Wieners piled into a single room rented from one of Jakub's brothers in the village of Stary Wisnicz. "We had to sell our clothing in order to live," says Henry. "It was a very degrading living." Stary Wisnicz was a few miles from Wisnicz Nowy, where a well-to-do fur dresser named Abraham Schon and his wife, Malka, lived with their son, Meyer, and daughters, Tania and Salla, who's now called Sally.

In those days, every Polish city and town where Jews lived had a *Judenrat*, "so the Germans said, 'We want so many people every day,' and based on this, every household had to supply somebody to work. There were some Hasidim who didn't want to, so we were young, and for money, we would work every day. We didn't care. My brother and I were working for the Germans, and one day a week, for ourselves." They chopped wood, picked strawberries, even bottled wine, "so we were drunk every day."

This is where Henry met Sally Schon, "and it was love at first sight." Henry—with dark, wavy hair and bright blue eyes—was so smitten with the sixteen-year-old Sally that he convinced his family to move to Wisnicz Nowy. When it came to wartime courtship, "you had to be inventive. We danced. They didn't have electricity, but we had a [crank] Victrola, and we danced to swing music." Sally threw her beau a birthday party when he turned nineteen. On her birthday, he gave her a manicure set and powder box, which she still has.

At that time, the Schon family lived in their own house. "There was no actual killing," Henry says, "but there was a ghetto, and you had to have a special pass" to enter and exit. Then in June 1942, "the Germans issued an order that all this area had to be *Judenrein*. We all knew more or less what it meant.

"My father and I went to Sally and said, 'We're going into hiding. You better do the same thing.' We went into hiding with a farmer in a basement. My brother was working for a German in the ghetto Bochnia, and he was sort of secure in his position [building truck frames].

"After it all cooled off, he sent a message to come to ghetto Bochnia. Whatever it was, at least Jews were living there. After a while, I sent a message to [the Schons] that it was bearable."

The Polish family hiding the Schons decided they could only risk keeping one person. "So they chose Sally because their daughter was friends with her." The rest of the family made its way to Bochnia. That ghetto, like the one in Kraków, had A and B sections. Those with work permits—including Maniek Wiener—lived in A. Everyone else lived in B.

"We stayed for one year in the ghetto," says Henry. "During this time, there were shootings to death in certain areas of the ghetto. We went into hiding in the ghetto itself."

In the spring of 1943, Maniek learned of a planned *Aktion* in Ghetto B. "We dug a bunker under one of the rooms. My brother covered us up with earth, leaves, and other things. Then my brother came and dug us out [after the *Aktion*]. Jewish blood was flowing in the streets."

Henry was caught and sent to Julag I, a Kraków-area labor camp, a precursor to Płaszów. He was put to work building roads for Siemens-Bauwerke.

"I was fluent in German, so I got friendly with one of the Germans who were instrumental in issuing passes. I said, 'Look, people are going sometimes home and coming back,' so he gave me a pass and I did come back. I was going then almost every week to Bochnia."

During one visit, Jakub Wiener was caught in a roundup of men headed for a labor camp. Henry went to the local Jewish police and offered to change places with his father. "They sent us to Kraków to the airport to work. I produced the pass, and, in no time, I was home again. I did this three times, but the third time, they sent me to Płaszów, and that's how I got stuck there."

At Płaszów in the fall of 1943, Henry Wiener lived in Bochnia Barracks, named after the ghetto where so many of its residents had dwelled. He drew the unenviable assignment of digging graves on Chujowa Górka, "Prick Hill."

"They would bring young Jewish girls who had [used] false papers, and we had to bury them. . . . One time, a young boy managed to escape. The Germans took ten people from our barracks and shot them dead, and we were forced to bury them. . . . One more time, another young man escaped from the camp and this time they took twenty people from our barracks and shot them and we had to bury them."

Of course, the Nazis wouldn't waste anything of value, "so they came and pulled out the gold teeth. One guy showed me gold teeth, and said, 'Why should I give it to [the guard]?' " At first, he says, "You felt like vomiting. It was just awful. But the SS guy was right behind you with a gun. I never saw anybody having a nervous breakdown in all those years. In my case, I said, 'I don't give a damn what they gonna do. We have to keep going and see their defeat, in spite of what they do to us.' "

But when there was a third escape from Bochnia Barracks, Henry Wiener figured his time was up. "I said, 'Oh my God,' and I didn't wait till they called us. I ran away to a coal depot with another guy. I said, 'I don't care what they do to me later; I'm not staying around now.' I was hiding until I heard shots. I knew the execution was over. When I came back, I was punished with a beating from a *Kapo,* but I was alive."

Alive, but heartbroken. Word reached Płaszów that Bochnia's Ghetto B had been liquidated. His parents and fourteen-year-old sister were dead. "I felt very lonely in this world, only hoping that somehow my brother was still alive, and my dear Sally also."

In fact, Maniek might still have been alive, but he wouldn't survive the war. Henry would later learn that Maniek was arrested "because he belonged to the underground. He went to Montelupich [the infamous Kraków lockup]; then he was sent to Auschwitz, and somebody told me he died of typhus there."

Sally ultimately spent eighteen months in hiding with a Polish farmer who'd been saved by Jews during World War I (they'd dressed him as a milk-maid). The farmer built a double wall, "the width of a small bed, and a small hole for the intake of food and outtake of refuse." There was no light. When soldiers came searching for a rumored hidden Jew, the farmer's family distracted them with vodka, and their killer German shepherds with salami.

Sally was liberated by Soviet soldiers in January 1945. She couldn't walk for five weeks or see for three months. She weighed seventy-five pounds.

One day, Henry Wiener noticed a line forming in the Płaszów camp. "I found out that this was for people registering to work in a pot-and-pan factory called Emalia, owned by a German called Oskar Schindler. Who was Schindler? We didn't know, but whatever it was, it meant getting out of the barracks. So we stood in line—[me and] my friend Abush Reich."

Schindler needed one hundred people. Henry and Abush stood per-haps four hundred deep. "The Jewish police were keeping order," he re-members. "They were hitting and hitting. I heard one of them calling another one, 'Hey, Steiner!' I remembered that my mother came from the Steiner family, so I took a chance. I said to my friend, 'Hold my place in line; I have to talk to him.'

"Before I opened my mouth, he wanted to smack me. I said, 'Wait a minute: Are you by any chance from Bielsko-Biala?' He said yes. I said, 'I think you are my mother's cousin.' He said, 'Who is your mother? Where you come from? What you doing here?' I said, 'I'm waiting for a bus; what do you *think* I'm doing here?' I saw already that it clicked."

He told the OD man that he feared dying under the rule of "the devil himself: Amon Goeth" and would do anything to get out. "So he took us both—Abush and me—and put us to the front. As it turned out, this was a lifesaving move."

The Emalia workers continued to live in the barracks for a time, until Schindler got permission to build his subcamp. In the meantime, the workers walked to the Lipowa Street factory and back daily, under guard. Henry got an outside job in construction at Emalia. He recalls that Schindler would pass by and actually greet the Jews: " 'Hello. How are you? How you doing?' He said to one guy, 'I let you play ball in the afternoon.' "

To the soccer-loving Henry Wiener, this was manna. "The average guy, you didn't understand that you were so hungry for something else in life besides, 'There is soup and bread today.' A you-don't-live-by-bread-alone-type thing. So everybody wanted to play. I said, 'Where I come from is the capital of soccer, and I scored the most goals.' "

Henry Wiener got a KL tattoo at Emalia, administered by one of the factory's Jewish doctors: Samek Rubenstein—now Stanley Robbin, who lives a few blocks west of Wiener in Long Beach, Long Island. "I still kid him about it," says Wiener. "I scrubbed it with sand until blood came out, but we had to show it every month, so I took a pencil and on that spot, I put it back."

One night, an Allied plane crashed into one of the empty barracks in the subcamp. After that, most of the Emalia workers had to move back to Płaszów and walk to work.

"One day, we had a Ukrainian guard, a young guy. I talked to him. We were walking near the [Płaszów] gate. I said, 'Listen, I'm starving. There are some people who have money who want to buy bread. If I buy bread for them, I'll have it for me. I have nothing to give you. I'm just telling you what it is.' He said, 'OK. Tomorrow, when we come, you go ahead and buy bread.' He even told the guy at the store to have bread for us. I got one full bread. Bread was life! This I did once or twice, but I didn't do any other 'business' [at Płaszów]."

When the camp was ordered closed in the fall of 1944, Schindler decided to move his operation to Brinnlitz. Henry recalls helping load *Herr Direktor's* two automobiles on a railroad car and camouflaging them with freight. The cars went to Brinnlitz; the men went to Gröss-Rosen. "This was a hell on earth," he says. "Thank God, we spent less than a week there."

At Brinnlitz, "we were setting up machines," Henry remembers. "We were never finished. Schindler saw to it we never were. In the beginning of April 1945, a group of thirty mechanics arrived in our camp, and, much to my joy, [one] was Nathan Krieger, now my brother-in-law!" Nathan had married Tania Schon, Sally's sister. They live in Cedarhurst, Long Island.

They were in bad shape, Henry says, but nowhere near as wretched as a group arriving about the same time: the frozen skeletons—living and dead—from Goleszów. He remembers how Emilie Schindler cared for the frozen men, and for Krieger.

Henry Wiener recalls a Czech partisan—a young woman—riding up on a horse on May 8, 1945, as their harbinger of freedom. He says Brinnlitz's mayor came to the camp and asked the inmates not to "plunder" the town. "He said, 'We are Czechs, and just like you, we are victims. We will bring you every day food.' We stayed one week. We wanted to recuperate a little," and try to figure out what to do next.

"When the war was over and you started to be human again, you asked yourself questions: 'Where are you going, now that you're not just looking for a piece of bread?'"

He and Abush Reich decided to go to Kraków. "There I found out nobody from my family was alive, but they told me Sally was alive!" They headed for Wisnicz Nowy, which was also Abush's hometown. Henry went to find Sally, and Abush went to a farmer who'd kept some of his family's belongings. The farmer, says Henry Wiener, hacked Abush Reich to death with an ax. Reich was twenty-three years old. "I felt horrible. After all that we suffered together. This was our first encounter in Poland."

Sally Wiener, who is sensitive and emotional, hardly can bear to listen. Tears flood her eyes. She wrings her hands. "He was such a beautiful boy!" she sobs, softly.

Henry describes his relief on finding his sweetheart: thin, pale, weak, but alive—and available. "A lot of people, to save their lives, married those who saved them, but she was free, thank God. In the meantime, her sister and brother came back, so she went to stay with them. I went back to my hometown.

"I rang the bell at our apartment. Whoever was there opened the door. From the accent, I recognized she was German. I said, 'Oh, sorry! Wrong house,' in German. I went to the city hall. I told them, 'This is my [survivor] pass. I lived over there—you can check. I want my apartment back.'

"I told them my furniture was still there. They said, 'Look, we understand what you're saying. If it was a Polish family, we could not do anything about it. But a German family? Tomorrow morning, you will have a key. Come at nine o'clock.' I was the only one who came back of all my friends."

He retrieved Sally from her family in Łódź and brought her to the Chorzów apartment. She says she went right to the nightstand, opened the drawer, and found the platinum-blond curl Henry's mother had snipped from his head as a boy.

The apartment quickly turned into a kind of survivor crash pad. "My uncle [Isidore Federgrin], came back, and everybody moved in," says Henry. And then he and Sally moved out. Jews straggling back to their hometowns all over Poland quickly realized the Poles hated them as much as ever. And, now that they'd helped themselves to so much Jewish property, they would stop at nothing to keep it. Anti-Semitic violence wracked Poland. The Wieners wanted none of it.

Uncle Isidore wanted him to stay. "He said, 'Where you going? We can make money here.' I said, 'You want to, you stay! Keep the apartment. We're getting out of here right now.' The Poles were at their best killing Jews. They didn't change. At that moment, we decided to leave Poland forever. Too much Jewish blood was spilled there."

In September 1945, they went to Usti nad Labem in Czechoslovakia, where Henry got a job at a soap factory and played for the factory's soccer team. They'd written to Henry's uncle Oscar Wiener in Brooklyn "in Polish, German, partly Yiddish, and a few words in English, which I remembered from high school days. He was a real American uncle. He came to the United States in 1905 and sent once a thousand dollars for my cousin who was getting married, for a dowry. A thousand dollars! Four weeks later, we got an answer: 'Go right away to the American zone. I can't do nothing for you in Czechoslovakia.'"

They made their way to the Displaced Persons camp at Furth where, on January 20, 1946, a Hungarian rabbi performed the camp's first wedding ceremony for Sally Schon and Henry Wiener. "You had to wait a month and you had to advertise," says Henry, "because in a lot of cases, the spouse came back."

Sally wore a borrowed blue dress. Henry wore a borrowed suit. "Oy, was I crying!" says Sally. "The rabbi said, 'I am in place of your mom and the whole family, and I bless you.'" Only her sister, Tania, survived.

Neither is likely to forget their wedding anniversary. The vanity license plate on their white Nissan Maxima reads: JAN 20 46. They married exactly twenty-six years after his parents' wedding day.

Before the newlyweds left Germany, Henry attended the war crimes tribunal at Nuremberg, just south of Furth. When asked for his court pass, he pretended to be a Polish journalist. What he heard enraged him.

"I was listening to this stupid American justice asking questions of [Franz] von Papen, the German ambassador in Turkey. They knew

Henry and Sally Wiener's wedding, January 20, 1946.

he was guilty! What was this, asking questions? The guy was *guilty!* Hang him! I couldn't take it. It was too obvious and boring. I stayed one day. They were all there: [Hermann] Göring, the rest of them."

Sally was pregnant with the Wieners' first child when they boarded the USS *Ernie Pyle* bound for New York City. A strike marooned them in Bremen for two months. They arrived on January 16, 1947, and moved in with cousins on Long Island. Son Jack was born that May, followed by Mark two years later, and Judy in 1955. Judy, her husband, and three kids share Henry and Sally's duplex. An intercom connects their second-floor apartment with the Wieners'. Mark, Jack, and their families also live on Long Island. Henry and Sally have eight grandchildren.

Henry's first job in America was with a company that bought war surplus. Uncle Oscar "paid under the table" for a small Brooklyn apartment for his nephew. Then Henry worked for three years as a cutter for the Durable Under-

Henry and Sally Wiener, Long Island, New York, 1994.

garments Company. At seventy-three, he still commutes every day to a Brooklyn garment factory that produces private-label women's clothes for high-end retailers like Neiman-Marcus and Bloomingdale's. He runs the cutting department. Sally owns Sally's Discount Center, a sportswear store in Long Beach.

It didn't take Henry Wiener long to find himself a soccer team in America. One Sunday, as he and Sally were pushing the baby carriage near Brooklyn's Jefferson High School, Henry noticed a banner proclaiming the name of the team on the soccer field: Hatikvah.

"So I asked someone, 'Who is the manager?' I talked to the manager, and he said to me, 'So I guess you were a star in Europe? Everybody who comes to me was a star in Europe.'

"I said, 'Give me a pair of shoes.'" Henry Wiener showed him just how right he was: "I knocked in two goals."

JACK MINTZ

On page ten of the list of the Schindler *Manner*—the men—is number 584, *Haftling* #69441: Anschell Freimann, born on October 6, 1923, occupation *Malergeselle* (painter's apprentice). The job, at least, was correct. "Anschell Freimann" was actually Jehuda Minc, brother of Iser Minc, prisoner #69440. The Holocaust's unique brand of situational ethics generated a plethora of life-saving lies, and this Płaszów identity swap was one of them. (Deconstructing the misspellings is another matter.)

The man who is now Jack Mintz, a tailor in Cleveland, Ohio, explains. "It wasn't planned. It was in a minute. We were in my work group on the *Appellplatz*. Anschell came running. 'They put me to Schindler and my father to transport.'" The situation for the Minc brothers was reversed. Jack agreed to the plan: Each would pretend to be the other.

"Everyone went together as far as Gröss-Rosen," he remembers. Then the *Schindlerjuden* went to Brinnlitz and the others continued to somewhere near Berlin. Jack later learned that the arrangement cost the real Anschell Freimann his life. "I met his father after the war. He told me that Anschell ran away. They were marching someplace after unloading from the transport. He and another guy hid in a barn, and Germans got him the next day."

The ersatz Anschell fabricated a plausible explanation for the mismatched filial surnames. "People in the camp used to say: 'How come your brother is Minc and you are Freimann?' I used to say when he was born, my parents didn't have the [civil] marriage license, and when I was born, they had it." (In Poland at the time, children born of couples who held religious, but not civil, licenses carried the mother's surname.)

Jack Mintz tells this story on the afternoon of March 19, 1994, a frigid day in Cleveland. In a few hours, Steven Spielberg will learn if he'll finally get a Best Director Oscar. Jack Mintz already has seen *Schindler's List*, the movie, three times. But he has never seen Schindler's list, the document, and it captivates him. He pores over it for familiar names.

This one was a professor. This one got dysentery. This one went to Israel after liberation. This was a *Budzyner*—one of the political prisoners from the town of Budzyn brought to Brinnlitz by its Nazi commandant, the tough guys who ran the kitchen and organized the camp's underground. This one was a Płaszów policeman.

"This Goldkorn I remember, and Baruch Posner. He was a neighbor from home. Poznyiak—he was a baker, also a *Budzyner*. He killed a German after the war. They hanged him, but the string broke, so [Pozniak] got a rifle and he shot him." He chortles.

He points to a Goldstein. "He was a little guy. And Ritterman—I knew him! He was sorting diamonds and gold at Płaszów. He put them in his clothes, and at Gröss-Rosen they told you, 'Take off your clothes, you'll get them afterward,' but you never saw them again. He was handsome, strong. He was a swimmer, a soccer player.

"Bernard Kornhauser. He was head of the electric department at Płaszów. He was one of those who created the committee to keep order in the camp. Salpeter! When I came in 1956 to Israel, he was a bigshot. He got a drugstore in Jaffa. I had a tailor shop on the other side of the street. When I applied to get reparations from Germany, I needed witnesses. I went in to him and asked him. He said, 'I don't sign for nobody.' I had to go to a guy in Beersheba."

There is Kerner, the OD man. "His pleasure was to hit women on the naked behind with a whip. Goldberg, Gross, two Greuners, Zefte, Haubenstock—they were all ODs. Kerner was from a nice Orthodox family. Some people wanted to survive, so it didn't matter how many they killed on the way."

He finds the Rosners, Wilhelm and Leopold. "Our bunk beds were standing against the wall in the same line," he recalls. "They were always playing music. Everybody liked it. Schindler sent somebody to Gröss-Rosen to get their instruments that were taken away from them. Bill Rosner—he was a good thief. What nobody else could steal, he could. And Willie Krantz, a nice guy, a policeman, too. He used to make people laugh. If somebody make him mad, he says, 'Take your nose and stick it up my ass and tell me whose nose is wet.'" That still makes Jack Mintz laugh.

He spots Marcel Goldberg, the notorious OD man who raked in bribes to secure spots on the list. "My bed was next to Marcel Goldberg's. He should die before he was born. He was an SOB. But to me and my brother, he was good. He was head of the labor department [at Płaszów]. One time, they were sending out people for a good place to work, next to Schindler's [Emalia] camp. Goldberg said he had room for one person on the list, and my brother and I wanted to go. He said, 'Oh, let the sons of bitches go together.'"

Again and again, he scans the fourteen-page men's list for his friend Allerhand, who now lives in Haifa, Israel. It's one of the list's many mysteries: some names simply don't appear.

Born on September 13, 1924, in Miechów, Jehuda Minc was the youngest of Tobiasz and Ida Minc's eight children. Before him came Benjamin, David, Iser, Hela, Bela, Esther, and Rachel. Like the other Jewish youngsters of Miechów, they belonged to sports clubs and the Zionist groups so popular in prewar Poland.

Ida was a shirtmaker. Tobiasz, a housepainter, was a Hasidic Jew. On Friday nights, he would bring home a beggar or a stranger from *shul* for Shabbat dinner. "We worked hard," says Jack, "but to help poor people, always."

His parents wanted their youngest child to get an education and "become something. I was their last chance to be a professional." But the war intervened. The Germans closed the schools. That, of course, didn't stop the kids of Miechów from enjoying life. "We were not cautious. We used to go sled riding, play soccer, and the Germans used to hunt us. They'd catch you, you'd run away, they'd shoot after you."

The Mintz family, circa 1929: (standing, rear) Hela, Benjamin, Bela, David.
(front) Iser, Ida, Rachel, Tobiasz, Esther. Jack is in front.

Tobiasz and Ida thought it might be a good idea if Jack found an activity that kept him off the streets. He'd already survived one life-threatening episode—polio, at the age of ten—and they didn't think he needed exposure to other risky situations. (The disease hospitalized him for a couple of months. "They gave you massages and electrical shocks that pinched you like needles," he recalls. "I couldn't walk. In our town, there was no [electric shock] machine, so I went to the hospital in Kraków.")

His parents apprenticed him to a tailor named Josef Plotez, who was about seventy. Mintz believes he and his family died at Belżec. "So I started sewing. My mother said, 'You be a tailor.' It's not like today. Even when you didn't like a job, you did it." In time, he realized how valuable a skill it was.

Mintz and his wife, Ethel Szwarcman Mintz—a tiny woman who survived the war in hiding—still sew professionally. They work out of their basement on two commercial sewing machines, surrounded by racks of clothing. Theoretically, they're retired, but as she explains, "People who work all their lives can't stand still."

Until the release of *Schindler's List*, they'd kept such a low profile that longtime customers were astounded when Jack Mintz, *Schindlerjude*, made the news. Now he's even done a little speaking in area temples and schools.

"For thirty-one years, I've gone to this man, and I never knew!" exclaims a woman bustling in the door with an armful of alterations. "Is this for another interview?" She beams. Jack Mintz beams back and shrugs.

The Miechów ghetto, created in 1941, closed officially on September 3, 1942. Jack Mintz says the Jewish policemen stayed, along with the *Judenrat* members. But others insinuated themselves back inside. Two months later, soldiers surrounded the ghetto and captured everyone.

"They got us the first time," says Jack. "The whole family." Tobiasz, Ida, and their daughters "were shipped away in closed cars to somewhere near Lublin, and we never heard [from them] again." Jack, Benjamin, and David ended up at Prokocim, a labor camp on the east bank of the Vistula at Kraków, also known as Julag II. At least one man they knew, a taxi driver, not only escaped, but spilled Nazi blood in the process. "He was from the last people in the ghetto. They took him and his wife and children in the forest. When they killed his wife and kids, he grabbed a knife and jumped on a German. Stabbed him in the neck. They were shooting after him, but he ran away."

Such acts of resistance were infrequent. "This was easy for the Germans to do because the Jews were law-abiding citizens, and people were so poor, busy struggling, and religious. What kind of fighter would be a father with five children? If he didn't work, he was going to the synagogue. There weren't six million fighters. Our town was one hundred percent religious, so whatever it is, is God's will. . . . The Germans had 'God is with us' written on their belt buckle. You talked to one of them, he said, 'Your God is by us a prisoner, and He's doing what we tell Him to do.' "

In any case, resistance brought instant retribution, not just to the bold one—"you took such a beating you were begging to be shot"—but to others made to pay for the "crime." Under such duress, the will to fight quickly drained away. "You were all the time under so much pressure, you were stunned, like somebody hit you over the head. They used psychology. They didn't let you concentrate. Things would change so fast: the pushing and beating and screaming."

Jack Mintz in the Miechów Ghetto.

When the brothers arrived at Prokocim, they found themselves guarded by black-uniformed Ukrainians. Fellow Clevelander John Demjanjuk, tried in Israel as "Ivan the Terrible," in the early 1990s, was a "Black." "They were the best killers," says Jack Mintz.

After a few weeks of building railroad bridges, he ran away, intending to head home. But Iser, who'd been assigned to a work detail at the Kraków military airport, intercepted him. Benjamin and David made it back to the ghetto, only to be caught in the final roundup. Jack believes they died at Bełżec, as did David's pregnant wife, a Miechów girl named Eisenstein.

Escaping Prokocim wasn't difficult, he says. "You took off the armband and you left. There was a time when you got civilian clothes and hair like everybody else, so you weren't in trouble, unless they caught you and you didn't have papers. My brother had papers from the SS," because he worked at the airport. His boss, a German named Shultz, "was a good man. For him, a worker was a worker, so he gave them permits."

Iser's papers allowed him an occasional trip home to Miechów, during which he would collect a few family photos. They survived the war, thanks to a friendly Pole.

At the end of 1943, the brothers (Iser was six years older than Jack) moved from the airport to Płaszów. Among their jobs was excavating the camp's mass graves. The German high command didn't want the advancing Russians to discover the thousands of corpses rotting under Płaszów soil. The bodies had to be burned. Jack Mintz modifies the scene, as depicted in *Schindler's List:* "There was no conveyor. We were bringing the bodies on stretchers and putting on the wood to make the fires with tar paper."

Iser happened to unearth the victims of Płaszów's best-known massacre: the Chilowicz contingent, shot by Amon Goeth on September 13, 1944. "My brother found Chilowicz's gold watch," Jack recalls. "[There was an inscription] in German: 'For his good service.' The Jewish residents gave him a gift for his birthday. The *Kapo*—his name was Ivan—was drunk all the time. He took a knife and scratched it. But instead of scratching on the back, he scratched on the face, and he said, 'It's not gold,' and threw it back to my brother. [Iser] sold it for bread: two or three loaves. Then we found Michael Pacanower's silver and pearl cigarette box—he was an OD, shot with Chilowicz—and Mrs. Chilowicz's compact."

Ivan, the drunken *Kapo*, "used to grab a handful of [gold] teeth and buy vodka," says Jack. He also liked to hit prisoners over the head with a shovel, but favored Iser Minc because he was tough. "My brother took a whole body on the shovel and put it on the stretcher. He was a hard worker." This earned him the privilege of fetching the work detail's soup kettle and scooping out the first bowl, from the bottom, where anything of nutritional value might have sunk.

Jack Mintz believes that "the rich guys" had a much harder time of it in captivity than boys like his brother, who were accustomed to physical labor. Iser, like his father, was a housepainter. "It wasn't the same being a painter then as it is now," Jack explains. "There were big brushes, and you had to scrub walls, wash walls, and the buildings were one hundred years old and falling apart. They were schlepping the ladders, so he was conditioned."

The camp was divided into living quarters and working quarters. Jack Mintz remembers that Jews would walk by the kitchen refuse pile. "You could always find a little tiny potato, frozen, on the heap, or even the peeling. There was a time when the Black Uniform was standing there, hunting, waiting for someone to start digging, and they got shot. But the next day, another group went by and one was shot. It didn't matter. They kept coming."

Once a fire broke out in the kitchen. Jack remembers Amon Goeth shrieking, " 'Next time this happens, I will kill you all! Not one will stay alive!' He was talking to the Jewish police. We put it out like a chain, with buckets of water."

He had another close call on Wieliczka Street, Camp Płaszów's eastern boundary. "When we were working outside [the camp], taking apart railroad tracks that they took to Germany, I was picking up the salvage. You could buy bread, then sell it. The Polacks used to bring something and sell it to us. The Ukrainian guard saw everything we did. He went straight to the packages. He told the SS sergeant, who called the main gate. The *Lagercommandant*, Yohn, came with guns and grenades. He was short and fat. They started beating everybody with whips and rifles."

Those who could flung contraband into the reservoirs Goeth had ordered built after the kitchen fire. "A few weeks before, they caught guys and shot one on the spot." According to Jack, this group got off easy.

The guards "used to shoot everything. They saw a cat, they killed it. A bird? They killed it. One SS shot a crow, and [an inmate whose] wife was sick caught that bird, cooked it a whole day to make a little bit of 'chicken' soup for his wife."

For a time, Jack worked in the camp's metal shop, making chandeliers, doors, and handcuffs. "They were so smart, the guys who worked there. They took the [metal] drums and made an oven. Under the cover was another cover, so when they were cooking something, you couldn't see anything."

He and Iser also were assigned to a crew dismantling the barracks at Wieliczka, the salt-mines town near Płaszów. Across the security fence, the brothers struck up a conversation with a Pole. "He asked where we were from; we told him. He said, 'My brother-in-law is a teacher in the schools in Miechów.' We asked him a favor, because a Hungarian SS told us, 'They gonna ship you to Germany, and take away everything, so if you can hide something, hide it.' So we asked him if he could hide a few pictures.

"We tied everything in a handkerchief and when the guard [wasn't watching], my brother threw it over the fence. After the war, we got it. He was a good man. I ask if I have to pay him, and he says no."

Then Anschell Freimann made his urgent plea. Jack and Iser were off to Gröss-Rosen, then, ultimately, to Brinnlitz. Jack Mintz again studies his copy of Schindler's list.

"People think Schindler was almighty God, but he wasn't," he explains. "Schindler was a nice guy. But when I came to Brinnlitz, I saw who [else] came there. I would say if you selected from the eleven hundred, maybe three hundred should go in a concentration camp after the war. There were a lot of crooks and *Kapos* [on the list]."

He holds Marcel Goldberg responsible. "He got more power [over the list] than Schindler. Schindler asked for the people he knew, but the rest he didn't know." Finagling with the list apparently continued until the last minute at Gröss-Rosen, when Goldberg crossed off a man named Stockman, a former Polish army officer and the leader of the *Budzyners*.

"The Kraków people from Płaszów thought they would be in charge of everything," says Mintz, "but Liepold took the guys from Budzyn." Liepold was the new Brinnlitz commandant. The *Budzyners* and the *Krakówers* "were always arguing."

Even Schindler couldn't prevent what happened to the men at Gröss Rosen. "They [gave] everybody a number. They took us to a trough with faucets. They made everybody have a bowel movement, so they could see if we had something in the rectum. It didn't go so fast. Some people brought some bread, and they started eating. The [veteran] prisoners said, 'Today you eat; tomorrow you go through the chimney.'

"There were two guys at the tables. They checked to see if you had gold teeth, they lifted up your arms, your feet, wherever you could have something stuck. The Russian POWs were the barbers. You knelt down and they shaved you with the 'louse promenade' [a bare strip down the center of the skull]. One guy had a little bit of wash powder. The water was a little trickle. Then the delousing, with one towel for ten, and by the second one, it was soaking wet.

"Out you went, with no clothes. They showed us a big tent, and inside was straw. Somebody fell down and grabbed the tent and pulled it down. They became crazy and started hitting and chasing us. It was like steps, and the walkways [were covered] with cinders. People fell down. I fell down. My back was burning from these scratches. They beat and beat everybody, and everybody tried to be in the middle. Finally, an officer came out and said, 'This is an *Arbeitshaupten* [work camp]. In the morning they'll all be dead! What are you doing?'"

At Brinnlitz, Jack and Iser worked setting up the factory: "moving machines, bringing in cement, bricks, making foundations for machines. Then I had a job to deliver boxes with metal to the machines." From scrap metal, he made a knife and a spoon. One of the mechanics made him a sewing needle and a tinsmith made him a thimble. With these implements, he was able to help his brother keep warm. He made mittens for him and an ingenious pair of long underwear.

"In Brinnlitz, they took my brother to cut branches so the guards [in the towers] could have a good view. Once he cut a big branch and landed [with it] in the water. For this he got a pair of long johns. He gave them to me. I found a pair of ladies' underpants and silk stockings. I cut off the feet and sewed [the stockings] to the panties for my brother."

Iser was assigned once to the *Straffcommando,* a punishment squad consigned to breaking rocks. Why? "He found a frozen turnip. The SS man stopped him and asked him, 'What you have there?' He sent him to four weeks in the *Straffcommando,* from six in the morning till late at night."

The *Straffcommando* was supposed to get half rations, but Iser ate well. "When he worked outside, he could find [food]. When they stored potatoes in the field, they dug a ditch, put them in, covered them with straw, and put dirt on top so they didn't freeze. The ditch was ten yards or longer, covered with straw. To get potatoes, you just took out straw.

"All the men were hungry. The guard was a sergeant with one eye and a machine gun. My brother talked to him every day. He always was in front. He told him, 'We're hungry, so when we pass by the potatoes, why can't we take some?' He said, 'I can't. I'm afraid. It's against the order.' But my brother felt he was a good man. So one day he told the boys: 'When we pass by, you run and grab, and I'll take care of him.' [The guard] tried to take the machine gun from his shoulder, but my brother grabbed him in a bear hug. He was very strong."

When the commando reached its mountainside destination, the prisoners baked their purloined potatoes. "This sergeant ate more than anyone, because he was hungry, too. My brother brought for me every day a baked potato."

Food was in such short supply at Brinnlitz that people would grub for the discarded potato eyes and eat them, as well as the beet peels Schindler fed his horses and cows.

As soon as the Soviet soldiers liberated the camp on May 9, 1945, the Minc brothers went looking for food. "Some Czech people invited us for dinner. A

woman was standing there, and she gave us rolls she baked." Someone gave
them chicken noodle soup; someone else gave them sugar.

"There was a big storage [warehouse] for the soldiers across the street,
and we ran in and grabbed things. One guy was an artist, and he made a Russian flag. They went on the roof to put it up, and somebody was shooting.
One guy was shot. Someone cooked a cow in the yard. It was chaos."

As for clothing, no one wanted the available German uniforms. "So I
asked a [Czech] policeman to go with me. He got a suit and shirt. I still had
opened shoes, so I tied up the shoes with string. With six guys, I caught a horse
and a little wagon and started going east until we caught the train to Poland.
We went to Miechów." Like many survivors, the brothers got a frigid welcome
at their old home. " 'Where were you that the Germans didn't kill you?' " one
former neighbor asked.

Iser and Jack heard that the city of Reichenbach held some promise. They
went there—"there was a Jewish culture center and Jewish police"—and got an
apartment. Iser got married, and Jack went to work at a newly established survivors' sewing cooperative. ("We got so many *shmattes* from America, you could
drown!") Everyone drew a check, "and at the end of the year, we divided [the
profits]. The government gave us a few sewing machines, and the Joint sent a
few."

Jack met Ethel Szwarcman, the seventeen-year-old daughter of Golda and
Solomon Szwarcman. The family of eight came from Sokołów Podlaski, about
thirty miles east of Warsaw. Soldiers shot her father, a tailor, in his synagogue
at the beginning of the war. The remaining family fled to Russia. Ethel's
mother, who lived into her eighties in Israel, never stopped looking for her dead
sons. Two sisters who survived live in Israel.

Ethel came for a job at the cooperative. Jack thought she was adorable, as
did several other young men, who competed mightily for her hand. He per-
sisted, and won.

"We had nothing to offer each other except ourselves," says Jack Mintz.
And that seemed to be enough. "A cantor married us. He was working as a
shoemaker because no one needed a cantor. He wrote up a paper and signed it,
with witnesses, and it was kosher. But it was not good enough for the govern-

ment. They didn't want to marry us till she was eighteen. But her mother said, 'Get married or get lost; it's no time to date.'"

Most survivors were searching for someone to love to help replace what they had lost. "We were like a branch cut off from the tree," says Jack. "We were lonely. We were looking for someone to trust."

They stayed in Poland until 1956, living in Breslau, and then immigrated to Israel. "[In Breslau] I used to work at home," Jack explains. "It was a communist regime. I started making clothing for the stores. They used to check on me because this was illegal. I always had five hundred [złotys] in my pocket. I was bribing everybody, and I survived. When I came to Israel, I went to look for a job. I couldn't get in a big factory, so I went from one store to another and asked for work. Finally one place gave me material. I took it home, made a couple of jackets, and got work from a big store."

Life in Israel was difficult, but Jack and Ethel Mintz arrived with an advantage: two tons of belongings, including a piano. "I thought my kids would play or I'd sell it. We had one hundred kilos of goose down to sell, a washer, a dryer, stove, fridge, a hide-a-bed sofa, all brand-new. Plus thirty kilos of dried salami, five kilos of butter—melted—dry bacon, dry mushrooms, twenty-five kilos of apples, and chocolate we bought in Vienna. We still have the down comforters. This was very expensive in Israel." Jack worked in Tel Aviv and commuted home to Haifa on weekends.

The Mintzes applied to go to America but were told it could take five years. "I forgot about it," says Jack. "Then after two years, they sent me papers." He went to Cleveland, where he had relatives. He hated it, but didn't have enough money to return to Israel, so his family joined him.

They were relieved to get their son, Toby, then fifteen, out of Israel before he'd become obligated to the army. "Israel is like your parents," says Jack Mintz. "You run away from home. You don't agree with your mother or your father, but you know you can always come home. The door is always open for you. A Jew is not different from the Irish who leave Ireland. My son is not a fighter; he would have been in danger."

Toby Mintz joined the U.S. Army Reserve during the Vietnam War, and wasn't called for active duty. If he had been, his father wouldn't have let him go. "I told them, 'He is my only son, and I am a survivor.'"

Jack Mintz with his wife, Ethel, in their basement sewing shop, Cleveland, Ohio, 1994.

Toby and his sister, Adina, asked few questions about their parents' pasts when growing up. "The movie is like a wake-up call for everybody, and it happened to them, too. They asked me to write it down, to make a tape. Up to now, if they'd bring it up, I wouldn't talk. My thinking was, When the war was going on, nobody was here to help, not the people who we lived among so many hundreds of years, not the democracies of the world. We came out beaten, broken, and nobody wanted to help. What's there to talk about?"

Toby Mintz is an electrical engineer. Adina Mintz Gelbman is a student. They both live in Cleveland. Jack and Ethel have four grandchildren.

Even in Israel, among other Jews and survivors, discussing the war years seemed risky. "My brother's brother-in-law was chosen to work by the crematorium. Everybody who worked there got shot, but he got sick and they didn't find him in the hospital. He used to tell this story in Reichenbach, and somebody reported him for burning people. The police came to arrest him. He hid himself till the president of [the Jewish] Federation came and straightened it out.

When I worked in the co-op, and refugees from Russia came back, an old Jewish man said to me, 'You killed other people in camp, otherwise you wouldn't survive.' So we didn't talk too much."

In Cleveland, Jack got a job making suits at Richman Brothers. "They had all ethnics, and maybe five Jews, [who were] the master [tailors]. In 1963, I started there at one dollar sixty an hour, and a good lunch for thirty cents. My cousin and I went to [the Jewish] Federation. I told them I came from Israel, and they didn't want to talk to me. They had an agreement [to discourage emigration from Israel]. Now they're sending me letters to give donations."

Several years ago, Cleveland's survivor community "started talking [about] organizing a museum here. It's a big community: fifty percent in the cemetery and fifty percent alive. I'm not interested in it."

It's still hard for Jack Mintz to understand why Europe's Jews had to suffer so much. "People didn't do anything. At the time, we didn't know if they could do something. After the war, I found out more. The [American] Jews didn't want to demonstrate because they didn't want to [stir] up anti-Semitism. I compared the American Jews to the German Jews—they didn't want to have anything to do with the Eastern Jews. 'They are *shmutsich* [dirty]. They have the beards, the long black coats.' And the Americans, too—they thought we were Yankees. They never saw me, and they hated me."

It's now late at night. The Academy Awards drone on from a small television in Jack and Ethel Mintz's kitchen. He is leaning on a cooking island, sipping tea, still perusing the list. His wife went to bed hours ago.

Jack Mintz barely notices as Steven Spielberg accepts the Best Picture award for *Schindler's List.* Where are the Kesslers, he wonders, the wealthy family who converted to Catholicism well before the war, but in Adolf Hitler's perverse genealogy remained as Jewish as their great-grandparents?

"Here is Shubert, the dentist. Ettinger—he was a professor. But where is Allerhand? I don't understand why I can't find him."

SAM BIRENZWEIG

When he moved from New York to a California retirement home in 1992, Sam Birenzweig, a childless widower, brought two suitcases, some books, and his memories.

A niece in Encinitas, a northern suburb of San Diego, wanted him nearby, so he took a room at Seacrest Village, a state-of-the-art branch of the San Diego Hebrew Home. It's a large room that looks out on a parking lot. He decorated sparsely, with a few simple pieces of blond wood furniture and an adjustable bed. Sam is comfortable there: supper at five-thirty in the dining room, in-house sabbath services, shopping trips, videos, musicians, speakers, and someone always up for a card game. Niece Miriam Wisniewski, who is married to a doctor and has two children, picks him up several times a week to spend time with the family.

Mostly, she says, he just wants to rest, and that's what he does . . . except when someone wants him to talk about the Holocaust, which he certainly never imagined he'd be doing at age seventy-nine. Once in a while in New York, a Jewish organization might have asked him to speak, but that was many years ago. "I used to tell them the harsh things, and I stopped because I got dreams," he says. "Everything goes to your body."

Not long after the release of *Schindler's List*, Sam Birenzweig dropped an idle comment at Seacrest Village. "I hear people talking about *Schindler's List*,

Sam Birenzweig, Encintias, California, 1994.

and I say, like a joke, 'I was on Schindler's list.' " Soon, he was addressing high-school kids in the heavily Chicano area who probably had never heard anything like his Old-World Polish accent. The kids would be calling him "Uncle Sam" before the hour was out. "Them, I don't tell the harsh things, and just what I myself saw."

Sam Birenzweig was born in June 1915 in Ostrowiec, an industrial city of 120,000 near Warsaw, noted for it steel and liquor. His parents, Miriam and David, had a wholesale glass business. He had three sisters and three brothers: Alta, who survived; Leah and Feige, who probably died at Auschwitz; Moshe and Mark, who also survived in Poland. Another brother, Josef, had gone to Palestine in 1934 but came back right before the war. "He had his wife and child over there. It cost a lot of money to get him out again [in 1940]."

Perhaps two months after the German invasion, the Gestapo rounded up forty of Ostrowiec's leading citizens—gentiles, he says—and hanged them in the marketplace. The whole town was called to watch "so that the people should be afraid to do anything against them—to revolt or sabotage. After that, they made a ghetto for the Jews." Over the next two years, transports decimated the ghetto population of about nine thousand.

"I went to the nearby town of Sandomierz; they said this ghetto would hold out longer," Sam explains. "I had one brother there—Moshe. The rest stayed with my parents." But the rumor that Sandomierz was safe turned out to be a ploy to get "everybody [to] come out from the hidden places. They got them all in one place, and sent them all over."

He and Moshe went to work on a road-building crew for Bomer & Lesch, a German company out of Mielec. "It was hard work, but we didn't have a problem with the Gestapo," says Sam. "We had cots. It was not so strict. The food was not so much, but in the beginning they still had some clothing for sale. There was a small town, and some people could go to the farmers and sell clothing for bread."

His parents and two sisters were taken to camps in the fall of 1942. He'd been able to see them from time to time, though it was illegal for Jews to travel. "But for money, you could get a pass."

He stayed with the road crew until early 1943. At that time, "Russia gave the German army its first big hit, near Stalingrad. It was the real McCoy." The Germans guarding his work detail had newspapers. Sam could see the headlines. "They got so nervous: 'We lost the war and this is the end now.' They saw already what would happen. This was a real satisfaction, to see that."

That June, he was transferred to Hankelwerke, a war-plane factory at Mielec, where he installed windshields. "From this factory, when they liquidated it, they sent us to Wieliczka in July 1944. Our group was painters and glaziers. They started to build there inside [the salt mines], big holes, underground." But they never finished. The Wieliczka tunnels were to have housed factories, but the environmental salts rusted the machines. In any case, the Soviets were bearing down, and by the summer of 1944, the Germans were dismantling it.

"There were eighteen hundred Jews," says Sam. "They figured out that they needed a few hundred people to take apart the barracks: young and healthy. There was a Jewish *Lagerführer:* Stockman, a marvelous guy. He didn't know what to do. How was he going to take out this guy and not that guy? He [put it this way]: 'Here will be really hard work. If anybody feels sick, old, not able to work, there is a transport that goes away tomorrow. Maybe you should take the transport. Anybody who feels young and healthy and can do hard labor, should stay.' This way, the people made the selection themselves. You had to make a selection, you had to send this guy to life, this guy to death." (Stockman, leader of the *Budzyners,* would later be knocked off Schindler's list by Marcel Goldberg in a power struggle.)

Sam and a friend from Sandomierz discussed the options. "I said, 'Don't go to the transport. Here, already, you know you get something to eat, even if you work hard. Over there, you don't know what's doing.' So we [Sam and his brother Moshe] stayed, and it was hard work. From there, they took us to Płaszów at the end of August." His friend, who "didn't want to work so hard," went with the transport and disappeared.

Płaszów "was practically empty," Sam recalls. "It was already a mishmash. Goeth was gone. It was chaos." But the men got to work outside the camp, guarded by "regular" soldiers, who had lost their taste for the Nazi excesses.

"They sent us to build trenches. We were building trenches here, and the Russians were building trenches from maybe two, three kilometers away. The soldier guarding us didn't work too hard. He was so depressed. He didn't have the will to hit us. There were warehouses with clothes they took from the dead people. The Polish [prisoners] used to take every day shirts and pants to sell on the black market. Outside you couldn't buy nothing, so the Polish women used to come over to make business. A few guys took five, ten shirts and put them on."

Their German guard didn't object. It meant extras for him, too. "He told me, 'If the Polish women can get you one kilogram butter and one liter vodka [for him], then you can make business with the shirts.' " The "business" included trading in a Płaszów-area store that still stocked luxury items like vodka and salami. It was for show, says Sam, because the Germans wanted to maintain the illusion that they were winning the war. These things were nearly impossible to buy elsewhere. And at Camp Płaszów, "they were like diamonds. . . . I didn't eat good food like this for three or four years! I brought it inside Płaszów. People there had money. This was terrific!"

But "business" was short-lived. "After two weeks, they took us by train to Gröss-Rosen. They took everything. You were naked like when you were born. They hit us a little bit there. We saw people hanging by the hands from the beams of the roof. They told us, 'This is Polish people, they made a revolt from Warsaw in 1944 against Germany.' "

Somehow, he got onto Schindler's list. "When they picked us up to go to Brinnlitz, I had no idea where I was going. I had never heard of Schindler. I was lucky." Before they left for Gröss-Rosen, he remembers that someone tried to buy his spot in the Schindler line. "This rich guy said, 'I'll give you five thousand dollars American.' He showed me the money. I didn't say nothing to him. I stayed [in line]." The man, says Sam, must have been "a tough guy from Kraków, but Schindler couldn't take all of them from the Emalia factory." He also didn't take Moshe Birenzweig, who went to another camp.

At Brinnlitz, Sam Birenzweig was "just a plain worker. I didn't work too hard. I made cement to put in the machinery. There were cliques there, and I was a stranger." One thing he noticed about his Brinnlitz coworkers: "They were not too depressed. They were feeling a little bit freer."

Certain people were sent every day to a grain mill near the plant. He asked to go. "They didn't let me. Later, I found out these people knew how to handle a rifle. [Schindler] connected them with the Czech underground. He was afraid that when Russia came closer and he had to close up the camp, [the Germans] would kill all the people."

Sam remembers what Schindler said to his workers on the day before liberation: " 'You should pray for me, I should get out alive. I get out alive, you all be alive.' "

Schindler got out alive and so did his workers. "The first few days, everybody was confused. We didn't go too far. The Czechs brought us food." Then he headed for home. "I wanted to see who was left alive. . . . I found Mark. He used to work in a steel factory that had a labor camp. When they started to liquidate that camp, he ran away with my sister [Alta] and hid with Polacks for five months." (Josef died in Israel and Alta in New York. Moshe died in Germany only three years after the war ended, following a car accident. Mark lives in New York.)

Sam went to Munich, where he studied chemistry. He immigrated to the United States in 1950. "I was involved in rubber chemicals. I can put together any formula. I took the [New York] telephone book and went looking for places that made rubber. I knew how to read 'rubber' in English. I found four places."

He got a job at a tire retread plant in the Bronx. "It was two Jewish people. One showed me an item, I took out a pencil and made the formula. They paid me sixty-five dollars a week. That was a lot of money." Five years later, he met a woman named Ann Liebman at a party. They married, but never had children. Ann was not able to sustain a pregnancy. "She was hidden by Polacks. She was not healthy when she came out, even though in the beginning it didn't show."

He left the retread plant for a glass shop, where he did chemical etchings on mirrors. "I didn't spend nothing. I saved five thousand dollars to go into the wholesale cosmetics business with a partner [on Manhattan's Lower East Side]. Ann helped in the business, just to kill time." They lived in Brooklyn's Canarsie section and traveled a lot. She died in 1985.

"We didn't talk much about the war," he says. "In the beginning, it was really hard. The whole thing went like a merry-go-round in your mind. Thank God, it didn't affect me mentally." Indeed, he seems in remarkably good spirits. During the spring and summer of 1994, he appeared on local television and on the front page of a San Diego newspaper.

All this attention gets a chuckle out of the man who believes he survived because he had a certain policy: "I never go first. I never go last. I always try to be in the middle, 'cause you never know what's gonna happen. That was a good policy."

Sam Birenzweig on a motorcycle driven by his brother, Mark, Germany, 1946.

DR. STANLEY ROBBIN

This is the story of a man and his monument. The man is Dr. Stanley Robbin. The monument is a fourteen-foot inverted pyramid of black Brazilian granite. It stands in front of the Long Beach, Long Island, City Hall, a few blocks from Robbin's home, and it is his obsession.

Its purpose is twofold: to honor four men—two of them "Righteous Gentiles"—and to stand as a symbolic tombstone for the lost millions. One panel bears the names of Oskar Schindler, Raoul Wallenberg, and Father Maximilian Kolbe. Another represents Janusz Korczak, surrounded by Jewish children (an SS soldier at his back). The third depicts the burning bush, bisected by a length of barbed wire dripping blood. Robbin, an accomplished amateur photographer, designed it.

The inverted pyramid rests on a three-sided slab. Etched into it, under the names of Schindler, Wallenberg, and Kolbe, is the inscription: "Their Brothers' Keepers." Inscribed under the illustration of Korczak, who accompanied 192 Jewish children from his Warsaw Ghetto orphanage to the Treblinka death camp, is "To the sacred and eternal memory of the million Jewish children who perished in the Holocaust." Under the bush is chapter three, verse two, from Exodus: "The burning bush was not consumed."

The retired cardiologist was once Samek Rubenstein, the doctor at

Dr. Stanley Robbin with the monument he erected, Long Beach, Long Island, 1994.

Emalia, and later an inmate at Mauthausen. In the worst of times at Mauthausen, his practice consisted of walking among the doomed in his death-camp rags, telling them lies: " 'You will survive. Don't be so upset.' I was an optimist. This was my medicine." In the best of times at Schindler's enamelware plant, he could at least provide the occasional bandage or aspirin.

Robbin began raising money for the monument and a small library in 1982, after vandals defaced nearby temples and Jewish homes. Someone painted swastikas on the Lido Beach Synagogue, an Orthodox house of worship.

"The breaking out of anti-Semitism is a horrible thing, after you went through what we went through," says Robbin. "This generation is forgetting it. When I started to see the swastikas on the houses in Long Beach, I said, *'I am going to do something about it!'*"

And he did. Five years and three hundred thousand dollars later, the monument was unveiled at Long Beach's Kennedy Plaza. A multiethnic, bipartisan crowd of political and community leaders stood beside Robbin and other survivors for its dedication.

Born in January 1914, Robbin grew up in Kraków, where his father, Manes, owned a brick factory. By 1920, his mother, Regina, was widowed, raising three sons alone. (His brothers, Mark and Arthur Rubenstein, live in Florida and Arizona, respectively.)

When he Americanized his name, Stanley Robbin chose the middle name Reginald to honor his mother, who was taken from the ghetto on a transport. Before the war, she kept a cheese shop in their apartment at 46 Dietal Street. "In front was a beautiful promenade," he recalls. "In back of the house was a gigantic garden for the army."

He attended Jewish schools on scholarship, and was one of only ten Jews who were admitted to the University of Kraków medical school (which, he says, used Jewish cadavers exclusively).

The young doctor went to work in the Kraków ghetto's Jewish Hospital during a 1941 typhus epidemic. "At that time, they [had] started to build Płaszów. Nobody [on the hospital medical staff] wanted to go there to be with them. They sent me. I was the youngest."

For a while, conditions at Płaszów weren't too bad. He was even permitted to take a patient who needed X rays to see the roentgenologist in Kraków. But things quickly degenerated under the authority of Amon Goeth. Robbin says he couldn't stand the brutality, so he asked Wilek Chilowicz, head of the camp's Jewish police, to transfer him to Emalia. Chilowicz, whom he'd known for years, did him the favor, and Robbin stayed there until the Płaszów complex broke up. Several Emalia veterans recall it was he who tattooed their arms with the KL that stood for *Konzentrationslager*—concentration camp. Lola Krumholz remembers that he drained an infection for her.

"In Emalia, they had a small room and three beds. There were a few supplies." And there was Schindler. "There was a boy, about sixteen, complaining of headache. He was resting in a bunk, and suddenly one of Goeth's people came to see the place with Schindler. They saw the [boy]: 'What is he doing here?' They wanted to kill him because he didn't look sick." Schindler talked the Nazis out of it. ("This boy still writes to me," says Robbin. He is now Sam Soldinger of Phoenix.)

"I felt I knew Schindler. [Once,] he called me in at two at night; he wanted to talk to me in his office. He had a radio. He was listening to what was happening on the Russian front. He said to me, 'Let me tell you what I did.'"

According to Robbin, Schindler then proceeded to tell him about helping two rabbis escape from the Germans. Drinking his way through the story, Schindler told Robbin all the details. "He said to me, 'Why they kill the Jewish people? Let them live!' He knew exactly what was happening. He said to me, 'Remember: I did something for the people.' After two hours, he put a glass of rum in front of me and said, 'Drink!' I never drank. He put a gun on the table. 'You drink!' For thirty-six hours, I was out cold." Apparently, the voluble Oskar realized he'd said too much.

But even Schindler couldn't prevent Stanley and his brothers from being transferred to the death camp Mauthausen. "I was in my white uniform," Robbin remembers. "They had one hundred forty people in a car. In a few minutes, we could not breathe. It was a freezer car! I started to knock at the door, and the SS said, 'Stop knocking. If I open the door, I will kill you.' But I realized we were going to die anyway. So he hit [me] with the rifle, here"—he points to his skull—"and the blood started to drip. Schindler saw me. He asked me what happened. I told him, and they changed the car" to one with some ventilation.

Robbin says he saw Schindler in Germany after the war, and asked him why he and other longtime Emalia workers didn't make the list. "He told me he was not responsible for it. He never arranged this, and he apologized."

When he got to Mauthausen, Robbin showed someone in authority papers proving he was a doctor. This, at least, entitled him to a shirt and shoes. Everyone else, he says, got only pants (which got shorter and shorter, as inmates ripped off strips of cloth for toilet paper).

In the war's waning months, bodies piled up at Mauthausen like so much compost. Stanley Robbin says he witnessed cannibalism. "They delivered some Russians, and everybody got a spoon and filed it to make a knife. They used the knife to open the belly of the bodies, and removed liver and ate it."

Only on Yom Kippur, when even many nonreligious Jews fast, did the cynical Nazis make sure to offer the ravenous *Haftlinger* treats they couldn't resist: "a whole piece of bread and marmalade."

The SS permitted Robbin to maintain an infirmary, of sorts, in Barracks Six. There was little he could do for the sick, but he says he once managed to save someone from death by camouflaging him. "Every six weeks, they would kill the guys on gas-chamber duty. One guy came to me, and I took black salve and covered his whole body. They were looking for him, but they didn't recognize him. Then he disappeared." In extreme cases, he was sometimes able to get permission to "prescribe" some oatmeal or a glass of milk.

The camp had its own version of Auschwitz's Dr. Mengele. "To cut parts of the body, he [used] people instead of animals." Robbin can barely gag out the sentence. He once watched the doctor excise a patient's neck tumor, and then deliberately not treat it so that he could watch how it grew back.

Among the wasted ones who came his way was Simon Wiesenthal, who survived to become the famous Nazi hunter. "He was very sick when he was brought to Mauthausen. I think he weighed maybe eighty pounds. I couldn't give food because I didn't have it. I was just talking. Every night, there was a thousand American planes, so to me it looked like, How long it can last? So I was talking and talking, and this was my job."

His greatest surprise was running into one of his medical school professors, a Dr. Albrecht, who wasn't Jewish. "The Germans came to him about four people they killed—not Jewish people. They wanted him to write on the death certificates that they all died a natural death, and because he refused, they sent him to Mauthausen." Albrecht survived.

Robbin says that for a time the Barracks Six "nurse" was Józef Cyrankiewicz, who became the Polish premier in 1947. He was a political prisoner, sent from Auschwitz.

Americans liberated the camp on May 5, 1945. Robbin says they didn't realize it would do more harm than good to feed the famished prisoners "plenty of bread and butter," so by the hundreds, the inmates developed terminal cases of dysentery. "When I saw what they were doing, I went to this general and said, 'Please—don't do it, you are killing them!' and they stopped."

Stanley Robbin came to the United States in 1946, through Austria and France. He met two women in Paris who asked him to visit their brother in New York. The man would later become his father-in-law. "I got there on a Friday, he asked [me] to come on Sunday, and that's when I met my wife." He proposed to Ruth Eliaser one year later, on a bench in Central Park, at midnight. Married in February 1948, they now have seven grandchildren. Son Mark, who lives in Attleboro, Massachusetts, followed in his father's medical footsteps: He is a gastroenterologist. Daughter Rhona Smith, of Fairfield, Connecticut, is a senior editor for McGraw-Hill. is and daughter Joan Kurtz, who lives on Long Island, is a teacher.

Armed with his medical-school records from Poland, Robbin secured residencies, and then a medical license. An early and ardent antismoking campaigner, he specialized in cardiology, with a practice at New York's Mount Sinai Hospital and an office on Park Avenue.

When the Robbins moved to Long Island in 1956, he shifted his practice to Long Beach Hospital. He retired in 1984. He and Ruth also have a condo at Century Village in Boca Raton, Florida.

Now that everybody knows about Oskar Schindler, Stanley Robbin wants to make sure the others aren't forgotten. Raoul Wallenberg, the aristocratic Swedish diplomat who saved more than 100,000 Hungarian Jews with Swedish "protective passports" and safe houses, vanished forever into the Soviet gulag in 1945.

Janusz Korczak is far less known. The pediatrician/educator was actually the Polish Jew Henry Goldszmit, who wrote pioneering child-development books. Korczak went to death with his orphans, after rejecting several offers to save his life.

Maximilian Kolbe was a Franciscan friar and journalist who was declared subversive by the Nazis. He was arrested in February 1941 and sent to Auschwitz. Five months later, he voluntarily substituted himself for a man sentenced to die in a starvation bunker. When he was still breathing two weeks later, a camp doctor finished him off with a lethal injection.

In a 1971 beatification ceremony, Pope Paul VI said Kolbe "represents all the unknown victims who suffered a cruel death in those barbarous years at the hands of cruel men." On October 10, 1982, Maximilian Kolbe was declared a saint.

LOLA AND RICHARD KRUMHOLZ

There was a slight interruption in the September 1939 wedding plans of Lola Kornfeld and Richard Krumholz: the German invasion of Poland.

When they finally married in January 1942, it was with considerably less pomp than the proposed double wedding with Lola's brother, Israel, and his fiancée. Instead, Lola and Richard had a Jewish ceremony in secret, then a civil transaction in the small town of Skala, where the Kornfelds had been lying low. Before the year was out, Lola's parents, Hermina and David, would disappear into the Belżec death factory.

Lola Kornfeld Krumholz, who is seventy-seven, has intriguing, khaki-colored eyes. They still run with tears for her lost parents. "Even this morning she was crying," says Richard, on a balmy May afternoon in Los Angeles, where they live near the Santa Monica airport. Their sons, David and Steven, run the Los Angeles–area chain of Richard's Luggage stores that their father established in 1951.

"We were a very close-knit family," Lola says of her own prewar clan in Poland. "They didn't know where they were going, and it bothers me that they didn't know if they were going to be gassed. We didn't find out for years what happened to them."

Richard, two years his wife's senior, came from the resort town of Kry-

Lola and Richard Krumholz, Los Angeles, 1994.

nica, where his grandfather built the *shul.* "Queen Juliana [of the Netherlands] spent her honeymoon in our town," he notes, with a certain pride. When his father died in 1936, Richard—the only child of Markus Krumholz's second marriage—took over the family business. It was what would now be called a gourmet grocery, "the only Jewish deli in town selling ham," according to Richard. "Saturday, the front door was closed and the side door was open."

When the musical Rosners played Krynica, they always patronized his store. "In the winter, we had tomatoes and peaches. You only could get it in my store. It was very exclusive."

Richard Krumholz also was one of the top luge drivers in Poland, an old Maccabi sports club chum of Leopold Page, who played hockey, handball, and water polo. They still play poker on Tuesday nights.

Richard and Lola met in 1934, when he was visiting relatives in her hometown of Bielsko. Her father, David Kornfeld, owned a carpet factory. Lola and Richard belonged to Betarim, the right-wing Zionist youth group. "I went to the place where they were getting together on Saturday afternoons," Richard remembers. "She came late, and I saw a good-looking girl. In 1935, I went on vacation to a place not far from where she lived in Silesia. She was passing by in front of the villa where I stayed! I recognized her and ran to her and said, 'We know each other.'"

The lame line apparently wasn't any more effective then than it is today. "Don't tell me a story like that," she sniffed. But soon they began corresponding, "which was not so easy," according to Richard, "because she didn't speak good Polish. In her school and home, only German was spoken. Her town was ninety-nine percent German."

In the spring of 1939, Richard celebrated Passover with the family of an aunt in Bielsko. "I said to Lola, 'What do you think if we get married?' She didn't say yes or no," which was not surprising, because she had another boyfriend at the time ("but he was too much of a playboy").

Bielsko, near the German border, southwest of Kraków, was hardly a hospitable venue for Jews in the early months of the occupation, so the Kornfelds relocated to Skala. Richard and his mother, Isabella, fled east, to Lvov. His five older half-siblings scattered. Only one brother in Siberia would survive the Holocaust.

But even marauding Germans couldn't keep the lovers apart. Richard discovered the Kornfelds' whereabouts, made his way to Skala, and married his sweetheart. Four months later, he was taken to one of the *Julag* camps that Płaszów eventually would absorb. The gourmet grocer found himself laying railroad track.

Lola and her mother-in-law (Isabella was by then also living in Skala) got passes to visit Richard at the *Julag.* They happened to be visiting during the August weekend *Aktion* in Skala that swallowed David and Hermina Kornfeld.

The women went to the Kraków ghetto, where Richard's friend Schenker, the shoemaker, would do them the first of several favors. "They slept in his kitchen," says Richard. "A month later, I escaped from the *Julag.* I was bringing boots from the shoemaker to Müller, the head of the *Julag.* I got a pass that I could go out by myself anytime; I didn't have to go with a group. One Sunday, I said I'm not coming back. With a pass, the Jewish police let you into the ghetto. Very shortly, I got the job at Schindler's."

The job was Schenker's second favor. He made boots for Oskar Schindler too. When he heard that the aspiring tycoon needed Jewish laborers, Schenker suggested Lola and Richard. In September 1942, they signed on at Emalia.

Schenker made the tall, shiny black boots that every SS man wore. They brought him leather; he fashioned their footwear . . . and some extras. "I was bringing SS boots from him to Schindler," says Richard, made from "surplus" SS leather. (Today, Schenker lives in New Jersey.)

Richard Krumholz says he had "the worst job in Emalia. I was at the furnace, burning the pots. It was like big forks, and you put from one hole to the other running. A few times I fainted. Lola was carrying boards to the drier."

Richard learned that his mother had been selected for transport. Once again, he beseeched Schenker for help. Schenker's wife, Ryvka, had worked for years at the Krumholzes' deli, "and was like a daughter to us. [Schenker] walked in to the head of the ghetto and said, 'This [Isabella] is my mother,' so he took her out from [the transport manifest], and the next day she had to [sign] all the papers 'Ryvka Schenker.' I told Schindler my mother remarried." Isabella Krumholz appears on the April 1945 Brinnlitz list as Ryvka Schenker, born on January 8, 1888. (On the list, Lola's birth year is correct: 1917.)

They all lived at Płaszów until Schindler built his subcamp. None of them was accustomed to physical labor. Lola remembers that Edith Wertheim, another Emalia pioneer, "was skipping work, and she got away with it."

Once they moved to the subcamp, both men and women could stay fairly clean—there was plenty of hot water because of the furnaces, and even soap. "Couples did get together at Emalia," according to Richard. "She came to my barrack and could sleep. There was no strict separation. Schindler didn't go for that."

In 1944, Richard got his wife lighter work as a spot welder, attaching handles to the pots. In the late summer of 1944, the three Krumholzes had every reason to believe they'd go with Oskar Schindler wherever his next move took him. After all, Lola and Richard had been with him since the beginning. What the men didn't realize was that Marcel Goldberg was brokering a list at the Płaszów main camp, "kicking us out and putting others in," as Richard tells it.

"All of a sudden," says Lola, "I knew he was not here. I didn't find out for a long time what happened to him."

Most of the Lipowa Street subcamp workers had been moved back to Płaszów. From there, the hundreds "dropped" from the list pushed out in all directions. Richard remembers being stuffed into a cattle car, on the scorching day in August 1944 when Murray Pantirer helped hose down the train. "One hundred fifty guys in one car. We had enough bread, but it was steaming."

Nonetheless, Richard Krumholz was in decent shape when they got to Mauthausen, "still physically strong from Schindler, not undernourished." He was nearly thirty years old.

The Germans living in and around Mauthausen would later claim ignorance of a death camp in their midst. Richard Krumholz scoffs. "When we came out in fives through the village of Mauthausen, they saw us, and if you did not march properly, you got hit by the SS. We were in striped suits." Once at the camp, "they put us in the shower. You got the louse promenade [reverse Mohawk haircut]. You slept three in one bunk, head and foot. The latrine was

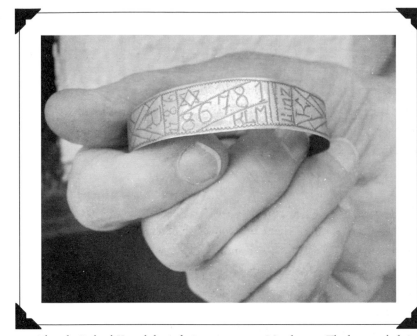

A bracelet Richard Krumholz made from scrap tin at Mauthausen. The design includes his inmate number, his initials, and a Star of David.

open, a hole. We didn't get too much to eat, and seven times a day, we went to the quarry to lift and carry stones. If you didn't take a really big one, they gave you a stone one hundred pounds. You didn't make it one hundred eighty-six steps, they pushed you down. We did that around two weeks."

Richard Krumholz notes that on a visit several years ago to the scene of so many crimes, Sam Wertheim, one of his campmates, couldn't make it up all the steps empty-handed. He shakes his head in amazement that any of them survived.

"Then we went to Linz II, one of the best camps in the Mauthausen system. They were not killing. An Austrian foreman [at the machine shop] liked me because I didn't speak German like Jewish. He gave me two apples every morning, which I smuggled to the *Kapo* of the barracks. I ate one, and for the other, I got extra soup. I was getting extra cigarettes. You got ten a week, so eight I gave back to the foreman, and two I smuggled to the camp. For that, I got two pounds of bread. The guys who smoked were giving the last piece of bread, and some perished. But I got twenty-five [lashes] there for using a towel [around the neck] like a muffler. I couldn't sit for a week or so."

Lola and Isabella couldn't imagine what had become of Richard, and he had no idea that they had gone to Auschwitz. Isabella, by then well into her sixties, found herself shunted to a barracks for those deemed ancient and irrelevant by Final Solution standards. Lola remained with the younger Schindler women.

"We were standing in front of the crematorium," Lola recalls. "I didn't know what it was. How should I know this is an oven that burns people? Somebody told me there is going to be a list. I ran to her [Isabella], to the other barracks, and brought her to where we were. I don't know where I got the courage and nerve to do it. When I brought her back to our side, they were reading the list, and we were all on it."

The U.S. Third Army liberated the Mauthausen camp system during the first week of May 1945, about the time Russian soldiers reached Brinnlitz. Richard Krumholz and Sam Wertheim were set free at Linz II, just in time. "They took the whole camp to caves in the woods and were supposed to blow up the caves during the night, but the Americans came," says Richard, who weighed eighty-two pounds at the end of his captivity.

Lola Krumholz says she was the first woman to find her husband in Linz. She had hopped a train from Brinnlitz to Prague. "All of a sudden came a message: 'Everybody has to leave the train; it is not going any farther today.' We went into the station, and I heard a train came back from Dachau, Buchenwald, Mauthausen. So I said, 'Oh—that's where my husband went! I heard a voice: 'Lola! Go back to Linz; your husband is alive!' He said who he was. He knew me from Emalia. So I went back to Brinnlitz. My mother-in-law was waiting for me. I yelled out, 'Richard is alive!'

Lola's brother, Israel, also might still have been alive in May 1945. "He became an officer in the Polish army, a good friend of Menachem Begin. He was probably killed by another Pole" in the army. In any case, she never saw him again.

Lola and Isabella—armed with the goods each of the *Schindlerjuden* carried away from Brinnlitz—returned to Prague. Lola bartered it to a Red Cross worker who drove her to Linz in a truck. Richard says she went to the Jewish center and announced, " 'I am Krumholz.' The day before, one Krumholz died." It was someone else.

Richard was recovering in a nearby private Catholic hospital for prisoners of war, thanks to a Red Cross worker. "When I came from the camp, I asked her, in German, where I could sleep overnight. She said, 'I'll take you home, but you are too sick. I will try to get you into hospital.' I said, 'I'm not going to a general hospital.' She took me [to the Catholic hospital] for six weeks, to rest and eat."

Lola Kornfeld and Richard Krumholz, Poland, 1939.

When Lola materialized at his bedside, Richard could hardly believe it. "We both cried. I said, 'Don't tell me the story that Mother is alive.'" But it wasn't a story. Isabella Krumholz was alive and well. She died in 1970.

The Krumholzes stayed in Linz until June 1946. They moved to Munich, then sailed from Hamburg to New York. Eight days later, they arrived in Los Angeles, where three of Lola's uncles lived.

When Oskar Schindler visited California in 1962, "He looked good," Lola remembers. "But I wasn't surprised he failed in business. He was not a businessman." By then, she and other survivors had some perspective on his deeds.

"Now we understand him more. From the beginning, he did not know how it would turn out."

PHOTO CREDITS

Pages xxviii, 218, 219, 226, 227: Courtesy of Victor Lewis
Pages xxix, xxx, xxxiii, 280, 282, 284, 287: Courtesy of Pola Yogev
Pages xxxv, 157, 240, 278: Photos by Beth A. Keiser
Pages 3, 4, 6, 7, 8, 9, 10, 18, 19, 31, 33, 37: Courtesy of Manci and Henry Rosner
Pages 15, 205, 229, 253, 288, 404, 428: Photos by Eddie Hausner
Pages 42, 43, 45: Courtesy of Ryszard Horowitz
Pages 51, 328, 343, 369: Photos by David Rose
Pages 55, 69, 73: Courtesy of Helen Sternlicht Rosenzweig
Pages 63, 389: Courtesy of Sam and Edith Wertheim
Page 71: Courtesy of Betsy Schagrin
Pages 76, 108: Photos by Jill Freedman
Pages 78, 80, 85, 95: Courtesy of Leon Leyson
Pages 93, 117, 118, 119, 311, 325, 380, 420, 438, 440: Photos by Adrienne
    Helitzer/STILL Productions
Pages 100, 104: Courtesy of Julius Eisenstein
Page 110: Courtesy of Celina Biniaz
Pages 124, 137: Photos by Stan J. Turkula
Pages 138, 320, 322: Courtesy of Maurice Markheim
Page 139: Courtesy of Margot and Chaskel Schlesinger
Pages 144, 153, 163, 172: Courtesy of Rena Ferber Finder
Page 177: Photo by Gerard Simonetti
Pages 181, 183, 194, 195: Courtesy of Murray Pantirer
Pages 188, 199, 204: Courtesy of Barry Tiger
Pages 208, 209, 214: Courtesy of Moshe Taube
Pages 216, 417: Photos by Melissa Farlow
Pages 233, 234: Courtesy of Igor Kling
Pages 245, 250: Courtesy of Sol Urbach
Pages 256, 260, 267, 275, 277, 332: Courtesy of Rena and Lewis Fagen
Pages 296, 297: Courtesy of Milton and Irene Hirschfeld
Pages 302, 309: Courtesy of Lola and Stanley Orzech
Pages 329, 331, 333, 334: Courtesy of Sally Huppert
Pages 338, 341: Courtesy of Moses Goldberg
Page 346: Photo by Jay B. Mather
Page 354: Courtesy of Henry Slamovich
Pages 358, 359, 365: Courtesy of Bronia Gunz
Pages 372, 374: Courtesy of Edith and Henry Silver
Page 385: Photo by Chrystyna Czajkowsky
Pages 394, 403: Courtesy of Henry and Sally Wiener
Pages 408, 410: Courtesy of Jack Mintz
Page 425: Courtesy of Sam Birenzweig
Page 434: Courtesy of Lola and Richard Krumholz